WAR
OF
SHADOWS

WAR OF SHADOWS

Codebreakers, Spies,
and the Secret Struggle
to Drive the Nazis
from the Middle East

GERSHOM GORENBERG

PUBLICAFFAIRS

NEW YORK

PublicAffairs
Hachette Book Group
1290 Avenue of the Americas, New York, NY 10104
www.publicaffairsbooks.com
@Public_Affairs

Printed in the United States of America
First Trade Paperback Edition: October 2022

Published by PublicAffairs, an imprint of Perseus Books, LLC, a subsidiary of Hachette Book Group, Inc. The PublicAffairs name and logo is a trademark of the Hachette Book Group.

The Hachette Speakers Bureau provides a wide range of authors for speaking events. To find out more, go to www.hachettespeakersbureau.com or call (866) 376-6591.

The publisher is not responsible for websites (or their content) that are not owned by the publisher.

Print book interior design by Linda Mark.

The Library of Congress has cataloged the hardcover edition as follows:
Names: Gorenberg, Gershom, author.
Title: War of shadows : codebreakers, spies, and the secret struggle to drive the Nazis from the Middle East / Gershom Gorenberg.
Description: First edition. | New York : PublicAffairs, 2021. | Includes bibliographical references and index.
Identifiers: LCCN 2020022031 | ISBN 9781610396271 (hardcover) | ISBN 9781610396288 (ebook)
Subjects: LCSH: World War, 1939–1945—Africa, North. | World War, 1939–1945—Middle East. | World War, 1939–1945—Secret service. | Espionage—History—20th century.
Classification: LCC D766.82 .G575 2021 | DDC 940.54/850961—dc23
LC record available at https://lccn.loc.gov/2020022031

ISBNs: 9781610396271 (hardcover), 9781610396288 (ebook),
        9781541702677 (paperback)

LSC-C

Printing 1, 2022

*In memory
of forgotten heroes*

We were eavesdroppers, strangers reading stolen scraps of other people's correspondence.

—*The History of Hut 3 (Top Secret Ultra)*

God delivers his will as visible in events, an obscure text written in a mysterious tongue. People toss off instant translations of it, hasty translations that are incorrect, full of faults, omissions and misreadings. Very few minds understand the divine tongue. The wisest, the calmest, the deepest, set about slowly deciphering it, and when they finally turn up with their text, the job has been done; there are already twenty translations in the marketplace. From each translation a party is born, and from each misreading a faction; and each party believes it has the only true text, and each faction believes it holds the light.

—Victor Hugo, *Les Misérables*

Contents

Cast of Characters

* Aristocratic titles appear only when the person was primarily known by that title.

** A list of intelligence and security agencies appears below.

UNITED STATES

Prescott Currier: officer and codebreaker in the US Navy's OP-20-G signal intelligence agency

Dwight Eisenhower: general, deputy chief, then chief of army planning; later commander of Operation Torch

Bonner Frank Fellers: military attaché in Egypt

William Friedman: codebreaker, director of the US Army's Signal Intelligence Service

James Fry: assistant military attaché in Egypt

Genevieve Grotjan: codebreaker, Signal Intelligence Service

Solomon Kullback: codebreaker, Signal Intelligence Service

Alexander Kirk: ambassador to Egypt

Charles Lindbergh: aviator and isolationist leader

George Marshall: general, army chief of staff

Russell Maxwell: general, commander of US military supply mission in Egypt

William Phillips: ambassador to Italy

Franklin Delano Roosevelt: president

Leo Rosen: officer and engineer, Signal Intelligence Service

Frank Rowlett: codebreaker, Signal Intelligence Service

Henry Stimson: Republican politician, secretary of state under Herbert Hoover, secretary of war under Franklin Roosevelt

Sumner Welles: undersecretary of state

BRITAIN

Jean Alington: Bletchley Park translator

Claude Auchinleck: general, British commander in chief, Middle East

Ralph Bagnold: army officer and explorer, founder and commander of the Long Range Desert Group

Alan Brooke: general, chief of the Imperial General Staff

Herbert Cecil Buck: army officer, commander of the Special Interrogation Group, SIG

Neville Chamberlain: prime minister until May 1940

Winston Churchill: prime minister from May 1940

Joan Clarke: codebreaker at GC&CS

Dorothy ("Peter") Clayton: aviator and explorer, wife of Robert Clayton

Pat Clayton: explorer, later officer in the Long Range Desert Group

Robert Clayton: navy pilot and explorer, husband of Dorothy Clayton

Alan Cunningham: general, commander of the Eighth Army in Libya, 1941

Andrew Cunningham: admiral, commander in chief, Mediterranean Fleet

Alastair Denniston: naval officer, codebreaker, first director of GC&CS, Government Code and Cipher School, British signal intelligence

John Dill: field marshal, chief of the Imperial General Staff, later British military's representative in Washington

Russell Dudley-Smith: naval officer, codebreaker at GC&CS

Aubrey (Abba) Eban: army officer, Special Operations Executive liaison in Palestine

Anthony Eden: Conservative politician, secretary of state for war, then foreign secretary

Ian Fleming: assistant to the director of British naval intelligence, younger brother of Peter Fleming

Peter Fleming: author and army officer

Lord Halifax (Edward Frederick Lindley Wood): foreign secretary, afterward ambassador to the United States

John Haselden: army intelligence officer

John Herivel: codebreaker at GC&CS

Harry Hinsley: codebreaker and traffic analyst, GC&CS

Dillwyn (Dilly) Knox: codebreaker, original head of the Enigma section of GC&CS

Jacqueline Lampson: half-Italian wife of Miles Lampson

Miles Lampson: ambassador to Egypt

Mavis Lever: codebreaker at GC&CS

Percy Loraine: ambassador to Italy

Harold MacMichael: high commissioner of Palestine

Raymond Maunsell: army officer, head of Security Intelligence Middle East, SIME

Stewart Menzies: director of MI6, alias "C," after Hugh Sinclair

Stuart Milner-Barry: codebreaker, GC&CS

Alan Moorehead: war correspondent

Philip Neame: general, commander of British forces in Palestine, later commander of British forces in Libya

Francis D'Arcy Osborne: envoy to the Holy See

Reg Parker: codebreaker at GC&CS

Hubert Penderel: aviator and explorer

George Pollock: director of Special Operation Executive's Middle East office

Guy Prendergast: explorer, Bagnold's successor as commander of the Long Range Desert Group

Hermione, Countess of Ranfurly

Daniel Knox, Earl of Ranfurly: Hermione's husband, army officer

Neil Ritchie: general, commander of the Eighth Army

Hugh Sinclair: admiral, director of MI6, alias "C," until his death late in 1939.

Margaret Storey: enemy intelligence analyst, GC&CS

Arthur Tedder: air marshal, commander in chief of the Royal Air Force in the Middle East

John Tiltman: army officer, veteran codebreaker, GC&CS

Edward Travis: naval officer, deputy director, then director of GC&CS

Alan Turing: codebreaker, GC&CS, inventor of the British version of the bombe

Peter Twinn: codebreaker, GC&CS

Valentine Vivian: head of MI6's counterespionage unit

June Watkins: cipher officer, Women's Auxiliary Air Force in Egypt

Archibald Wavell: general, first commander in chief, Middle East, replaced by Auchinleck

Gordon Welchman: codebreaker and head of Hut 6 at GC&CS

B. T. Wilson, general: "number one" for Palestine in the Special Operations Executive

Henry Maitland ("Jumbo") Wilson: general, commander of British Troops in Egypt, later of the Ninth Army

NEW ZEALAND

General Bernard Freyberg: commander of New Zealand forces in North Africa

POLAND

Marian Rejewski: codebreaker

Jerzy Rozycki: codebreaker

Henryk Zygalski: codebreaker

FRANCE

Gustave Bertrand alias Godefroy: army officer, director of cryptological services in French military intelligence

Pierre Koenig: general, Free French commander in North Africa

Philippe Petain: leader of the collaborationist Vichy regime after France's surrender to Germany

Susan Travers: British-born Free French soldier, Koenig's driver

EGYPT

Abdul Rahman Azzam: politician, diplomat, and cabinet minister

Kemal el Din: prince and explorer, cousin of Farouk

Farouk: king from 1936

Fouad: king, father of Farouk

Hassan Gaafar: half brother of Johann Eppler

Abbas Halim: prince, cousin of Farouk

Nevine Abbas Halim: princess, daughter of Abbas Halim, cousin of Farouk

Ahmed Hassanein: explorer, later diplomat, mentor of Farouk, chamberlain of the royal household, and head of the royal cabinet

Ali Maher: politician, adviser to Farouk, prime minister

Aziz el-Masri: military figure, mentor to Farouk, briefly army chief of staff

Khaled Mohi El Din: army officer

Mustafa Nahas: leader of the Wafd party, prime minister

Gamal Abdel Nasser: army officer

Nazli: queen, wife of Fouad, mother of Farouk

Antonio Pulli: Italian-born palace electrician, Farouk's close confidant and reputed procurer

Anwar al-Sadat: signals officer

Ernesto Verucci: Italian-born architect at the royal court, confidant of Farouk

Youssef Zulficar: Farouk's father-in-law, ambassador to Persia

PALESTINE

Yisrael Galili: socialist Zionist political and military figure

Eliahu Gottlieb: German-born soldier in the British Special Interrogation Group, SIG

Hajj Amin el-Husseini: exiled former mufti of Jerusalem

Moshe Shertok: head of the political department of the Jewish Agency

Maurice Tiefenbrunner: German-born illegal immigrant to Palestine, soldier in the British Special Interrogation Group, SIG

IRAQ

Rashid Ali al-Gailani: politician: prime minister after 1941 coup, afterward in exile

GERMANY

Werner Best: deputy to Heinrich Himmler

Wilhelm Canaris: commander of the Abwehr

Hans Entholt: actor, later junior officer, lover of Laszlo Almasy

Johann Eppler, alias Hussein Gaafar: Abwehr agent

Erwin Ettel: ambassador to Iran, afterward Middle East expert in Foreign Office

Hermann Göring: senior Nazi figure with multiple positions, confidant and personal envoy of Hitler

Reinhard Heydrich: head of the Gestapo and the SD, later of the RSHA

Heinrich Himmler: head of the SS

Adolf Hitler: the Führer, Nazi dictator of Germany

Albert Kesselring: Luftwaffe field marshal, commander of German forces in the Mediterranean

Franz von Papen: German ambassador to Turkey

Walther Rauff: SS officer, inventor of the mobile gas chamber

Joachim von Ribbentrop: foreign minister

Nikolaus Ritter: Abwehr officer

Erwin Rommel: general, later field marshal, commander of Axis forces in North Africa

Heinrich Gerd Sandstede, alias Sandy, Peter Muncaster: Abwehr agent

Alfred Seebohm: army officer, commander of frontline signal intelligence company under Rommel

ITALY

Pietro Badoglio: field marshal, governor-general of Libya, army chief of staff

Italo Balbo: prominent Fascist, aviator, air marshal, governor-general of Libya

Ettore Bastico: general, nominal commander in chief in Libya

Ugo Cavallero: field marshal, army chief of staff after Badoglio

Galeazzo Ciano: foreign minister, son-in-law of Mussolini

Italo Gariboldi: general, briefly commander in Libya after Graziani

Rodolfo ("the Butcher") Graziani: general and vice governor of Libya; later field marshal and commander of Italian forces that invaded Egypt

Orlando Lorenzini: officer in Libya

Pietro Maletti: general, commander of an army group in Libya

Serafino Mazzolini: ambassador in Egypt

Paolo Monelli: war correspondent

Benito Mussolini: the Duce, Fascist dictator of Italy

Umberto Piatti: general and landowner in Libya

Manfredi Talamo: commander of the paramilitary Carabinieri's counterespionage center and of its Removal Section, the P Squad

HUNGARY

Laszlo Almasy: explorer, aviator, later officer in the German army in North Africa

Gyula Gömbös: fascist and anti-Semitic politician, premier 1932–1936

Laszlo Pathy: honorary consul in Egypt

INTELLIGENCE AND SECURITY AGENCIES

Abwehr: German military intelligence

B-Dienst: German Navy signal intelligence

GC&CS: Government Code and Cipher School, British signal intelligence

GCHQ: Government Communications Headquarters, previously GC&CS

ISLD: Inter-Services Liaison Department, MI6 station in Cairo

MI5: British domestic security and counterintelligence

MI6: British overseas intelligence, officially the Secret Intelligence Service

OKW/Chi: German High Command signal intelligence

OP-20-G: US Navy signal intelligence

RSHA: Reichssicherheitshauptamt, Nazi roof body of the SS, Gestapo, and police

SD: Sicherheitsdienst, Nazi Party intelligence bureau

Sezione Prelevamento: Removal Section (P Squad) of Italian counterintelligence, responsible for thefts from foreign embassies

SIG: Special Interrogation Group, German-speaking British commando unit

SIM: Servizio Informazioni Militari, Italy's Military Information Service

SIME: Security Intelligence Middle East, British counterintelligence in the Middle East

SIS: Signal Intelligence Service, US Army signal intelligence

SOE: Special Operations Executive, British agency responsible for training and directing partisans in Axis-occupied countries

SS: Schutzstaffel, feared Nazi security, combat, and genocide force that grew out of Hitler's personal guard

Note on Names and Spellings

NAMES OF PLACES and countries are given in the form common at the time of the events. There are many ways to spell Arabic and Hebrew names in English. The spellings here are ones commonly used at the time or, when available, that individuals used when writing in English.

Not only do British and American spellings vary, but in some cases more than one form was used. For instance, both *cipher* and *cypher* appear in direct quotations from British documents.

THE MEDITERRANEAN THEATRE

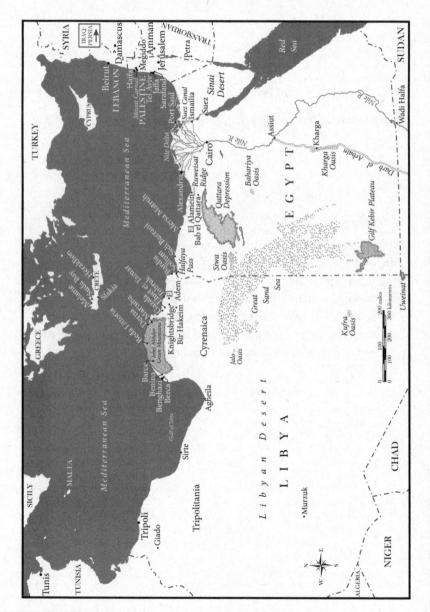

AUTHOR'S NOTE

Over lunch in Jerusalem, my friend Daniel Avitzour mentioned that his father had been a British officer in Palestine during World War II, and that the British army offered to evacuate his mother to South Africa. Or perhaps it was a demand that she leave the country, since Palestine was likely to soon be a battlefield. In either case, she refused.

That conversation set me on a journey that lasted years—to Rome, to Cairo and the sands of El Alamein, to London and the once-secret huts of Bletchley Park, to archives in places from Tel Aviv to Palo Alto, to the homes of the children and grandchildren of people whose names have been forgotten though they changed the direction of history. It was also a journey of the mind, of countless long days and nights spent fitting together the recently declassified or long-lost or long-secret documents of one country with espionage reports of another, of following one lead to another to find someone who still remembered the face and voice of a mysterious woman who'd once tracked spies—obsessed, I admit, amazed as I watched established facts unravel and new ones take their place. In the end, I was able to create a distinctly new portrait of one of the great turning points of the last century.

This is a true story. It is drawn primarily from the documents of the time, official and private. Some papers had remained classified for as long as seven decades. I have also consulted, carefully, even warily, the later memories of people who played a part, and have benefited from the research of many other historians. If a conversation appears here, it was recorded by someone who took part; if the temperature on a certain morning appears, it was written down by someone who suffered the heat or cold. To avoid breaking the flow of the story, the attributions and some technical information about codebreaking appear in the notes.

One human lifetime ago, the battle for the Middle East was one of the critical fronts of World War II. Much of what determined the outcome of that battle, and therefore of the war as a whole, remained secret. Quickly shaped legends turned into accepted memory. Today even that misleading memory is fading. Yet what happened then shaped the Middle East, and continues to shape it today.

Stories have lessons. But lessons are best told after the story, not before. Thus have I done.

Daniel, to my great sorrow, is no longer here to read this. Still I thank him for sending me on the journey.

CURTAIN RISING: LAST TRAIN FROM CAIRO

Early Summer, 1942. Cairo.

THE WORLD AS everyone knew it was coming to an end.

In the vast desert west of the Nile, the Eighth Army of the British Empire was in full flight from the German and Italian forces commanded by Field Marshal Erwin Rommel.

SMOKE ROSE FROM the grand British embassy facing the Nile. Smoke rose a few hundred yards down the river from the mansions of Garden City that war had transformed into British General Headquarters Middle East. In the Cairo heat, privates fed bonfires with all the paper that must not fall into enemy hands—cables from London, lists of arms, reports radioed in cipher from the battlefield, maps, and codebooks. The flames were too hot, the updraft too strong, and half-burnt secrets floated out over the city.

Smoke rose from the office of the Special Operations Executive, the secret undisciplined unit that backed partisans throughout the occupied Balkans and now was trying to erase its chaotic records. At Royal

Air Force headquarters, too many papers were dumped too quickly down a chute to an incinerator. Some wafted whole over the fence and into the streets, which were packed with dusty trucks pouring in from the desert carrying exhausted soldiers, and with convoys evacuating rear units east to Palestine, and with the cars of wealthy Alexandrians who'd fled to Cairo and the cars of rich Cairenes trying to get through the traffic to flee south or east. Everyone honked, as if the horn were the gas pedal.[1]

The pillars of smoke stood over the city and gave no guidance to the exodus.

ON THE MORNING of her nineteenth birthday, June Watkins emerged from the Metropole Hotel in downtown Cairo. That's where the Royal Air Force had tucked its cipher office. Around a long table, officers of the Women's Auxiliary Air Force worked as fast as they possibly could, turning words into opaque groups of numbers to be sent out in Morse code by radio, or translating equally opaque numbers from field units back into words. In the summer, the room was too hot, even at night, even if you were wearing a thin cotton tropical uniform. Watkins's commander was "quite old," meaning at least twenty-seven, and had once deciphered a list of pilots who'd been shot down. It was from the squadron in which the commander's boyfriend served. His name was on it. The commander passed on the list and said nothing. No one ever gets a medal for that kind of heroism.[2]

Watkins's father had wired her £20 for her birthday, a fortune, two months' salary for a woman officer, and she headed for the bank to see if it had arrived. The lines outside stretched for blocks.[3] When she got inside the grand marble-walled lobby, she found it packed with Egyptian businessmen trying to withdraw their money.

By sheer chance, a large South African captain, an old friend, recognized her and helped her shove through the bedlam to the counter. The man in front of her ranted steadily in French through the grating at the clerk who was counting out his money. The banks had run short of cash and were handing out worn banknotes while waiting for the government map department to improvise printing an emergency supply.[4] The man grabbed his notes, accidentally tore some, and started weeping as he cursed the clerk. Calmly, the clerk got Watkins her money. The captain plowed back out through the crowd for her.

Outside they met another South African officer. "What are you still doing here?" he demanded. Women soldiers were supposed to be gone. Five hundred South African women had already been evacuated up the Nile to Aswan.[5] Watkins was billeted in the Cairo YWCA hostel, a palace with marble floors outfitted with iron camp beds for soldiers—but nearly all the women were gone.

Her team would remain till headquarters pulled out, she said. "And I want to stay," she added. "I can look after myself." She tapped the bulge of a pistol under her shirt. She did not tell him that the same week, on the roof of the Metropole, the women of the cipher room had received a lesson in using pistols.

Among other things, they learned how to shoot themselves. Women who knew the ciphers were not to fall into enemy hands.

Her friend the South African captain took her to Groppi's café, a favorite among British officers. They wanted to drink iced coffee in the garden but were told it was closed, so they sat inside. From the window of the ladies' room, Watkins looked into the garden. The restaurant staff was out there, painting welcome signs in German for Rommel's officers.

At stores that sold suitcases, as at the banks, crowds of people pushed to get in.[6]

OUTSIDE CAIRO'S TRAIN station stood the granite colossus called *Egypt's Awakening*—a sleek, angular sphinx rising on his outstretched forelegs, facing east toward the dawn, next to the taller figure of a woman lifting a veil from her face. The woman was inspired by Egyptian feminist Huda Shaarawi, who in 1923 had returned from a women's conference and demonstratively removed her veil in the train station.[7] The station itself, studded with arches and intricate carved arabesques, was modeled on the mosques of Cairo's medieval Mamluk sultans.[8] Together, the sculpture and the railway hall formed a temple to Egypt, its future, its incomplete independence.

Inside, the god of chaos ruled. Trains from Alexandria disgorged anxious mothers and fathers dragging suitcases and children. They had to shove their way out through the wave of soldiers and families from Cairo trying to board trains headed south or east. South lay Aswan in Upper Egypt and, much further, Khartoum in Sudan. East lay the port of Suez, for the fortunate who had managed to book passage to Eritrea, Kenya, or South Africa.[9] Or you could gamble on safety in Ismalia, on the Canal. Even if the Eighth Army lost the Nile, surely it would hold the Canal.

If that seemed a poor wager, there was the all-night express to Jerusalem.

For Palestine, you needed the right papers. Halfway across the Sinai, police boarded the train to check everyone.[10] The British consulate, war correspondent Alan Moorehead found, was "besieged with people seeking visas to Palestine."

The British ambassador, Sir Miles Lampson, reported to London that "there has been a panic among the Jews, who are naturally apprehensive of their fate in the event of a successful Axis invasion."[11]

Jews taking refuge in Palestine, however, might end up staying. This was a risk that British authorities did not want to take. Since 1939 British policy had been to allow very little Jewish immigration, in the hope of keeping Palestine's Arabs from supporting the Axis. "If we must offend one side, let us offend the Jews rather than the Arabs," Neville Chamberlain had declared while he was still prime minister.[12] For July, August, and September 1942, the government of Mandatory Palestine allocated just nine hundred permits for Jews to immigrate. A permit, or "certificate," could cover a whole family, but most were reserved for Polish Jewish refugees who had made it through the Soviet Union to Tehran.[13]

"The number of Egyptian Jews who desire . . . visas for Turkey is increasing every day. As at present, no arrangements have been made for these, please let me know what should be done," the head of the Turkish legation in Cairo cabled the Foreign Ministry in Ankara.

The answer came three days later. Say no, it said.[14]

At General Headquarters, the British war cabinet's Cairo representative, Minister of State Richard Casey, met with military commanders. There were people who had to be evacuated, they decided—technicians whose expertise was too valuable to lose, "anti-Fascist Italians and anti-Nazi Germans . . . Egyptians whose lives would be in danger on account of their pro-British attitude . . . compromised persons, agents." The British embassy compiled the lists. Over three nights, sixteen hundred people boarded trains for Jerusalem.[15]

By one account, Mandatory officials in Jerusalem vetoed bringing the hundred or so German and Italian Jews on the lists from Cairo; the crisis in Egypt was no reason to change policy. A defiant captain in Cairo began ferrying them across the Sinai in his own car. The Jerusalem bureaucrats demanded to send them back. An Italian Jew tried to kill himself rather than return to Cairo. At last, the Jews were allowed temporary refuge, as long as they promised not to stay permanently.[16]

"The situation is very serious," the Persian ambassador to Egypt cabled Tehran. "Alexandria is in danger." The diplomats of the Albanian, Yugoslavian, and Czech governments-in-exile left for Palestine. Air raid sirens sounded every night in Cairo, but no bombs fell. The Saudi ambassador stayed in Cairo. King Abdulaziz ordered him to report daily on "the truth about conditions . . . Be diligent about this."[17]

The messages were sent in the secret codes of their nations so that they could be read only by the people for whom they were intended in scattered capitals. At an unmarked government building on Berkeley Street in central London, men and women broke the codes, translated the messages, printed them on paper marked "most secret" in red letters, and sent them to a tiny elite list of addressees.

The SOE, the Special Operations Executive, moved its Middle East headquarters to Jerusalem, despite a cable from London warning that Palestine "may also be occupied by the enemy." The SOE's work included preparing for what to do if a country was overrun. This meant destroying things that could help the enemy and training locals to act as partisans. As late as April 1942, an order from the main office had said to give a "post-occupational" plan for Egypt low priority. Concentrate on Turkey, Iraq, Persia, Syria, and Palestine, it said. If the Nazis invaded the Middle East, they'd come from the north through Turkey, or from the sea, or from the air as they had come in Crete. In April, it had seemed that Egypt wasn't in immediate danger. Everything had changed too quickly.

Before pulling out, the SOE left instructions for how to set fire to stores of cotton, Egypt's prime export. "The stocks of cotton in

Egypt . . . amount to two years' supply for the Axis," the memo said, and the Axis was short on textiles.[18]

"WOUNDED ARE POURING into Palestine because the hospitals in Egypt are overflowing," Hermione, Countess of Ranfurly, recorded in her diary. Hermione's title came from her husband, Daniel Knox, Earl of Ranfurly, who had the rank of lieutenant and the present status of prisoner of war in Italy. Her position as assistant private secretary to Sir Harold MacMichael, the high commissioner of Palestine, resulted from following Daniel to the Middle East when war broke out and staying on in hell-bent defiance of every effort of the British high command to get her back to England.

Now she left the office to spend four hours every day in the hospital wards, "washing soldiers, making beds and emptying things. Today I washed four heads which were full of sand." The wounded men were constantly joking, she wrote. "Only when they ask me to help them to write home do I glimpse their real misery: some of them are so afraid their families will not want them back now they are changed."

Evacuees from Cairo and Alexandria kept arriving in Jerusalem, by train and in caravans of cars. Many were second-time refugees— Greeks, Czechs, Poles, Belgians, and Serbs who'd fled the Nazi conquest of their own countries and settled in Egypt. The YMCA in Jerusalem filled up, then the hotels and pensions, then apartments in the city and in Bethlehem and the summer hilltop resort town of Ramallah. "People are sleeping on the floors in the passages of the King David Hotel," Ranfurly recorded. Convents in Bethlehem took in two thousand of them.

In the evening, Ranfurly went to farewell parties for men leaving for the front. The battle was "now only 400 miles away," she wrote. Rommel's tanks had covered nearly that distance in the last week.

General Henry Maitland Wilson, commander of the Ninth Army, which held Syria and Palestine, passed through Jerusalem. Wilson, known to all as "Jumbo," was coming from the Sinai Desert, where he "was preparing a line . . . in case the Germans break through" in Egypt. In Syria and Lebanon, his army had defensive positions facing north, against invasion via Turkey. Wilson ordered them turned southward, in case the Germans took Palestine.[19]

Tel Aviv's buses, several hundred of them, were outfitted with stretchers strapped to the roofs. By quickly removing the seats, the buses could be transformed into ambulances. The Palestine government issued a decree "empowering it to take over control of any enterprise in the country . . . for the efficient prosecution of the war." The chief rabbis announced that to help the war effort, religious Jews could put aside the normally strict prohibition against working on the Sabbath. Factories producing military supplies upped employees' workweek to sixty-four hours. "The question of whether the Middle East is reaching its 'zero month'"—like the zero hour—"is on the lips of every resident of Palestine," the Jewish Telegraphic Agency reported.[20]

A few days earlier, the agency had carried an item from London. "More than 700,000 Polish Jews—a third of the entire Jewish population—have been massacred in Poland since last summer," it said, citing a report "received here . . . through underground channels" by a Jewish member of the Polish government-in-exile, Samuel Zygelbaum. "In the city of Lodz alone 35,000 Jews were executed in gas chambers carried in trucks," it said. Elsewhere Jews were loaded onto sealed trains headed for an "unknown destination."[21]

Hebrew newspapers in Palestine published the story—and doubted it, as they had earlier reports of atrocities in particular towns. "These items," said the editorial in the Tel Aviv daily *Hatzofeh* after the Zygelbaum report, "come as rumors taken from the air, passed from one informant to another, one writer to another." News agencies should behave more responsibly, the editorial said. Such stories were likely to lead to despair or to apathy. The Nazis were certainly murdering Jews, but these numbers defied belief.[22]

DOWNTOWN CAIRO WAS put under curfew from 8:00 at night to 7:00 in the morning. Officers were told to carry their pistols at all times. The two orders were like signal flags announcing "Situation Dire." They came from General Headquarters, from the officer temporarily filling in for General Claude Auchinleck, commander in chief for the Middle East.[23]

Auchinleck had flown to the desert to take personal command of the Eighth Army. His departure was another distress flag. Ambassador Lampson sent an urgent cable asking the Foreign Office to get the BBC to stop using "Battle for Egypt"—a term he called "singularly unhappy"—to describe what was happening. "We have a highly sensitive and excitable public to consider here," he said.

In subsequent cables, Lampson himself sounded less excitable. Despite "panic amongst all classes," Egyptians "have taken [a] fatalistic attitude" toward the Axis advance, he reported. If unrest broke out, it would be over the shortage of wheat, sugar, and maize.[24]

Colonel Bonner Frank Fellers, the American military attaché in Egypt, painted the picture in stronger colors. "Although life is always very hard for ninety percent of the people, today in villages wages are low[er], prices higher, people hungrier than normal," he reported. "Should Axis advance on the Delta, first reaction [of] the masses is likely to be looting of warehouses containing food."[25]

Most Egyptians were desperately poor. The poor do not have cars, and do not buy train tickets. They are the last to flee in war. They wait, and they trade rumors. The rumors, according to informants run by a British secret office called Security Intelligence Middle East, said that the British "had begun to seize all essential commodities, such as wheat and vegetables." Among the peasants, it was said that "after the German occupation, there would be a general and free distribution of agricultural implements."[26]

Lampson told London that he was sending brief assessments of the military situation to Egyptian prime minister Mustafa el-Nahas, who passed them on to King Farouk. A worried answer came back: Since they were going to the palace, was Lampson sure that they "contain nothing that could in any way serve the enemy?" Not to worry, they were "worded . . . so as to give nothing away," Lampson answered. The twenty-two-year-old Farouk was dithering about what to do if the Germans occupied Egypt, the ambassador said: whether to leave with the retreating British "and lose his throne in the event of a final German victory, or to stay and lose his throne in the event of a final British victory."

Unstated in Lampson's cables was the question of where Farouk's loyalties actually lay. Perhaps the ambassador believed the king when he said that "bygones were bygones and everyone must now pull loyally together." Or perhaps Lampson only thought he heard Farouk say that. Lampson had a tendency to believe that conversations ended with everyone agreeing with him, and with Rommel at the gates he did not need another bout with the king of Egypt.[27]

FOR MORE THAN two years, the war had been a constant but distant fear in Cairo.

Men and machines fought out there, in the desert, hundreds of miles from the narrow band of green country along the Nile. The armies pushed back and forth across Cyrenaica, the eastern half of Libya, Italy's colony. They paused, exhausted, and shoved onward again. At the end of May 1942, the Panzer Army Africa—the German and Italian force under Rommel's command—attacked once more. The Axis and British armies ground each other down.

Then Tobruk fell.

Tobruk was a small Libyan town with a deep-water harbor, ninety miles from the border with Egypt. In 1941, Rommel's army besieged it for nine months but failed to conquer it. Without the harbor, the Axis forces couldn't advance into Egypt. They needed it to get fuel, food, and ammunition by sea, and they couldn't risk the British breaking out of Tobruk and cutting them off from behind.[28]

Britain had retreated from France, lost Greece, lost Singapore. But Tobruk stood for British tenacity and victory.

"British" in a very wide sense: the Tobruk garrison was originally Australians; they were relieved by Polish and English brigades. The Eighth Army was an international legion. Besides units actually from Britain, the roster of the Eighth Army also included New Zealanders, Indians and South Africans, Free French and Greeks, and others.[29]

In 1942, Tobruk fell in twenty-four hours.

At dawn on June 20, the Panzer Army attacked. The next day, at the first sunrise of summer, the garrison surrendered. Thirty-five thousand South African, Indian, and British soldiers went into captivity.[30]

Moorehead, the war correspondent, had passed through Tobruk shortly before this. He saw thousands of British military vehicles parked in the town, ammunition dumps, fuel that "lay around in flimsy square tins—millions of gallons." The food dumps held "tinned toma-toes, peas and potatoes, tinned American bacon and Argentine beef . . . sacks of tea and sugar, big tins of cheese . . . fresh onions and dates." Before surrender, the garrison managed to destroy only some of the supplies. Rommel's army—hungry for food and ammo, thirsty for wa-ter and fuel, and very short on trucks to carry what it needed—took the rest of the treasure, even before it could use the port.[31]

Tobruk the symbol was also in Axis hands. "Defeat is one thing; disgrace is another," Prime Minister Winston Churchill would say of Tobruk.[32] Churchill told Auchinleck to mount "stern resistance" at the Egyptian border. Auchinleck answered, "This position is untenable because of our weakness in armor." He and Lieutenant General Neil Ritchie, commander of the Eighth Army, decided the only hope was to retreat to the tiny port of Mersa Matruh, 150 miles further back on the desolate Egyptian coast.[33] Their army was unravelling. It fled at full speed eastward with Rommel pursuing it.

Auchinleck flew from a Cairo airfield to the new battle headquar-ters near Mersa Matruh, abruptly dismissed Ritchie, and took com-mand in the field.[34] On June 29, after another battle, the Panzer Army overran Mersa Matruh and continued chasing the British forces east-ward toward Alexandria.[35]

Late that night, Lampson dined at the residence of Alexander Kirk, the American ambassador. Kirk "solemnly assured me that tonight was the night and Alexandria was going to be bypassed and Cairo occupied, and that a parachute landing in Cairo" to seize General Headquarters Middle East "would take place before the morning." So Lampson re-corded the dinner conversation in his diary. He had poked holes in Kirk's rumors. "While we were thus discoursing in the moonlight on his roof, the [air raid] sirens went." Lampson waited half an hour for the "all clear" siren, heard nothing, and ordered his driver to take him home through the empty streets.[36]

EVERYONE TALKED ABOUT Rommel. He was always pictured with cap-tured British sand goggles strapped onto his cap, to show he was mas-ter of the desert.[37]

The press, in Arabic and in European languages, said too much about Rommel's abilities, SIME complained. The reports "have convinced Egyptians that he is the greatest military genius of the war."[38]

Yet the papers were telling what the British thought, from Churchill down. "We have a very daring and skillful opponent," the prime minister had declared in the House of Commons, "a great general."[39] Auchinleck had sent out an order to his officers, warning them not to call the enemy "Rommel." It made soldiers think he had "supernatural powers," which hurt morale. "We must refer to 'the Germans' or 'the Axis powers' or 'the enemy,'" Auchinleck commanded.[40]

It was a futile order. The British were awed by Rommel. He was the reason for their collapse—his boldness, and his preternatural ability to predict where the Eighth Army would be, to evade it, to strike where it was weakest.[41]

But Fellers, the American military attaché, wrote as if he had stood watching the debacle from another angle, from a separate hilltop, through other binoculars, and had spotted a different culprit. "Under their present leadership," he reported to Washington, the British army could not win, no matter how much equipment the United States sent.

The "Eighth Army failed to maintain morale . . . Its tactical conceptions were consistently faulty . . . Its reactions to battlefield changes [were] sluggish," Fellers said. The infantry, armor, and air force fought separate battles. "The German Air Force has complete control of the Eastern Mediterranean. The Royal Navy is impotent."

The only hope for holding the Middle East was new British commanders with new methods and American reinforcements, Fellers wrote. He did not use exclamation marks; all of his words were exclamation marks.[42]

ROMMEL WROTE TO his wife after passing Mersa Matruh: "Dear Lu . . . There will be a few more battles to fight before we reach our goal, but I think the worst is well behind us. I'm fine."[43]

Italian dictator Benito Mussolini flew to eastern Libya. "About a dozen" planes carried his entourage, Italian war correspondent Paolo Monelli wrote. By some accounts, one of them carried the white charger on which he intended to enter Cairo.[44] At last he would have the new Roman Empire he sought. Rommel, and Adolf Hitler, were looking much further than the Nile and even the Suez Canal—to the oil fields of Iraq and to Persia, where the Panzer Army Africa would meet victorious German forces coming south from Russia.[45]

At midday on July 1, 1942, Rommel's forces reached another set of British defenses, prepared in haste, running south through the sands from a minor railway stop on the coast called Two Flags—in Arabic, El Alamein.

Alexandria was a little more than sixty miles away. In Cairo, soldiers were burning papers, and the train station was mobbed.

THE MANSION STOOD halfway between Oxford and Cambridge, in the damp green English countryside, two thousand miles to the northwest of Egypt. It looked like an architect's sampler of styles offered to wealthy Englishmen: turrets and classical columns, round bay windows and square ones, plain red-brick and stone masonry. On the lawns an infestation of squat brick and wood huts had sprung up. The place was called Bletchley Park.

Margaret Storey and Russell Dudley-Smith worked in one of those huts. They were studying messages not meant for their eyes—radiograms sent from Berlin to German army and air force headquarters in North Africa, and from headquarters to officers in command of divisions and brigades.

Storey and Dudley-Smith wanted to know if someone in Cairo was still sending out the secrets of British General Headquarters Middle East—secrets that had served Rommel so well.

Much depended on this question, much more than Dudley-Smith and Storey could imagine. The fate of the Middle East hung on the next battle. It might determine the outcome of the war.

Act I

ALL QUIET
ON THE NILE

1

"REPORT FOR DUTY, IN ACCORDANCE WITH THE INSTRUCTIONS YOU HAVE RECEIVED"

September 1939. Cambridge–Berlin–Warsaw.

NEVILLE CHAMBERLAIN'S VOICE came out of every wireless set in Britain at 11:15 on Sunday morning. It was September 3. Two days earlier, Germany had invaded Poland.

At first, the prime minister's pauses lasted longer than his words. He swam slowly through the quicksand of his exhaustion.[1] That morning, he said, Britain's ambassador had delivered an ultimatum to Germany: Agree by 11:00 to withdraw from Poland, or Britain will go to war. "No such undertaking has been received," Chamberlain intoned.

"Consequently this country is at war with Germany."

He spoke for less than five minutes. By the end, as he prayed for God to "defend the right," he'd found his rhythm. He sounded like a leader calling a nation to victory.

But first he admitted personal defeat. It was "a bitter blow," Chamberlain said, "that all my long struggle to win the peace has failed."

The lesson that Britain had learned from the trench warfare and endless slaughter of the Great War was to avoid another Great War. Chamberlain, more than anyone, had believed the way to do that was to keep a smaller war from breaking out anywhere in Europe, lest the conflagration spread.[2] It was a sensible lesson for a sensible world, one that did not include Adolf Hitler. In Munich almost a year before, Chamberlain had given away part of Czechoslovakia to Hitler. Instead of "peace in our time," he got some months for Britain to start to create a wartime military, and for him to accept whom he was facing. "There is no chance . . . that this man will ever give up his practice of using force to gain his will," Chamberlain said. "He can only be stopped by force."

The radio speech was anticlimax. The children of London and the rest of Britain's cities were already lining up, school by school, on the platforms of railway stations and boarding trains for the countryside, where they would live with strangers who were required to take them. Parents had received notice the day before.[3] German bombers were expected in the skies immediately, possibly carrying poison gas. The BBC announced that sports events were prohibited, cinemas shut. Too many people would die if a bomb found a crowd.[4] Parliament met that day and passed a law requiring all men between eighteen and forty-one to register for conscription.

GORDON WELCHMAN WAS at home in Cambridge when the prime minister spoke. The line in the speech that mattered most immediately to him was the one telling members of the "fighting services" to "report for duty in accordance with the instructions you have received." Welchman had neither rank nor uniform. But he had instructions.

Welchman was a thirty-three-year-old Cambridge don, which is to say a professor of mathematics. He was writing a textbook on algebraic geometry, an abstract field unsullied by real-world applications. A photo of him from this time shows his wavy hair meticulously combed, his moustache trimmed. He wears a tweed jacket, rests his head against one hand, and smokes a pipe: he looks like a Hollywood heartthrob in a poster for a movie about a Cambridge professor. War had broken into his life once, when he was a boy, when his much older brother was killed at Mons, in Belgium, in the first battle the British fought in the Great War. The closest he'd come to violent death himself was a motorcycle accident, from which the only lasting effect was to end his trombone playing.

That night an air-raid siren went off in Cambridge. Welchman and his wife, Katherine, grabbed their one-and-a-half-year-old son and took shelter under the staircase, considered the safest place in a house. "Cambridge could hardly be considered a prime military target," he wrote of the incident. "Katherine saw the absurdity of the situation before I did." The siren was a false alarm.[5]

A Cambridge fellow who rushed back to the university when war broke out found several of his colleagues "digging a zigzag trench in the playing field of King College School as a makeshift air-raid shelter." They were "fortified by a large beer barrel set in one of the classrooms."[6] Welchman missed this. On the morning of September 4, he drove to Bletchley Park to report for duty. Another Cambridge mathematician, Alan Turing, arrived the same day.[7]

Welchman's real-world life was about to begin.

THE UNSCHEDULED TRAIN, code-named "Amerika," left Berlin on the evening of September 3. It was the mobile headquarters of Adolf Hitler—a dozen or so railway cars that included his personal quarters, his communications center for keeping in touch with Berlin and his field commanders, and the rolling war room with the maps where orderlies could mark the advance of armored divisions. Hitler was heading eastward, into Poland. He wanted to see the work of his hands.

A special security battalion, with its own antitank and antiaircraft guns, traveled with Hitler and his retinue. The Führer had personally chosen the commander: Erwin Rommel.[8]

Three times before, Germany's absolute ruler had pulled Rommel away from other duties for this purpose: after the Anschluss in March 1938, when Hitler made his triumphal entry into Austria; again when Hitler rode into the Sudentenland to survey his newly seized territory; and then in March 1939, when Germany overran the rest of Czechoslovakia and Hitler entered Prague. Hitler was very taken with the forty-seven-year-old officer. For the occasion of invading Poland, he promoted Rommel, retroactively, from colonel to major general.

Rommel gloried in each moment of attention from the supreme leader. He wrote home to his wife proudly that he'd been invited to sit next to the Führer at lunch, and that he "was allowed to chat for almost two hours with him about military problems yesterday. He is extraordinarily friendly towards me."[9]

(These letters did not make it into a collection of Rommel's papers, published years later. Perhaps this was because they did not fit the legend that Germans and, strangely enough, British writers built around Rommel—that he was a worthy opponent on the playing field of a team sport called war, a "brave, able and scrupulous" general who patriotically fought for Germany but was unsullied by Nazism.[10])

Rommel's name was already known in Germany. In 1937, he published a best-selling book, *Infantry Tactics*. The title suggested a textbook, but mostly it told stories of battles that Rommel fought as a young infantry commander in the Great War.

The lesson that Rommel had learned in that war was that ramming an army against the trenches of the enemy was senseless. The skillful commander would find a weak point, dash through or around enemy lines, and throw his opponent into confusion. Speed, daring, and the power of the will would bring victory.

Rommel wrote about commanding foot soldiers. But tanks—still an experiment in the last war—could move much faster. Rommel, like Hitler, believed that tanks were the weapon of modern war, and his ideas matched the new form of warfare that Germany unleashed in Poland: blitzkrieg, massive armored divisions breaking through enemy defenses and overrunning a country.[11]

There was a problem: to direct an offensive, headquarters had to keep in touch with the commanders of those tank forces, who needed to keep in contact with the units under them. The key to blitzkrieg was "speed of attack through speed of communications." The only way to do this was by radio—but to send battle plans by radio was to shout them out loud to the world.

A way had to be found to put the messages into a code that the enemy could not break. It had to be simple and quick. It had to be portable. The solution Germany found was a machine called Enigma.[12]

A FEW HOURS after the train called "Amerika" pulled out of Berlin, President Franklin Roosevelt addressed the American nation by radio. Because night came later to the United States than to Europe, it was still Sunday evening for him and his listeners. His fireside chat consisted of carefully poised contradictions.

"It is easy for you and me to shrug our shoulders and to say that conflicts taking place thousands of miles from the continental United States . . . do not seriously affect Americans," he said. And a moment later, "Let no man or woman thoughtlessly or falsely talk of America sending its armies to European fields."

"This nation will remain a neutral nation," Roosevelt said. And then, "Even a neutral cannot be asked to close his mind or close his conscience."

He knew which side he was on, which side the country should be on. He also knew that the lesson that most Americans had learned from the Great War was to stay safely on their own side of the ocean. In line with that sentiment, the United States had remained resolutely unready for war. The year before, the army chief of staff estimated that America had the eighteenth-largest army in the world. "As long as it remains within my power to prevent, there will be no blackout of peace in the United States," Roosevelt concluded.[13]

The president's practical proposal for taking sides while staying out of war was to sell arms to Britain and France. That required Congress to repeal the 1935 Neutrality Act. The country's best-known isolationist, aviator Charles Lindbergh, gave his own national radio broadcast to rally opposition. The speech was tinged with Nazi talking points on the injustice of the post–Great War borders. The only kind of war that America should enter, Lindbergh said, would be one to preserve white supremacy.

"These wars in Europe are not wars in which our civilization is defending itself against some Asiatic intruder," Lindbergh said. "This is not a question of banding together to defend the white race against foreign invasion."[14]

ON SEPTEMBER 7, Walther Rauff sat in a meeting at the SS Main Office in Berlin. There are no minutes of his thoughts, no record of whether he engaged in any self-reflection.[15]

If he did, Rauff could well have been amazed at how his life had turned around. Two years earlier, his father had died—the imperious man, unsparing of the rod, who had come home badly wounded from the Great War. Walther Rauff's wife and the German navy got fed up with his drinking and his womanizing. She divorced him; the navy dismissed him. At the age of thirty-one, he went from being in command of most of Germany's minesweepers to being out of work and alone.

Then a navy friend asked Reinhard Heydrich to help Rauff out. Heydrich, the unofficial deputy to SS chief Heinrich Himmler, was head of both the Gestapo and the Nazi Party's intelligence service, known as the SD (for Sicherheitsdienst, "security service"). Both organizations were part of the SS, and they competed in fanaticism in pursuing the Third Reich's political and "racial" enemies. Heydrich had something in common with Rauff. He, too, had been cashiered from the navy after getting engaged to one woman while having an affair with another. The Nazi Party had given him a new career.[16]

In January 1938, Rauff joined the SD. He took off in his new position. He was put in charge of the SD's mobilization plan for war. He received special dispensation from Himmler to remarry, even though his new wife's first marriage had been to a Jew. He'd vaguely sympathized with National Socialism, but his first loyalty had been to the navy till it threw him out. Now he gave his everything to the Führer and the discipline of the SD.

A later US intelligence report describes Rauff as "medium height, clear white skin, blue eyes."[17] It might as well say "generic SS officer."[18] A purported "Aryan body" was a prerequisite for the job. In a photograph from his early SD days, he has been given back his navy uniform. He has a wide face, a cleft chin, and a straight, expressionless mouth.[19]

Heydrich's deputy, Werner Best, presided over the early-September meeting with Rauff and five other division heads at SS Main Office, and laid out the plans for the subjugation of Poland. Germany would annex much of the western part of the country and put the rest under its direct rule. The goal was to expel Jews and Poles from the annexed areas to the Polish reserve further east.[20]

Werner Best didn't need to go into the plans for settling Germans in the Lebensraum of the East. The job of the SS was to clear the space. But Nazi bureaucrats did have a model in mind that they had closely studied: Italy's colonization of Libya and Ethiopia. Nazis were impressed that their Fascist ally was turning its African empire into "white man's country." The colonial effort built the "warrior spirit," and by mixing Italians from all parts of the country in its settlements, it created a new and better "racial type." Germany would subjugate the Poles as Italy did Arabs and Ethiopians. To the Italian blueprint, the Nazis added an innovation: eliminating the Jews.[21]

The SS forum met the next week with Heydrich, and the week after. Hitler had approved more detailed plans. In the short term, Jews would be consigned to ghettos until they could be expelled. There would be three categories of Poles in the annexed territories—political leaders, to be put in concentration camps; mid-level Poles, to be deported immediately; and all the rest, who would first be exploited as laborers, then pushed eastward. If mass murder was not yet the main theme, it was a very clear motif.[22]

Until now, Rauff might have been a Nazi bureaucrat as a solution to his career problems. From this point, "his participation in the inner circle of decision makers . . . marked a break, in which Rauff transformed himself from a possible follower to a perpetrator."[23]

THE ORDER TO leave Warsaw came on September 5. By the next day, Marian Rejewski and his colleagues closed down the German Section of the Polish military's Cipher Office, and were listening to the rhythmic click of train wheels on their way to Brest in eastern Poland. From there they zigzagged southward, seeking sanctuary, to the small town of Wlodzimierz Wolynski.[24] They got out of the capital with very little time to spare. Germany had plunged its armies into Poland like swords from the north, west, and south. By September 8, German tanks were on the outskirts of Warsaw, the heart of Poland.[25]

Rejewski was carrying a secret weapon. Indeed, it would be better to say that he *was* Poland's secret weapon.

Photos of Rejewski show a man with thick hair combed back from his round face. He wears small circular glasses over smiling eyes.[26] On the train, he surely wasn't smiling. Besides being in danger himself, he had been forced to leave his wife, his three-year-old son, and his infant daughter in Warsaw.

Ten years before, when Rejewski was writing his master's thesis in mathematics at Poznań University, another student had come up to him and said that the department head had put him down on a list for a meeting. The students, it turned out, had been selected by the Intelligence Section of the Polish General Staff. They were invited to a course in codebreaking, held in a fort in the city. Poznań had been under German rule until the Great War, so it was a good place to re-cruit German-speaking Poles. By 1931, Rejewski was working for the Cipher Office, at first part-time in Poznań, then full-time in Warsaw. He was assigned the bureau's greatest challenge. Two even younger mathematicians, Jerzy Rozycki and Henryk Zygalski, soon joined him.[27] They, too, were on the train out of Warsaw.

The test of the codebreaker begins with the problem facing the code maker: how to send a message that can only be read by the per-son it's intended for. One solution is to replace each word with some-thing else—for instance, a random group of five letters or numbers. "Warsaw" could be 36504 or YKRBI; "tomorrow" could be 85327 or MQMYT. The sender finds each word in the codebook and writes down the group; the receiver uses the opposite side of the book, which lists code groups and their plain-language meaning.

One risk is that your rival might get a copy of the codebook—delivered by a spy, or stolen from a diplomat's hotel room, or captured in the headquarters of an enemy unit. The professional term for this is "physical compromise," which sounds like an entirely different kind of espionage. Nearly as good is to get hold of a message both in its plain-language and coded form. Line them up, and you have a piece of the codebook.

Even without such glitches, if you send many messages in the same code, especially about a known subject, a skilled codebreaker can look for repetitions, think of possible meanings, see if they fit together into sentences, and begin to piece together the codebook. One of Rejewski's first assignments was cracking a German naval code. "You just . . . keep manipulating the material over and over again, you see, and you look [at it] and make guesses—it's a little like . . . crossword puzzles, like riddles, you have to figure out what this [code] group could mean," Rejewski would later explain.[28] Solving a code requires marathon patience. It requires holding a huge amount of information in your head, and extraordinary reasoning ability, and something beyond reason—sudden flashes of intuition, sparks leaping between two charged points in the clouds of half-consciousness.

A standard way to protect a code was to make the groups look different each time. For a code that gave groups of numbers, you could provide another long table of random numbers. The sender's code clerk added the first random number to the code group for the first word, the second random number to the second group, and so forth. The receiving clerk took the same list and subtracted the numbers. For the next message, they could start at a different, mutually agreed point on the list.

Like the codebook itself, the subtraction table—the list of random numbers—lost its value the moment it fell into enemy hands. Besides that, the method was cumbersome, slow, and prone to mistakes, especially in messages sent by soldiers on the battlefield while shells were falling. (June Watkins of the Women's Auxiliary Air Force would learn this about subtraction tables in her code officers' course in Cairo, and use them in the basement of the Metropole Hotel—and she would complain in code-room slang that the "gremlins have certainly been at work" when messages arrived garbled from units in the desert.[29])

The alternative to a code is a cipher—replacing each letter of the original text with another letter. To hide the original words and create what looks like code groups, you take out all the spaces, spell out punctuation, and divide the text into groups of five.

A simple cipher, though, can be broken in minutes if the codebreaker has a long enough message. The most common letter in English is *e*. If replaced by *z*, then *z* will be the most common letter in the enciphered message. Code writers came up with methods to overcome this. But those techniques slowed up the process of enciphering and deciphering. Sometimes they did little but increase the number of messages that a codebreaker needed in order to break in.

But what if the code clerk sending a message could use a different cipher for every letter? What if you typed "EEEEE," and it came out "YBNWQ," and so on, an apparently unconnected stream of letters, ad infinitum? A would-be codebreaker looking for the most common letter in this message would be lost. To have any value, of course, the receiving clerk would need to have the same cipher for each letter. Yet the method would have to be quick and easy to use.

The new era of telegraph and radio made the need for a convenient but unbreakable code much more pressing, for businesses as for governments. Messages sent by Morse code in electrical pulses could too easily be read by the wrong people. Who knew who might be working at the cable company, or who might listen in, uninvited, to wireless transmissions? Say, for instance, you were at the Marconi Radiotelegraph Company office on El Madabegh Street in central Cairo, sending your partner in Buenos Aires a particularly attractive offer you'd gotten for a consignment of cotton. Would you want the message to fall into the hands of a competitor?

"If you have no good coding system, you are always running a considerable risk. Transmitted by cable or without wire, your correspondence will always be exposed to every spy . . . your intended or settled contracts, your offers and important news to every inquisitive eye," read a mid-1920s sales brochure from the Chiffriermaschinen (Cipher Machines) company of Berlin, advertising its new business device, the Enigma.[30]

The pamphlet showed something that looked like a close relative of the typewriter, sitting in a wooden box. The keyboard had twenty-six keys, for letters only. Behind the keyboard was a lamp board showing the letters of the alphabet, arranged in the same pattern as on the keyboard, each with a tiny electric light under it. At the back, instead of a place for paper, three toothed wheels stuck out of a lid. With the oak box and the battery, the whole thing weighed under fifteen pounds.[31]

Hidden inside each wheel was a web of wiring. The Enigma's German inventor, Arthur Scherbius, designed his machine so that each time you typed a letter, a pulse of electricity followed a tangled path through all three wheels and lit up one of the letters on the lamp board. A second clerk would watch and write down the letters as they lit up, creating the enciphered message. To write a number or punctuation mark, you spelled it out.

Hitting a key also made one of the wheels in back move a notch. Twenty-six keystrokes made it come full circle—and move the next wheel one notch. When the first wheel did another full circle, it moved the second wheel one more notch. When the second wheel went all the way around, it moved the third wheel once. It took over seventeen thousand keystrokes to bring all three wheels back to their original positions.

Since the wheels kept moving, the path changed each time you hit a key. Every position created a different cipher. If you typed "ZZZ," it might come out as "WMY" or "UGB." The one certainty on an Enigma was that Z would never come out as Z.

The elegant thing about Scherbius's code-department-in-a-box was that it worked both ways. If the clerk at the receiving end set the machine to the exact same starting position and typed in the meaningless string of letters she'd received, the original message appeared, one letter at a time, flashing from the little lights. At any other setting, the message remained a mystery. In the original design, there were close to two billion possible settings.[32]

In 1926, the navy of the Weimar Republic began using Enigma machines for its communications, followed by the German army in 1928. Nazi Germany's air force, the Luftwaffe, adopted the machine in 1935.[33] Other inventors created cipher machines in those years, but they were big and bulky—fine for embassies or stationary military headquarters. Enigma was perfectly suited for the new, fast-moving warfare that Germany was developing.

The German military upgraded Enigma in a way that upped the possible settings into the quintillions. This was actually a small number compared to the total possible ways to wire three different wheels. Rejewski would calculate that this came out to a number written as five, followed by ninety-two zeroes, a quantity beyond imagination.[34] The wires were the riddle wrapped inside the Enigma.

Obviously, no codebreaker was ever going to look at messages and figure out the wiring—not in a trillion years.

Rejewski did it in less than three months. No one else ever matched the feat.

He started working on the equations in the autumn of 1932, and solved the puzzle of the wiring by January 1933. Rozycki and Zygalski joined him to work on discovering the daily settings. By the time Hitler came to power in 1933, they could read every German military message that a Polish radio man at an interception station, straining to listen for Morse dots and dashes on the right frequency, could write down.[35]

The Warsaw office in which Rejewski and his two colleagues worked was on the third floor of an eighteenth-century Polish castle that had become the Polish General Staff building. From their window, they could look out at the Tomb of the Unknown Soldier. Diplomatic protocol required foreign dignitaries on official visits to pay respects at the tomb. The codebreakers could watch German foreign minister Joachim von Ribbentrop or Hitler's personal emissary Hermann Göring lay their wreaths without ever suspecting that three young mathematicians had found a back door to the Third Reich's military secrets.[36]

As Germany prepared for war, it kept adding twists to how it used Enigma to make it even more secure. Rejewski and his two coworkers kept breaking in. The job got more time-consuming, and there were only three of them.[37] The information they gleaned could not make up for Poland's military weakness. And the radio messages did not include the final betrayal—the secret provisions of the Molotov-Ribbentrop Pact between the Soviet Union and Germany, signed a week before Germany invaded Poland.

On September 17, under those provisions, the Soviet Union invaded eastern Poland. Rejewski and the rest of the German Section fled again, this time southward by truck to the Romanian border. Evading an internment camp, Rejewski, Rozycki, and Zygalski reached Bucharest and came to the British legation for help. A diplomat told them he'd have to check with London first.

The three Poles didn't want to take the chance of waiting in a city where they weren't supposed to be. They headed for the French embassy. French intelligence knew them. The embassy gave them passports, visas, and tickets, and they boarded yet another train—this time across the southern rim of Europe, through Yugoslavia and Italy to France.[38]

Poland was doomed, but its secret weapon had escaped with his life.

2

THE SEDUCTIVE CURVES
OF THE DUNES

September 1939. London-Cairo-Gilf Kebir.

THE TROOPSHIP HAD been a luxury liner till war broke out. Ralph Bagnold had been a civilian. Now Bagnold was back in the Royal Engineers uniform he'd worn nearly half his life, with the major's insignia on his shoulders, heading out yet again for a corner of the British Empire.

By the imperturbable unreason of the military, though, his destination was East Africa, rather than Egypt.[1] Bagnold knew the empty stretches of Egypt as well as any man alive, with the possible competition of Laszlo Almasy, the ambiguous Hungarian explorer.

Bagnold had followed his father into the Royal Engineers. He made officer by age nineteen, sped along by the voracious hunger of the Great War. After surviving the trenches, he completed a three-year degree in engineering at Cambridge in two years and returned to the military.[2] In 1926 he arrived in Cairo with his two-seater Morris automobile—Bagnold liked cars—to join the signal corps of the BTE, the British Troops in Egypt.[3]

The BTE was a minor military appendage of the empire, with little to do unless a rebellion broke out against the Egyptian government or against Britain's role in ruling the country. If you wanted no more than to play polo at the Gezira Sporting Club on its island in the Nile, Cairo was a fine posting.

Bagnold was bored. No one ever left the Nile Valley for the desert on either side. A fellow lieutenant bought a Model T, and Bagnold bought one like it, since his Morris wasn't built for roadless rock and sand. They started with several forays eastward. On a map of Transjordan, Bagnold saw the name Petra, the legendary ruins of a city that the ancient Nabateans had carved, not built, out of the walls of a red rock canyon. So he and his friend drove there on an untried route through the Sinai, with four other young officers to help push the cars out of sand when they got stuck. Bagnold was falling in love—with taking off with five other fellows and three cars to drive a thousand miles across land no one had ever driven, with the absolute silence of the desert night, with the "secret joy" of crawling beneath the car in mid-desert to change a broken spring with his own grease-covered hands.[4]

On the other side of the Nile lay terrain far harsher. Bagnold wanted to go there. The part of the Sahara known as the Libyan Desert stretched a thousand miles westward from the river, and a thousand miles from the Mediterranean southward. Herodotus wrote of the Persian army of fifty thousand men, sent by Cambyses, son of Cyrus the Great, which marched into the desert and was swallowed entirely by a sandstorm.[5] In the 1920s much of the desert was blank space on maps, calling seductively to explorers.

Kemal el Din, a millionaire Egyptian prince and cousin to the future King Farouk, ventured into the desert with cars riding half on wheels, half on caterpillar tracks. At the southwest corner of Egypt, near the border with Libya, he discovered a sandstone tableland the size of Switzerland rising out of the desert. He named it the Great Plateau, Gilf Kebir. The Great Sand Sea, a region of dunes hundreds of miles wide, ran from Gilf Kebir nearly to the Mediterranean. Together they created a barrier between Libya and Egypt much more substantive than the border that European diplomats had drawn on a map with a ruler. The waves of the Sand Sea were slow-moving sand dunes, as high as three hundred feet. The nineteenth-century explorer who named it concluded that his camels would never make it across the dunes. Kemal el Din reached the same conclusion about his half-tracks.[6]

Another Egyptian aristocrat, Ahmed Hassanein, led a camel expedition from the Mediterranean along the western side of the Great Sand Sea to a Libyan oasis called Kufra, and from there to Darfur in Sudan. Beyond Kufra, he came to a mountain called Uweinat, half-mythical till then, a mass of sandstone rising out of the desert that looked like "some colossal crumbling citadel surrounded down below by the mounds of its ruined town."[7] Uweinat was so massive that it caught rare clouds and knocked the rain out of them, so it had two pools at its base. In a gorge in the mountain, Hassanein found drawings of lions, ostriches, and giraffes and men with bows and arrows from a prehistoric era before a climate change burned savannah to desert.[8]

Hassanein made his eight-month, twenty-two-hundred-mile journey while on leave from the Egyptian Foreign Office. In his account of the expedition, he wrote of how the desert had bewitched him: he was like a man "deeply in love with a very fascinating but cruel woman. She treats him badly and the world crumples in his hand; at night she smiles on him, and the whole world is a paradise. The desert smiles, and there is no place on earth worth living in but the desert."[9] Afterward the Foreign Office sent him to represent Egypt in Washington and London. He returned from the diplomatic stints to become an adviser to kings, spending his life in meeting rooms and intrigues in Cairo, exiled from the desert.[10]

The Royal Engineers moved Bagnold to India, but he kept thinking about the Libyan Desert. There were areas out there the size of whole European countries, and no one knew anything about them.[11] This thought possessed him. On leaves, he came back to Egypt and set out into the emptiness.

To lighten their cars for traveling on sand, he and his friends stripped them of hoods, bumpers, and radiator covers. To save water, they designed a way to funnel the steam boiling out of the radiator into two-gallon cans on the running boards, where it cooled and could be reused. The dilettantes became professionals, who became pioneers of desert travel. The sands were devoid of landmarks, and the steel of the vehicles deceived compasses. Bagnold invented a solution: a sun compass. It looked like a sundial but worked in reverse. A sundial stays in one place, and the shifting direction of a shadow as the sun moves in the sky tells the time. Bagnold's sun compass rode on the dashboard. The navigator's watch told him the time of day. His readings of the stars at night provided each day's starting location. With that information and the shadow cast by the compass's needle, the navigator could calculate the precise direction for driving for days across blank, lifeless sands.[12]

Pictures of Bagnold from life outside the desert show him clean-shaven but for his precise moustache. The part in his dark hair is a sharp line; his expression is usually serious. In a photo from his 1929 expedition, he wears a wide-brimmed hat, a beard, and a delighted smile.[13] The beard was a necessity; water was too valuable for shaving. Even for drinking it was rationed to four pints per day.[14] On that trip, he and a new friend, Lieutenant Guy Prendergast, and their companions made their first foray into the Sand Sea. When they couldn't find a hoped-for passage between the waves of sand, Bagnold aimed his stripped-down Ford truck directly at a dune and pressed the accelerator. "Suddenly the light doubled in strength as if more suns had been switched on . . . The lorry tipped violently backwards . . . We floated up and up on a yellow cloud." Rather than sinking, they found themselves at the top.[15]

The next year, better prepared, they set out again. Prendergast, as infatuated with the desert and with automobiles as Bagnold, had become his constant partner. In five days, they and their companions crossed four hundred miles of dunes and came out on the Libyan side of the Great Sand Sea. The barrier was not impassable. But it contained mysteries. Bagnold wondered how the dunes could "behave like living things"— how a dune miles long could slowly march forward in a straight line, keeping its shape, like some immense worm, and how mature dunes could give birth to baby dunes that would run ahead of their mothers.[16]

From the Sand Sea they headed south to the Gilf Kebir, and beyond to the haunting rock paintings at Uweinat. Near the mountain, the transmission in one of their cars gave out. Bagnold was a careful man; the expedition traveled in three cars so that the loss of one didn't strand them. But "it was a mournful business leaving that car behind," Bagnold would recall.[17] "It looked so small and pathetic . . . it had carried me so far and struggled over so many obstacles."

From Uweinat, they turned east through Sudan, and reached the town of Wadi Halfa on the Nile. There Bagnold and his friends chanced on Pat Clayton, an Englishman who worked for the Egyptian government mapping the desert. In a Greek cafe, the thirsty men drank beer together and declared themselves the founders of a club dedicated to finding Zerzura—the Oasis of the Little Birds—a lush, legendary place known from unreliable medieval texts and from stories that earlier explorers heard from the scattered Arabs of the interior. Bagnold was still mourning his car. Clayton agreed to look for it, and Bagnold said he'd send spare parts and new tires.[18]

Searching for Zerzura would not be easy. Descriptions of the place and of its location contradicted each other wildly.[19] The one constant was water, flowing from the springs. Daughters and sons of the desert longed for a place of rushing streams and green trees. Sons and daughters of cloudy forested lands in the north came south and gave their hearts to sunlight and dunes. Their dreams met in the stories of Zerzura.

The Bagnold crew drove back into the desert and headed north toward Cairo. For the last part of the journey they followed the Darb el Arbain, the abandoned caravan route once used by traders bringing spices and human beings from sub-Saharan Africa to sell in the markets of Egypt. It was marked by the skeletons of camels that died along the way. There were no human skeletons; the single mercy of the slavers had been to bury the bodies of their merchandise.[20]

THE SPARE PARTS from Cairo arrived in Wadi Halfa by railroad and riverboat. In February 1931, Clayton set out toward Uweinat with his local drivers on his next surveying mission. Near Bagnold's car, they spotted the "tracks of a large party of Arabs, with camels and horses," Clayton reported. "Careful examination of the tracks showed footprints of women and children." This was a riddle: horses suggested a Beduin raiding party; footprints of women and children said the opposite.

Clayton left some men to work on the car and went on to one of the pools at the base of Uweinat, where he found a family of ten Beduin "in a starving and pitiable condition. The women's feet were so raw they could only crawl on hands and knees." They'd come across two hundred miles of lifeless land from the oasis of Kufra in Libya. They "had had no food in days, and no chance of either getting food or making their way on foot to any inhabited spot." They were fleeing Italian troops under General Rodolfo Graziani, and the machine guns of his airplanes that had pursued them.

Bagnold's car, it now seemed, had been deposited at Uweinat by providence. Clayton's men succeeded in repairing it. He loaded up all ten members of the family and drove more than two hundred miles through a sandstorm to his campsite. From there he sent them with one of his drivers on the two-day journey to Wadi Halfa, where the local hospital managed to save all of his passengers. In the weeks that followed, Clayton and his men covered five thousand miles in the desert, searched for tracks, personally rescued another twenty-seven people, and helped hundreds of others find paths to safety. And he learned of many others who lay down in the sands and died.[21]

Their bodies were small dots that made up part of a much larger picture. In 1911, Italy had gone to war with the Ottoman Empire and invaded Libya, the last piece of Africa still ruled from Constantinople. Libya was also the part of Africa closest to Italy. More importantly, other European powers had already grabbed almost all of the continent; Italy came late to the feeding frenzy. Its tenuous hold on the African coast nearly vanished during the Great War. When Benito Mussolini took power in 1922, he ordered the *riconquista*—the reconquest—of Libya. General Graziani, chosen to carry out the mission, called the Arabs and the Berber population *barbari*, barbarians, a term borrowed from the Roman Empire that the Fascist regime sought to renew.

Graziani became known as the Butcher. His forces not only killed armed rebels but murdered children and old people. Death often came from the sky; the Italian air force struck villages with poison gas and machine guns. The terror escalated when Mussolini appointed Field Marshal Pietro Badoglio governor of Libya in 1928. He and Graziani drove the inhabitants of inland Libya into concentration camps, where disease and starvation ruled. Badoglio ordered his soldiers to be "ferocious and inexorable." An estimated eight hundred thousand people lived in Libya when the Italian campaign began. One in eight—one hundred thousand people—died directly at the hands of Graziani's troops or starved to death in the *riconquista*.

The strongest guerrilla resistance came from the Senussi, an Islamic religious order that had spread among the Beduin in Cyrenaica, the eastern half of Libya. Kufra, a cluster of oases deep in Cyrenaica near the border with Egypt, was the Senussi religious center and stronghold. In January 1931, two columns of Graziani's forces converged on Kufra, supported by warplanes. Hundreds of men, women, and children with their camels and horses fled toward Egypt, Sudan, and the Chad province of French Equatorial Africa. The family near death that Clayton found at the Uweinat pool was a human communiqué to the outside world of Graziani's lopsided victory.[22]

The Italian conquest of Kufra shifted the meaning of exploring the desert. The border between Libya and Sudan—the latter officially under joint Egyptian and British rule—was disputed. In which territory did Uweinat lie, with its pools of drinkable water on the way to Wadi Halfa? The border between Egypt and Libya was merely a line drawn through vaguely known lands. And if Mussolini wanted a new Roman Empire, it was quite obvious that the old empire had ruled the Nile and the Levant. The Duce's dreams did not stop at an unmarked line in the sand.

BAGNOLD WASN'T THE first explorer to travel the Darb el Arbain—the Forty-Day Path—in an automobile. Laszlo Almasy did it the year before as the last part of a seventy-five-hundred-mile journey from Mombasa in Kenya to Cairo, with a millionaire adventurer as his companion and a Beduin guide.[23] His companion survived the trip. This wasn't always the case with Almasy. In an earlier venture driving wealthy tourists into the desert, he'd lost at least one.[24]

Almasy was the son of wealthy but titleless Hungarian aristocrats. He was a tall, thin man with a right triangle of a nose and a receding chin that together gave his face the profile of a large-beaked bird, such as the sparrow-lark of the Sahara.[25] Almasy longed for flight. As a gymnasium student during the very early years of aviation, he'd built his own aircraft—and crashed it, and spent months in a hospital.[26] He started the Great War as a cavalry officer in the Austro-Hungarian army but was transferred to the newly created air force. In a mission over the Italian Alps in 1918, his plane was hit by Italian fire. He made it back over the lines, crashed, and again found himself in a hospital bed. This didn't cure him of flying.[27] His later career suggests that surviving two crashes made a stronger impression on him than the crashes themselves.

Almasy had more bad luck: he'd fought for an empire that no longer existed when the war was over. In 1921, he took part in two failed attempts to put Charles, the last Habsburg emperor, on the empty throne of now independent Hungary. Charles rewarded Almasy by making him a count. The title came from an uncrowned king and was never confirmed by the Hungarian parliament. In Hungary, Almasy didn't use it.[28]

More misfortune: he was the second son, the one who didn't inherit. After the failed restoration, he worked as a bishop's private secretary. He led hunting parties, and drove in road races for the Austrian automobile company Steyr. He became an official of the Hungarian Boy Scouts, which may merely have shown attraction to "manly" pursuits. Then again, the scouts were tied to the paramilitary Hungarian National Defense Association, led by Hungarian fascist and anti-Semite Gyula Gömbös.[29]

Yet Gömbös had led the opposition to the royalist restoration.[30] Had Almasy switched right-wing factions, or simply found a convenient patron? His precise loyalties could be as uncertain as his title.

In 1926, at the age of thirty-one, Laszlo Almasy met the desert. It took time for him to realize that he had discovered the love of his life, to be convinced that "the desert is terrible, and it is merciless, but to the desert all those who once have known it must return."[31]

(Almasy wrote those words in a travelogue in Hungarian, saying they were a Beduin proverb. He'd actually taken them from Hassanein's book in English. Almasy's accounts of his own exploits also flare and flicker like lights on unreliable current.[32] He did not, however, steal Hassanein's metaphor of the desert as a "fascinating but cruel woman." It spoke to him less.)

Almasy came to Egypt as the representative of Steyr Automobiles. Away from Hungary, he began calling himself Count Laszlo de Almasy.[33] The job included driving the company's cars into roadless territory to show off what they could handle. On his first trip, he and a Hungarian prince followed the Nile into the Sudan. Where the river takes a wide bend, they cut across rocky desert, then continued south for big-game hunting. The shortcut introduced him to the desert. The next year, on impulse, he took a Beduin guide and drove 220 miles from Cairo across the sands to the Bahariya oasis, carrying two and a half gallons of water and no food. Getting there and back alive rivaled surviving an airplane crash.

These were flirts. The Darb el Arbain trip, he wrote, "was when the desert made me captive forever."[34]

In his telling, his Beduin guide on the caravan route first told him about Zerzura. Naturally he wanted to find the lost paradise. Almasy decided that the oasis must be in Gilf Kebir and that the way to find it was from the air. He went to England, bought a Gypsy Moth, a light plane, and flew in hops through Europe to the Middle East. Caught in a storm in northern Syria, he crash-landed, wrecking the plane.

But word of his planned expedition reached a wealthy twenty-three-year-old British baronet, Sir Robert Clayton, who was a newly trained Royal Navy pilot. He was no relation of desert surveyor Pat Clayton, rescuer of the Kufra refugees, who was recruited as the expedition's navigator. Almasy also brought in a Royal Air Force pilot, Hubert Penderel. They headed out to Gilf Kebir in the spring of 1932.

From a plane above the desert plateau, one could in fact see a hidden wadi lush with trees. But it was the British pilots who first spotted it. Almasy was away at the time, on a dash across the desert to Kufra to get water and fuel, of which he hadn't taken enough. There the Italian military commander of the oasis hosted him and the soldiers cheered him.

Unknown to his British friends, Almasy promised the Italian commander the map he was preparing of Gilf Kebir. Hungary's one dependable ally at the time was Fascist Italy. Yet Almasy also gave Pat Clayton photos of the Italian headquarters in Kufra. Perhaps he was still working out his allegiances. Perhaps he wanted to bank favors with everyone who controlled part of the desert.[35]

A year later, Almasy arrived in Kufra again, this time as a scheduled supply stop on yet another expedition. Back in Hungary, fascist leader Gyula Gömbös had just become prime minister. Almasy told the Italian intelligence officer at Kufra he'd received a message from Gömbös to provide "all help possible to Italy." He did. He turned over the map he'd promised of Gilf Kebir. It showed a pass that he and Penderel had discovered, which cut all the way through the plateau.[36]

In Italian military hands, the pass was a potential shortcut from Kufra to Upper Egypt. It would save an invading force the long loop southward around Gilf Kebir and Uweinat. Almasy may or may not have known that in the fall of 1932 Bagnold and Prendergast had met an Italian military patrol at an isolated well, in a piece of desert claimed by both Egypt and Italy. The Italian commander, Major Orlando Lorenzini, turned old fuel barrels on their sides, laid a tabletop across them, and served Bagnold's group a dinner of chicken, spaghetti, and Chianti spread on a white tablecloth. Rather indiscreetly, Lorenzini mused out loud, "The Nile at Aswan is only 900 kilometers from Uweinat. If there is a war, what fun it would be to take a battalion to Aswan and seize the dam. What could you do?"[37]

FOUR DECADES AFTER his death, "Count de Almasy" would come back to life as the central character in Michael Ondaatje's novel, *The English Patient*. In the novel, Almasy discovers a cave deep in the desert with prehistoric paintings of people swimming in since-vanished water. Just as war is about to erupt, he's on an expedition with an English couple—a pilot and his wife, Geoffrey and Katherine Clifton. The name is a slight shift from "Clayton." Almasy and Katherine fall in love; Geoffrey tries to kill his rival by crashing an airplane into him. Instead, Geoffrey is killed and Katherine mortally wounded. In his attempts to rescue her, Almasy is mistaken at one point for an Axis spy.

Within this fiction lies a seed of fact. Almasy's most famous discovery was the Cave of the Swimmers, on the west side of Gilf Kebir.[38] But he found the wall paintings in the autumn of 1933. By that time, Sir Robert Clayton had died—at the age of twenty-four, shortly after returning to England from his single expedition with Almasy. By one account, he came down with polio. In Almasy's telling, he died of blood poisoning from the bite of a fly in the desert.[39] Robert's wife, Dorothy—curiously nicknamed Peter—did in fact reach Gilf Kebir, but soon after his death, on an expedition in search of Zerzura with the surveyor Pat Clayton. She did not want to go with Almasy, possibly because she shared with others in the small circle of desert explorers a fear of his recklessness and the distaste of their day for his homosexuality.[40]

Dorothy Clayton was indeed mortally wounded in an aviation accident—taking off in England in a small plane in 1933, a year after her husband's death.[41] Almasy went on exploring Gilf Kebir, convinced that he had found Zerzura in deep wadis fed by rare rainfall.[42]

Almasy was secretly in love in the late 1930s, just not with Dorothy Clayton. The letters to him from his lover, the young German actor Hans Entholt, may be the only map, lightly sketched, of Almasy's inner world. In one letter, Entholt writes, "I told you long ago that all your adventures were only an escape." Another letter hints that Almasy is bothered by Hans's apolitical failure to share his enthusiasm for National Socialism.[43]

What is most truthful about *The English Patient* is that it is explicitly fiction. In Almasy's conflicting reports written in different languages, as in the countless accounts of the war that unintentionally celebrated the wrong people as heroes, or that intentionally did so, in the memories of people who knew only part of what happened or who misheard what were anyway rumors—in all these the line between fact and imagination is less definite.

Beneath each well-known piece of history is another story that was preserved in long-secret documents or in papers that men brought home and left in attics, or that died with women whose generation was widowed by the war. What has been told so many times that it is bright and definite and unambiguous may turn out to be a coded message from the past, meaning something else entirely, waiting to be deciphered.

THE ROYAL ARMY next shunted Bagnold to Hong Kong, where in 1934 he finished a book, *Libyan Sands: Travels in a Dead World*. The last chapter argues that the wadis found by Almasy in Gilf Kebir were not a true oasis fed by springs. Zerzura, wrote Bagnold, was not a real place, but a "wish-oasis," waiting to be found, "difficult of access, if one is enterprising enough to go to look." Zerzura was a destination worth searching for and always out of reach, which would vanish on the day when the entire earth had been explored.[44] Almasy said he'd found Zerzura. Bagnold was happy not to have.

Along with articles Bagnold had written in the *Times* of London about his journeys, *Libyan Sands* established him as a celebrity explorer. Meanwhile, army doctors determined that a bug called tropical sprue that he'd caught in Hong Kong, or perhaps on his journey to the ruins of Angkor Wat in Cambodia, had destroyed his stomach's ability to produce digestive acid, rendering him an invalid for life. He was discharged from the military, moved into a gentleman's serviced flat in London, ate his dinners at a club, and inexplicably recovered completely from his illness. So he set out to answer the questions he'd brought home from the desert about sandstorms and dunes that seemed to be alive. In the summer of 1939 he completed *The Physics of Blown Sand and Desert Dunes*, a scientific work mapping a previously unexplored field.[45] Decades later it would be used to understand the movement of dunes on Mars, where perhaps Zerzura was now to be sought.[46]

Bagnold finished his *Physics* just in time. Soon after, the army called him back. His troopship's intended route was to the Suez Canal, then down the east coast of Africa. In the Mediterranean, though, another ship collided with it. The damaged troopship put in at Port Suez, Egypt, at the north end of the Canal, where its passengers were to wait for the next convoy. Bagnold preferred to spend the accidental leave with friends. He got on the train to Cairo, a city trying to figure out whether it was at war.[47]

By then, Almasy had left.[48] Hungary was not at war, but its alliance with both Germany and Italy may have been reason enough for a well-known Hungarian to feel safer elsewhere—or to be told to leave. Besides Hans's letter, there's other testimony that Almasy firmly chose sides well before the war. It comes from shipping magnate Laszlo Pathy, who was Hungary's honorary consul in Egypt for the decade before the war. According to Pathy, in the mid-1930s he requested an audience with King Fouad to introduce Almasy. The king, it was known, wanted to create an Egyptian Desert Institute; Almasy wanted to head it and submitted his plans. Eight or ten days later, Pathy got a phone call from the king's chamberlain, curtly rejecting the Hungarian explorer. Later, Pathy would recount, he invited Trevor Evans, the private secretary of Ambassador Miles Lampson, for tea. Lampson's man explained the king's decision.

Both the British embassy and Egyptian intelligence, Evans said, had told the king that Almasy "was acting on behalf of the Nazis" and wanted the position to make it easier to do "spying in the desert" for Germany.

This is hearsay—a suspicion repeated by Evans, as Pathy remembered it long afterward.[49] Maybe until the summer of 1939, the dubious count's only solid allegiance was to the desert. In September, people had to make choices. Henceforth, Almasy's loyalties were finally certain.

3

NEXT KING OF THE NILE

September–October 1939. Cairo–Rome.

FAROUK, KING OF Egypt, had reigned three years when Germany invaded Poland.[1]

With his ascension to the throne, Farouk had inherited his late father Fouad's seventy-five thousand acres of fertile Nile Valley fields, making him the owner of the largest landholdings in Egypt. He inherited his father's palaces and compulsively acquired collection of weaponry—from daggers to pistols to cannons—to which Farouk compulsively added. The rifles in the collection did get used; Farouk liked to hunt big game in Sudan, nominally part of his realm. He collected rare coins, too, and cars, starting with the Austin sports car his father gave him when he was eleven to drive around the palace grounds, and including the Mercedes Benz that Adolf Hitler gave him as a wedding gift, the same make used by high Nazi officials.[2] All of his cars were red. No one else in Egypt was allowed to own a red car.

Nonetheless, Farouk was a popular monarch, in part because he was the first of his dynasty who could give a speech in Arabic, the language of his country.

Farouk was nineteen years old in 1939. He could have whatever he wanted, except full rule of Egypt.

Farouk's great-great-grandfather, an Albanian officer in the Ottoman army named Muhammad Ali, arrived in Cairo in 1801. A French army originally led by the ambitious young general Napoleon Bonaparte had occupied the Ottoman province of Egypt for three years. When the French foray into the Middle East collapsed, Egypt was left in chaos. Muhammad Ali and his skilled Albanian soldiers were supposed to bring the Nile back under Constantinople's control.

Instead, he brought Egypt under his own control. In the course of his rise, Muhammad Ali forced Ottoman sultan Selim III to recognize him as governor. He massacred the Mameluke aristocrats whose families had dominated Egypt since long before the Ottomans came. He seized their land and the land held in trust by Islamic institutions, much as Henry VIII had seized the holdings of British monasteries. He developed cotton as Egypt's export crop. He built schools and sent graduates off to study in Europe so they could return as technocrats before the term existed. He built a conscript army on European lines, put down a revolt in Arabia for the sultan, and then sent an army into the Levant, intending to take Constantinople so he could replace the sultan. Britain forced him to retreat. As quid pro quo, it forced the sultan to make Muhammad Ali's governorship hereditary. In name, the Ottomans were still sovereign. In reality, Egypt was independent—but the new lords of the land still spoke Turkish.

Muhammad Ali's grandson Ismail set out to build a new European Cairo, a Mediterranean Paris with wide avenues and grand villas, with parks and museums and an opera house, next to the old Cairo. Wealthy Egyptians lived in the new town along with immigrants from around the Mediterranean drawn to the rising metropolis: Italians, Greeks, Jews and Christians from the Levant, and others. The two Cairos stood for two Egypts: one where people spoke French, Italian, and Greek, sent their children to European schools, and traded with the world; another where people spoke Arabic, owned tiny bits of land or worked the land of the wealthy, and for the most part went to no schools. The American Civil War gave Ismail a windfall: the Union blockade of the South sent world cotton prices climbing fourfold. When the war ended and the cotton bubble burst, he went on spending. He hired out-of-work Confederate officers in his bid to expand his realm southward to create his own African empire, another step toward matching European monarchs.

In the process, Ismail virtually mortgaged the country to European banks. He sold his family shares in the new Suez Canal at fire-sale prices. Britain and France took over Egypt's finances, then forced Ismail to abdicate in favor of his son, Tewfik, in 1879. Ismail went into exile in Italy. Conditions for Egyptians worsened. In 1881 a revolt broke out against Tewfik. In September 1882, British troops took Cairo, this time to stay.

It was a bizarre conquest. Tewfik remained the *khedive*, the viceroy, ostensibly for the Ottomans. In reality, Egypt was under military occupation, and the British consul general ruled the country. The cotton went to Britain, as did the profits, with the added value for the occupier that British military rule guaranteed the defense of the Suez Canal, the short route from Britain to India, Singapore, and Hong Kong. When the Great War broke out in 1914, the fiction of Ottoman sovereignty became impossible to maintain. Tewfik's son, Khedive Abbas Hilmi II, publicly urged Egyptians to support the Central Powers. Britain declared Egypt a protectorate and replaced Abbas Hilmi with another of Ismail's sons. When he died, Ismail's youngest son, Fouad, who'd grown up mostly in Italy with his exiled father, took his place.

After the war, a group of prominent Egyptians formed a delegation—a *wafd* in Arabic—to attend the Versailles peace conference. In Europe, the victors were breaking up the defeated empires and granting nations their independence. US president Woodrow Wilson's Fourteen Points endorsed the hopes of the age: it promised borders and statehood based on nationality—a country for Polish speakers, a country for speakers of Czech and Slovakian.

Egypt, though, had the misfortune to be ruled by a victorious empire, and to be in Africa, not Europe. Britain blocked the delegation and exiled its leaders. Cairo's streets filled with demonstrations, followed by riots. British troops stamped out the revolution, but sparks kept bursting into flame. Wilson's recognition of the British protectorate over Egypt in the midst of the uprising added American betrayal to British repression.[3] The segregationist US president apparently did not think that the progressive principles of self-determination should apply to Africa.

In 1922, Britain compromised and proclaimed Egypt an independent country, at least in name. Fouad was crowned king. The delegation to Versailles established a political party dedicated to full independence, the Wafd, which won a landslide victory in the first elections. On paper, Egypt was now a constitutional monarchy, modeled on Britain. What became known as Egypt's liberal age began.

In reality, the Wafd was committed to the "constitutional" part of that description, the palace only to "monarchy." And the protectorate remained. Britain had dictated the terms of Egypt's faux independence, pending an agreement someday in the future on relations between the two countries. Britain's representative, the high commissioner, played the king and the Wafd against each other. The British Troops in Egypt stayed on. The Egyptian army "was kept in the requisite state of tranquility by the British officers seconded to it and by depriving it of artillery, modern arms and . . . ammunition," as Raymond Maunsell, who became the intelligence officer of the British Troops in Egypt in 1932, would write. The European Department of the Egyptian Interior Ministry, headed by British officials, "was, in fact, in control of the entire security apparatus of the Egyptian government."[4]

(Maunsell was unusual among junior officers for getting out beyond the Gezira Club and Cairo's bars. He spoke Arabic and had been one of Bagnold's exploring companions before getting the intelligence post.[5]) Cairo drew more foreigners—some of them refugees from dictatorships rising in Europe—and more landless peasants. For the poor, Egypt was a Dickensian nightmare under very bright sunlight. In Egypt as a whole, one out of every two children died by age five. Just one-seventh of the population was literate. Meanwhile, most members of parliament owned large tracts of land—feudal lords wearing the suits of democratic politicians. In Cairo, wealthy Egyptians shopped at the same new department stores as foreigners. Men could spend long evenings at bars, or in Cairo's red-light district. The liberation of better-off Egyptian women proceeded only as far as attending school and not wearing veils. The women of the royal family, descended from Muhammad Ali and intermarried with Ottoman royals, wore low-cut gowns to balls—except for the young Queen Nazli, wife of Fouad, who was kept a near-prisoner in the palace, out of sight of other men.[6]

Princess Nevine, one of Farouk's countless cousins, recorded in her memoirs that her parents did not let her and her siblings "learn Arabic too early as it would ruin our pronunciation" in European languages. When her grandmother got around to teaching her Muslim prayers, Nevine had to memorize the sounds by rote. The real native language of the royal clan was mutual resentment, since all the princes thought that "at one point or the other they or their fathers should have reigned" if the succession had proceeded properly.[7]

WHILE PRINCES BICKERED, a different succession took place: in 1933 a new high commissioner, Sir Miles Lampson, moved into the British Residency. Lampson was a career diplomat, fresh from seven years in Peking, and a recent widower. The word "imperious" could have been invented for Lampson, and not just because of his dedication to the British Empire. He stood six feet, five inches and weighed 250 pounds. Two motorcycle outriders, blasting their whistles, escorted his car on Cairo streets. He did not carry money, or his own cigarette case or fly whisk; lesser beings handled those things. He had a secretary whose job was to take down the diary entries that he dictated to record his meetings, dinner guests, and the precise number of birds he and his guests had killed in his frequent excursions to the British Residency's private hunting grounds.[8]

In Cairo, Lampson met a high-society visitor, Jacqueline Castellani, daughter of a famous Italian physician and his English wife. When they married at the end of 1934, she was twenty-four; he was fifty-three.[9]

Farouk often appeared in Lampson's pages as "the boy."[10] True, Farouk really was a boy of sixteen when King Fouad died suddenly in April 1936, and his smooth, round, pale face looked even younger. Farouk was in London at the time, studying part-time at the Royal Military Academy at Woolwich, accompanied by two chaperones, the former diplomat and desert explorer Ahmed Hassanein and Aziz el-Masri, an Egyptian military man. In early May, Farouk returned to Egypt, to the cheering of orchestrated crowds at whistle-stops between Alexandria and Cairo.

Parliamentary elections had just been held; the Wafd won over three-quarters of the seats. Lampson discreetly met with Wafd leader Mustafa el-Nahas and leaders of lesser parties about who would sit on a three-man regency council, which would reign in Farouk's place until he came of age. Lampson told each politician that he "had no desire to get mixed up in purely Egyptian affairs." Asked if he insisted on seeing the names of the regents in advance, Lampson replied that "insistence was too strong a word." In diplomacy, the strongest way to confirm something can be to deny it very softly.

Nahas wanted Farouk to go back to England to complete his education. The young king was popular and—Nahas thought—dependent on the British. Lampson agreed with Nahas that having Farouk around was bad for parliamentary power and for Egyptian independence. For just those reasons, Lampson kept the king in Cairo, and arranged for Eton College to send him a tutor from England.[11]

A few months later the tutor complained to Hassanein, now the chamberlain of the royal household, "As to my job . . . I had never been given an opportunity even of trying to do it. I neither lived in the palace nor saw the king more than once or twice a week if I was lucky." Hassanein, the closest thing that Farouk now had to a father figure, was sympathetic but "dislikes doing even the gentle amount of scolding which he can hardly avoid." The tutor observed that Hassanein was "largely preoccupied" with Queen Nazli, Farouk's mother, who was liberated by the death of Fouad. This observation was shared by virtually all of Egyptian high society.[12]

Farouk was powerless, the regents compliant. For Lampson, this made it easier to wrap up negotiations with Nahas, now prime minister, on the long-delayed treaty between Britain and Egypt.[13]

The agreement, signed in August 1936, opened by proclaiming that "the military occupation of Egypt . . . is terminated." What came after qualified this. Sudan, until further agreement, would still be joint Egyptian-British territory. (Sudan was the southern part of Ismail's old kingdom. Officially Egypt shared sovereignty there with Britain. In reality, a British general ruled it as a colony.) Britain would keep ten thousand troops near the Suez Canal to protect the waterway, but would gradually remove its army from Cairo and Alexandria. The two countries would have a military alliance. If either were at war, the other would "immediately come to [its] aid." And if Britain were at war, "His Majesty the King of Egypt" would give Britain the use of his ports, airfields, and territory, and would censor the press and declare martial law.[14]

War was more than an abstract possibility. Mussolini's Italy had just conquered Ethiopia. An Italian marching song from that war went,

> *We want to renew*
> *the great Empire of Rome*
> *marching on the path*
> *that the Duce has shown us.*[15]

With Ethiopia subdued, Mussolini proclaimed that Italy was now a "Fascist empire."[16] In Europe, Mussolini's new foreign minister, his thirty-three-year-old playboy son-in-law Galeazzo Ciano, was meeting Nazi leaders to create what would become known as the Rome-Berlin Axis. (The name was coined by Hungary's fascist prime minister, Gyula Gömbös.) Separating Italian East Africa and Libya, obstinately and temptingly, lay Egypt and Sudan.[17] This threat may explain why Nahas agreed to the military provisions that left British troops in Egypt. He wanted a free Egypt, not Italy taking Britain's place. Nahas had a cold, sober view of fascism.[18]

The treaty said Egypt was independent. So Lampson's title switched from high commissioner to ambassador. His home was now officially the embassy, but the old name, the British Residency, stuck to it. Lampson's view of his job remained that discreetly, but "with tact and firmness, British influence should remain the governing factor" in Egypt.[19]

The most "important but secret" Egyptian desire and goal, according to Raymond Maunsell, was abolishing the British-run European Department of the Interior Ministry. A free Egypt couldn't have another country running its security services. Britain conceded the point—more or less.

With the Ethiopia crisis, Maunsell had been promoted to major and given the new post of "district security officer," the DSO, which meant the representative of Britain's MI5 counterintelligence agency in an overseas British territory. During the treaty negotiations, Maunsell "visited the European Department . . . two or three times a week, armed with a capacious briefcase which various British officials helped to fill with files." As far as MI5 was concerned, Egypt was still British turf, and its man in Cairo needed the written memory of the European Department. He also needed ongoing Egyptian cooperation. So "it became necessary and expedient," Maunsell would write, "to give certain Egyptian officers in the secret police 'subsidies' . . . and this helped considerably to oil the wheels."[20]

Another part of the deal was that Britain would expand and train Egypt's own army.[21] It needed more officers, so in the autumn of 1936, for the first time, the Egyptian military academy in Cairo accepted some cadets who came from middle-class or poor families.[22] Anwar al-Sadat, the village-born son of a low-level government clerk, got in.[23] Gamal Abdel Nasser, son of a postal worker, was turned down at first but got accepted a year later and managed to graduate with Sadat. Later accounts by the students of those years describe the academy as an incubator of intense Egyptian nationalism, sharply spiced with resentment of the academy's British military advisers.[24] According to Maunsell, Nasser never came to the DSO's attention as a potential subversive.[25]

In the summer of 1937, Farouk reached the age of eighteen according to the lunar Islamic calendar, in which each year has 354 days. As he rode from his palace to parliament for the ceremony making him king, crowds lining the streets showed "wild enthusiasm, such as the country rarely has seen before" for "the beloved young monarch," the *New York Times* reported in a glowingly royalist item. Ignoring centuries of medieval Islamic history, the newspaper proclaimed him the "first independent ruler of Egypt since the days of the pharaohs."[26]

Farouk *was* popular, and cocksure. He despised Nahas, his rival for power in Egypt, insulted him, and took "what he thought was innocent pleasure in baiting him," according to a British diplomat.[27] Farouk's closest adviser was Ali Maher, a master of backroom dealing who had served his father. The Wafd, meanwhile, was suffering from ailments common to independence movements after they achieve their goal: corruption, divvying up of government positions between the faithful, and absence of a new program.

Encouraged by Maher, the king dismissed Nahas's government and called elections. Ballot stuffing, gerrymandering, and throwing Wafd voters out of polling places reduced the party to a few seats in the new parliament.[28] Farouk picked a new prime minister who would be loyal to the palace. But Ali Maher, as chief of the royal household, was the voice whispering closest to the king's ear—along with the court architect, Ernesto Verucci, an Italian also inherited from Farouk's father. Fouad's nostalgia for Italy showed in the servants and advisers he bequeathed to his son.[29]

IN AUGUST 1939, in Cairo as in Paris, London, and Warsaw, you could feel the hurricane of war rushing toward the coast of the world.

Farouk's prime minister was ill and wanted a rest cure at the Mediterranean beach town of Mersa Matruh. Farouk took the opportunity to replace him with Ali Maher. The new cabinet appointed Aziz el-Masri, Farouk's former chaperone in London, as chief of staff of the Egyptian military.[30] The name Masri means "Egyptian" in Arabic. It testified to his own underconfidence about that identity. Masri was born in Cairo in 1879, but his family was Circassian—an ethnic group that fled the Caucasus Mountains in the nineteenth century to escape genocide at Russian hands and became a warrior class in the Ottoman Empire. He changed his last name to Masri as a student at the military academy in Constantinople to stress his Egyptian and Arab loyalties. During the Great War he served briefly as chief of staff to Sharif Hussein, the ruler of Mecca who launched the Arab revolt against the Ottomans. They fell out because Masri urged an improbable alliance with Germany. Hussein preferred the alliance with Britain offered by T. E. Lawrence, known as Lawrence of Arabia. When the war ended, Masri returned to his native city.[31]

As for Maher, the British considered him a good administrator but a suspect character. An embassy expert on Arab affairs described him as "a small ravenous wolf driven by furnace-heats of ambition." (However justified the suspicions that Maher was pro-Axis, it also appears that the British did not approve of ambition in local leaders, and that they sometimes judged a man's character by his height.) Lampson worried that Maher might pass military secrets to the Germans. But the imperious ambassador didn't want to interfere openly in Egyptian politics. It would make Egypt's independence look false, and could ignite unrest when Britain had bigger problems.[32]

On September 1, Lampson went to see Maher. Britain was about to go to war. The pledges in the Anglo-Egyptian Treaty had come due, Lampson said. The prime minister agreed. Maher and Farouk declared a state of siege in Egypt. For practical purposes, Britain's military occupation of Egypt would remain in place. Two days later, though, Maher had bad news for the ambassador: he couldn't join Britain that day in declaring war on Germany. The reasons that he gave shifted: Maher said he needed a unanimous cabinet vote, and some ministers were holding out. They feared Germany would respond with "an aerial attack on Egypt," and as a result "the country would turn on the government." Britain didn't have enough troops in Egypt to defend it, and "might contemplate a strategic sacrifice" of the country after pulling it into the conflict. Besides, declaring war would look like taking orders from London. Parliament might not go along. The public wouldn't understand why Egypt needed to get involved in a distant war.[33]

But was it distant? That depended on what Italy would do.

On August 30, Benito Mussolini ordered nightly blackouts in Rome, and air-raid siren tests, and closing of cafes and public entertainment. On August 31, the Duce reversed himself and gave "orders that the lights of the city be turned back on," Galeazzo Ciano wrote in his diary.[34]

The ambassadors in their ornate buildings in and around the Ludovisi district of Rome did not need a codebook to read the message signaled in the city's lights: Mussolini knew that Hitler was going to war and kept changing his mind about whether to join him.

Ciano spent all August arguing against it. In 1936 he had been the matchmaker of the Axis. Germany's promise to recognize Italy's empire helped sway him. So did the shared belief in dictatorship and in the destiny and vitality of the "young nations"—Italy, Germany, and Japan too—that had come late to the fifteen-sided chess game of global power politics.[35]

Germany's takeover of Czechoslovakia ignited Ciano's doubts. He didn't object to conquest as such. He'd fought in Ethiopia and wrote the year after, "I miss that war."[36] When Hitler entered Prague, Ciano was planning Italy's conquest of Albania, which took place the next month. Ciano was plotting to foment an insurrection in Croatia that was supposed to end with Italy taking it from Yugoslavia. He was a dedicated Fascist, even though his father-in-law, Mussolini, accused the bourgeoisie of "cowardice, laziness and love of the quiet life," and he, Ciano, was a rich man's son who spent much of his time at the golf course, often at the clubhouse bar.[37] He worshipped his father-in-law as he worshipped his own father.

But Germany, he concluded, was a dangerous, undependable ally. It grabbed up countries without forewarning Italy. It promised Italy the Balkans and the Mediterranean for its empire but couldn't be trusted. Hitler might have his own eyes on Croatia.

Germany, Ciano wrote after meetings with Hitler and his foreign minister, Joachim von Ribbentrop, in early August 1939, was "possessed by the demon of destruction." In a meeting with Ciano near the end of the fateful month, Mussolini said that Germany was evading diplomacy over its demands of Poland because Hitler didn't want Italy to get in the way of his war, as Mussolini had the year before by proposing the Munich Agreement. Ciano wrote that he had a "simpler explanation, namely, that the Germans are treacherous and deceitful." He added, "Could there ever be a more revolting pig than von Ribbentrop?" Ciano was right about treachery, but this time Mussolini read Hitler accurately. The Führer did not want to get any older before going to war.[38]

Mussolini dithered. He often agreed with Ciano, but was very afraid of looking like a coward.[39] On September 1, he decided at last on "nonintervention." Ciano did not relax. In his diary he recorded, "The Duce is convinced of the need to remain neutral, but he is not at all happy."[40]

MUSSOLINI'S CHOICE ALLOWED a man named Major Manfredi Talamo to go on doing what he did best: breaking, entering, and safecracking. His targets were embassies, especially Britain's. War would have inconvenienced him.

Talamo pulled off one of his early jobs during the Ethiopia campaign. He and his men entered the British embassy on Via Venti Settembre.

(A fifteen-minute walk in one direction on the avenue would take you to Mussolini's residence, the Villa Torlonia; a fifteen-minute walk the other way would bring you to the War Ministry.) They opened the ambassador's safe, removed documents, photostatted them in a nearby War Ministry studio, and returned them the same night. The temporary theft went undetected.

The booty included the secret Maffey Report, written the year before, when Italy was threatening to invade Ethiopia but had not yet struck. The report concluded that it would make little difference to British interests in Africa whether the country was independent or not. In practice, the British government had rejected that conclusion and opposed the Italian conquest. To embarrass Britain, Mussolini had the report leaked to the Rome newspaper *Il giornale d'Italia*. From there it spread to the press around the world.

The risk of a propaganda coup based on espionage is that the injured country will investigate, change codes and locks, hunt down spies. To protect its source, Italy's Military Information Service—Servizio Informazioni Militari, or SIM—spread a rumor that someone had photographed the report in the British embassy in Paris, and from there it had reached the Italian government.[41]

Talamo had come up through the ranks of the Carabinieri, Italy's national paramilitary police. In 1933, he was assigned to the Carabinieri's counterespionage center, which operated under SIM. Then or soon after he became the center's commander.[42]

Even before Talamo's arrival, SIM was recruiting collaborators among Italians who worked in foreign embassies. Francesco Costantini, employed at the British embassy, had for years been filching papers and turning them over to the Italian intelligence service.[43] His brother Secondo, another embassy employee, helped him. Unknown to SIM, the brothers Costantini made a double profit by providing copies to the Rome station of Soviet intelligence agencies. This did not reduce the value of British secret documents that landed on Mussolini's desk.[44]

Talamo turned a scattershot method into an ongoing, meticulously run operation: the Removal Section—the Sezione Prelevamento, or P Squad. Under Talamo worked a dozen or so noncommissioned officers. Each was assigned an embassy, perhaps two. Over months, even years, they got to know Italians who worked there and identified who might be turned into agents. Their candidates were invited to the War Ministry, where they were interviewed by a man dressed in civilian clothes, who had dark, wavy hair, a pudgy face, and a southern Italian accent, and who gave his name as something other than Talamo. He offered a salary, which was not open to negotiation. If they said no, they were warned never to talk about the meeting. If they said yes, they were told to learn everything about the layout of the embassy, its schedule, and the habits of its denizens. And they waited, patiently, for the chance to make wax impressions of unattended keys to doors and safes, which they delivered to Talamo so that he could make copies.[45]

At the Argentine embassy, Talamo recruited a chauffeur. At the Portuguese legation, he enlisted a servant, and another at the residence of the Portuguese minister—in practice, the ambassador, but with a diplomatic rank one rung lower. At the Swiss legation, a servant named Peppino worked for him. At the French embassy, Talamo's man, or at least one of them, was a porter. A typist at the Turkish embassy worked for Talamo, as did the maid of the Turkish military attaché. A doorman at the American embassy was on the P Squad's payroll, and a doorman at the Japanese embassy, where Talamo also recruited the head messenger, who doubled as an embassy typist and made copies of all the ambassador's cables and reports to Tokyo. A footman at the British embassy named Paesano was on Talamo's payroll; either he or someone with a very similar name was also employed as a messenger for the US military attaché.[46]

The maid at the home of an Egyptian diplomat made wax impressions of his keys while he was taking a bath. The P Squad signed up an Italian man whose lover was a secretary at the Swedish legation, and who convinced her to type up extra copies of documents for him. To get keys from one of the Balkan embassies, a P Squad agent arranged for a woman to invite a diplomat home.[47] The agent hid under the bed, extracted the keys from the diplomat's pants, pressed them into wax, and put them back in the man's pocket while the diplomat was engaged in a frank and cordial exchange with his hostess.[48]

Talamo's NCOs were ordered not to discuss their work with each other. Between themselves, they whispered the rumor that their commander had made his own connections with diplomats rather than servants, but they never knew for sure. Talamo strictly followed the rules he set for secrecy; he told them nothing but what they needed to know.[49] They did know for sure that their commander was the maître d' of a hotel called Rome, in which the rooms were embassies. He had keys to nearly all of them.[50]

Francesco Costantini lost his job at the British embassy in 1936, possibly due to the Maffey Report theft. But his brother stayed on. At the start of the next year, in Ambassador Eric Drummond's personal quarters, Secondo Costantini opened what was known as a "red box"—a wooden lockbox ornately clad in red leather, used to carry secret documents. Inside, instead of papers, lay Drummond's daughter's diamond necklace. Secondo was not one to spit in fortune's eye. He took the jewelry.

When the theft was noticed, Britain's Secret Intelligence Service—otherwise known as MI6—sent Major Valentine Vivian, the head of its own counterespionage unit, to Rome to investigate. His report described a thief's paradise. All the embassy's keys, Vivian wrote, had surely been copied, since the diplomats "habitually" took them to their residences, where Italian servants could make wax impressions. At least six staffers had identical keys that opened all the red boxes. The embassy did have a safe with a combination lock, where keys should have been left at night. Vivian found the combination on a piece of paper—stored in a red box.

If a thief nonetheless lacked a key, he could open the embassy press officer's wooden cabinet by removing six screws. Among the documents stored there was the "confidential print," a secret Foreign Office digest of papers from key British embassies around the world. When the embassy was closed at night and during the long Mediterranean afternoon break, the only guard was a Carabinieri soldier at the gate. Vivian described him as "a menace rather than a safeguard."

Britain had a separate legation to the Holy See. Since the Vatican was too small for embassy buildings, the legation was located elsewhere in Rome—on the grounds of the Guardia di Finanza, the Italian financial police. The Vatican legation also received the confidential print from London. "The legation premises . . . are entirely unoccupied at night and afford no protection whatever for the documents they house," Major Vivian found.

MI6's man saw local employees—Italians, or British subjects who were longtime Italian residents—as the greatest threat to security. "Certain countries—Italy, Germany, the USSR and Japan in particular—must be treated as 'enemy' countries," the MI6 man wrote, and it had to be assumed that their intelligence agencies would exploit every opening to bribe or pressure locals working at embassies. In Rome, Vivian said, there was "at least one traitor" on the embassy payroll, and he strongly suspected Secondo Costantini. Major Vivian's report included a long list of recommendations, from replacing cabinets to replacing Italian workers with people sent from the United Kingdom.[51]

None of this was done. Later in the year "a further leakage came to notice," and Vivian's instructions were repeated. Nothing happened.[52]

Vivian went on to inspect the British embassy in Berlin and wrote a similarly scathing report. The British ambassador took two months of vacation every summer, leaving his German porter free to access the embassy at night when the offices were closed. "The Gestapo could . . . introduce nightly and for a practically unlimited period each night any number of locksmiths and experts in safe-breaking," Vivian wrote.[53] The ambassador, however, thought very little of MI6, and the results of Vivian's Berlin report apparently matched those of the Rome report.[54]

Employing the reckless Costantini brothers stood in contrast to Talamo's usual micromanaged precision. He took care of every detail of each entry. In most cases, Talamo went in personally, leaving his men outside to keep watch. He would open the targeted safe, note the precise arrangement of the contents, take what he wanted to the War Ministry photo studio, supervise the photostatting, and return everything to its position.

Sometimes, instead, Talamo gave the copied keys to a safe to his agent inside the embassy, who removed the documents and gave them to Talamo for copying. Once everything was back in place, Talamo took the keys. That's how he raided the Belgian legation twice in 1937. The Belgians did not like to work late. The operations took place between five and six in the evening, and yielded codebooks along with other documents. Talamo stole the Portuguese legation's cipher books and the Turkish military attaché's cipher.

SIM had its own codebreakers, but too few of them. Safecracking was quicker.

The two operations complemented each other. If you know how a country builds its codes, and what phrases repeat in its messages, unraveling a code is much easier. The Portuguese legation got a new cipher the year after Talamo's raid, but the information gleaned from the old cipher helped SIM break the new one.[55]

In May 1939, the Duce instructed the Servizio Informazioni Militari to pass any new British papers it acquired to Germany.[56] Whether or not Talamo's own commanders told him this, he had acquired a new client.

Three months later, Germany went to war. Mussolini reluctantly stayed out. Talamo stepped up the frequency of thefts from the British embassy.[57]

ON SEPTEMBER 4, *Al Aharam*, Egypt's largest-circulation newspaper, reported that it still had no word from its Rome correspondent on Italy's intentions. But it put together the clues. Rome radio stations, it said, had carried British prime minister Neville Chamberlain's speech on going to war. Italian diplomats in Cairo hadn't been told to close their legation. "The Italian liner Marco Polo is today sailing from Italy to Alexandria," it reported. All this indicated that "Italy is not yet ready to range herself alongside Germany."[58]

As the days passed and that prediction held true, the Foreign Office in London reluctantly accepted Lampson's view: it wasn't worth pushing Ali Maher and Farouk to declare war.[59] In practice, Britain prepared to defend Egypt as part of the empire. Officially, Egypt was a "nonbelligerent."[60]

The morning after Ralph Bagnold got to Cairo, he dropped in at General Headquarters Middle East to see a friend from his days serving there. The friend was now chief signals officer of the British Troops in Egypt.

"Just the man," his friend said. "Wavell wants to see you at once."

Bagnold was baffled. As far as he'd known, he was uninvited and unexpected. He couldn't figure out how General Archibald Wavell knew he was in Egypt or what Wavell himself was doing there.

It turned out that a reporter for the English-language *Egypt Gazette* had spotted him the evening before. The morning paper reported correctly that the famous desert explorer was back in town, and incorrectly that the War Office had assigned him to the right place. As for Wavell, he'd been appointed to head the new and still mostly theoretical Middle East Command, for the moment consisting of the small British forces responsible for internal security in Egypt, Sudan, and Palestine. Wavell was supposed to turn them into an army, but to be quiet about it and avoid provoking Italy.

The signals officer took Bagnold to a small upstairs office, where he found "a rather stocky man with a grim weatherbeaten face, with one very bright eye." Wavell asked if he'd like to serve in Egypt, and arranged for the War Office to transfer him. He was sent to Mersa Matruh on the coast, where Britain's single armored division in Egypt—incomplete, inexperienced, and untrained for desert fighting—was deployed to stop an Italian invasion.[61]

4

THE MACHINE IS THE FUTURE

Autumn 1939. Bletchley Park-Warsaw-
Paris.

A LINE OF trees protected the country estate from the rumble of the
trains passing by on the London-Scotland and Cambridge-Oxford
lines. A fence ran around the estate—no barbed wire yet—and a sentry
stood at the gate when Gordon Welchman drove up. On his first day,
his name was most likely on a list for the sentry. After that he'd need
the daily password, though the sentries weren't strict about this once
they knew a face.[1]

Up the drive from the gate stood the mansion, with its improbable collection of gables, arches, stonework, peaked roofs, and a cop-
per dome. A stockbroker who'd been rewarded for his riches by being
made a baronet had lived there for over forty years. He'd completed
his pose of country gentleman by planting a maze on the grounds and
hundreds of trees including a sequoia redwood from California.[2]

The mansion now housed confusion. MI6, the Secret Intelligence
Service, had set up its wireless communication station in an attic. An
aerial ran from the top of the house to the towering redwood. MI6
took over the bedrooms on the second floor for its offices. Ground-
floor rooms went to the telephone exchange and the teleprinters

and to workspace for the people who broke army, navy, and air force codes for the half-euphemistically named Government Code and Cypher School, Britain's signal intelligence agency. The director of the GC&CS, Alastair Denniston, established his office in the morning sitting room of the lady of the estate, where the picture window looked out on the lawn, the circular carriageway, and the lake.[3]

The prewar staff had moved into Bletchley Park in mid-August. In early September, after Britain went to war, new people kept arriving, asking where they were supposed to go and looking for other people they knew, as if GC&CS really were a school and this was the start of the term. Space ran out in the mansion, despite it having twenty-three bedrooms, and in the cottage behind the stable yard, probably the former home of the groom. MI6 bought the small private grammar school that neighbored the estate, and the section that worked on diplomatic codes moved in.[4]

The year before, when the Sudentenland crisis boiled over, MI6 director Admiral Hugh Sinclair had decided his agency needed a location safer than central London. When people in Britain thought of war with Germany, they thought of Guernica, the town that the German air force had shattered in a single day during the Spanish Civil War. So Sinclair went looking for real estate in the countryside. The widow of Bletchley Park's baronet had died, and his son had sold the place to a developer. Sinclair found it before the new owner had time to tear down the mansion and start building houses. The War Office and the Foreign Office each thought the other should pay. Sinclair felt greater urgency, and put out £7,500 of his own money, a fortune, and bought the estate in his own name. (Sinclair respected agency traditions: his predecessor's last initial had been *C*, so Sinclair went on using that letter as his alias; his predecessor wrote in green ink, so he did too.)

The administrative officer of MI6, Captain William Ridley, directed a trial run of moving from London to Bletchley in September 1938. Staffers from MI6 and GC&CS moved into hotels around Bletchley Park and said they were part of "Captain Ridley's shooting party," out for a hunt. The plan was that if war broke out, everyone would stay. The mix of young female secretaries and Great War veterans led locals to guess all the wrong secrets. Then came the Munich Agreement, and everyone returned to London.[5]

One story that grew around Sinclair's purchase of Bletchley said that he was attracted by the junction of the London rail line with the Cambridge-Oxford track. This may be myth; Sinclair may simply have taken the first country estate he found on the market.[6] Still, the midpoint between the two universities was precisely where GC&CS belonged, physically and in spirit.

In 1929 in America, President Herbert Hoover had picked Henry Stimson as his secretary of state. Stimson discovered that the State and War departments were jointly funding a tiny codebreaking agency, officially called the Cipher Bureau and unofficially known—at least by its flamboyant director, Herbert Yardley—as the Black Chamber. Eight years before, Yardley and his crew had broken Japan's diplomatic codes in time for a conference between American, British, Italian, French, and Japanese representatives on limiting the sizes of their respective navies. The Black Chamber decoded the message from Tokyo to its negotiators telling them that their rock-bottom offer should be that Japan would have 60 percent of the battleship tonnage of the US Navy. American negotiators naturally refused every offer from Japan until its representatives lowered their demand to this number.

Stimson regarded the Black Chamber as a violation of diplomatic ethics. He immediately cut his department's funding, and the bureau shut down. Stimson later explained, "Gentlemen don't read each other's mail."[7]

The six employees of the bureau found themselves jobless just as the American economy collapsed. Five nonetheless kept their silence. Yardley, however, wrote a tell-all book, *American Black Chamber*. Besides its English-language success, it sold thirty thousand copies in the Japanese version. "The jolt which his book gave to Japanese cryptographers," according to a secret US report eleven years later, led "them out of their blissful ignorance" and caused them to develop their own Enigma-type cipher machines.[8]

Stimson's puritanical stuffiness never afflicted his British counterparts. Another kind of stuffiness did. Their recruiting policy has been aptly described by a historian as "Only gentlemen should read each other's mail."[9]

Codebreaking, that is, was a job for people of the proper class, and sufficiently brilliant gentlemen were to be recruited at Cambridge and Oxford. This practice dated back to the Great War, when the Royal Navy's codebreaking office, informally known as Room 40 for its place in the Old Admiralty Building, enlisted classicists and linguists, on the theory that if you could make sense of faded handwritten ancient Greek or Latin, you could unravel a German military or diplomatic code.

The experiment proved the theory. Room 40's successes included decoding the telegram in which German foreign minister Arthur Zimmermann offered Mexico an alliance against the still-neutral United States. Mexico was to regain Texas, Arizona, and New Mexico as the payoff. The message was sent in January 1917 to the German ambassador in Washington in Germany's most sophisticated diplomatic code, but the British intercepted it. From Washington, the German embassy forwarded it to the German legation in Mexico in an older code, and in slightly different words. Britain didn't turn over the telegram to the US ambassador in London till it could steal a copy of the reworded version in Mexico City, in order to keep anyone in Germany from guessing that the newer code was now an open book. The telegram did not propose that Mexico get California, perhaps because Zimmermann also proposed adding Japan to the alliance and was saving some booty for that country. Once published in America, the telegram helped bring America into the war.[10]

The Royal Army had its own unit for reading the mail of officers and gentlemen. When the war ended in 1918, the two units were merged to create the GC&CS and were put under the control of the Secret Intelligence Service. The money-saving merger gave Britain an edge over other countries: its codebreakers weren't divided into separate agencies working for competing branches of the military that didn't want to talk to each other. In its first years, GC&CS devoted its energies to the diplomatic messages of ever more countries—a task made easier because British companies owned much of the worldwide web of telegraphic cables. The cable firms had a quiet, gentlemanly arrangement, authorized by the 1920 Official Secrets Act, to turn over to the British government copies of messages between ambassadors, attachés, and their capitals.[11]

As far as Alastair Denniston was concerned, the Munich Agreement meant only that he had peace for a little more time. He used it to recruit geniuses from Oxbridge, and added mathematicians to his list of candidates. So a letter came in the post one day in late 1938 for Gordon Welchman, politely and unexpectedly inviting him to join the Government Code and Cypher School. The next March, just after Hitler dismembered Czechoslovakia, Welchman went to London for a two-week introduction to the arts of cryptography—that is, creating codes—and cryptanalysis, breaking them.[12]

John Tiltman taught some of Welchman's classes. Tiltman really had been a schoolteacher once, until the Great War pulled him from the classroom to France, where he was badly wounded. War takes those who survive, whirls them around, and flings them in directions they never imagined. A bit of Russian he'd picked up landed Tiltman in the business of breaking Soviet codes.

From there he went on to creating new codes for Britain. Unlike many in that line of work, he searched out the weak points in his own codes and used them as clues for how to solve those of other countries. While insisting he was bad at languages, he taught himself Japanese and broke Japanese codes, including the one used by military attachés. He did it over and over, because the Japanese kept changing their codebooks. In 1939, Tiltman headed the military section—which, in British terms, meant specifically the army section—of GC&CS. One thing he hadn't accomplished was deciphering German Enigma messages.[13] No one could do that, as far as anyone in Britain knew.

A photo from that time or soon after shows Denniston and Tiltman on a London street. Denniston's suit is tailored tightly to his narrow build; the brim of his homburg casts a shadow that hides his eyes; the crown of his hat reaches Tiltman's shoulder. Tiltman wears the tartan trousers of the Scottish infantry unit in which he fought on the Somme, with a wide leather belt around a military jacket that looks at least one size too small for him, or perhaps he is two sizes too big for the street. He swings his arms as he strides toward the camera.

One man looks like a whisper; the other, a gale.[14]

After the London course, Welchman got five more months of Cambridge calm. The day he reported to Bletchley Park, he was sent to the cottage behind the stable yard. The cottage was the kingdom of Dillwyn Knox, head of the Enigma section of GC&CS. It was a small kingdom, and drab. The rooms of the cottage were whitewashed; if you rubbed against the wall, you'd find a splotch of white powder on your clothes. A closet connected the two downstairs rooms. Dilly Knox regularly limped into the closet when he meant to go outside. Dilly had a poor sense of direction in the physical realm and an inclination toward accidents. His love of motorcycles had ended with him alive but with one leg permanently damaged. In 1939 he was fifty-five years old, tall, with unkempt black hair retreating from his high forehead. His black-framed glasses seemed to serve as a divider between the world and his thoughts.

In the realm of obscure symbols, on the other hand, Dilly had a supernatural sense of direction. As a young Cambridge scholar, he'd dedicated himself to deciphering a set of papyrus fragments bought by a British Museum scout from tomb robbers in Egypt. The fragments bore the lost, lewd work of the obscure third-century-BCE Greek poet Herodas.

In 1915, Room 40 had needed him more than Cambridge did. Actually, Dilly worked in Room 53, the only one in the Old Admiralty Building with a bathtub. Hot water helped him think. He unraveled the code used by the commander of the German navy. He and a colleague decoded the Zimmermann Telegram. After the Great War, Dilly completed his translation of Herodas but went on working for GC&CS. He acquired an early commercial Enigma machine, though a British expert analyzed the device and decided Britain shouldn't use Enigma for its own communications. Other countries did adopt the Enigma. Dilly Knox spent years on their messages.[15]

Dilly's Enigma section numbered just four people when it moved into the cottage, out of the 110 GC&CS prewar staff who came to Bletchley Park. A year earlier, the Enigma section had consisted only of Dilly and his secretary.[16] Size was a statement. The resources devoted to a particular code depend on the value of the information sent in it—but also on the odds that investing people's time will pay off with a break. Enigma carried freight trains full of German secrets. But could anyone crack the riddle?

Dilly did find his way into the versions of Enigma that the Spanish Nationalists used during the Civil War and those that Italy's navy used.

These were older, simpler machines. Germany's upgraded Enigma remained impenetrable. Peter Twinn, a twenty-three-year-old Oxford mathematician who started working with Dilly in February 1939, was "not sure whether [Dilly] had any chance of success." But it was hard to know since Dilly Knox was "notorious for being very secretive." Knox treated a code as a puzzle to be solved alone—one more reason for his small team. Denniston, though, had enough hope to bring in Twinn, Turing, and Welchman.[17]

When Welchman came to the cottage, someone showed him a copy of a German Enigma machine with the correct wiring and explained the format in which messages were sent. The machine and the explanations, he was told, came from "the Poles." He wasn't told any more details. Dilly didn't take to Welchman. He gave Welchman "some sort of test and appeared annoyed that I passed." In fact, Dilly was suffering from a chronic stomach illness. Besides, he generally did not like men. He preferred the company of women.[18]

Sinclair was in much worse health, dying of cancer. Nonetheless, he sent a chef to Bletchley Park at his own expense. Until the staff grew and war rationing set in, everyone ate lunch in the mansion's dining room, at tables laden with chickens, hams, and beef puddings, with sherry trifles and bowls of fruit for dessert. They were billeted in the countryside, in private homes and tiny inns. Welchman and Patrick Wilkinson, a mathematician working on Italian naval codes, were given rooms in a pub called the Duncombe Arms, down a country road, on a hillside with a view of a wide green valley. In the pub's billiards room, they spent their evenings with friends from work. In the daytime, they lived in a strange world, trying to work magic on incomprehensible missives from a far-away war, forbidden to speak a word of what they did to anyone outside.[19]

WELCHMAN WAS SOON moved from the cottage to a classroom in the old school at the edge of the estate. He connected the move to Dilly's hostility. The room was furnished with a few wooden chairs, a long table, blank walls, and much empty space. Bundles of German radio messages were piled on the table. On the lower part of each slip of paper, the coded message was written—rows of block letters in pencil that looked like gibberish, as if a schoolchild had recopied a text pounded out by the mythical monkey at a typewriter.[20]

Above the rows were a few shorter lines of letters and numbers, not enciphered by Enigma but nearly as opaque. They contained instructions for Enigma operators. Welchman's job was to see if he could squeeze meaning out of the top lines, known as the preamble. At first he shared the classroom with Alex Kendrick, a member of Dilly's tiny prewar staff whose trousers were dotted with holes burned by ash that fell from cigarettes or a pipe while Kendrick's mind focused on a problem. Welchman and Kendrick felt "a bit lonely" in the big room. Then Kendrick was transferred to a different job and Welchman was totally alone.

The slips of paper came from the army's intercept station at Chatham, a town in southeast England facing across the Channel toward Europe. There, operators with wireless sets and headphones scanned shortwave frequencies for the clicking of Morse code. An intercept operator had to be able to hear rapid dots and dashes and automatically write them as letters. Highly skilled operators could hear the pattern of Morse when anyone else heard silence or static. The very best ones could recognize the personal rhythm of the hand of an individual German radio man on the telegraph key, the way you'd recognize a voice you heard over and over while eavesdropping at the door of a room, even without knowing the name or face that belonged to the voice.

They had their ears pressed to the door of the Third Reich. All around Germany and what had been Austria and Czechoslovakia, and in a piece of Poland that grew daily as German armies advanced, radio operators were sending messages up and down chains of command.

In his first days at Bletchley Park, Welchman picked up from Kendrick and others how the Enigma system worked and what was known about the preambles. Once a month, the German code clerks got instructions on how to set their Enigma machines each day. Different parts of the military got different instructions. You could only read a message meant for the air force if you had air force settings—the "key," as the tiny Enigma team at Bletchley Park called the daily settings for a particular part of the military.

Part of the preamble was a three-letter code, called the "discriminant," that told what key a message was in—for instance, that it was in the air force's settings. For security, the Germans used four different discriminants for each key, like using four different codenames for the same spy, and changed them every day.

If this sounds confusing, it was meant to be—for an enemy trying to listen in.

The key, Welchman learned, told the clerk which wheels to insert in the three slots in the Enigma each day, and in what order. The Germans now had five different wheels to use in the machines. In each one, the maze of wiring was different and would scramble the message differently. Today the order could be wheels A, B, and E; tomorrow, it could be D, C, and A. Altogether there were sixty possible wheel orders.

Each wheel had a metal ring around it, inscribed around the outside with the letters of the alphabet. The operator could rotate the ring around the wheel, so that any letter could be lined up with a starting mark on the wheel. The key also told him where to set the rings. With twenty-six positions on each of three rings, there were seventeen thousand possible ring settings. Multiply that by sixty wheel orders, and you had over a million combinations.

The Germans decided that this wasn't safe enough. To the original Enigma design, they added a plugboard. It looked like a telephone switchboard, but with a socket for each letter of the alphabet. If the Enigma operator connected the A and G sockets with a cable, then A would be enciphered as if it were G and vice versa. The daily key included a list of ten pairs of letters to be connected. The number of ways you could create ten pairs on the board came to an astounding 150,000,000,000,000. Multiply this by the number of wheel orders and ring settings, and there were 150 quintillion ways to set up Enigma.

The Germans reasonably figured that even if a machine and all five wheels fell into enemy hands, no one would ever be able to test all those settings to find the right one.

And yet, the Germans added another security measure. When the clerk inserted the day's three wheels in the proper order, with the letter rings set to their proper place, the top letter on each wheel showed through a window. Every time a code clerk sent a new message, he chose three letters and turned the wheels so that they showed through the windows. This became the starting position for the turning of the wheels. To decipher the message, you needed to set the whole machine to the same key—and then put the wheels in the same starting spots.

Somehow, though, the sending clerk had to communicate his wheel settings to the receiving clerk in a way no uninvited listeners could understand. This is how the Germans solved the problem: the sending clerk would use Enigma itself to encipher his starting wheel positions. First, he chose two sets of three letters—let's say "ABC" and "XYZ." As the last part of his unencoded preamble, he sent ABC, known as the indicator. Then he set his wheels to the starting position ABC and typed in "XYZ XYZ." The pulses ran through the maze of wire. With each letter he typed, one or more wheels moved, and the maze shifted shape. A garbled series of six letters lit up on the lamp board of his Enigma. It could be "TRABQW" or "VGDZGL" or anything else. He'd send those six letters at the start of his enciphered message.

At the other end, the receiving clerk saw the "ABC" at the end of the preamble, and set his wheels with ABC showing at the top. Then he typed in the first six letters in the message. On his lamp board "XYZ XYZ" lit up.

Aha, he'd say, that's the starting position of the wheels for the rest of the message. Since the first three letters and the next three matched, he knew he hadn't messed up. He moved his wheels so that "XYZ" showed at the top and typed in the rest of the enciphered message. In place of nonsense, words lit up on his lamp board, one letter at a time.

To this, the Germans added a standard precaution. Code clerks had to break long messages into shorter pieces and send them separately. For each piece, the operator chose a different wheel setting.

Welchman wasn't really supposed to concern himself with the wheel settings; he'd been banished from working on Enigma. His assignment was the unencrypted stuff that came before the wheel settings.

Welchman sat in the empty classroom, puffing his pipe and studying the preambles. The first mystery was what kind of pattern he was even looking for. Most people, faced with a mountain of unintelligible detail, get anxious, get headaches, look away. Welchman got curious. He began "making lists of this and that." Things connected. Like vines, patterns started growing.

One showed up in multipart messages. When a German code clerk at an airfield cut a long report into pieces to send it to the air force command, he usually used a different discriminant in each piece to identify the air force key. It seemed so obviously safer not to repeat the same one. Welchman realized that if he followed a four-part message, he'd often find all four of that day's discriminants for a key. Then he could identify every message in that key that Chatham had intercepted on that day. The security precaution turned out to be a security breach.

The Germans were not stupid. They were human. They'd come up with a system. Each time they checked their logic, it came out reassuringly correct. They'd built a fortress in their minds, with high walls, a moat, and a bolted gate. Every time they looked at it, they saw it was impregnable.

Welchman wasn't one of them. He looked at the fortress: it shimmered in front of his eyes and came into focus, and he could see that the gate was a drawbridge lowered across the moat, inviting him in.

Enigma appeared unconquerable. Its fundamental flaw was that human beings built it, and other human beings could see it differently.

The same law governs codebreaking and safecracking: any lock that one human mind can design, some other human mind will eventually see a way to break. The first mind snaps shut around its solution. The second mind must be unlocked and open.

On his daily lists, after he figured out which three-letter discriminants belonged to which key, Welchman marked them with colored pencils. From then on at Bletchley Park, the names of Enigma keys were colors. He used his red pencil a lot, along with blue and less often green. Red was the key used by the Luftwaffe, the German air force.[21]

Curiosity doesn't stop where it's told. Welchman also made lists of the wheel settings, the first six letters of the enciphered text. Again, patterns bloomed. Sometimes, the "X" in "XYZ" would be enciphered by the same letter both times, so that the message might begin GBD GWL. The same stutter could happen with the second letter, or the third.

The mathematician began calculating. Only about half the combinations of wheel orders and ring settings could make one of those repetitions happen. If another repeat showed up the same day in the same key, it cut the number of settings by half again. With twelve such pairs, the potential settings dropped from a million to just 250—few enough to check individually.

He designed a method for taking the patterns and finding the daily settings. The machinery would consist of hundreds of sheets of thin cardboard, each punched with holes in precise spots on a grid. The holes represented settings that could produce a particular repeat. It might take months to punch the holes, a couple million of them altogether. But once the full set of sheets was ready, they could be used daily, stacked in accordance with the repeats in each day's messages. Where the holes lined up, light would shine through, indicating potential solutions. You could try them on an Enigma machine with that day's intercepts. In a matter of hours, you'd have the day's settings.

It would work only because the German clerk had to type his wheel setting twice. Again, the safety measure opened the gate to the Enigma fortress. Welchman rushed to the cottage and told Dilly Knox his brainstorm.

"Dilly was furious," Welchman would write. "What I was suggesting was precisely what he was doing . . . Dilly reminded me that I had been told to study discriminants and call signs" and not to break Enigma.

What Dilly did not say was that Welchman had just kicked his self-respect where it was already bruised.

IN FACT, DILLY told Welchman nothing about his secret journey to Warsaw at the end of July—just a few months earlier and in an entirely different era, when he and Alastair Denniston could still take a train across Germany.

The invitation came from the Polish Cipher Office. More than anyone, Polish codebreakers could taste how close war was. They decided to risk sharing their secret in order to share the impossible burden of their work. The matchmaker between the Poles and GC&CS was a man who often appeared in British documents under the alias Godefroy—Captain Gustave Bertrand, director of cryptological services in French military intelligence.[22]

Britain's commitment to defend Poland was born only in March 1939, when Hitler seized Czechoslovakia. The alliance of France and Poland against Germany, the dangerous country that lay between them, dated to 1921. It led to cooperation—cautious and selective—between their codebreakers.

In 1931, a German named Thilo Schmidt walked into the French embassy in Berlin and offered to sell secret documents. Germany's economy had collapsed. Schmidt had a wife, children, and mistresses and was not getting by on his salary from the job that his brother had landed him at the Defense Ministry Cipher Office. The French intelligence agent assigned to him generously helped out. Schmidt showed his value by filching German army manuals on Enigma procedures. After that, he provided lists of settings that the army was using for Enigma.

Bertrand went from ecstasy to angst. His staff understood much better how Enigma worked—but still didn't understand a single day's messages. He took his Enigma papers to Warsaw, gave them to his Polish counterpart, and went home with a promise that the Poles would share any breakthroughs.[23]

By then mathematician Marian Rejewski had come up with equations that would reveal how Enigma wheels were wired. But there were too many variables; solving the equations threatened to be very slow work. The French treasure changed that. In those days, the Germans used the same settings throughout their military, and only changed the wheel order every three months. The September 1932 settings stolen by Schmidt gave the summer wheel order; the October settings gave the order for autumn. Rejewski could fill in several variables, and he quickly solved the equations.[24]

Rejewski and his two even younger colleagues, Jerzy Rozycki and Henryk Zygalski, were soon deciphering Germany's perfectly protected military secrets daily. Long before Welchman heard of Enigma, they noticed the German practice of enciphering the wheel setting twice and the clues it provided to discover the daily settings. Rejewski came up with a machine that looked like two Enigma machines tethered together. It could rapidly check settings to see which ones could produce the patterns they found. They called it a *bomba*, a bomb, perhaps because it ticked, or because it dropped weighted pendulums when it found a likely setting, or because the three of them were eating the molded ice cream treat called a bombe, a *bomba* in Polish, when Rejewski got the idea. When the Germans started making more connections on the plugboard, they unknowingly defeated Rejewski's *bomba*—but not an invention by Zygalski. He came up with using cardboard sheets with small holes cut in them, and lining them up to find the daily setting.[25]

For six years, their agency never told Bertrand of their success.[26] The simplest explanation is fear: what you share with an ally, you also share with whoever is spying on your ally. If the French didn't know, a French traitor couldn't tell the Germans.

And then, in December 1938, the Germans added two new Enigma wheels to the original three, creating sixty wheel orders in place of six. Rejewski figured out the wiring. But now they would need ten times more of Zygalski's sheets. The three men on the team were cutting the holes in the sheets themselves with razorblades. The job was impossible. German radio networks chatted war preparations in a language that had gone back to being incomprehensible.[27]

The Poles asked for help.

Bertrand and one of his codebreakers checked into the Bristol Hotel in Warsaw on July 24, 1939, along with Denniston and Dilly Knox.[28] The next morning, they were picked up at 7:00 and driven to a clearing in a forest near the village of Pyry, where the Cipher Office had its new building, heavily guarded and partly underground. For the next three hours, Major Maksymilian Ciezki—head of the German subsection and Rejewski's boss—laid out how his men had broken Enigma. "I confess I was unable to understand completely," wrote Denniston, who'd been cracking codes since Room 40 in the Great War. Only when "we were taken down to an underground room full of electronic equipment did I fully grasp the results of their reasoning."

Dilly "accompanied us throughout but maintained a stony silence and was obviously extremely angry about something. It was only when we got back into a car that he suddenly let go and . . . raged and raged that they were lying to us," Denniston wrote.

"The whole thing was a pinch"—a theft, Knox insisted. No one could have reasoned out the Enigma wiring. "They never worked it out," he exploded. "They must have bought it or pinched it."[29]

Other British codebreakers would have the same reaction.[30] If you weren't looking at the problem the way Rejewski had, it appeared unsolvable. And Dilly was about one-tenth right. Rejewski never saw a stolen machine, but the stolen papers did help him.

Denniston now had to clean up a diplomatic difficulty. Bertrand was in the cab, and even if he didn't speak English, he could hear rage. In a note afterward, Denniston asked the French officer to "understand my big problem in the shape of Knox. He is a man of exceptional intelligence but he does not know the word cooperation. You surely must have noticed that off duty he is a pleasant chap loved by all. But . . . in Warsaw I had some deplorable experiences with him. He wants to do everything himself . . . He can't stand it when someone knows more than him.

"Unfortunately, I cannot do without him," Denniston wrote. Knox knew more about Enigma than anyone in Britain, he said.[31]

By the next day Dilly had sailed through his mind's storm into calm waters. Zygalski and Rozycki explained their methods to him. Dilly decided that the Polish mathematicians were "charming young men," and Rejewski happily saw that "Knox grasped everything very quickly, almost as quick as lightning." Denniston and Knox promised that GC&CS would manufacture a full set of Zygalski's sheets; the Poles promised to send their British and French friends each a working copy of the German military Enigma.[32]

This time, promises were kept. On August 16 Bertrand stepped off a train in Victoria Station in London. With him was a courier bearing a Polish-made working copy of a German Enigma. Stewart Menzies, the deputy of dying MI6 chief Hugh Sinclair, came to the station himself to receive it. The Rejewski team also sent technical drawings of their bombe, as it was called henceforth in English.[33] The gifts arrived just as GC&CS was moving from London to Bletchley Park in readiness for oncoming war.

In September, during their flight from Warsaw, Rejewski and his colleagues had to destroy all their equipment—the bombes, the Zygalski sheets they'd dedicatedly cut by hand, the Enigma replicas.[34] The meeting in the forest clearing at Pyry preserved their years of work. It made everything that Bletchley Park did possible.

HITLER FLEW TO Warsaw on October 5, 1939. With him came the commander of his security battalion, the man already known as the "Führer's general," Erwin Rommel.

In scattered corners of Poland, the country's last troops were still fighting. Warsaw had fallen a week before, after the government fled to Romania, after German artillery ground the city down like a pestle grinding seeds in a mortar, after the German air force showed that Guernica had only been a training run. Most of Warsaw, a foreign correspondent reported, "was in ruins, buildings and streets battered to charred wrecks." There were "huge craters in the middle of main thoroughfares and tram rails twisted into geographical patterns." The reporter said nothing about seeing corpses. Perhaps they'd all been removed from the streets in honor of Hitler's visit.[35]

Nor did the foreign correspondents see the daily reports of Reinhard Heydrich's SS *Einsatzgruppen* as they followed the frontline troops into Poland. Heydrich ordered them to erase Poland's elites. On an inspection tour early in the invasion, Heydrich especially urged his men to kill Jews or terrify them into fleeing to the Soviet Union. Speaking with Admiral Wilhelm Canaris, head of the Abwehr, German military intelligence, Heydrich described his mandate from Hitler: "The nobility, the Catholic clergy and the Jews must be killed." This was only loosely a secret. The chief of the Army General Staff, General Franz Halder, told one of his officers that Hitler and his closest lieutenant, Hermann Göring, aimed "to destroy and exterminate the Polish people." The officer wrote in his journal that Halder told him more but that it was too appalling to write down. No plan or bureaucracy of mass murder yet existed; Heydrich's men improvised. By the time Hitler landed in Warsaw, they had executed between twelve and sixteen thousand people, about a third of them Jews.[36]

The Führer himself made repeated trips to Poland in September. In the morning, he'd hold a staff meeting in the conference room of his train. Rommel attended, listened, and was sometimes honored by being asked to speak. (Heydrich's work may not have been on the agenda, but generals were talking about it. Rommel almost certainly heard something. Only a determined effort to preserve Rommel's innocence could lead one to conclude otherwise.) After the meetings, Hitler went out in an open Mercedes Benz, wearing a pistol in his belt, with Rommel's soldiers before and after him. The convoy rode through newly conquered towns, where Polish snipers were still shooting, to posts under artillery fire, to the very line of battle where German units were pushing across rivers.[37]

"I had a lot of trouble with him. He always wanted to be with the advance units. It seemed to give him pleasure to be under fire," Rommel wrote, not as a complaint but in admiration. Rommel believed in commanding from the front, from the midst of the battle. Like Hitler, he thrilled to danger. They were gamblers who played another hand, and another, to prove what they already believed—that they would always draw the right cards, that the odds did not apply to special men like them.[38]

On October 5, Hitler came to Warsaw only for a few hours, not to command but to exult. A reviewing stand had been built on a central street in the diplomatic quarter, where the buildings were relatively whole. Row upon row of troops marched before him, their rifles shouldered, their legs goose-stepping as if they were all driven by gears of the same clockwork. Cavalry troops rode by with arms aloft in the Nazi salute. Hitler's own arm jerked up, dropped, and stabbed up again, as if propelled by the same invisible springs and gears.

Back at the airport, Hitler shook hands with the foreign newsmen and used the rubblescape of Warsaw as a warning. "I only wish certain statesmen in certain countries who seem to want to turn the whole of Western Europe into such a shambles could have the opportunity of seeing, as you have, the real meaning of war."

Rommel wrote to his wife, "About every tenth house is burned out and collapsed . . . There has been no water, no light, no gas and no food for two days now . . . The Lord Mayor is estimating 40,000 dead and wounded." As if blind to how all this had happened, he wrote, "The inhabitants draw a breath of relief that we have arrived and rescued them."[39]

As WELCHMAN WOULD remember the blowup over his brainstorm, he didn't get angry himself, despite Dilly Knox's fury. He was too exhilarated: he wasn't alone; other people also believed that Enigma could be cracked.

When he brought his idea to Dilly, it turned out, a team led by Cambridge mathematician John Jeffreys was already busy in the cottage, punching sheets with a machine built for the purpose. The noise was driving Alan Turing nuts. Turing moved to a loft in the cottage where the stable boys once slept. He climbed up by rope ladder and lowered a basket tied to a rope when he wanted coffee sent up.[40]

A loft and a coffee cup lowered by rope to the world of people: this arrangement fit Alan Turing. He was twenty-seven. He had not fit into his English boarding school as a boy. He did not like to play cricket. He ran long distances, mostly alone. Contrary to myths that grew up about Turing, he did not have a problem understanding people's feelings. Rather, he could not bear the illogic of society. He was unkempt, probably because he did not see the logical need to tuck his shirt in or shave closely. Since he suffered terribly from hay fever, it was logical to ride his bicycle wearing his war-issue gas mask during pollen season. He was shy, apparently because conventions made no sense to him. They were full of contradictions. The greatest contradiction may have been between the private upper-class acceptance of homosexuality, like his, especially at Cambridge, and the public horror of it.

At twenty-four Turing had written a paper in which he imagined a machine that could be directed by instructions on punched cards to solve any mathematical problem. The machine was not the point of the paper; its imagined existence was part of his proof that no mathematic calculation could solve the paradox of the sentence "I am lying." The paradox would remain, and Turing's idea of a machine that followed programmed instructions would transform the world. But this was later.[41]

The bombe drawings from Poland, it appears, ended up in Turing's loft. He seized on the idea of a machine that spun the wheels of multiple copies of Enigma. But he took it in a new direction. Rejewski's bombe had exploited the same flaw as the punched sheets did: the German practice of enciphering the wheel settings twice. Turing's bombe would instead exploit a piece of text you could expect to find in a message—what was known as a crib.

A German code clerk who received an enciphered message and knew the day's settings used the machine to produce the original words. Turing's idea was that you could reverse the process: if you had an enciphered message and a very good idea of a few of the original words, you could use them to find the settings. The machine would spin through one setting after another until it found one that could have turned the guessed words into the gibberish taken down by the intercept operator.

This wasn't the programmable machine Turing had imagined in his paper. The bombe would be hardwired to do just one thing. Turing's design called for a machine with thirty copies of Enigma, their ninety wheels all spinning at once, to run through thousands of settings quickly.

There was a catch: to use Turing's method, you'd need to break Enigma some other way first. Only then would you know which phrases insistently repeated.

Logically, Turing concluded, it could be done. It would be done. On this, Welchman and Knox could agree. A memo they all signed from November 1, 1939, only two months after the war began, says they had two machines now punching the Zygalski sheets and planned to go up to six. Turing's "30 enigma bomb [*sic*] machine, adapted to use for cribs, is on order and parts are being made at the British Tabulating Company."[42] A report a week later said that the German military was using Enigma "universally . . . wherever there is no great danger of capture," and added, "It is believed that messages can be read in considerable quantity when the machinery is complete."[43]

Welchman thought about quantity and had another big idea.

Poland had fallen. Britain and France were not fighting anywhere; neither was Germany. People were already talking about the "phoney war." They knew better. It was the anxious war. Something would happen, at a place not yet known, on a date not yet set. Yet, even in that time of waiting, the motorcycle dispatch rider from the interception station at Chatham brought hundreds of messages every day.

In the past, Welchman saw, codebreaking had been an artisanal pursuit. A cable or radiogram was intercepted, or a paper stolen from a diplomatic bag. A brilliant person worked on it, single-minded, occasionally inspired, and broke the code or cipher and translated the message. Now the Germans were radioing enciphered text in industrial amounts. The abundance would only grow when the fighting began again.

If GC&CS cracked Enigma, it would also need to create an intelligence assembly line. It would need to break the job into pieces, to grow, to add people, to create separate teams to register the messages, break keys, decode, and translate, working three shifts a day, around the clock. Chatham wouldn't be enough. They'd need more intercept stations, more operators, more wireless sets, more, much more of everything.

The future, Welchman saw, was turning intelligence into an industry.

Welchman thought of this, and Knox did not, because Knox was an artisan, a master craftsman proud of his trade. He was a lone knight doing battle with the dragon named Enigma. Welchman liked being with people, and was beginning to imagine that fitting them into teams and directing them could be even more fun than solving equations.

In mid-November, Welchman took a plan for massive expansion to Denniston's deputy, Commander Edward Travis. Welchman sensed, correctly, that Travis would be more interested than Denniston would. Denniston had written to "C" that he would be "greatly relieved" when he could get done with the management tangles of moving to Bletchley Park, confiding, "I am most anxious to take my share of the work on the . . . cryptographic problems confronting us."[44] He wanted to break codes, not manage an empire. A draft of Welchman's plan proposed dividing research and production. Knox would head a small research group, working on the German navy's more secure Enigma system and other unsolved problems. Travis took the job of going to government offices at Whitehall in London. He would talk, wheedle, beg, and get funds.[45]

The confidence was radiant. It was glorious. The Enigma section hadn't yet deciphered a single German message.

POLAND PROVED TO Rommel what he already wanted to believe: Hitler was a brilliant strategist. Hitler, like Rommel himself, was free of the outdated caution of the Prussian aristocrats of the General Staff, which made sense because neither man was Prussian, and neither had General Staff training. The best commander led from the front; the best commander fought by rushing forward—and now the best way to do that was with tanks.[46]

Rommel asked for his next command to be a panzer division—an armored division. The army's personnel department wanted to give him a mountain infantry division, because that's where his past lay. Hitler, it seems, overruled the personnel officers, and Rommel got his wish. He and Hitler agreed: tanks were the future. Tomorrow belonged to machines.[47]

5

THE FLAW IN THE MACHINE IS THE MAN

Winter 1940. Cairo-Rome-Bletchley Park.

IN CAIRO ON the last day of 1939, "Our big hotels were crowded. At Shepheard's and at Mena House, New Year's Eve was celebrated as brilliantly as in other years. The creations (from Paris and London) worn by the ladies, the gargantuan menus washed down with unlimited champagne and whisky and good company, all helped one . . . 'drive away dull care,'" wrote Jean Lugol, the Swiss editor of the Cairo daily *La bourse egyptienne*. "We drank, ate and danced till the small hours."[1]

Lugol's "we" referred to foreigners and wealthy westernized Egyptians. For the poor, which meant most Egyptians, the war felt closer. The price of everything had gone up, especially the kerosene they used to cook their food. "There is already a genuine background of popular discomfort and resentment" that could make people receptive to Axis propaganda, Ambassador Miles Lampson told the Foreign Office in London.[2]

Lampson's reports rippled with diplomatically restrained anxiety. When the war began, he said, most Egyptians were "wholeheartedly in favour of the democratic powers." But Prime Minister Ali Maher had dismissed "numerous . . . senior government officials, popularly regarded as pro-British." At the palace, King Farouk created an "increasingly anti-British atmosphere," ignored warnings to get rid of his Italian hangers-on, and only listened to Maher. Aziz el-Masri, the army chief of staff, was undermining the British military, and he organized sporting clubs that were really "quasi-military formations . . . to serve political ends in the future." Lampson demanded that Maher force Masri out. The prime minister leaked the demand and "represented himself as the staunch patriot resisting . . . this British attack on Egyptian independence."

Lampson took offense at a cartoon published in a comic paper that showed the rector of Egyptian University "in a suppliant attitude before me" begging *not* to be given the honor of knight commander of the British Empire that he'd recently been awarded. Government employees who wanted to keep their jobs would do best to maintain distance from the British, the cartoon suggested.

Lampson and Maher met. The prime minister agreed to force Chief of Staff Masri into retirement. But when Lampson demanded that Maher tighten censorship of the weekly comic papers, Maher gave him a typed reply accusing him of "dictatorial methods." Lampson angrily told him to tear it up. "The common belief," Lampson wrote, was that the "prime minister is not always entirely balanced or normal."[3] Maher's view of Lampson is not recorded.

MI5's man in Cairo, Raymond Maunsell, had one or two explanations of Maher's actions. In 1939, Maunsell got promoted to lieutenant colonel and became head of Security Intelligence Middle East, SIME, a new office responsible for counterintelligence all the way to Persia. In Cairo, Maunsell "had an agent—a Jewess believe it or not—in the telephone exchange of the Dresdner Bank," which had close ties to the Nazi regime. She could plug an extra line into conversations; it ran to an "observation flat," where Maunsell's agents eavesdropped.

SIME "strongly suspected" that until September 1939 Maher was in contact with the Abwehr, Nazi military intelligence, and probably getting money from it through the Dresdner Bank. Maunsell conceded that Maher's pro-Axis position might have reflected what "he thought was right for his country"—but even so, Maher didn't mind getting paid for it.[4]

On the other hand, Maunsell's men appear to have missed General Masri's meeting with Italy's ambassador in Egypt, Serafino Mazzolini, in October 1939. Masri wanted to cooperate with the Italians and push out the British. He also suggested that Egypt follow the German and Italian example and institute a race policy. In Egypt's case, that would mean expelling "colored elements" southward to the Sudan. Masri asked for a promise that Italy wasn't out to take Britain's place by conquering Egypt. Whatever Mazzolini's response was, Masri went on seeing his enemy's enemy as his friend.[5]

At Mersa Matruh, Major Ralph Bagnold looked out at the Western Desert and cultivated his own crop of fears. The commander of the British Troops in Egypt, the BTE, and his staff officers showed "total ignorance of the desert country" that lay beyond the narrow green band of fields and villages along the Nile River. Bagnold had once gone looking at the Cairo headquarters for a map of Egypt that extended to the Libyan border. The only one he found "faded out to the west with the inscription, 'Limits of sand dunes unknown,'" as if none of Bagnold's and Hassanein's and Almasy's expeditions had ever happened.

Bagnold thought about a dinner of chicken, spaghetti, and Chianti served deep in the desert seven years earlier, and about his Italian host Major Lorenzini's careless warning. What if the Italians did, in fact, send a light desert force south of the Sand Sea to Aswan or to Wadi Halfa? They could cut Egypt off from the Sudan, which was now threatened by Italian forces in Ethiopia.

The commander of the armored division at Mersa Matruh, General Michael O'Moore Creagh, asked Bagnold to show him the territory they were supposed to defend. They drove out to the Libyan frontier, getting close enough to see Italian forts. From there they drove south to the edge of the Great Sand Sea, then eastward again to look at the cliffs dropping to the Qattara Depression and its salt marshes. Qattara was shaped like a jagged leaf, the wide part in the southwest near Libya, the tip closest to the coast in the northeast, reaching almost to the Nile Delta. It was two-thirds the size of Belgium and impassable. Together the Sand Sea and Qattara blocked much of the desert to armored forces, leaving a coastal corridor that got narrower on the eastern end. When Bagnold and Creagh got back to base after three days in the desert, Creagh found a note from BTE commander General Henry Maitland Wilson—asking him why he'd left his headquarters.

Bagnold wrote up a short proposal: the British army should buy some American trucks and cars, fit them for the desert as he'd done for exploring, and train a small group of "officers and men in the art of cross-country driving." Rather than wait for an Italian attack, they'd slip across the dunes into Libya and explore what the Italians were up to. In January 1940, Creagh sent the proposal to General Wilson in Cairo. This was actually the second time Bagnold had suggested the idea. It was rejected, again. An official account explains that the high command "considered that Italy was unlikely to come into the war against us."[6]

HUTS SPROUTED ON the groomed grounds of Bletchley Park. The rose garden was uprooted to make room. The green maze was cut down. The lake and tennis courts survived. From the outside, the huts looked like something thrown up in a factory yard to house machines. Inside, thin walls of board or asbestos divided the rooms from a center hallway just wide enough for two people to pass.

At the start of 1940, Huts 6 and 8 were halfway built. Hut 8 was designated for Turing, who'd head the team working on the German navy's Enigma system. Welchman would move into Hut 6 with the operation that was supposed to break air force and army Enigma.[7]

Welchman needed more people. GC&CS was still informal, practically a club to which you were invited by a member, or that you might hear very vaguely about if you knew the right kind of people or came from the right university. Welchman recruited a friend from his student days, Stuart Milner-Barry, who'd studied classics at Cambridge. Now he worked unhappily as a stockbroker and more pleasurably played chess for the British national team. Milner-Barry, in turn, brought *his* friend, Hugh Alexander, who'd been a mathematics student at Cambridge and was now working in London as director of research for a department store chain, a job for which he was "ill-adapted; he was far too untidy even to look like a businessman." Milner-Barry knew him from chess. Alexander was the British champion.[8]

Next came Welchman's students. He signed up Joan Clarke, whom he'd supervised the year before in geometry. He warned her the pay would be low. "Girls"—as women were almost always called at Bletchley Park—were paid less than men, even with the same job title, and started at lower ranks as a matter of course. A male Cambridge student recruited earlier that year got £5 a week as a Foreign Office "temporary junior assistant." When Clarke started work after her last exams, she was listed as a "linguist" at £3 a week and assigned to Turing's Hut 8. Almost immediately she moved from the clerks' room to where Turing, Peter Twinn, and Alex Kendrick worked on Enigma. One of them said, "Welcome to the sahib's room." In her task, though not her pay, she was now their equal.[9]

One night in January, John Herivel heard a knock on his door in Cambridge. He opened it; Welchman slipped in. Welchman had supervised the young mathematician from Belfast for two years, then vanished at the beginning of the third. Herivel was fit for army service but had permission to finish his honors exams that year before being called up. Welchman asked his student to join him in "very important war work" at Bletchley Park instead.

Herivel said yes. The university had become "a ghostly place," with everyone leaving. He was on the train a few days later, though Welchman hadn't actually explained what the work was.

Job offers for the Government Code and Cypher School were always cryptic. Only when you got to Bletchley Park and signed the Official Secrets Act, to acknowledge you were bound by it, could you be initiated into the esoteric knowledge of your job—and of no other job. Another twist was that once in, you couldn't get out. "A girl who had broken her heart and wanted to get away to give it a chance to mend" could apply for a transfer, one staffer wrote. She "might find sympathy but would not get release." A man couldn't decide he wanted to go fight in the war, even if he was embarrassed to have a desk job he couldn't describe while other men were dying, even if his old headmaster wrote to him and told him he was a disgrace to his school, as happened. No one would let him take the chance of being captured.[10]

There's no trace of how Margaret Storey got to Bletchley Park in the early part of 1940. The trace she left in life was the work she did there, which she never wrote about or spoke about. People who knew her assumed she had a university education. If so, it was not from Cambridge or Oxford, the usual recruiting grounds for GC&CS. She and her sister Penelope may have been recommended by one of the people of the right class, those who assumed that their class was best suited to keep secrets. They may simply have applied for work at the Foreign Office when the war began. She was born in Ceylon, where her father owned a tea plantation. As befits a colonial gentleman, he wrote a book called *Hunting and Shooting in Ceylon*. Her colonial childhood may explain her ability to absorb languages; she eventually spoke at least nine fluently. Someone who worked with her mentioned Turkish, another said Russian.

In any case, Margaret Storey started at Bletchley Park at the rank of untrained clerk. She was a slight woman, twenty-two years old and extremely shy, who dressed in browns, spoke the precise English of a BBC announcer, remembered every word she heard and read, and identified flowers and birds by their Latin names. She had a sense of humor, but she treated it as if it were covered by the Official Secrets Act. To her good fortune, a cloister of peculiar geniuses was a place where a woman like that could be noticed.[11]

GALEAZZO CIANO, MUSSOLINI's son-in-law and foreign minister, appointed the son of Field Marshal Badoglio, the chief of the general staff, to an ambassadorship. "He is no ace, but his father adores him, and I intend to keep his good will at all costs. He is a valuable ally in the cause of non-intervention," Ciano logged in his diary at the start of the year.

Badoglio's erstwhile partner in the *riconquista* of Libya, Field Marshal Rodolfo Graziani, the Butcher, was now the army chief of staff. He "favors war at the side of Germany and tries to persuade the Duce to hasten it," Ciano wrote in his precise handwriting. Graziani had "more ambition than brains," Ciano fumed. Pietro Badoglio, on the other hand, understood that Italy was short on raw materials, that rearming "would take all of 1941, and not even in 1942 will we be able to take offensive action." If Ciano had any scruples, which is a matter of debate, they were not about invading and conquering countries. He opposed only trying to do it without an army fit for the job.

He thought of nothing but convincing the Duce to stay out of war. The usual gossip went missing from his diary entries. At times he thought he was winning. Mussolini "at last has become well acquainted with the state of the army," his son-in-law wrote in mid-January. "The number of divisions that are ready are ten; by the end of January there will be eleven. The others lack everything more or less. Some are 92 percent lacking in artillery. Under these conditions it is crazy to speak of war.

"Mussolini . . . is discouraged to the point of feeling the symptoms of a new stomach ulcer."

In those words, one could also hear what Mussolini ached to do. The Duce let out his frustration at the Germans. Ciano wrote of a conversation with his father-in-law: "He says, 'They should themselves be guided by me if they do not want to make numerous unpardonable faux pas. In politics it is undeniable that I am more intelligent than Hitler.'" In his diary entry, Ciano added what he had kept to himself: "I must say that until now the Chancellor of the Third Reich doesn't appear to share this opinion."

Italy was desperately short of both foreign currency and coal. Britain offered a trade deal that would include coal. "The terms are not bad," Ciano wrote in early February. A memorandum from the British ambassador said that an absolute condition for the deal was that Italy sell arms and ammunition to Britain. Britain's gambit was that an agreement would speed its own preparations, while keeping Italy out of war. Ciano was in favor. The Duce vetoed the deal. Italy needed the arms, he said. Besides, he'd made promises to Germany, and "morality and honor" required keeping them. Ciano passed this on to British ambassador Percy Loraine in mid-February. Loraine replied—in Ciano's paraphrasing—that "relations between our countries are really moving to a period of greater difficulties."

(If Loraine sent that assessment to the Foreign Office in London, and if it ricocheted from there to the War Office and onward to headquarters in Cairo, it did not lead General Wilson to reread Bagnold's proposal.)

Germany did supply coal to Italy but could not transport enough by land. It had to come by sea in Italian ships. At a social affair, Loraine told Ciano that as of March 1, Britain would enforce its blockade of German trade and interdict the ships.

Sumner Welles, the US undersecretary of state and President Roosevelt's personal emissary, came to Rome to convince Italy to remain neutral. Ciano found him "distinguished in appearance and in manners," a gentleman, in contrast to "the pack of vulgarians that make up the German leadership." Mussolini met Welles. Afterward he told his son-in-law, "Between us and the Americans any kind of understanding is impossible because they assess problems on the surface and we go deeply into them."

The day before the British blockade on coal began, Ciano wrote of hearing that Mussolini had said, "There are still some criminals and imbeciles in Italy who believe Germany will be beaten. I tell you Germany will win!"

Ciano commented, "I accept 'imbecile' if it is for me, but I think 'criminal' is unjust!"[12]

JOHN HERIVEL WAS billeted in a house down the road from Bletchley Park. The landlady gave him a sitting room where she served him dinner. This was awkward, because he knew well that "landlady" meant "the lady of the house who had been required by an all-powerful war-time government to give *me* board and lodging in *her* house." After she cleared the dishes and shut the door each evening, he settled into a plush armchair that may have dated to Queen Victoria's reign, smoked his pipe, and listened to the hiss of the coal fire in the fireplace and the crunch now and then of someone slogging through the snow outside. All day he'd been thinking Enigma. If you've been arranging and rearranging pieces of a puzzle for many hours without getting them to fit, and then you relax in front of the fire, all you can think of are puzzle pieces.

One night in late February he dozed off. He woke with a dream fleeing his mind. "I was left with a distinct picture . . . of a German Enigma operator." He had double good fortune: For one thing, the picture ignited ideas. For another, his pipe had not set fire to the rug while he dozed.[13]

Two months earlier, at the end of 1939, Dilly Knox had mixed a strong punch and held a party in the cottage: Alastair Denniston, as the director, ceremonially cut the last of two million holes in the cardboard sheets, completing one set for Bletchley Park and one set for the Poles.[14] The cottage team searched intercepted messages and found repeats in the first six letters of messages. They arranged the sheets—and came up with nothing. No Enigma breaks.

The best suggestion of what to do next was to ask Rejewski, Rozycki, and Zygalski for technical help. The three mathematicians, along with other members of the Polish Cipher Office who'd succeeded in reaching France, were now at what was called Command Post Bruno, in a chateau at Gretz-Armainvilliers, twenty-five miles outside Paris. There they worked with French military intelligence under Gustave Bertrand. Denniston wrote to Stewart Menzies, who was now "C" because Sinclair had died. Menzies wrote to the head of French intelligence and asked that Bertrand send the Polish trio to England.[15]

Bertrand said no. He explained that the French government was now paying the salaries of the remnants of the Polish army who'd regrouped in France, and "therefore the Poles must work in France."[16] Bertrand apparently feared that once in England, they wouldn't come back, and he would lose his assets.[17] Britain's chance to get Rejewski and friends had evaporated the autumn before in Bucharest when an anonymous British diplomat said he'd have to wait for instructions before helping them.

Dilly Knox offered to go to Paris. Denniston turned him down, perhaps recalling the "deplorable experiences" with him in Warsaw. Turing went instead, alone, in mid-January. Evidently, Denniston considered him quite capable of navigating people's feelings. By some accounts, it turned out that the Poles had sent mistaken information about the recently added fourth and fifth Enigma wheels.[18] When that was straightened out, the sheets worked. It's equally possible, though, that the British simply needed better instructions in how to use them.

Either way, the Poles and Turing managed to solve an Enigma key, probably for January 17. For the first time since the war broke out, they read new messages. A few days later, Turing was back, and Dilly's team was breaking keys in the cottage.[19]

Dilly sped up the process by noticing two habits of German operators. When they chose their indicator and a wheel setting at the start of a message, they were supposed to pick three random letters for each. But people aren't random creatures. They like letters that join up, that mean something. So German operators would use sets like "HIT-LER" or "BER-LIN" or girls' names, such as "MAR-THA" or "CIL-LIE." The last of those apparently gave rise to the Bletchley Park term "cillies" for such telltale patterns.

Then, when sending a message in several parts, they sometimes looked at whatever letters were showing at the top of the wheels at the end of one part, and sent that, unencrypted, as the indicator for the next one. Looking out for those mistakes, you could cut down on the number of possible settings, and using the sheets became much quicker. Milner-Barry, the classicist whom Welchman rescued from stockbroking, kept a catalogue of German security breaches. Instead of studying the tragic flaws of Sophocles's characters, he became expert in the fatal errors of anonymous Nazi code clerks.[20]

By the time Herivel got to Bletchley Park on January 29, Welchman's crew had moved into Hut 6. Next to it, in Hut 3, a new team—an officer each from the air force, navy, and army and a Foreign Office man—had the job of translating the messages to reveal the treasure of useful intelligence.

When they read the deciphered messages, they found that the treasure was usually still hidden.

Blue was a practice key, used for training operators. The text was often nursery rhymes. Red was a richer vein: the key of the Luftwaffe, the German air force. But the German words "still bristled with obscurities." The Germans wrote in their own abbreviations and military jargon. They used codenames. They used numbers that stood for bases, targets, airfields, trains, and coordinates on German maps. They sent lists, in which only the quantities appeared because sender and receiver knew what item came first and second and tenth. So the number 423 in a list could mean that many airplanes or troops or tons of fuel.

"We were eavesdroppers," a Hut 3 man wrote, "strangers reading stolen scraps of other people's correspondence."

Knowing German wasn't enough. They needed to learn a new language, with no one to teach it. They needed to keep track of words and names and find connections. The translators had to become code-breakers themselves.[21]

Besides that, with the sheets and Dilly's cillies combined, Hut 6 was having only "occasional successes" at finding the daily settings.[22] In late February, in his armchair in front of the fire, Herivel was looking for a new way in.

He was a mathematician. His dream, though, told him to think not about numbers but about a person—about the clerk with the machine, a soldier, still awake at midnight or half awake before dawn, when he had to rotate the letter rings on his three Enigma wheels. The new day's settings specified which letter on each ring had to line up with the starting mark on the wheel. After setting the ring, the soldier had to put the wheels into the machine. Because of how the Enigma was built, the easiest way to insert the wheels was with the three letters from the daily ring settings on top.

Five minutes after midnight, or maybe at dawn, an officer would hand him the day's first message to encipher. Before sending a message, he was supposed to move the wheels so that three other letters, chosen randomly, would show. Those would be the indicator, which he would send openly, unencrypted.

But if he was tired, or under pressure, or both, it would be so easy not to move the wheels. In that case, his indicator would be the same as his ring settings—the ring settings for everyone using that key. If it were Red, for instance, he would openly send the ring settings for the entire German air force. Or maybe, being both lazy and careful, he'd move each wheel by a letter.

If a couple dozen or thirty or fifty operators did that, Herivel thought, someone looking at a stack of intercepted German messages would see an unnatural concentration of very similar indicators. The ring settings might just be inside that cluster. You might be able to test just those couple dozen variations and find the settings for that day.

The flaw in the machine was the man. The flaw in the machine's design was forgetting that people—tired people, stressed people, people who don't think randomly—would use it.

Herivel told Welchman his idea. Welchman lit up, and told him to start charting indicators. It was the beginning of March. Herivel started looking for clusters.

The idea didn't work. He was unable to find clusters of very similar indicators that revealed the daily key.

In the meantime, the British Tabulating Company delivered the first of Turing's bombes in mid-March. It did work, with the spinning wheels testing one hypothetical wheel setting and then another to see if any of them could have turned a likely snippet of German text into what appeared in a message. But testing one setting at a time turned out to be much too slow to be useful.

Welchman sat down one day with his colored pencils. An idea had flashed in his mind for a way to rewire the bombe so that it checked twenty-six hypotheses at a time. He rushed to Turing to show him his drawing.

He got a much warmer response than he had from Dilly with his previous brainstorm. "Turing was incredulous . . . as I had been, but when he studied the diagram he agreed the idea would work, and became as excited about it as I was. He agreed that the improvement . . . was spectacular." Or rather, that it would be, once the factory could build a new bombe. They had months to wait.[23]

Herivel, for his part, kept making his charts every day. He wouldn't be able to explain why, except to say that "I may simply have felt in my bones that such a beautiful theory . . . must be right." When he had an evening shift, someone on an earlier shift would fill in the chart for him. The thing to do, if you'd tried an idea and it hadn't worked, was to keep trying till it did.[24]

6

THE ORACLES

Spring 1940. Bletchley Park-France-Rome.

ON APRIL 7, Harry Hinsley turned a crank on an old-fashioned telephone that connected him to the Operational Intelligence Center at the British Admiralty. Hinsley's job at Bletchley Park was tracking the wireless traffic of the German navy. He read the call letters of intercepted messages, and their frequencies, and information on the direction from which the radio signals had come. The autumn before, as he was about to start his third year studying history at Cambridge, two of his instructors put his name down on a very short list of top students for GC&CS. John Tiltman and Alastair Denniston, the gale and the whisper, came to the university, interviewed him, and offered him a job without telling him what it was. Now he puzzled out the locations of ships and land stations, and who talked to whom. He became the "leading expert outside Germany on the wireless organization of the German Navy," for the simple reason that no one else knew anything. He couldn't read the messages, but knowing who was talking, and from where, was the next best thing.

On this particular day, he phoned to say that German ships were talking by wireless in North Sea waters west of Denmark and in the narrow passage that led out of the Baltic Sea. This was something completely new, Hinsley said; he hadn't seen traffic from there before. Afterward, he'd figure that the intelligence officers at the other end of the line hadn't paid attention because he was a young civilian and because what he was doing, a craft called traffic analysis, was new to them.[1]

Alan Turing's team had yet to break into German naval Enigma. But the Naval Section at Bletchley Park had solved some more conventional codes and ciphers. One was used by merchant marine ships that had been put under the command of the German admiralty. In early April, a codebreaker named Christopher Morris deciphered a message telling ships sailing toward the Norwegian port of Bergen to report their positions to the army high command in Berlin. He was told he'd made a mistake; ships wouldn't report to the army; he should decrypt it again. He did; it still said the same thing. The translation wasn't passed on.

On April 9, German ships entered Norwegian ports—Oslo and Kristiansand in the south, Bergen and Trondheim further north, all the way up to Narvik beyond the Arctic Circle. They brought infantry troops. More ships unloaded invasion forces in Copenhagen, while German units crossed the land border into Denmark.

The Phoney War in the West had just turned real.

Until that day, both Norway and Denmark had carefully stuck to neutrality. Germany now said it was invading them in order to protect their neutrality from Britain. The sliver of truth in this irrationale was that seizing Norway really was a means to fighting Britain. Germany, with its own ports on the nearly landlocked Baltic Sea and the British-dominated North Sea, wanted Norway's harbors as bases for war in the Atlantic. Besides that, the iron ore on which Germany's arms factories depended came by rail from Swedish mines to the sea at Narvik. Taking the harbor guarded the supply line. As for conquering Denmark, that was a means to the end of taking Norway.

The Danes surrendered the same day. Norway, outnumbered, tried to stop the invasion. Belatedly, Britain and France sent infantry forces to landing points north and south of Trondheim, and to Narvik.[2]

HARRY HINSLEY'S INFORMATION wasn't ignored because of his youth. His phone call was actually one item in a long list of intelligence clues of the coming invasion, beginning months beforehand and multiplying as the date approached. All were ignored. Three days before the landings, the top British diplomat in Copenhagen cabled the Foreign Office with information from his US counterpart: the American had a source who said the Germans intended to take Narvik. A Foreign Office desk officer added a memo, dismissing the report: "A German descent on Narvik is surely out of the question." Two days before the landings, Britain's naval attaché in Copenhagen sighted German warships heading north past Denmark. He cabled the Admiralty in London. A duty officer immediately showed the telegram to First Lord of the Admiralty Winston Churchill. Churchill read it and said, "I don't think so." Churchill did not believe Germany had the military ability to take Norway, and assumed the ships were intended for naval missions.

The warnings went unheeded in part because they were reaching different offices and often weren't shared. (Hinsley himself later wrote about this.) The Admiralty's Operational Intelligence Center, at the other end of Hinsley's phone line, was not getting full reports from MI6 or the Foreign Office. None of the clues were as explicit as they would later seem. They required interpretation. They had to be balanced against other signs, and they did not fit what the people reading them expected. The European division of Military Intelligence assessed that Germany would need at least 25 divisions to invade Norway and Sweden, and had information on only six deployed where they'd be needed. This assumed that a German offensive in Scandinavia would necessarily target Sweden and Norway together. The assumption was treated as a fact.[3]

Beforehand, the clues of invasion were like the first symptoms of a rare disease. The doctors look for ailments they know well. Each receives lab reports from different tests, full of extraneous information. Afterward, when the patient is dead, when the autopsy takes place, all the doctors look negligent. All but the pathologist, who is proud of his judgment.

For the invasion of Norway and Denmark, the German army and air force issued a new Enigma key for joint use. Hut 6 named it Yellow, and by April 15 was breaking it daily, often by dawn. After that, the translators in Hut 3 sometimes received intercepted messages less than an hour after a German wireless operator tapped them out in

Morse code. The messages—about one thousand in little more than a month—told how German forces were organized, and what supplies they had and needed, and what they had done, and, most important of all, what their plans and orders were to do next.

Both huts went over to three shifts a day, operating around the clock. Teleprinter lines were installed from Hut 3 to MI6 headquarters in London; from there, translated messages were forwarded to the three separate ministries responsible for making war: the Admiralty, the Air Ministry, and the War Office, which despite its name only administered the army. A safe way to get information from London to commanders fighting in Norway still hadn't been devised.

Before the serial number of each teleprinted item, the letters "CX" appeared. This was MI6's standard label for reports from human agents. The messages from Bletchley Park would say things like "Source saw a document saying . . ." or, if the translator had only been able to puzzle out part of it, "Source saw a half-burned telegram . . ." The supposed source was code-named Boniface. He was said to be an anti-Nazi German, leader of a spy ring in the Nazi military.

Here lay a paradox: The enemy's purloined letters only have value if commanders and high officials know about them and trust their authenticity. Yet the process of stealing information is most secure when the fewest people know about it and, even then, don't know how orders for tomorrow's bombing missions could get from a German airfield outside Narvik to the Air Ministry in London.

Denniston, Knox, and Welchman knew that "in theory Enigma was unbreakable; in practice it was broken only because the Germans [were] confident and careless." If the Germans ever suspected that Enigma was being read and they cracked down, making sure everyone using it followed the rules, the game was up. So even when Bletchley Park sent out information read directly from German communications, it disguised the intelligence as reports from a spy. Yet British commanders and ministry officials didn't put full trust in human agents—even the terribly knowledgeable Boniface.

Not that it entirely mattered. "Had it . . . been possible to fight a campaign in Norway with a fair chance of winning . . . [Boniface] might have made all the difference," a Hut 3 report concluded. As it was, the nominal agent's information showed "the extent of the German strength" that Britain's forces were inadequately fighting in the snowfields of Scandinavia.[4]

GALEAZZO CIANO RETURNED to his office at the Foreign Ministry in Rome after a bad flu and met his father-in-law. "After ten days I found Mussolini more warlike and more pro-German than ever, but he says he will do nothing before the end of August, that is, after improvising preparations and after the harvest. Thus only three months remain to give us a ray of hope," he scrawled in his notebook in late April.

Ciano's diary entries read like an excruciatingly slow-motion shot of a man hanging from the windowsill of a tall building, his fingertips slipping toward the edge. The American ambassador, William Phillips, came to the Duce with a message from President Roosevelt. It was "dressed in polite phrases," but the gist was that if Italy entered on the German side, "some states that intend to remain neutral"—meaning America—"will need to revise their positions at once."

The warning only angered Mussolini, who wrote a "cutting and hostile reply" to Roosevelt. The news from Norway at the start of May that the Royal Navy had evacuated the British forces outside Trondheim, on the other hand, "literally exalts the Duce who, with ever-increasing emphasis, says he is certain of German victory." Hitler wrote Mussolini a letter, in which he complained sardonically—as Ciano paraphrased him—"about the excessive speed of victory" in Norway, "which did not allow him to draw in the English forces more effectively to destroy them completely."

One bit of Rome gossip did make it into Ciano's notes, but it could only add to his gloom. Luigi Barzini, a journalist for *Corriere della sera* who'd ghostwritten an autobiography of Mussolini, had been arrested. Ciano knew Barzini as one of the young and famous in Rome, like himself. It turned out that Barzini had told a British diplomat that Italy had agents inside Britain's embassy, and also that "Mussolini is insane."

The incriminating evidence against Barzini came from "the usual documents we took" from the embassy, Ciano wrote. Manfredi Talamo and the P Squad were silently at work, and the keys to Britain's embassy were still in their hands.[5] The British embassy staff did nothing about Barzini's warning.

THE CHANGES IN Enigma messages showed up in the last days of April, in all the keys but Yellow. Till then, German operators had encoded the starting position of their wheels twice at the beginning of their messages. At Hut 6, the method of using punched sheets to break the daily key depended on that pedantic repetition, and it was the only method that consistently worked.

Now, in everything but Yellow, the operators were only encoding wheel positions once.

"At one blow a catastrophe had fallen," an internal account says. Yellow could still be read. But Red, the key of the German air force, was locked again. And really, no one knew how long Yellow would last. The entire Enigma project, all the work done till now, could crumble.[6]

Like German merchant ships reporting to the army, the change in Enigma methods was an omen, an encoded message about the future. No one at Bletchley Park decrypted it.

"THE WITHDRAWAL FROM southern Norway is not comparable to the withdrawal from Gallipoli," Neville Chamberlain told the House of Commons. The prime minister had been putting this moment off; now he was trying to explain the failed campaign. He was right that the price of failure in Norway was less than the price of the disastrous attempt to take Constantinople during the Great War. Britain had committed far fewer troops to the landings near Trondheim. But then, one reason for that was Chamberlain's long delay in preparing for war, which meant that Britain had fewer forces available, and France was a higher priority.

Another difference from Gallipoli: Winston Churchill had borne the blame for that catastrophe, and it nearly ended his career. Churchill, once again first lord of the Admiralty, the cabinet minister responsible for the navy, had misread evidence of Germany's intentions in Scandinavia. But the honorable members of the house aimed their fury at Chamberlain, who had misread the danger posed by Hitler for years.

"I do not think that the people of this country yet realize the extent or the imminence of the threat which is impending against us," Chamberlain said now, as if carrying on a dialogue with himself rather than the Commons.

From the floor, someone shouted, "We said that five years ago."[7]

The next day, Chamberlain survived a no-confidence vote, but it was still a defeat: dozens of MPs from his own party voted against him or abstained. His time was over. The obvious replacement was the foreign secretary, Lord Halifax—who in a meeting with Chamberlain and Churchill turned down the job. He gave technical reasons, which would forever leave the question of whether he did not feel capable of the task, or perhaps did not want the blame for what he believed was coming.

Churchill, the third man in the room, was quite willing.[8]

The fall and rise of Winston Churchill deserves to be seen as it appeared at the moment. It was uncanny. The summer before, the American ambassador to Britain, Joseph Kennedy, relayed Chamberlain's comment that Churchill was a "fine two-handed drinker and his judgment has never proved to be good." Franklin Roosevelt's emissary Sumner Welles met Churchill in his office in the winter of 1940 and reported, "When I was shown into his office, Mr. Churchill was sitting in front of the fire, smoking a 24-inch cigar and drinking whisky and soda. It was quite obvious that he had consumed a good many whiskies before I arrived." Other American diplomats said that Churchill was old, tired, a has-been—showing that they were listening carefully to what Britain's stuffy political class thought.[9]

Churchill was sixty-five years old, indeed old by the standard of the time. He was habitually on the losing side of debates: he had opposed self-rule for India, opposed the abdication of King Edward, opposed cutting off Jewish immigration to Palestine—and opposed appeasing Hitler. He was stained by military failure, astoundingly combative, brutally witty, popular among the public, disliked by people who knew him, wildly imaginative, able to seize men and women's emotions with his bursts of staccato sentences, and, most of all, ready to seize the hour when everyone else feared it. He'd fought without allies, been defeated, and was ready to claim his personal victory. Britain was now a battered country at war. Churchill shone with the confidence Britain needed.

Churchill was burned out, insatiable, and suddenly young.

It was May 9, 1940. The next day Chamberlain would go to the king and recommend that Churchill succeed him.

"Dearest Lu," Erwin Rommel wrote to his wife that night, "We're packing up at last . . . You'll get all the news for the next few days from the papers. Don't worry yourself. Everything will go all right."[10]

In the dark early hours of the next day, Rommel's Seventh Panzer Division crossed the border from Germany into the Ardennes forest of southern Belgium. Rommel had a regiment with two hundred tanks under his command, as well as two regiments of infantry, an artillery regiment, and a varied list of other units. All this put Rommel, as division commander, just above the rank of anonymity. The division was part of a corps, the corps was part of an army, and the army was part of one of the three army groups that burst into the Low Countries on their way to France.

Britain and France had expected Germany to attack through the open plains of Holland and northern Belgium. The Allies were ready to fling their own divisions northward, and did so as soon as the invasion began. What the Allies didn't expect was for the main German attack to come through the Ardennes. It was impassable for an army, or so they believed. By taking the narrow roads of the forest, the Germans sliced into the weakest spot in the Allied defense. The plan depended on moving fast.

Rommel moved very fast. On the third day, his division crossed the Meuse River. He was, by some accounts, at the very front of his troops, in the river, under fire, as they made the crossing. He pushed on with his tanks, leaving behind other German divisions on either side of him. At one point, he ignored a radioed order to halt by feigning that it never reached him. He reached the town of Avesnes, his assigned goal, and decided on his own to rush onward through the night with the first of his tanks to grab a bridge over the next river, the Sambre, at daybreak. On the far side of the river, the lead tanks ran low on fuel and had to stop. The rest of his division was strung out helter-skelter on the road, a long, terribly exposed finger stuck into the collapsing French defense. He drove back in a command car through French lines to collect his regiments and fight the way back to his stranded tanks.

At the town of Arras, British tanks finally counterattacked his overstretched division. Rommel ran between his artillery and antitank positions to direct the defense. His aide-de-camp, alongside him, was shot and killed. His defense held. Rommel's report said that he'd faced "hundreds" of enemy tanks.

The actual number was less than ninety. An admiring account explains that the overstating of enemy strength is "a facet of every battle and every army." A less admiring account notes that his reports also failed "to give credit to other formations which had contributed to his successes."

Rommel was a very modern general who "practically courted the attention of the photographic and film crews of the propaganda companies." He built his own legend. He would win the Knight's Cross, the highest Nazi military award, for taking the Sambre bridge. The propaganda writers of the German newspapers wrote about his "Ghost Division" that vanished and reappeared. The propagandists made Rommel the symbol of blitzkrieg. An artist assigned to his division painted a portrait of Rommel as the Aryan racial ideal, with "a high forehead, a strong, forceful nose, prominent cheekbones, a narrow mouth with tight lips and a chin of great determination." Printed on postcards and posters, copies of Rommel's portrait were churned out for German troops.[11]

Yet Rommel's report on Arras, with its exaggeration of British armored strength, added to his commanders' fears that their tanks were advancing too quickly. A larger British and French counterattack would cut through their overstretched lines, they thought; they needed to rest, reorganize, and let supplies catch up with the tank brigades. Hitler ordered a halt.

The pause lasted three days. In that time, the British Expeditionary Force retreated toward the small port of Dunkirk, set up defenses, and got ready for rescue by sea.[12]

At four o'clock on an afternoon in May, John Herivel showed up for his evening shift at Hut 6. Welchman was standing at the door, waiting for him. He had news: Someone else had filled in Herivel's chart for him. That day it yielded results: among the three-letter indicators used by German Enigma operators, the chart showed a very clear cluster. As Herivel walked in, one of his colleagues was sitting at a table, working out the day's settings for Red. After three months of disappointments, his idea was working splendidly.

In past tense, it was easy to see that the Germans had changed the Enigma procedure at the end of April to tighten security before the invasion. When the huge operation began, the volume of messages increased drastically. One reason blitzkrieg worked was that the German air force worked tightly with the army. Orders, responses, reports went out constantly by wireless in the Red key. Enigma operators had to work faster. They had officers shouting at them. Some saved time by using the day's ring settings as their first indicator. Herivel's charts of the indicators showed where to look for the settings.

Accounts of when the "Herivel tip" first succeeded are based on memories and give dates anywhere from May 11 to May 22. What matters is that after the first time, it kept producing results. Day after day, the tired overworked code clerks of the German air force unknowingly passed the day's settings to the tired overworked men and women of Hut 6. In Hut 3, translators strained at messages garbled in the heat of battle and squeezed words out of them.[13]

Denniston sent out a polite demand that no one try to save up the weekly day off to have enough for visits home. The strain of working continuously was too much. "You *must* have your rest day—you need it," he wrote.[14] In a step forward since the Norway campaign, the most important information from the German texts was now sent via MI6 to British army and air force headquarters in France. As in Norway, it made little difference in the face of military collapse.[15]

On the other hand, Churchill was informed that Bletchley Park was peeking over the shoulders of the German air force. Churchill had a passion for espionage, which was lacking in the generally less passionate prime ministers before him. Room 40, predecessor of GC&CS, was born when Churchill was first lord of the Admiralty at the start of the previous war. He believed in reading other people's mail.[16]

In Churchill's terrible first weeks as prime minister, the secret intelligence success was a very rare encouragement.[17] Publicly, the evacuation of nearly 340,000 Allied troops from Dunkirk was the single event to which he could point as a victory. He did not know that Rommel's overstated report of Allied strength at Arras had contributed to the rescue.

Roosevelt sent a message to Mussolini to talk him out of war. Ambassador William Phillips was supposed to bring it to the Duce, but Mussolini refused to receive him, so Phillips came to Ciano. The message said that if Mussolini would "inform me of Italy's legitimate aspirations" in the Mediterranean—meaning his demands for British and French colonial territory—Roosevelt would try to negotiate an agreement. Ciano told Phillips it was useless. "It takes more than that to dissuade Mussolini," Ciano said, or so he wrote of his side of the conversation afterward. "In fact, it is not that [Mussolini] wants this or that; what he wants is war, and even if he were to obtain double what he claims by peaceful means, he would refuse."[18]

The French campaign had erased Mussolini's last hesitations. He could not bear being left out. He summoned the chief of the general staff, Pietro Badoglio, and Italo Balbo, the governor-general of Libya, to his office and told them he'd decided to go to war.

Badoglio tried one last time. "We have no arms, we have no tanks, we have no airplanes, not even shirts for our soldiers. It's suicide," he said.

"You, marshal, are not calm enough to judge the situation," the Duce said. "I can tell you everything will be over by September and that I only need a few thousand dead so as to sit at the peace conference as a belligerent."[19]

Mussolini ordered a blackout in Rome on the night of June 9, 1940. The next day, near sunset, he stepped onto the balcony of the Palazzo Venezia, the fifteenth-century palace where he had his office. Below him, filling the great plaza, thousands of Romans had gathered at his orders. They were the extras in the Duce's drama. The location was a propaganda stage set, shouting the glory of Italy. On Mussolini's right on a high marble plinth, the bronze image of Vittorio Emanuele II, the first king of united Italy, frozen forever on horseback, rode toward him. Below the statue was the tomb of the unknown soldier, known as the Altar of the Fatherland. Next to the monument a wide avenue had been ripped through the city to the ancient Colosseum, so that Mussolini could see it from his balcony. The palace itself had once been the embassy of the proud republic of Venice, which for centuries had dominated the Mediterranean.

"We go into the field against the plutocratic and reactionary democracies of the West, who have repeatedly blocked the march, and even threatened the existence of the Italian people," he proclaimed. The war, he said, "is the struggle of a poor people against those who wish to starve us with their retention of all the riches and gold of the earth. It is a struggle of the fecund and young peoples against barren peoples slipping to their sunset."[20]

The crowd, as ordered, applauded.

"I am sad, very sad," Ciano wrote. "The adventure begins. May God help us."[21]

THE MESSAGE TO General Archibald Wavell came unencoded via the Cairo office of the Marconi Radiotelegraph Company of Egypt. It was from John Dill, chief of the Imperial General Staff in London. "Wish you and Jumbo [Wilson] and all under your command good luck in whatever may lie ahead," it said.

"Many thanks," the commander of Britain's small forces in the Middle East radioed back. "We will do our best."[22]

Act II

THE WAGER

1

THE KEYSTONE IN THE ARCH

Spring 1940. London-Cairo-Washington-
Benghazi.

"THE BATTLE OF France is over. I expect that the Battle of Britain is about to begin," Winston Churchill told the House of Commons on June 18, 1940. "Upon this battle depends the survival of Christian civilization," he said.[1]

Churchill was understating the war's drastic transformation. The day before, the new French government under military hero Philippe Petain had asked Hitler for an armistice. Barely a week had passed since Mussolini spoke from his balcony. No longer was Britain part of a great-power alliance against Nazi Germany. It now stood virtually alone against both Germany and Italy. Western Europe was lost.

In America, still neutral, the black-and-white newsreel pictures of smoke rising from cities suddenly seemed to be in sharper focus, and the wind carried a harsh scent, still distant but hard to erase.

And already the contagion had spread beyond Europe. Italy's entrance extended the war beyond the lands of "Christian civilization" to Africa and the Middle East.

In Cairo, British ambassador Miles Lampson suffered in the ferocious, sand-heavy, late-spring wind from the desert as his mood about Egypt's king and government inched downward.[2]

Italy declared war on a Monday.

On Wednesday, Lampson talked with General Wavell. Egyptian prime minister Ali Maher hadn't broken relations with Rome or expelled Italy's ambassador in Cairo, Serafino Mazzolini. Wavell proposed sending "troops to surround the [Italian] legation" to force the ambassador to leave. Lampson—uncomfortable with Wavell's military directness, still seeking a subtle form of imperial rule—said such a public display was perhaps "a little hasty." He'd talk to Maher.

By Friday, Lampson dictated into his diary, "There is no doubt to my mind whatsoever that this man [Maher] is double-crossing us." In parliament, Maher had said that an Italian invasion was reason for Egypt to go to war—but he also said that an attack on British airfields in Egypt was *not* cause to join the war. A pro-British prince of the royal house, commander of Egypt's single armored brigade, came to Lampson to warn that "the rot was spreading fast and it was only a step to [the] Egyptian Army refusing to fight on the side of the Allies."

(Lampson's suspicions that Maher was conspiring against Britain had a more solid basis than he knew. A month earlier, Italy's Mazzolini had reported to Rome that the prime minister supported Italy's claims on the French protectorate of Tunisia. Egypt would stay out of the war, Maher had told Mazzolini, as long as Italy didn't directly attack it.[3])

Meanwhile, Wafd leader Mustafa el-Nahas was "genuinely convinced of Italian peril, hates totalitarianism and, I believe, looks upon Great Britain as Egypt's only hope." So Lampson wrote to the Foreign Office. In fact, Nahas was the most popular politician in the country precisely because he and his party represented Egyptian nationalism, born of the passion to be rid of England. Nahas, clear-eyed, was willing to postpone that fight in the face of a greater danger. Opposing Italy did not hurt his public standing—not after the Italian atrocities in Libya, not after Italy's conquest of Muslim Albania.

On the day France's Petain asked for an armistice, Lampson met Farouk at a royal palace on the Alexandria shore, told him that "we were in deadly earnest" about having a friendly prime minister, and warned that General Wavell "was anxiously awaiting my return." Farouk was supposed to understand how the general would deal with a misbehaving boy king. Farouk—possibly having heard the news from France—told the ambassador, ominously, that "it was his duty to keep his people out of war on the losing side."

Lampson flew back to Cairo, where he first heard of France's capitulation. In the privacy of his residence that night, the imperious ambassador considered the news, and wrote a melancholy telegram wondering whether Britain could hold Egypt after France had "run out." Italy no longer needed to defend Libya's western border with French-ruled Tunisia. Now it could turn all of its "250,000-odd" troops in Libya eastward against Egypt.

Lampson decided it would be best to wait until the morning before sending such a text. In the morning, it seems, he thought better of sharing those thoughts with his superior, Lord Halifax, the foreign secretary. Sharing them with Farouk never crossed his mind.

Lampson and Halifax had actually agreed that they could accept Egypt not declaring war. What they wanted was an Egyptian government they could trust to support the British war effort—and that they did not suspect of covert collusion with Italy. The British war cabinet approved Lampson's plan: If the king did not appoint such a government, Lampson would threaten to use military force. Then either Nahas would replace Maher—or, if Nahas refused to become prime minister, "we should have to administer the country under martial law."[4]

Lampson went to see the king again. Farouk seemed compliant. He said he'd form a new cabinet based "entirely on what England thinks is good for both countries." Then again, he said that France and King Leopold of Belgium had been right to surrender. They ended the meeting, Lampson recorded, by joking about Farouk's obesity. (The thin, handsome king of 1936 had seemed to inflate physically as his popularity waned.)

Lampson heard from "a confidential source inside the palace" of talk that "if things got to their worst, King F. will try to hop it to Italy" in a Hungarian plane. Wavell said it would be excellent to "let the boy go . . . thereby showing he was a poltroon . . . deserting his country." Lampson answered that the Foreign Office orders were to prevent Farouk from reaching Italy, "where he would become pretender to the Egyptian throne," a loudspeaker of Italian propaganda.

Knowing just what was going on in the young king's mind is difficult, especially because people often don't know half of what is going on in their own minds. Farouk's motive could have been sympathy with Italy inherited from his father, or personal pique with Lampson, or real preference for the Axis. It could have been an honest assessment that Britain might lose and that siding with the loser could be costly. He could have believed the Italian propaganda of the late 1930s that Mussolini was the "protector of Islam" and that Italy had "respect for the independence" of Arab countries.[5] Wanting to be rid of Britain, Farouk might have believed that his enemy's enemy was his friend, a bit of logic that ignores the possibility that your enemy's enemy might be an even greater enemy. Very possibly, all these thoughts were jumbled in the mind of a young king who as a boy had been handed exam answers in advance and now was trying to find his way in a chaotic world.[6]

At last, Mazzolini and his diplomatic staff of a hundred Italians left Egypt.[7] At the end of June, Farouk suddenly told Lampson that he'd chosen a new prime minister, the former Egyptian ambassador to Britain, Hassan Sabry. Farouk's move was meant to preserve his sense of being in charge while disarming Lampson. Sabry was known as pro-British. But the king had defied Lampson's instructions to consult Nahas, Farouk's rival for power and for the claim to speak for Egypt, on forming the new government.

Lampson and Wavell's plan to force Farouk to make Nahas prime minister unraveled. It depended on the threat of British military force. At the last moment, Nahas decided that he couldn't come to power that way. Wavell and the local commanders of the Royal Navy and the Royal Air Force also turned hesitant. They had too few forces, and now they had too many threats to face, as the French colonies in North Africa and the Levant declared allegiance to the new pro-Axis French government in Vichy. The map of the Middle East now showed a shrunken British realm squeezed between much larger Axis lands.

Lampson and the king retreated into their corners with their half victories. Maher was out, as the ambassador had demanded. Yet Farouk had used his limited power to avoid committing Egypt to war against the Axis. In the hour of decisions, he had successfully evaded a choice.

At the palace, Farouk held onto a small circle of Italian cronies to whom he'd granted Egyptian nationality, including Ernesto Verucci, the court architect he'd inherited from his father, and Antonio Pulli, who'd risen from palace electrician to Farouk's closest companion, especially during the king's increasing visits to Cairo night clubs. Pulli's services to Farouk reputedly included procuring belly dancers who caught the king's eye and bringing them to the palace.[8] Of all Farouk's commitments, his loyalty to pleasure couldn't be questioned.

THE THIRD AND last copy of Major Ralph Bagnold's twice-rejected memo landed on Wavell's desk shortly after Mussolini declared war. Bagnold now had a staff job in Cairo. In less than an hour, he was called to Wavell's office, told to sit, and commanded, "Tell me more about this."[9]

Bagnold explained: small, specially trained units with desert-fitted trucks could cross the supposedly impassable Sand Sea, move anywhere in the Libyan desert, and watch for signs that the Italians were readying an attack on southern Egypt.

"What would you do if you found no such preparations?" the stern, one-eyed general asked.

"How about some piracy on the high desert?" Bagnold improvised.

Wavell broke into a smile, and asked, "Can you be ready in six weeks?"

Bagnold wasn't ready for this question. "Yes, sir, provided . . ." he started.

"Yes, of course," Wavell said. He pressed a button on his desk that rang a bell. His chief of staff, Lieutenant General Arthur Smith, came in. "Arthur, Bagnold needs a talisman. Get this typed up," Wavell said. "To all heads of departments and branches. I wish any request by Major Bagnold in person to be granted immediately and without question." As for soldiers, Wavell said he'd talk to Jumbo Wilson—the commander of the British Troops in Egypt, who'd previously turned down Bagnold's proposal. "You'll find him very helpful," Wavell said.

Bagnold, stunned, left the office and got to work. He put out word to his old exploring companions. Pat Clayton, the surveyor who'd rescued the refugees from Kufra, came from Tanganyika in East Africa to become an officer in the unit. They scoured Egypt for the Chevrolet trucks they wanted to rebuild. Wilson, now cooperative, asked for volunteers for an "important but dangerous mission" from a newly arrived division of New Zealanders. Half the division volunteered; 150 men were chosen. They had to give up their boots for sandals. They had give up the brown felt slouch hats that made a man a New Zealand soldier, and instead wear kefiyyehs, borrowed from the Palestine police under a pretext, because nothing but the Arab scarf could protect them from sand "as fine as baking powder," driven by wind, that could batter your face and invade your nose and mouth. They had very little time to learn how to drive trucks over dunes, to live on a meager water ration, to navigate in daytime by the sun and at night by the stars. In August, Clayton led the first foray of the Long Range Desert Group, otherwise known as Bagnold's Boys, into Libya.[10]

"PIRACY ON THE high desert" appealed to Wavell because an unexpected British attack on an outpost in the depths of southern Libya would give Italian commanders the impression that he had much larger forces than he did. Given the actual condition of his command, illusion was the most powerful weapon he had.

The summer before, when Wavell was appointed head of the new and nearly theoretical Middle East Command, he gained responsibility for an area stretching from the Persian Gulf to the Western Desert of Egypt, and from Cyprus in the Mediterranean south to the Horn of Africa. He found himself begging for a modern airplane. The plane he originally had at his disposal took over three hours to make the 250-mile flight from Cairo to Palestine, one of the shortest hops in the region of his command.

At scattered British headquarters, he found an "almost entire absence of any detailed and coordinated war plans . . . other than measures of pure defense." In Egypt, the plan in case of invasion from Libya was to retreat eastward along the coast toward the Nile. General Wilson's staff considered it "doubtful whether even [Mersa] Matruh could be held," meaning that the defensive battle might be on the outskirts of Alexandria. Sudan, Kenya, British Somaliland, and the British colony of Aden at the south end of the Arabian Peninsula were all threatened by the Italian army in Ethiopia and Eritrea, which meant that British access to the Red Sea was also in jeopardy.

Politically, Wavell feared "the possibility of hostility of the Arabs in Iraq, Syria, Saudi Arabia and elsewhere." Palestine, at least, had calmed down after three years of Arab revolt. Wavell predicted that leaders of the Jewish minority would ask to raise their own armed force to protect Palestine, thereby freeing British troops for elsewhere. They had pursued the goal of a Jewish military, he wrote, "with their usual racial pertinacity for many years." Short as he was on troops, Wavell opposed this. Moshe Shertok, head of the political department of the Jewish Agency, came to Cairo to make his case to Wavell. For practical purposes, Shertok's title meant he was the foreign minister of the organized Jewish community in Palestine. Wavell told him that granting the request would probably have "political repercussions" in Palestine and the surrounding Arab countries that could "far outweigh the military value of such a force."

On the other hand, at the end of 1939 Wavell had asked the Imperial General Staff in London for "small amounts" of equipment for the Egyptian army even though it might be "wasted as far as waging this war is concerned." There was, he explained, "a certain amount of intrigue in the Egyptian Army" against the British military presence, and denying equipment could make the Egyptians "sour and sulky."

In the conventions of his time and his class, Wavell didn't stand out by talking of groups as races, by using adjectives for Egyptians that were fit for schoolboys, or by describing Jews as ill-mannered. His political logic, however, led to denying arms to committed allies against the Axis and providing them to uncertain partners.

The dangers he faced multiplied, and the directions from which they could come. After Germany and Russia divided Poland, Wavell got a message from the Imperial General Staff about the potential for Germany and Russia to launch a joint offensive south through the Caucasus toward either Egypt or the oil fields of Iraq. On the eve of Italy entering the war, Wavell wondered whether he would have to defend the Greek island of Crete.

He expected an attack on Malta. The rock island jutted from the sea, like an eastern sister of Gibraltar, in the straits between Sicily and

Tunisia. Malta was both dangerous and tempting to the Italians: its narrow, deep harbor served the Royal Navy, its airfields the Royal Air Force.[11]

Wavell's forces had not grown at the same pace as the threats. In January 1940, the First Cavalry Division had shipped out from England to Palestine. It was the last unit in the British army still using horses, and the horses came along. It would be summer before the division finally began its metamorphosis into an armored force.[12]

Weaponry was in short supply throughout Wavell's command. The arms from Britain's factories were going almost entirely to the British Expeditionary Force in France. Then came the evacuation from Dunkirk. The British left behind—in Churchill's listing—"7,000 tons of ammunition, 90,000 rifles, 2,300 [artillery] guns, 82,000 vehicles," and more.[13] After that loss, the armies in Britain itself desperately needed supplies to face the expected German invasion.

When British war correspondent Alan Moorehead came to Cairo in late spring, he found that staff officers at headquarters had not yet woken up to the war. "No one worked from one till five-thirty or six, and even then work trickled through the comfortable offices borne along in a tide of gossip and Turkish coffee and pungent cigarettes." The long siesta break was understandable, perhaps, given the "roasting afternoon heat," but the heat didn't keep the officers from their afternoon polo matches. "Slowly, painfully, reluctantly"—after the first air-raid sirens in Cairo, after the French commanders in Lebanon and Syria lined up with Vichy, after the first skirmishes on the Libyan border, "the Middle East dragged itself out of its apathy." By "Middle East," he meant the British there, especially the staff officers whom Wavell inherited.

The numbers were absurdly imbalanced. Lampson's figure of 250,000 Italian troops in Libya was not the highest estimate. Wavell had 36,000 in Egypt and less than 28,000 in Palestine. The Seventh Armored Division, deployed in the Western Desert of Egypt, was supposed to have 220 medium tanks. It actually had only 65 and was short on spare parts. Wavell had been given a division of the Indian army, the colonial army of British India made up of Indian soldiers under British and Indian officers. The Indian division lacked the artillery it was supposed to have. Moorehead got word that the Australian division training in Palestine was so ill-equipped that "they were using sticks tied with red flags as anti-tank guns and sticks tied with blue flags as Brens." The New Zealand division from which Bagnold drew his volunteers reached Egypt without its weaponry, which had gone down at sea.

Wavell's initial strategy was to bluff, to "make one tank look like a squadron, make a raid look like an advance." He sent small units on short stabs into Libya at night to attack, blow up munition dumps, hold a position for a few hours or days, and retreat.[14] These operations took place just across the border with Egypt. Bagnold's Boys would expand the realm of surprise much further into Libya. They were a gift that fit Wavell's desires and exceeded his hopes.

WAVELL DID NOT expect bluff to work forever. On the last day of July 1940, in the war cabinet in London, Secretary of State for War Anthony Eden read a telegram from the general saying that the Italians looked ready for a major offensive. Wavell thought trying to hold the Egyptian coastal village of Sollum near the Libyan border would be too costly. "The lack of equipment in the Middle East now necessitated a withdrawal," at least as far as Sidi Barani, fifty miles further back, Wavell warned. Eden told the war cabinet that a convoy with ammunition would leave Britain for Egypt in a few days, possibly also carrying "some armored cars" and spare parts. Beyond that meager commitment, he said, "it was impossible at the present time to spare any considerable reinforcement in the way of tanks, etc."[15]

In that "present time," Britain was preparing for German landings on its beaches. In mid-July Eden summoned General Alan Brooke and appointed him commander in chief of the Home Forces, responsible for the defense of all Britain. "The idea of failure at this stage of the war is too ghastly to contemplate," Brooke wrote in his diary. Brooke was violating the security rule against generals keeping diaries. But he longed to write letters to his wife, which would have been a greater violation. He was terribly alone. The terror of the job was that his forces and supplies were insufficient, and that he could never show his own fear to anyone. Brooke visited Churchill at the Cabinet War Rooms, an underground bunker near 10 Downing Street, "where I may have to be near the PM if an invasion starts," and found him "full of the most marvellous courage." Inspecting his units could be less inspiring. "Found it in a lamentable backward state of training . . . and deficient of officers," Brooke said of one division.

Wavell flew home. Churchill wanted to hear him in person. Brooke left a meeting with Eden and Wavell on August 10 dismayed by the decisions made. He'd been forced to part with three tank regiments. Those regiments, he'd note, constituted "a large proportion of my total armored forces" for defending Britain against the expected invasion.[16]

Let us note the timing: two weeks after Eden said that tanks could not possibly be spared, Churchill himself told the war cabinet that, "now that we were so much stronger" at home, the regiments could be sent to Egypt. Without them, he said "we might find ourselves in serious trouble in the Middle East."[17]

Whatever had been churned out of British factories or arrived from America in that brief time—however confident Churchill was that the combined strength of the Royal Navy and stormy Channel weather would defeat an invasion before it began—the real meaning of the decision was that Egypt and the Middle East were worth taking a potentially fateful risk to defend. They were the keystone in the long arch of the empire. Churchill believed passionately, without qualms, in the empire, in the right and duty of Britain to rule over supposedly lesser peoples around much of the globe.[18] But the reasons for defending Egypt were more than emotional or ideological. They were also strategic. The Middle East was what still gave Britain a hold on the Mediterranean and a chance to threaten Italy and Germany from the south. The Suez Canal and the oil fields of Iraq and southern Persia were prizes that had to be kept from the Axis.

Yet sending reinforcements was still the kind of choice whose weight is known only to leaders in time of war. "The decision to give this blood-transfusion while we braced ourselves to meet a mortal danger was at once awful and right," Churchill would later write.[19]

It was a wager, with the very existence of Britain as the stakes.

And however much it was made in Britain's imperial interests, however incidental or irrelevant the millions of people who actually lived in the Middle East were to the decision, it meant that Britain would seek to prevent their falling under Axis rule. It was a wager that changed the shape of the war, and of the Middle East then and after.

THE EUROPEAN WAR became a world war in another way. For every action in one place, there were distant unequal reactions.[20] Hitler did not intend to bring America's welders, riveters, and steelyard workers into the war. But he did. In mid-May, as Germany's tanks crossed from Belgium into France, Franklin Roosevelt spoke before a joint session of Congress and asked for the spectacular sum of $1.2 billion in emergency military funds. Oceans no longer made America safe, he said. Airplanes could carry war to its shores at three hundred miles per hour. If the Germans seized Greenland, bombers taking off from there could reach New England in six hours. Instead of building twelve thousand warplanes a year, he said, America must build at least fifty thousand. Every arms factory and shipyard had to work twenty-four hours a day. "Nations that were not ready and were unable to get ready found themselves overrun by the enemy," Roosevelt said.[21]

Churchill cabled, pleading for weaponry from America's stores. Roosevelt agreed, but his old friend and isolationist secretary of war, Henry Woodring, stonewalled.[22] (In their personal dispute, they acted out the national argument: rearmament had wall-to-wall support; helping Britain divided the country.) The army chief of staff, General George Marshall, solved the problem by defining the supplies in US armories that the British needed as suddenly being surplus, and then selling it to two companies that sold it to Britain at cost. Two days after the Dunkirk evacuation, ships were carrying half a million "surplus" rifles, 130 million rounds of ammunition, 900 howitzers, and much more from America to Britain. Tanks were missing from the cargo. America didn't have enough of those, and wasn't yet making enough.

Mussolini did not intend to give another forceful shove on the rudder of American policy. But he did. "The hand that held the dagger has struck it into the back of its neighbor," Roosevelt declared in a speech the day Italy declared war, expecting an Italian invasion of France. "We will extend to the opponents of force the material resources of this nation," he promised.[23]

A week later, he appointed Frank Knox, who'd been the Republican candidate for vice president in 1936, as secretary of the navy. Roosevelt asked for Secretary of War Woodring's resignation, and replaced him with Republican Henry Stimson, who'd been Herbert Hoover's secretary of state. On the eve of their appointments, both Knox and Stimson had called for instituting a military draft and increasing aid to Britain. In effect, the president had created a bipartisan war cabinet, but without the Republican Party's assent.

That week *Life* magazine's lead illustrated feature was headlined "This Is How the U.S. May Be Invaded." The scenario, described as beginning in July 1941, opened with Japanese aircraft carriers launching a surprise attack on the Panama Canal Zone. It continued with an Axis landing in New Jersey, and concluded with a drawing captioned, "U.S. envoys sue for peace in Philadelphia's Independence Hall before a Fascist tribunal seated before a Nazi flag."[24]

The war changed Roosevelt's personal course as well. He was nearing the end of his second term, as much as any president had ever served. He'd had a minor heart attack, though it was kept even more secret than his inability to walk. Early in the year, he'd told Treasury Secretary Henry Morgenthau that he wouldn't run for reelection unless "things get very, very much worse in Europe." Now things were entirely worse. "With deep-dyed anti–New Dealers turning into Third-Termers overnight," an unsigned *Life* article said, "his chances of reelection rose rapidly."[25] In July, at a Democratic convention orchestrated to show that the party had risen as one to beg him to run again, he was nominated for another term.

"We are all agreed that Roosevelt seems determined to get us into the war as soon as he can," Charles Lindbergh wrote in his diary, after a meeting in Washington with isolationist members of Congress. At a rally in Chicago, Lindbergh was the headline speaker. The organizers were disappointed they'd only half-filled the seventy-five-thousand-seat Soldier Field stadium, but Lindbergh's speech was broadcast on national radio. The famous aviator mocked Roosevelt's claim that an air force could use Greenland, "with its Arctic climate [and] its mountainous terrain," as a base. (America would prove him wrong.) He dismissed the idea that the United States should take a side in the war, or that there was any difference between the sides. "In the past, we have dealt with a Europe dominated by England and France. In the future we may have to deal with a Europe dominated by Germany," Lindbergh declared. What mattered for America was to stop giving "grandstand advice to Britain," to stop making "accusations of aggression and barbarism on the part of Germany," and to stay out of European affairs.

On September 4, Lindbergh was back in Washington for a meeting with his closest congressional ally, Republican representative James Van Zandt, and a Yale law student named R. Douglas Stuart. That day Stuart founded the America First Committee to unite the isolationist movement, for which Lindbergh would become the spokesman. Lindbergh listed one other person at the meeting at Van Zandt's office: Major Bonner Frank Fellers of the US Army.[26]

It was Fellers's last day in the States before shipping out to Madrid, where he would become assistant military attaché. In a way, he was finally about to begin his career.[27]

Fellers was forty-five. He still looked trim, but his hairline had receded so far that "my forehead has practically crept up to the back of my neck," as he'd written to a friend. In his letters, he took himself lightly. In person, he relaxed people into saying more than they expected or really should have. In his reports, he stated his views with omniscient certainty. He'd grown up on a Midwestern farm, which was common for army officers of the day. He'd transferred to West Point from a Quaker college, a background that was anything but common. His curiosity, and his ambition, needed more space than Indiana and Illinois allowed. He got his commission on November 1, 1918, a moment before the armistice, and spent twenty-two years in the peacetime army as a lieutenant and captain, only making major that summer of 1940. This pace showed his unusual drive: he'd advanced three ranks in the time it took the average US Army officer to rise one step in the doldrums of the interwar years. In the peacetime army, old officers neither died nor faded away; they stayed and stood in the way of young officers.[28]

Assigned to Manila in 1922, Fellers took leave, sailed to Japan, fell in love with the country, and sent a report to the assistant chief of staff for military intelligence noting that he'd spotted machine-gun nests guarding the railway tunnels, that target practice was held four times yearly for the shore guns protecting Kobe harbor, and that schoolboys went on hikes in squad formation led by army officers. In the years that he spent stateside, he collected friends, including ex-president Herbert Hoover, celebrity journalist Frazier Hunt, and a top diplomat at the

Soviet embassy. In the late 1930s Fellers traveled from Paris across the length of the Soviet Union to Japan and then back again. His reports quoted Russian scientists, a Soviet general, Ukrainian peasants, a Czech officer, and a high Nazi official. He was invited back to West Point—to teach English. His prose, it seemed, won more attention than his strategic analysis.

In March 1940 Fellers wrote a paper against America entering the war. "The bitter criticism in America of Herr Hitler is strongly tinged with British and Jewish propaganda," he wrote. He decried immigration of Jewish refugees, a view that was unremarkable in the officer class. He attacked the ban on Japanese immigration, an exceptional position when "scientific racism" and the yellow peril were accepted truths in that class.[29] He went to the Republican convention in 1940 and favored isolationist candidate Robert Taft. He despised Roosevelt. But the mission to Madrid meant that he now was assigned full-time to military intelligence. Ultimately, it meant that Bonner Fellers would be one of Roosevelt's valued sources on a war that Fellers had opposed as fervently as Lindbergh did.

ACCOUNTS OF THE British bombing raid on Tobruk on June 18 mention only one plane shot down by Italian antiaircraft crews: an Italian bomber, piloted by Italo Balbo. An aviator whose international fame rivaled Lindbergh's, Balbo was also the governor and military commander of Libya, and was under Mussolini's orders to invade Egypt. He was returning from a reconnaissance flight and died in the crash.

Lindbergh's fame came from crossing the Atlantic alone. Balbo's fame came from the spectacle of group flight. His greatest exploit was leading twenty-five Italian flying boats together, in formation, across the Atlantic. That was in 1933, when he headed the Italian air force. The extravaganza expressed the Fascist ethic of turning individuals into cogs in the machine of the nation. One leg of the journey took them from Iceland through the fogs of Greenland to Labrador. When they landed in Lake Michigan off the Chicago shore, the mayor proclaimed Balbo Day. In New York, Balbo and his pilots got a ticker-tape parade. President Roosevelt invited him for lunch.

Back home, a jealous Mussolini appointed Balbo to the Libya post, a prestigious exile. Balbo was a prominent Fascist, one of the leaders of the March of Rome that had put Mussolini in power. Now, though, he was much too popular for Mussolini's tastes. As time passed he made himself even less popular in Rome by criticizing the alliance with Germany, and by dissenting from Mussolini's turn to anti-Semitism.

The latter policy was partly imitation of Hitler. But in Mussolini's own description, it followed logically from the conquest of Ethiopia, where he enacted race laws separating whites and blacks. What happened in the colony became a prelude to what happened in Italy. The 1938 Manifesto of the Race, signed by leading scientists, defined Italians as Aryans and declared Jews biologically inferior and unassimilable. Until that moment, Italian Jews may have been the most assimilated in Europe; many were members of the Fascist Party. The racial laws that followed excluded them from the party, from schools, professions, and marriage to Aryans.

The laws were supposed to apply equally in Libya, where a fifth of Tripoli, the largest town, was Jewish. So was 5 percent of Benghazi, the largest town in Cyrenaica, the eastern part of the colony. Balbo's own policy had been the opposite. He had sought to force the local Jews to become more Italian, with measures that included public whipping of those who closed their stores on Saturdays. He avoided implementing many of the race decrees. He was a Fascist of an obsolete variety; he had not kept up.[30]

All this led to reports that downing Balbo "may or may not have been accidental."[31] Evidence of a plot never surfaced. His death, however, did remove him as an obstacle to implementing Rome's policies against Libya's population.

Which is a reminder: Libya had a population. Desert war is often described as purer than war in other lands, as being more like a sea battle, involving only combatants maneuvering in uninhabited space. Yet there were inhabited islands in the ocean of sand. In fertile areas along the coast, there were entire archipelagoes. Tobruk was a town in June 1940. Benghazi was a small, flourishing city with elegant avenues. Civilians died when bombs fell, just as they did in Europe. And for those who lived, the battles determined who ruled them.

When Balbo died, the Duce sent General Rodolfo Graziani back to Libya to replace him. Mussolini had two great worries that summer. The first was that Britain would ask Germany for peace. The second was that Germany would conquer Britain quickly, before Italy could overrun Egypt and unite the pieces of its African empire. That fear grew in August as waves of Luftwaffe bombers pounded England and fought the RAF in preparation for landings.

In Italy the winter before, Graziani had wanted to join Germany in the war. In Libya, his enthusiasm dried up. Visiting Rome in August, he told Foreign Minister Ciano how unready the army in Libya was. "We move toward a defeat which, in the desert, inevitably becomes a rapid and total disaster," Graziani said. If he absolutely had to send his divisions forward, he wanted to wait for cooler weather.[32]

From Berlin, Mussolini got "significant hints" that "the decisive attack against Britain" was about to start. It did not occur to him that the British would last longer than the French. Mussolini expected both "victory and peace" by the end of September, and sent orders to Graziani that he must attack—certainly by the day when "the first platoon of [German] soldiers" landed on an English beach.

At last, the offensive was set for September 6. When the date came, Graziani asked for another month. Mussolini now thought that the war might last all the way into winter. But he'd been living in expectation for too many weeks. Graziani must attack or be replaced, he told his ministers.

The general followed orders.

On September 9, three months after Mussolini's decision to go to war, the Italian Tenth Army rolled toward the border with Egypt.[33]

2

WAR OF SHADOWS

Summer-Autumn 1940. Washington-
Bletchley Park-Rome-Budapest.

In one corner of the Munitions Building, the US War Department's massive warren of offices near the Lincoln Memorial, Roosevelt's appointment of a new secretary of war brought a surge of anxiety. As secretary of state in 1929, Henry Stimson had closed down the Black Chamber, which cracked codes and read other countries' diplomatic cables. In the summer of 1940, William Friedman and his small band of codebreakers at the army's Signal Intelligence Service feared that Stimson would shut their operation as well, just as they were on the obsessed, manic edge of a breakthrough.

Back when Stimson shut the Black Chamber, Friedman was left as the only code expert in the War Department. Like virtually everyone else who worked in cryptography in those days, he came to the field by accident.

Friedman was born in 1891 in Kishinev, a half-Romanian, half-Jewish town at the western edge of the Russian Empire. When he was a year old, his family emigrated to the United States to escape the threat of anti-Semitic violence in the tsar's realm. (Many years later, a psychiatrist treating him would note that Friedman lived with a constant, inherited fear of pogroms.) Overcoming the quieter but endemic anti-Semitism in America of his day, Friedman succeeded in getting into Cornell University. With his degree in genetics, he was hired by a millionaire who had set up an agricultural lab as a personal hobby. Then Friedman was put to work in his benefactor's other project, looking for the code in Shakespeare's writing that would supposedly reveal the "true" author. In the process of disproving that theory, Friedman invented mathematical principles for codebreaking. He also came to the understanding that applying rules could take you only to the edge of revelations. To crack a code, he'd write, you also had to "let your subconscious solve it." His own intuitions may have been picked up from his father, who'd been a linguist and translator before the move to America. Solving codes—as Dilly Knox best demonstrated in Britain—can be translation taken to a higher level: puzzling out meaning from a language about which you know nothing.[1]

In 1921 Friedman moved from the millionaire's estate to the Munitions Building on Constitution Avenue in Washington to become the chief cryptographer—and the only cryptographer—of the Office of the Chief Signal Officer of the US Army. A photograph shows Friedman with a high forehead, sculpted cheekbones, and a narrow chin. His wide-set, hooded eyes are melancholy, as if sending a coded message to ignore the smile on his lips. After the Black Chamber closed, he was allowed to hire three assistants. In contrast to their British counterparts, they did not come from exclusive universities or from an aristocratic old boys' club. US government rules required that Friedman hire only people who'd passed the civil service exam. Two of the three were young Jewish mathematicians who'd been teaching school in New York. They were old friends from City College, the academic paradise of New York's teeming immigrant masses yearning for higher education. Abe Sinkov brought Solomon Kullback a flyer he'd spotted, saying that the civil service was looking for mathematicians. Both were frustrated as schoolteachers; they wanted to *use* their math. The civil service, though racially segregated, was a refuge for Jews for whom jobs in corporations and universities were nearly off-limits.[2] The third man, Frank Rowlett, had been teaching math in the back country of southwest Virginia. When Rowlett got a letter offering him a job as "junior cryptanalyst," he couldn't find the word in the dictionary.

Friedman explained afterward that it meant "codebreaker" and that he'd invented it.

The Signal Intelligence Service, or SIS, grew very slowly. Officially, Friedman wasn't supposed to engage in "the solution of . . . secret or disguised enemy messages" in peacetime. He was only allowed to train his people to do that, so they would be ready for war. In the meantime, their task was developing codes for the army and government agencies. To create one—apparently the Military Intelligence Code, to be used by military attachés—they wrote the fifty thousand words that needed to be in the codebook on one set of cards and an equal number of meaningless groups of five letters on a second set. Then they went inside a room-sized vault, tossed all the cards of one set in the air, picked them up one by one, and matched them with cards from the other set.[3]

They used letters rather than numbers, apparently because attachés sent their reports to Washington via commercial firms. Radiograms came into Washington via RCA, the Radio Corporation of America. The companies had historically charged less for letters than for numbers. The catch was that with letters you couldn't use subtraction tables—lists of random numbers to subtract from the code groups in order to disguise them. Friedman came up with another solution: tables in which the alphabet from *A* to *Z* appeared at the top, followed by line after line in which the alphabet was scrambled. If the first letter of the coded message was *K*, the sender would replace it with the letter that appeared beneath *K* in the first line of the table. For the second letter, he'd use the second line. Tables could be produced quickly, unlike a new code. So each attaché could get a different set, and they could be replaced regularly. The system was a poor man's Enigma: slowly, by hand, each letter was encrypted in a different cipher.[4]

Meanwhile, under the cover story that they were only training at cryptography, Friedman and his SIS staff worked on the new codes that Japan adopted after Herbert Yardley had written his tell-all book *American Black Chamber*, which had warned the Japanese more than a decade earlier that their codes were compromised. In the mid-1930s Friedman's team succeeded in cracking the first, simple cipher machine that the Japanese used for diplomatic traffic. The Americans codenamed it Red, and it provided a stream of intelligence on Japanese intentions. Toward the end of 1938, a disturbing message appeared. It authorized "travel for a 'communications expert' named Okamato" to the most important Japanese embassies around the world, including Washington, London, Rome, and Berlin. His job was to set up a new cipher machine. On February 19, 1939, another intercepted Japanese message announced that the new device would go into use the next day. With American-Japanese relations growing ever more tense, the vital intelligence stream dried up.

SIS named the new machine Purple. Friedman's team could see that it was based on the Red machine, but was far more sophisticated. At the Munitions Building, the SIS mathematicians began looking frenetically for a solution. Friedman, whose job had slowly shifted to administrator, received orders to get back to work on codebreaking.

The characteristics of Red that carried over to Purple provided some clues. Both machines were used to send messages in Japanese transliterated into English characters. Red had encrypted vowels separately from consonants. Purple still encrypted six out of twenty-six letters in an easily broken method, though the six letters changed daily. If you figured out the six for a given day, it was sometimes possible to work out much more of the original, plain-language message. Occasionally, the Japanese made the cardinal error of sending the same message in Purple to the most important embassies and in Red to other diplomatic missions.

The mystery was how the other twenty letters were being encrypted. When war broke out in Europe, the SIS got a budget increase that brought Friedman two dozen new staffers, including Genevieve Grotjan, a brilliant twenty-six-year-old mathematician who'd been unable to get a college teaching job—very likely because of another endemic prejudice, against women. In contrast to its British counterpart at Bletchley Park, the SIS paid women the same as men.

Then Stimson became secretary of war.

The chief signal officer talked to Roosevelt's military aide, and received dispensation to keep the resurrected Black Chamber secret from the secretary. By mid-1940, the Purple team was working deep into every night, coming in on weekends, and borrowing staff from other projects. Friedman himself woke earlier and earlier, drinking coffee and pacing his kitchen for hours before going to the Munitions

Building. There, in the humid heat of the Washington summer, the sweaty codebreakers fought the fans in their rooms to keep the papers on their desks.

On a September afternoon, Gene Grotjan had a breakthrough. Staring through her rimless glasses at comparisons of Purple messages and plain-language texts, she realized that the twenty-letter sets each day were going through a triple scrambler, similar to the three rotors of an Enigma machine. She rushed into the next room, where the senior staff worked, to ask Rowlett to come see. "Gene has found what we're looking for!" Rowlett shouted moments later. Cheers erupted in the office. Grotjan's glasses enlarged the tears in her eyes. A week later, her insight allowed the codebreakers to decrypt and translate two messages.[5]

It was September 20, a week before Japan, Germany, and Italy signed the Tripartite Pact, binding them to mutual defense against attack on any of them. The timing of Grotjan's breakthrough was not coincidence: the negotiations apparently led to a surge in Japanese diplomatic traffic, providing the SIS with more raw material.

At the time, it appeared that the three Axis countries, especially Germany, created the pact to deter America from entering the war. The deeper explanation was that on the chessboard of Hitler's megalomania, the pact was a move meant to lead Japan to destroy the American navy while the Führer was busy with other plans.[6]

Three weeks later, under the direction of Lieutenant Leo Rosen, who'd been assigned to the SIS because he'd studied electrical engineering at MIT, a signal corps team had built an ersatz Purple machine. They'd never seen the real thing, but their copy could decode messages—if you knew the daily settings. The Japanese were only using a few hundred of countless possible combinations. Friedman's report from mid-October 1940 says that his staff had already worked out a third of the settings actually in use. The decrypted messages were appropriately code-named Magic.

Word of the wondrous SIS device reached the army chief of staff, General George Marshall. He visited the SIS to see it working. Then he brought Henry Stimson.

The secretary of war watched the making of Magic and liked it. He did not shut anything. As he'd later explain, "What you do in war

and what you do in peace are two entirely different things." Even if
the United States was not a belligerent at the moment, he'd been appointed to his current office to prepare for the looming possibility of
war. Magic allowed Marshall, Stimson, and Roosevelt to stand invis-
ibly behind Japan's diplomats in Rome and Berlin, Washington and
London, and read over their shoulders.

Friedman, who'd been in the army reserves for years, was called
up for active duty at the rank of colonel. Two weeks later, he had a
nervous breakdown and was taken to the army's Walter Reed Hospital. Extreme nervous fatigue, the doctors concluded, which perhaps
should be decoded as saying there is only so much sleepless strain the
subconscious can sustain. Having succeeded in his mission, Friedman
collapsed.

Marian Rejewski was now Pierre Renaud, a teacher from Brittany. So
his papers said. It's likely that whoever forged them chose Brittany in
the hope that no provincial Vichy policeman in the small town of Uzes
would realize that "Renaud's" accent was shaped by Polish, not by
Breton, a language that was still spoken in a far corner of France. Jerzy
Rozycki's documents said he was Julien Rouget. Henryk Zygalski had
become René Sargent. Gustave Bertrand of French military intelligence bought a chateau outside Uzes under his latest alias, "Monsieur
Barsac." Command Post Cadix, as it was known to a very few Frenchmen, began operating on October 1, 1940. To the Polish General Staff
in exile in London, it was Eksopytura 300—Field Office 300.

The journey that ended in Uzes had begun on June 10 at 1:40 a.m.
at another chateau, the one secretly known as Command Post Bruno,
at Gretz-Armainvilliers, twenty-five miles from Paris. By the time the
sun rose and set that day, Italy would have joined the war. Much more
important for Bertrand, German armies would be even closer to Paris.
Bertrand had orders to evacuate the fifteen members of the Polish
Cipher Bureau working for him on German Enigma, along with the
seven Spanish Republican codebreakers who decrypted the ciphers of
Italy and of the Franco regime in Spain.

Bertrand's orders did not come with vehicles. He commandeered
a truck and a bus, loaded them with the post's staffers and files and

Polish-made Enigma machines, and headed out into the churning current of refugees on the roads southward.[7] Rejewski, Rozycki, and Zygalski were fleeing a German invasion for the second time in nine months. Even more important than preserving their lives and their ability to break Enigma was keeping the knowledge that it could be broken from the Nazis.

A hundred miles south of Paris, at La Fèrte-Saint Aubin, they set up shop—and then fled further south after the fall of Paris to Le Chatelet, then onward to Vensat, and to Agen, moving almost daily. They were at yet another temporary refuge, a wide spot in the road called Bon Encontre, when news came of the French surrender.

The armistice required France to hand over to Germany the names of everyone engaged in signal intelligence. Bertrand managed to get his fugitive Poles and Spaniards onto three planes from Toulouse to Oran in Algeria. From there they moved on to Algiers, where they registered under false names at the Touring Club Hotel, avoided talking to locals, and remained in virtual confinement for close to three months. The Abwehr and the SD—the Nazi Party's intelligence bureau—were spreading out in the officially unoccupied part of France administered by the Vichy government and in Vichy-controlled Algeria.

Under the armistice, the French army had to shrink to one hundred thousand men. Within that small number, a large tangle of conspiracies and conflicted loyalties grew. Bertrand sided with a covert anti-German faction and decided to reestablish his intelligence operation on Vichy territory. His plan was approved by General Maxime Weygand, defense minister of the Vichy government, a man reasonably suspected by both the Allies and the Germans of working against them. Weygand served in the collaborationist regime, but wanted his own sources on what the Germans were up to.

With their forged papers, the Polish and Spanish codebreakers returned from Algeria and got to work. The only radio intelligence service that the Germans allowed in Vichy was an agency that was supposed to search for Resistance transmitters. Pro-Resistance officers working there instead monitored German traffic and provided intercepted messages to Command Post Cadix. Inside occupied France, the Resistance tapped telegraph cables and sent couriers to Uzes carrying encoded

Nazi telegrams. At the Uzes chateau itself, four Polish wireless operators listened through the shortwave static to the Abwehr and SD radio nets. Rejewski and his colleagues broke the codes. From Cadix flowed an underground stream of warnings to the Resistance of what the secret police were planning. Via a shortwave link, the Polish General Staff in London received intelligence it could share with the British.

But the personal link to Bletchley Park was broken. Bertrand could not come to England bearing gifts; Alan Turing could not cross the Channel to talk to the Poles.

In the summer and fall of 1940, Britain was engaged in two fateful battles. In one, the Battle of Britain, the German air force intended to destroy the Royal Air Force and break the British will before a Nazi amphibious invasion. In the other, the Battle of the Atlantic, Britain was trying to bring the convoys of arms and supplies from America that it needed to survive, as German submarines moving in packs hunted its ships. It was winning the first battle and losing the second.

Unknown to the Germans, the press, and the British public, the war of the mind at Bletchley Park also had two fronts: against the Enigma methods of the German air force and against German naval Enigma.

On the first front, Bletchley Park was gaining ground, as it began to fulfill Welchman's vision of industrialized codebreaking. The first of the new bombes was delivered in August, its key-breaking ability speeded up with Welchman's diagonal board. The bombe's limitation was that it depended on a crib, a very educated guess about a short bit of text likely to appear at the beginning of a message. The guess depended on knowing what was in earlier messages.[8] So it was most effective against the German air force key, Red, which Hut 6 had broken and read in the past.[9]

On the other front, against naval Enigma, German defenses were defeating the codebreakers, and the defeat meant that British ships and supplies were sinking and many men dying in the cold North Atlantic waters. The German navy imposed much stricter security rules than the air force did. A naval Enigma operator had to choose his wheel setting for messages from a list, and then used a code and a cipher to hide it before sending it. In Hut 8 at Bletchley Park, Alan Turing and Peter Twinn were stymied. Only by capturing the code and cipher instructions from a German vessel, they believed, could they learn the method.[10]

Ian Fleming, the young assistant to the director of naval intelligence, came up with a plan: repair a downed German bomber, man it with "a tough crew of five" wearing bloodied German uniforms, fly it over the English Channel, radio an SOS message, and crash the plane into the sea. When a German rescue boat picked up the disguised men, they'd "shoot [the] German crew, dump [them] overboard, [and] bring [the] rescue boat back to English port." Fleming expected to be one of the five. The scheme was approved, labeled Operation Ruthless, and then called off.[11] Ian Fleming was imaginative, but Ruthless was a plan fit only for a spy novel.

Frank Birch, the navy intelligence officer at Bletchley Park, sent a memo to the Admiralty in October. "Turing and Twinn came to me like undertakers cheated of a nice corpse two days ago, all in a stew about the cancellation of Operation Ruthless," he wrote. "The burden of their song was the importance of a pinch."[12] As a senior Bletchley Park figure wrote on another occasion, "As far as we are concerned, pinching is the best form of cryptography."[13]

Once before, Marian Rejewski had found the equations to unlock Enigma. The entire operation against the German machine began with that flash of insight. This isn't proof he could have done the same again to solve the naval Enigma problem, but the possibility was never tested. It's unlikely that anyone in England would have asked him. The best minds of Bletchley Park assumed that the Poles had pinched an Enigma machine with its wheels, rather than working out the wiring mathematically.

After the fall of France, in any case, Rejewski was beyond reach. Dilly Knox's health grew worse, as did Alastair Denniston's. Bletchley Park filled with new recruits who did not know how Enigma was first broken or by whom.

The magicians from Warsaw faded from the collective memory of Britain's codebreakers. Bletchley Park's history was a secret known to few. The Poles' contribution was an even deeper secret.

"Four SIM agents were surprised this evening inside the Yugoslav legation," Ciano told his diary on August 3.[14] "We must encourage the rumor that they were simply ordinary burglars."

For Manfredi Talamo, this was a rare and dangerous fiasco. His Removal Section and the whole Servizio Informazioni Militari, the SIM, could have inscribed "Pinching is the best form of cryptography" on their coat of arms. But if the identity of the intruders in the Yugoslav embassy became known among foreign diplomats, Talamo's game could be over.

Ciano's rumor spreading apparently succeeded, though. Security at embassies remained abysmal. Talamo's copied keys still worked. Many of the diplomats lived at the Hotel Ambasciatori, an ornate neo-Renaissance building on Via Vittorio Veneto, in quarters conveniently provided by the Italian government. The palace was around the corner from the US embassy and close to other legations in the posh Ludovisi district, which meant that diplomats could walk home from work and Talamo's men could easily keep track of when they were away from their offices.[15]

The British embassy to Italy had closed down, but plenty of others were left. Actually, another British legation remained open very nearby, in the world's tiniest independent state, the Vatican. A country of a little over a hundred acres didn't have much room for foreign diplomatic offices, so in normal times they were located elsewhere in Rome. After Mussolini declared war, British representative Francis D'Arcy Osborne moved to an apartment in Casa Santa Marta, a Vatican guesthouse in the shadow of St. Peter's Basilica. The French, Belgian, Polish, and other Allied diplomats joined him as guests, or as honored prisoners, at the Santa Marta. To communicate with London, they sent messages in the Vatican diplomatic bag to Bern. From neutral Switzerland, their reports could be radioed to London.

Talamo wasted no time. In June 1940, he assigned one of his men, Angelo Greffi, to Osborne's relocated legation. By August or September, Greffi had picked out two Italians working for the British, and they were called in for interviews with the man with a pudgy face and a southern Italian accent who, if he gave a name at all, did not give "Talamo."

The P Squad chief had his own contacts inside the Vatican. One was Giovanni Fazio, the pro-Fascist head of the "special section" of the Vatican police. Fazio's men followed each of the foreign diplomats and kept hour-to-hour reports on their movements. Fazio gave that information to Talamo. The reports on D'Arcy Osborne apparently showed that he habitually left his residence for several hours every Sunday morning. That was the time chosen for the P Squad's periodic break-ins. The Vatican police did not interfere. Talamo's men knew what to look for: they removed, photographed, and returned code-books, cipher tables, and coded messages on which the plain English text had been handwritten by whoever decoded them. It was all that Italy's own codebreakers could wish for.[16]

BUDAPEST WAS STILL a neutral capital, which made it one of the back alleys accessible from both sides of a divided world. Major Nikolaus Ritter of the Abwehr, German military intelligence, came there nearly once a month under the name Dr. Jansen; he used it as a meeting place with the agents he was running in the Balkans and the Middle East under the guise of representatives of Oriental Export and Import, purportedly a Hungarian furniture firm. Besides that, there was no war economy in Budapest, so he shopped there for clothes for his wife and got a bespoke suit for himself.

In Budapest, he'd been introduced to Captain Laszlo Almasy. Ritter's understanding was that Almasy served in the Hungarian Intelligence Service. Ritter appears to be the only source for this. Other accounts say Almasy was teaching at Hungary's air force academy. It's possible that Almasy was doing both. It's also possible that Almasy strayed from the truth to impress the German. Certainly Ritter took a liking to him and to the Almasy family mansion, and dropped by regularly on his trips to Budapest.

Though he'd returned to his home country, Almasy felt he was in exile. "If you ever need to know anything about Africa that I can help you with, let me know. I know the land and people like my vest pocket," he liked to tell Ritter. He backed that up with stories and name dropping. One time, in September 1940, he talked about Aziz el-Masri, who had been chief of staff of the Egyptian army until the British pushed him out. Almasy said the old Anglophobic general was a friend of his, and that "the general and his nationalist Egyptian friends were fervently hoping for a German victory" that would free them from the British.

Ritter blurted out what he considered an absolutely improbable idea. "Could this man, this general, perhaps be influenced to work with us against the British?"

Almasy didn't think it all improbable. He said this was just what he was leading up to.

Together they cooked up a proposal: they would smuggle Masri out of Cairo to Germany and use him "to persuade Egyptian revolutionaries to switch to the German side."

Almasy would be the smuggler.

At first Abwehr commander Wilhelm Canaris labeled this idea "crazy." A month later he reversed himself. In the meantime, Hitler was leaning on Budapest to align militarily with the Axis. On November 20, Hungary formally joined the Tripartite Pact. Soon after, Almasy got orders seconding him to the Abwehr, where he would retain the rank of captain but wear a German uniform. Or so Almasy would later describe the change of country that he served: as something imposed on him.

But the orders came from the commander of the Hungarian air force, who may have been a personal friend, and the move furthered his scheme with Ritter. The plan fit his passion for living dangerously, and it would take him home to the desert.[17]

3

SANDSTORM

Autumn 1940-Winter 1941.
Cairo-Haifa-Benghazi.

MARSHAL RODOLFO GRAZIANI, known as "the Butcher," ordered his troops forward toward Egypt in two prongs. The main force would attack along the coast. A smaller, more mobile group under General Pietro Maletti would leave its base in Libya and head south into the desert, cross into Egypt, then swoop around the British front line and attack from behind. Maletti had spent years in Libya. He'd fought under Graziani in the *riconquista* and the slaughter of the Senussi at Kufra. He knew the desert.

After giving the command to advance, Graziani told his diary, "Thus is accomplished what may well be recorded as a crime of historic proportions, against the commission of which I have fought with all my strength." In the mind of the Butcher, let us assume, the crime was not against Britain or Egypt. It was against the unready Italian army he led. But he absolved himself; he was only following orders. "For whatever evil may occur, I, before God and my soldiers, am not *responsible*."

Maletti, overconfident or careless, left his Arab guides behind and got lost in soft sands while still in Libya. By the time the Italian air force found him, he'd used up too much fuel, time, and water for his flanking action. He returned to the coastal road to join the rest of the army.[1]

On the Libyan side of the border, the land rose from the shoreline to a plateau. The coastal plateau ended just inside Egypt, where a cliff dropped six hundred feet to Sollum, a dot on the map with a customs post, thirty houses, and too few British defenders. The Italians had to descend from the high ground via a rocky path called Halfaya Pass. British soldiers called it Hellfire Pass. The rocks mostly hid the Italian trucks as they came downhill. Still, British gunners noticed that the Italians "caught the sun on their windshields at one exposed corner," war correspondent Alan Moorehead wrote. "A few seconds later each vehicle exposed itself again very briefly on another bend." The gun crews "had merely to note each reflected flash from the windshields and then aim at the lower corner." Shattered vehicles clogged the path, but the river of "water-trucks, guns, donkey teams, tanks, armored cars" kept flowing down the escarpment.

The outnumbered British abandoned Sollum, dropped back sixty miles to the deserted Beduin village of Sidi Barani, and abandoned it too. General Wavell's sunburned soldiers had dug their trenches in the sand at Mersa Matruh, eighty miles further on. The former resort village had a port and a paved road all the way to Alexandria to supply it. That's where Wavell hoped to stop the Italians before the river of men and machines could reach Alexandria.[2]

Instead, Graziani ordered a halt at Sidi Barani on September 16. He'd taken a strip of Egyptian coast; he'd taken casualties; he didn't intend to take more chances. The British could not see the chaos in the Italian multitude that had pursued them into Egypt: whole units that panicked, junior officers who "deserted their troops under fire," the general who "drove artillery lieutenants out of hiding and back to their guns with blows." Graziani told Rome that he was making logistic preparations for the next advance. He didn't say how long that would take. On the coast and in an arc into the desert, his soldiers began building fortified camps.[3]

At the end of September, the minutes of the British war cabinet included a laconic report from the chief of the Imperial General Staff, John Dill, that "there was nothing to indicate . . . that the Italian offensive would be resumed at an early date."[4] Seen from London or Cairo, it hardly made sense. Graziani, or perhaps God, had granted Britain time to send more men and tanks to Egypt.

Mussolini, at first, was "radiant" about the invasion, which gave Italy "the glory she has sought in vain for three centuries." His son-in-law recorded the Duce's words in his diary. Ecstasy evaporated into anxiety and then anger when Mussolini realized that Graziani saw the next stage as months, not days, away.

The Duce was even angrier when German troops began occupying Romania. Germany had too little petroleum to fuel a war. It depended on Romania's oil fields and produced an invitation from the country's new far-right government to protect them. Mussolini thought Germany understood that the Balkans were supposed to belong to *his* empire. Hitler was always surprising him, always snatching without inviting Italy to share. "This time I am going to pay him back in his own coin," he told Ciano. "He will find out from the papers that I have occupied Greece." He expected to seize the country easily, as he had seized Albania, as the Germans had grabbed Austria and Czechoslovakia.[5]

Major Bonner Fellers barely had time to unpack his suitcase in Madrid when he got orders "to proceed by first available transportation to Cairo." The Military Intelligence Division of the US Army had decided that it needed an attaché in Cairo more than it needed an assistant to the military attaché in Spain. The Franco regime in Spain might join the war on the Axis side, but in Egypt a war was now actually going on.

The decision to move Fellers was sudden, almost impulsive. It came within two weeks of Graziani's clumsy invasion.[6] Military Intelligence in Washington clearly hadn't been planning to post an attaché in Egypt. Fellers hadn't received codebooks, regulations on how to run an attaché office, or budget instructions.[7]

He left Madrid on October 18. Crossing Europe, he was in Berlin a few nights later. He heard sirens, which gave so little warning of approaching British bombers that he hadn't pulled his clothes on before he heard antiaircraft guns firing. He took note that the searchlights meant to help the gun crews were useless. The lights never found a plane, though Fellers was told that sixty British bombers had attacked the city. He did not report who told him this; he often left sources unnamed. From Berlin he traveled to Budapest, perhaps crossing paths on the street with Abwehr officer Nikolaus Ritter, in town to meet his agents. At the end of October, Fellers reported to the US legation in Cairo.[8]

By his fourth day in Cairo, he met with Britain's secretary of state for war, Anthony Eden. Churchill had sent Eden off to Egypt by flying boat because Wavell had not attacked the Italians yet despite all the tanks he had been sent; because Churchill found it "illogical" that Egypt hadn't declared war, and he wanted to remind King Farouk that "he was under the necessity of obeying our instructions"; because a Turkish military delegation would be in Cairo; and because of a telegram from Spain. The telegram contained a thirdhand report: the British ambassador in Madrid said that the Spanish foreign minister said that Hitler and Mussolini had agreed that the Germans would plunge their army through "Constantinople and Syria" to conquer Egypt. Churchill wanted Eden to persuade the Turks that they should side with Britain, not acquiesce to the Axis.

The warning from the ambassador in Madrid is recorded not in the war cabinet minutes but in the even more secret annex, in which Lord Halifax, the foreign secretary, warns that the thrust through Turkey could actually be aimed at the Persian Gulf, the territory of oil. The airfields and antiaircraft defenses that Germany was building in Romania might be part of the plan, he said.[9] In this war, neutrality lasted only till a country was overrun, or until it stabbed another in the back. Every map hid invisible invasion routes.

The earth hid sinews tying every front to every other far-away front. When German tanks wounded the soil in Romania, the ground shuddered in Egypt.

Eden was about to fly home when Italy invaded Greece from Albania. He delayed leaving. Between his urgent talks with the British commanders, Eden carved out time for the freshly arrived American major, Bonner Fellers. The meeting, it seems, testifies to how eagerly Fellers got to work, and how easily he made himself at home in people's confidence. In the spring he'd been teaching English to cadets.

Now he could radio home that Anthony Eden had pledged that "I would be permitted to see all British units and installations."[10]

The cabinet-level promise testifies to another thing: how important it was to Britain's leaders to make the Americans feel like they were already allies in a war they hadn't entered. Secrets, willy-nilly, bind giver and taker. In September, Fellers had belonged to the inner circle of American isolationists. In November, he was bound by shared secrets with Anthony Eden.

Fellers received an office on the second floor of the American consulate building in Garden City, the quiet enclave of aristocrats and ambassadors on the eastern bank of the Nile, in a separate universe from the din of the rest of Cairo. The building was the mansion of a recently deceased millionaire. The staircase Fellers took to his office each day was wide enough for a king's entourage. In late November he wrote his Report No. 1. Hassan Sabry, Egypt's prime minister, had stood a few days before in parliament to give the first speech of the winter session. He spoke softly, turned for a moment toward the king, staggered, and collapsed. He was carried out dead. The next day Farouk appointed a successor—who stuck to the policy of "nonparticipation" in the war.

The British, Fellers wrote, tried pressing the king to get off the sidelines, then "gave it up as a bad job." One of Fellers's sources was Jumbo Wilson, commander of the British Troops in Egypt. The British military, Fellers wrote, had "reported officially that at least eighty percent of the Egyptian officers were dead against war." A unit of less than a thousand men of the Egyptian army's Frontier Force held Siwa Oasis near the Libyan border. "Word came to the British Army that the Egyptian officers . . . would refuse to fight if attacked by the Italians . . . the oasis lies on a route by which the Italians might invade" through the desert, Fellers said.

Fellers also got an Egyptian cabinet minister, Abdul Rahman Azzam, to talk to him about the crisis. Azzam had fought in Libya with the Senussi against the Italians twenty years earlier. He "hated Italy possibly more than any other Egyptian," Fellers wrote, but "still violently opposed participation in the war." As described by Fellers, Azzam looked at the war as one between Britain and Italy, in which the fact that the gunfire and dying were taking place on Egyptian soil was a distant abstraction. Egyptians, Azzam told Fellers, "honestly desired to help Great Britain" as long as doing so didn't pull them into the conflict. Azzam had proposed to Wilson that the Egyptian army pull its units out of the desert "to police rear areas," freeing British troops for the front. As part of the arrangement, Wilson wanted the Egyptian army to turn over tanks, trucks, and artillery to the British. Azzam agreed to give cover by presenting this to Farouk as his idea.[11]

Second Lieutenant Khaled Mohi El Din of the Egyptian Cavalry Corps's First Tank Regiment arrived at his brigade's barracks one morning and "found several British officers inspecting tanks. I asked what was going on and the reply was like a fatal knife stab: 'The British are taking our tanks.'" Mohi El Din had graduated from the military academy just a couple of months before. He had felt caressed by admiring glances as he walked Cairo streets in his uniform. Now, "our bitterness and humiliation were indescribable. How could we be an army without arms? How could the occupiers take our weapons?" In his account, the British seized the tanks to make up for their losses at Dunkirk.[12]

At Mersa Matruh, Anwar al-Sadat was serving as the signals officer in an Egyptian artillery brigade deployed to stop the expected Italian advance. As Sadat saw things, "our enemy was primarily, if not solely, Great Britain," and to fight the Italians would mean "we were fighting for Britain, in violation of the 1936 treaty which had established the sovereignty of Egypt." On November 20, his brigade got orders to withdraw, and to turn over its guns to the British. He was "livid with rage" and, like Mohi El Din, felt humiliated. On the other hand, being sent back to Cairo allowed him to meet regularly with one of the men he most respected, the man he hoped would advise him on starting a revolution—deposed military chief of staff Aziz el-Masri. Sometimes they met at Masri's home, sometimes at Groppi's cafe in the center of Cairo.[13] Groppi's was either a daring or foolish spot to choose, since it was also a favorite meeting spot of British officers.

THE EMPRESS OF Britain sailed from the port of Suez, at the southern end of the Canal, on September 24, 1940. The Empress was an ocean liner converted to troop carrier, a fast ship that could make the journey from England around the Cape of Good Hope to Egypt in under six weeks. She had just delivered four thousand British soldiers for General Wavell's forces. On the return trip, very unwillingly, Countess Hermione Ranfurly was sailing homeward.

The title of countess had come with her marriage to Daniel Knox, Earl of Ranfurly, a member of the penniless gentry. He was a lieutenant in the Notts Sherwood Rangers Yeomanry, the last cavalry unit in the British military that still had horses. On their first wedding anniversary, in January 1940, his unit had shipped out for Palestine. War Office orders barred wives from following them, with absolutely no exceptions allowed.

Hermione Ranfurly got a job in London as a secretary with a boss who kept asking her out to dine and dance. On her lunch hour, she went to an obscure travel agency—"just one room with a man and a typewriter"—recommended by a friend. The man behind the typewriter had a brother who worked in the Passport Office. He got her the papers she needed to leave England, cross France, and enter Egypt. She pawned the family jewels, which brought her enough only for a third-class ticket. In her girdle she hid the .25 Colt revolver she'd bought when war broke out "for use against [German] parachutists," as she'd written on her request for a gun license. From Marseilles she caught a mail steamer for Egypt, then boarded the train for Palestine and "sat up all night on a hard seat being serenaded by the Australian soldiers singing 'Waltzing Matilda.'"

When Dan got leave for three days, they drove to Beirut. They were dancing on the seaside terrace of a nightclub when a Frenchman told them that Germany had invaded the Low Countries and that Churchill had become prime minister. "Dan thought perhaps he was drunk," she wrote in her diary.

At first the war was something awful she heard on the wireless. Then Italy joined, France fell, and the French colonial rulers in Lebanon and Syria sided with Vichy. Palestine was now "flanked by enemies," Ranfurly wrote. The Sherwood Rangers at last gave up their horses and redeployed to Haifa, Palestine's main port and industrial center, to man coastal artillery.

Ranfurly rented a spartan room in a Catholic hospice run by German nuns near the docks. One summer day she heard planes overhead and ran outside to wave at our "our wonderful RAF." Then came the "crump, crump, crump" of explosions. The bombers were Italian, from the wing of the air force whose insignia was three green mice. They'd flown across the sea from the Italian-ruled Dodecanese Islands off the coast of Turkey to strike Haifa's oil refineries. On their next raid, the Green Mice hit some of the refinery tanks—and a small open market near the harbor where, the countess wrote, "bits of bodies are spattered all over adjacent buildings."

The British command in Jerusalem decided that in the midst of the crisis, it didn't need the bother of "'illegal' wives . . . those who reached the Middle East . . . against military orders." They would be sent home. The order was a strange one. It treated the Middle East as a war front from which British civilians must be removed, either for their safety or perhaps so they would not distract their husbands. Yet when the order was given, swarms of German bombers filled Britain's skies. At first they struck the airfields of the Royal Air Force, so that its pilots would not be able to strike the boats that would be bringing German troops to British shores. British officers who would command the battles on the beaches were not banned from seeing their wives. Then the Luftwaffe switched to bombing cities. In London, if you had a pint with a friend after work and said good-bye, it might be good-bye forever.

Ranfurly's best friend, Toby, who'd used the same obscure travel agent to follow her husband, accepted the order to go home. Ranfurly did not. But even a letter from a general's wife in Cairo saying that Wavell himself thought Ranfurly's secretarial skills were essential to the war effort did not persuade the brigadier in Jerusalem who told her, "You can't expect me to believe that a countess can type."

"Brigadier, if I am forced to leave I will return," she said as she left his office. It was September 14. Outside, Dan told her that the Italians had invaded Egypt.

When *The Empress of Britain* docked in Cape Town, Hermione Ranfurly said good-bye to Toby and went to the Barclays Bank branch with a letter of introduction to the manager from his counterpart and old friend at Barclays in Haifa. She asked him if she could get a taxi from Cape Town to Cairo. He laughed. Even in peacetime, that was a drive for crazed adventurers, not cabbies. The only way she could get north, he said, was by flying boat, one of the big airplanes that took off from and landed on water and were the fastest and most luxurious means of long-distance transportation in the world. But she needed to do it quickly, before she was discovered. He said he "loved romance and adventure," so he lent her £125, actual riches, and equipped her with a letter to *his* friend, who worked for Cook's Travel in Durban.

The train to Durban took two nights and days. The Cook's man said flying boats were booked up for two months. "Mr. Hapgood, my journey is urgent and secret," she told him. "It is vital I fly out of Durban on the next plane for Cairo." Either her title, or her exotic looks—dark hair combed back to show a widow's peak, thin eyebrows flaring upward like a bird in flight, huge dark eyes, lavish smile—or her self-confidence, or all three convinced him that she was the secret agent she implied she was. He got her on the plane leaving the dawn after next and said, "Don't ask me how." It cost £115. The flying boat touched down at ports twice a day to refuel and at dusk for an overnight stay. On the third morning, at Lake Victoria halfway up Africa, the commander of the military police in Cairo joined the flight and sat behind her. "I thought all the ladies were going south," he began a question. She started to say she was airsick, then vomited into her handkerchief. He gave up.

The fourth evening they landed on the Nile at Cairo. She slipped into town and hid out with her husband's best man and his wife. Two mornings later, he handed her the morning edition of the *Egyptian Mail*. The front page said that *The Empress of Britain* had been attacked by enemy planes seven hundred miles from Ireland and had sunk.

Her hostess told her that the news was out in Cairo that she'd returned. The commander of the military police ordered his men to find her. A memo went out to all military offices not to give her a job. Dan, now the aide-de-camp to General Philip Neame, commander of the British forces in Palestine, got two days in Cairo. He told her that Toby had gone down with *The Empress of Britain*.

Ranfurly went for an interview with the head of Shell Oil in the Middle East. He had no opening but made a phone call, then gave her an address on Qasr el-Nil, one of the main streets in Cairo's central business district. It was for an office on the eighth floor. A tall, gray-haired man asked her questions, then told her she could start work the next day at £25 a month. The workday, as was common in the Cairo heat, was 8:30 till lunch and then 5:30 to 8:30 at night. She'd work seven days a week.

On the way out she thought to ask if this was a spy organization.

"You'll soon find out," he answered, smiling.

She said she was "prepared to do anything except sleep with people."

"Okay," he said.

Her diary says nothing of a name on the door. If there was one, it almost certainly did not say Special Operations Executive or more specifically, SO2, meaning the second branch of the SOE, the wing responsible for sabotage behind enemy lines, political subversion, and organizing resistance movements. She had come to the right place, though. The SOE was not an agency inclined to follow an order from General Headquarters Middle East. In fact, the order may have been an incentive to take her. Her new boss, George Pollock, was a London lawyer who'd been given the rank of lieutenant colonel and who answered to the SOE main office at the Ministry of Economic Warfare in London. The job meant she could repay the Barclays man in Cape Town and get a visa saying "civil servant" instead of "officer's wife," meaning she could stay. A week after she started work, she turned twenty-seven.[14]

RANFURLY'S DIARY DOES not include the worst of the Italian air attacks on Palestine, against Tel Aviv, a city that had no military targets. The bombs killed 125 people.

Hajj Amin el-Husseini, the former mufti of Jerusalem, congratulated Mussolini on striking the Jewish city. His message to the Duce ignored the Arab deaths in Haifa, a mixed city. Husseini had been the most prominent leader of the Arab revolt in the late 1930s in Palestine, which Ciano's Foreign Ministry and SIM, Italian military intelligence, had secretly subsidized. Now, in exile in Baghdad, he hoped that British defeats would help renew the revolt.

But the air raids had the opposite effect. The mayor of Jaffa, the Arab city next to Tel Aviv, came to the funerals for the Tel Aviv victims. The Jaffa Arabic newspaper *Filastin* slammed the "criminal Italian bombardment," and a campaign by the Jewish *Palestine Post* to help pay for building British warplanes brought donations from Arabs as well as Jews.[15]

In British security agency reports and in the minds of British generals and politicians, the potential for a new revolt loomed constantly. For good reason: it had taken Britain three years and an ever-growing contingent of combat troops to extinguish the previous uprising.[16] The Mufti—as Husseini was almost always called—was the face of the fears.

In the early days of the war, Jewish leaders in Palestine debated whether to encourage young Palestinian Jews to enlist in the British army or to build up their own underground militia, the Haganah, to fight a possible pro-Axis Arab uprising. There were really two arguments, tangled together—which danger you believed was more immediate, and how passionately you dreamed of Jews finally defending themselves, on their own. A militia would be useless against Axis divisions but could fight Arab irregulars. The Jewish Agency, the quasi-government of the Jewish community in Palestine, urged enlisting in the British military. The British insisted at first on mixed units with an equal number of Jews and Arabs, lest they appear to be creating a Jewish army and thereby push Palestine's Arabs into the arms of the Axis and the Mufti.[17]

In historical memory, Hajj Amin el-Husseini would virtually become the face of Palestine's Arabs during the war. Memory would mislead. The Mufti had been absent for two years when the war began. A British intelligence report may have been accurate when it said that the "Mufti's propagandists" organized secret meetings at the Nabi Musa religious celebrations in May 1940, "at which the villagers and tribesmen were told that the revolt must be renewed at the earliest opportunity." But no revolt followed.

Another intelligence report said that "representatives of the Mufti's followers" met in early 1940 in Lebanon with a messenger from Husseini. He told them to spread Husseini's instructions that "Palestinian Arabs were not to volunteer to serve with the British forces."[18] *Filastin*, on the other hand, prominently covered public meetings led by the Mufti's opponents urging men to join up. By the end of 1940, close to twenty-five hundred had done so—whether for money or adventure or because they believed that Italy and Germany were enemies worth fighting. There were fewer Arab volunteers than Jewish ones.

But Husseini hardly had long-distance control of Palestine's Arabs.[19] Indeed, one reason for the lower Arab recruitment level, according to the British military, would turn out to be a widespread "failure to reach requisite physical standard" among Arabs who did want to sign up.[20]

Meanwhile, the war was transforming Palestine. If you had a job building an army base, or you worked in an army workshop, or you opened a bar, you were better off. If not, the little money you had bought less rice or flour. Troops poured in from England, Australia, New Zealand, and India. The Australians made the strongest impression: they were huge, loud, and happy and drank prodigiously.[21]

ANTHONY EDEN RETURNED to London in early November with word from Wavell. A messenger was the only means of communication that Wavell trusted. Italy had cut Britain's undersea cables in the Mediterranean, and Wavell feared the treachery of wireless. Anything sent by it, even in the best code you had, could give you away.[22] Churchill heard the general's plans and "purred like six cats," as he said himself.[23]

By the light of a half-moon, the thirty thousand men of the Western Desert Force marched forward on the night of December 7, passing between Graziani's isolated fortified camps. When day came, they lay down on the cold sands. The big lumbering Matilda tanks stilled their double engines. The next morning the attack began, striking the Italian bases from behind. The Italians had far more men, but they were facing the wrong way, and when they got their antitank guns turned around, their shells were too weak for the heavy armor of the British tanks. Maletti, the Italian general who hadn't bothered with Arab guides, was wounded but kept firing a machine gun until he was killed in the Nibeiwa camp, where he had his headquarters.[24]

"I have been advised in strict confidence by the British General Headquarters that the Maletti group consisting of 2 regiments, 2 Libyan divisions, half the entire Italian artillery and half of all Italian mechanized units have been captured or destroyed," Fellers radioed the War Department in Washington at noon on December 12. Fifteen thousand Italians were prisoners, including four generals. Eight hours later, Fellers sent an update: the number of Italian prisoners had doubled.

Whole Italian divisions were annihilated. Sandstorms cloaked the battlefield in dust and deep yellow light, adding to the chaos.[25]

The news from Egypt "comes like a thunderbolt," Ciano wrote. It was made all the worse by the news from the Balkans. Ciano, like his father-in-law, had expected that grabbing Greece would be easy. Instead, the Greeks had counterattacked and invaded Albania.

"I visit Mussolini and find him very much shaken," Ciano wrote. "I have nothing to tell him, but desire only by my presence to make him understand that I am with him more than ever." The more reason he had to doubt the Duce, it seems, the harder Ciano tried to preserve his faith.[26]

Moorehead, the war correspondent, drove into Nibeiwa camp and found a soldier's vision of paradise disappearing under the wind-driven sand. Officers' beds were "laid out with clean sheets . . . Parmesan cheeses as big as small cart wheels and nearly a foot thick lay about in neat piles." There were bottles of cherries, and of red and white "wines from Frascati and Falerno and Chianti" and casks of brandy. Every Italian soldier had abandoned his personal espresso percolator. Maletti's armored division, Moorehead wrote, had been "as tame as an old lion in the zoo."

Sollum fell to the British a week after the offensive began. The surviving fragments of the Italian army fell back to Bardia, where a "picturesque Fascist settlement of white-walled houses" stood on cliffs above the first harbor inside Libya. Beyond Bardia on the coast lay Tobruk. Seventy-eight British soldiers had died so far in the desert. In a time of vast dying, it was a tiny number, for all but each of those seventy-eight men.[27] With secrecy, surprise, and better-built tanks, Wavell and Major General Richard O'Connor, commander of the Western Desert Force, were providing a very rare gift: British victory.

Ralph Bagnold's Long Range Desert Group, the LRDG, could act with even greater secrecy, since so few people needed to know what the small unit was up to. In late December, two LRDG patrols headed west out of Cairo under Captain Pat Clayton, the former desert surveyor. When they passed the pyramids, they'd already left the narrow green belt of the Nile for the desert. They drove thirteen hundred miles into the emptiness—across the Great Sand Sea into Libya, then in a wide arc to avoid the Italian garrison at Kufra oasis, all the way south to the border with the French colonial province of Chad. In all that way—a journey equivalent to driving from Miami to New York—they spotted three natives leading camels, and no other human beings.

Bagnold had come up with the plan. In Khartoum he had heard that the governor of Chad, Felix Eboué, was the rare French colonial official who had not yet come out for Vichy. Bagnold had decided it was time for a rogue diplomatic mission. He flew half the breadth of Africa to Fort Lamy, the capital of Chad, where he collapsed on the runway, apparently from a relapse of malaria. He woke in a bedroom in Eboué's residence. A few hours later, Eboué entered the room with a lieutenant colonel named d'Ornano. Eboué was a black man from Martinique in the Caribbean. D'Ornano, from Corsica, was a tall, pale redhead who wore the flowing cape of the camel cavalry and was deputy commander of the French garrison. The commander, who leaned toward Vichy, had refused to come. D'Ornano seized his place.

Bagnold told them he wanted to strike Italian outposts in southwest Libya, the far corner from Egypt, but his patrols could not carry enough fuel, food, and water to operate that far from home. He wanted their help.

"We've got to decide *now*," d'Ornano told the governor. "This is our chance." Eboué assented with a nod of his head. D'Ornano had a condition: he would go along, with a few men, and the patrol would fly both British and French flags. D'Ornano proceeded to write out a formal agreement with the British army, which he signed in the name of the French army of Chad.

So d'Ornano and nine of his men were waiting for Clayton at a nowhere in the desert that according to maps drawn in Europe was on the line between Libya and Chad. Four afternoons later, trucks rolled into Murzuk, a Libyan oasis town and former way station on the caravan route to Timbuktu. One patrol hit the tiny Italian airbase, destroying three fighter-bombers and a hangar, while the other attacked the Italian fortress at the edge of town. Soldiers caught outside were shot down. The Italian commander was returning from his lunch break to the fort when a shell blew up his car. But the soldiers inside the fort started firing back. After two hours Clayton decided to retreat.

He'd lost two men. One was d'Ornano. They were buried in the desert.

Afterward the combined force raided three more Italian outposts. The next target on their list was Kufra oasis. The Italians were on their guard now. An Italian plane spotted Clayton's patrol, opened fire, and wounded him. The man who'd rescued the refugees from Kufra a decade earlier was taken prisoner and shipped to Italy before he could take part in conquering the oasis.

The Free French later finished the job at Kufra, though. The French flag and another with the Croix de Lorraine—the cross with two bars that Free France had taken as its emblem—flew over the oasis. But Bagnold became military governor—the explorer now the prince of a piece of the desert—and the LRDG had a base inside Libya from which its patrols, navigating by the stars and sun, could vanish into the desert to watch the Italians or attack them. Chad was now firmly an Allied outpost in the center of Africa, and the Free French and Bagnold's Boys were sworn partners in desert piracy. The big war was still on the coast, but the Italian army never knew when it would be attacked elsewhere. It was like a man trying to fight a boxing match while swatting wasps away from his legs.[28]

On the coast, an Australian division took Bardia less than a week into 1941. Tobruk, another eighty-five miles up the coast, fell later in the month. By now, the British held one hundred thousand Italians prisoner. "Twenty percent," Moorehead wrote, "were found to be suffering some form of chronic dysentery," the enemy shared by all armies. In the town, he found the streets littered with clothes, toys, and chairs, the jetsam of Italian civilians who'd fled. Flames leapt from a furniture warehouse; wine from broken vats flowed in the street. "In the bay a ship kept burning steadily. By its light the wounded were being carried down to the docks." Moorehead's joy at victory evaporated, leaving "an unreasoning sense of futility."[29]

Tobruk's harbor, Bonner Fellers told the War Department, would allow the Western Desert Force to keep rolling onward into Libya. No longer would trucks from the Nile need to bring all the fuel, food, and ammunition that an army devoured. Fellers had driven those hundreds of miles from Cairo to the front himself. The Italians were losing, he reported, because they were fighting the wrong war, a war of fixed camps and roads. "The British daringly stretched the mobility of their armored units to the limit," he wrote. "The Italians avoided the desert . . . while [the British] found security in the desert and lived therein."[30]

The coastline of Cyrenaica, the eastern province of Libya, was shaped like a camel's hump. Derna, the next harbor after Tobruk, was near the top and marked the beginning of a range of coastal hills known simply as Jebel Akhdar, the Green Mountains, where real rain fell, trees grew, and fields could be farmed. At the far end of the mountains, on the other side of the hump, lay Benghazi, the largest town in the region.

After losing Tobruk, Graziani's broken forces fled, abandoning Derna and then Benghazi. Their only goal was to reach Tripolitania, the western province of Libya. They stuck to the long curve of the coastal road. One of O'Connor's divisions, Australians, chased the Italians. As if to demonstrate Fellers's thesis, O'Connor sent his other division nearly in a straight line across the desert south of the Green Mountains. There was no road. There were no maps to guide the truck and tank drivers for much of the journey. They made it. The Italians were "caught on February 7 between the Australian column . . . and the British armored division astride Benghazi-Tripoli road," Fellers radioed Washington. Except for three hundred trucks that British planes spotted heading west, "it is doubtful that any Italian forces escaped."[31]

The Italian burghers of Benghazi did make it down the road. The town of sixty-six thousand had been one-third Italian. Most fled, including the wealthy, the Fascist officials, and the police. The Italian mayor stayed to surrender. The British found the Muslim majority mostly friendly, especially members of the Senussi order. Many of Benghazi's thirty-three hundred Jews greeted the British as their liberators and the Jewish soldiers from Palestine in British uniforms as a miracle.[32] In the Jewish quarter, one soldier from Palestine wrote home, "A crowd surrounded me . . . they actually tried to kiss my hand." An old man touched him and recited, "Blessed be He who shares his glory with flesh and blood," the blessing dictated by tradition for a Jewish king.[33]

"Today I met Bonner Fellers, the U.S. military attaché here—an original and delightful person who seems to say exactly what he thinks to everyone regardless of nationality or rank," Hermione Ranfurly wrote in her diary in Cairo. "He has just returned from the desert and spoke with . . . admiration of how our attack was kept secret. 'General

Wavell told me they were going to do manoeuvres so up I went as an observer, and God dammit—it was the works.'"[34] She seemed to like a man who would curse to a countess. As for Fellers, after twenty-two years in the US Army, he was at last seeing battle.

Far to the south, a British force had invaded Ethiopia. Having gone to war with Britain to complete his African empire, Mussolini was losing the empire entirely. In Libya, "at present there is no chance of a counter-attack by the Italians. Between Tripoli and Benghazi there are no prepared [Italian] defenses. The Arabs are definitely hostile toward the Italians and the road is good," Fellers radioed home. "It is my opinion that an immediate pursuit will be undertaken by the British."[35]

4

HALF-SHARED SECRETS

Winter-Spring 1941. Bletchley
Park-Tobruk-Crete-Cairo.

"Now we're getting places," Bonner Fellers told Countess Ranfurly. It was March 11, and he'd phoned to tell her that President Roosevelt had just signed the Lend-Lease Act on the same day that the US Congress passed it. The law allowed the president to "sell, transfer title to, exchange, lease, lend, or otherwise dispose of" arms to "any country whose defense the president deems vital to the defense of the United States." Put differently, the law meant that Roosevelt could now give Britain whatever it needed to keep fighting.[1]

Roosevelt had announced the Lend-Lease idea at a press conference in December 1940, and followed up with the national radio broadcast in which he pledged that America would be "the arsenal of democracy." He'd just been elected to a third term, and he'd received a letter from Churchill explaining that Britain was running out of money to pay for American arms. Roosevelt did not want to go to war; he wanted Britain to win, and for that it needed American guns, tanks, bullets, airplanes, trucks, ships, shells, and more.[2]

Charles Lindbergh, the spokesman of isolationism, had testified in Congress, before the House Foreign Affairs Committee, against Lend-Lease.

"Which side do you want to win?" he was asked.

"Neither," Lindbergh answered.[3]

Lindbergh had been one of the last people Fellers met before sailing for Spain the summer before. Now Fellers had been granted rare access to Britain's secrets and watched its battles. He knew which side he wanted to win.

DEEPER SECRETS WERE being shared than Fellers knew about. One was contained in a two-hundred-pound box, part of the luggage of four American junior officers who boarded the British battleship *King George V* at Annapolis, Maryland, at the end of January 1941. Two were from the US Army's Signal Intelligence Service: Lieutenant Leo Rosen and Abe Sinkov, recently transformed from civilian to captain. (In his dress uniform, Sinkov looked like an intellectual masquerading as an officer; his rimless glasses emphasized his down-turned eyebrows and the distant, knowing gaze in his close-set eyes.) Sinkov was a late addition. Colonel William Friedman was supposed to go, but he was still in Walter Reed Hospital, recovering from his post-Purple breakdown.[4] The other two, Prescott Currier and Robert Weeks, were from OP-20-G, the navy's rival parallel organization. The pairs met each other for the first time at the dock. The army and navy codebreaking agencies treated each other at times practically as hostile powers.[5]

(The *King George V* had just brought Lord Halifax to America to become Britain's new ambassador.[6] Churchill preferred to have the former appeasement advocate in Washington rather than serving as foreign secretary in London—especially as the prime minister anyway handled the core of British-US relations directly with Roosevelt.)

The seed of the American codebreakers' visit was planted the summer before, with an offer through the British embassy in Washington to share military information. As with Anthony Eden's openness to Fellers, the point was to woo the United States into a closer alliance. Then something embarrassing happened: the Americans took the wooing all too seriously. The US Army's assistant chief of staff for intelligence, General Sherman Miles, hoped that gaining British knowledge of Axis codes and ciphers would make it possible to uncover plans for attacking the Panama Canal or Latin American countries, and to find German and Italian spies in America.[7] The number two man at the British embassy in Washington sent a cable home in October. "The proposal was made that full exchange should now take place . . . concerning crypto-graphic machines, codes and cyphers of Germany, Italy, Japan, Russia and possibly even other countries," he said.[8]

The request bounced through opulent London offices to the desk of Stewart Menzies, head of MI6 and therefore also responsible for the Government Communications Headquarters, GCHQ, the new name of the Government Code and Cypher School. He carefully offered a "pretty free interchange of cryptographic information," signing his name, as MI6 tradition dictated, "C," in green ink.

A cable came back from Washington. Both the War and Navy departments had noticed the words "pretty free." This didn't sound like, say, "completely free." They were unhappy.[9]

Menzies wrote a note that indicated squirming. "A full interchange on Germany and Italy could not be entertained," he wrote, meaning that the Americans must not be told about breaking Enigma. Americans were not good at keeping secrets. But, he added, expressing "any reservations will annoy the United States authorities." Menzies called GCHQ director Alastair Denniston to consult and then wrote a new memo, to Churchill. Tell the Americans yes, Menzies suggested, but make a "mental reservation" not to tell them about German Enigma. "That work is conducted in separate buildings," he said, which American visitors wouldn't be shown.

Churchill sent a question back, in his barbed-wire handwriting and his usual red ink: "What will they think if they find we have been reading their stuff?"

Apparently Menzies reassured him that GCHQ's work on American codes could also be kept from the visitors.[10]

On an afternoon in early February 1941, the four American officers disembarked at the Royal Navy base at Sheerness, at the mouth of the Thames. Two staff cars were waiting for them, along with a truck for their crates. They reached Bletchley Park at night. The mansion, with its blackout curtains drawn, was a dark shadow in a darker countryside. Inside, Denniston stood waiting to greet them in his office, with Tiltman towering over him, and with two other top staffers and a cask of sherry. From there, they were taken to the country house of the chairman of the Anglo-Persian Oil Company, where a butler, three maids, and a cook would make them at home for the next ten weeks. They often lunched at Tiltman's home near Bletchley Park, where Tiltman's wife served off-the-ration-card chicken and lobster. The extravagant hospitality, perhaps, was designed to show goodwill while diverting their interest from some of the huts on the Bletchley Park lawn.[11]

But then there was that big crate, sent as a dowry by Friedman's Signal Intelligence Service.[12] It contained a fully operative replica of Japan's Purple cipher machine. The Americans set it up and showed how it worked. Before being given anything, they'd offered up the greatest success of American cryptography.

John Tiltman was dumbstruck by the "magnificent gesture." He'd worked on Japan's codes and ciphers for years, since he'd taught himself Japanese. Purple had eluded him. The obvious quid pro quo was to tell the Americans about the Enigma work. Denniston wouldn't hear of it, so Tiltman went up the ladder to Menzies, who in turn went to Churchill with a compromise: show the US officers the machines used to decipher Enigma but not deciphered messages. "As proposed," Churchill scribbled in assent.[13]

Margaret Storey was working in Hut 6 that winter.[14] A standard task for young multilingual women was operating an improvised version of an Enigma machine. The device tested whether a setting suggested by the bombes was, in fact, the one in which a message had been enciphered. If it was correct, deciphering could begin. It was a repetitive, draining task, performed for many hours, assembly-line work of the mind, in shifts that switched from day to evening to the midnight-to-dawn run.[15] If Storey looked up from her work one day, she might have spotted two or four visitors in civilian dress, receiving quiet explanations from someone senior. If she had asked who they were, she would have been told they were Canadians. But in Hut 6—a small, separate universe of thick cigarette smoke and nicotine-stained ceilings, of linoleum floors and weak British sunlight made weaker by the blackout curtains around the windows and the brick blast walls around the building—you did not ask questions or talk to anyone about your work. The visitors would not have been taking notes; the deal worked out by Tiltman required them to commit what they learned to memory, not paper, and to reveal the Enigma secrets only to Friedman and the head of OP-20-G.[16]

The officers' visit had already produced two results: Tiltman was settling into the role of liaison with his US counterparts. Indeed, a life-long friendship had begun between Tiltman and "Abe and Prescott"— the army's Sinkov and the navy's Currier.[17] And reluctantly, GCHQ was sharing more than it had planned.

But not everything.

TILTMAN HAD OTHER new friends. By early spring, perhaps in time to meet the American visitors over lunch, Russell Dudley-Smith and his new wife, Joan, rented the ground floor of the Tiltman family's two-story house. Dudley-Smith was a thin man, nearly six feet tall, with a narrow face that made his Royal Navy officer's cap and his horn-rimmed glasses look much too large. When he left in the morning for the short walk to work at Bletchley Park, Tiltman's teenage daughter would remember, Dudley-Smith's uniform "always looked like an un-made bed."[18]

Dudley-Smith had been two in 1914 when his father died. His mother provided for him and his sister—so family lore would say—by moving from one relative's house to another every six months. Despite the wanderings, he got top marks in school. He enrolled at the University of London's Birkbeck College, where classes were given at night. It allowed him to work in the day as a lab assistant at the Royal Arsenal's research department in Woolwich in the southeast of London. In a poem, he called Woolwich "a town of guns and slime . . . and trams and touts and pallid whores." His poems were typed, or written in a handwriting so precise it could have been a printer's fancy font.

The mix of wanderlust and disgust with London that show up in his poetry may explain why he left the university, without graduating, for the Royal Navy. His thick glasses disqualified him for a combat role. His mathematic abilities qualified him to become a naval paymaster, a ship's accountant. The job was poor fare for a hungry mind. He read

The News from Tartary, adventurer Peter Fleming's account of his journey from Peking to Kashmir, and carefully copied out the itinerary. He taught himself Persian, arranged to get newspapers in that language, and joined the Royal Central Asian Society. He wrote a taxonomy of personality traits. He wrote a study of the causes of suicide.

In the first months of the war, he was serving aboard the HMS *Resolution*, flagship of a squadron in the North Atlantic. He wasn't allowed on deck (so family memory would say) lest the wind rip off his glasses. Some messages encoded in the Royal Navy's flagship code caught his bored eye.

When it came to his intellectual ability, he could overcome his shyness. He managed to talk to the admiral. I don't think our codes are safe, Paymaster Lieutenant Dudley-Smith said. Could he try decoding them? The admiral told him to try. In three weeks he'd broken them.

Early in 1940, the *Resolution* put in for repairs. Dudley-Smith came down with German measles and was given medical leave. At home, he received a letter saying that he was "wanted for a cryptographic appointment as he has made this one of his interests." He found himself at Mansfield College, Oxford, where navy and GC&CS experts designed British codes. The man in charge was Commander Edward Travis, who was also the deputy director of Bletchley Park.

Dudley-Smith's experiment with the flagship code had given him a calling in life, one that finally gave his mind ample sustenance: finding out whether Britain's own codes and ciphers could be broken, and whether the enemy was doing so.

In 1941, freshly married, he was moved to Bletchley Park to work under Travis and take the freshly created posts of cipher security officer and secretary of a new committee on the subject that brought together the navy, air force, army, and Bletchley Park. Travis, the reigning expert on finding flaws in British codes, was too busy as an administrator. Dudley-Smith filled the gap. During that year, his responsibility expanded to the communications of allies and almost-allies. He showed, for instance, that the US merchant marine cipher was "pathetically simple" to break, a warning passed on to the US Navy. Three months later he checked and found that the Americans were still using the transparent cipher. After the second warning, the cipher was finally switched.[19]

IN THE SPRING of 1941, the Foreign Office sent a query. Intelligence cooperation between Britain and the United States was growing, and there were two ways to trade information—via the American embassy in London or the British embassy in Washington. The US embassy would use American diplomatic ciphers to report home. But was that safe? At the Ministry of Economic Warfare, in charge of denying Germany raw materials, the man in charge of economic intelligence wanted to know. The Foreign Office asked Menzies, who forwarded the question to Travis, who would have most likely asked Dudley-Smith to get answers.

A note initialed by Travis came back to the Foreign Office. It said American diplomatic telegrams to Washington were safe from interception—by the Axis. The unstated implication was that American traffic traveled on an intact British undersea cable.

As for the wider question of US diplomatic codes and ciphers, this was delicate. The State Department had three code systems, the GCHQ note said. One system was used rarely, for the most secret messages. So far it was unbreakable.

"The second-best book," used more often, for material that was just slightly less secret, was "legible but patchy." GCHQ could read some messages that the enemy couldn't solve, but the opposite was also true. For "third-grade material," the State Department used another code. It was "probably fully legible," meaning that both British and Axis codebreakers could read anything sent in it.

The big difference, the note said, was that Britain was able to intercept many more American diplomatic cables than the enemy was.

So it would be a bad idea to tell the State Department to use its best code for anything that needed to be secret. Doing this would mean that "we lose *all* American traffic." The enemy would be denied less American information because it was getting less to start with.[20] Part of the job of the gentlemen and ladies at GCHQ was reading American mail. Knowing what an almost-ally thought, particularly what it thought about you, was valuable. No warning was sent.

Not then. But two months earlier in Madrid, British ambassador Samuel Hoare—another pro-appeasement former cabinet minister exiled to a diplomatic post—had passed a "hint" to American ambassador Alexander Wendell. Hoare had heard from "friendly sources on which I rely" that American codes and ciphers "generally used even for confidential matters are vulnerable." The US embassy in Spain rarely used the best, safest system, Hoare had heard.

The State Department had asked the Foreign Office in London about this. On this occasion, Menzies had apparently forgotten to check with his codebreakers. He had approved a letter recommending to State that when communicating with Madrid, it should use only its best cipher "for confidential and delicate subjects."[21]

If the State Department took this advice, it apparently did so only for messages to Spain. When GCHQ was finally asked about American security, US diplomats were still sending secrets in the second-best code, and both the British and the Axis were still breaking it. The British were breaking it more often.

STILL, BLETCHLEY PARK'S real war was with the enemy's codes and with Enigma most of all. It was a war that took place on paper, in the whirl of the bombe wheels, and most of all in the mind.

As the big war outside grew, so did the quiet war of the codes. Enigma keys proliferated, serving different tentacles of the Nazi military and bureaucracy. In the summer of 1940, Bletchley Park identified the key used by the German railway administration. It vanished, then reappeared early in 1941. The Nazi railway people used a model of the Enigma machine without a plugboard, which made it easier for John Tiltman to crack the key. By March the number of railway messages multiplied. Most gave instructions about moving German troops and supplies across Europe, to the east.

At the beginning of January, Hitler sent the German air force's Fliegerkorps X—the 10th Air Corps—to Sicily to lend support to the crumbling Italian army in Libya. The corps got its own Enigma key, which Hut 6 at Bletchley Park labeled Light Blue. German code clerks presumably used some of the same stock phrases in Light Blue as they had in Red, the main air force key. Those phrases could serve as cribs, the bits of text used to set up the bombes. Sometimes whole messages sent in Red or Light Blue were resent in the other, a gift to codebreakers. By the end of February, Gordon Welchman's crew at Hut 6 was reading the new key.[22] (Welchman was at home too little;

his wife would begin to believe he was seeing someone else. In fact, he was carrying on a love affair with his work. It was exciting; it served his country; he was superb at it. His Hut 6 team was "the happiest group at Bletchley," he would recall. And like a man with a secret lover, he could tell almost no one what he was up to.[23])

But the German army's keys remained unconquered. Radio messages, in any case, would not have revealed Hitler's meeting on February 6 with the general he had decided to send to Libya: Erwin Rommel.

At most, reading army Enigma would have allowed Hut 6 to hear the echoes of the orders given to Rommel. Rommel was to command two German divisions, one of them a tank division, along with Italian mobile forces already in Libya. His job was to prevent British conquest of western Libya. He was subject to the Italian high command, though he could appeal to Berlin if need be. His German troops would begin arriving in Tripoli by ship in mid-February. Rommel would fly in before them and begin reconnaissance. But his divisions wouldn't be up to full strength until mid-May. At least until he had one full division, he was to stay in the Tripoli area. Much further east, the Italians were supposed to hold a north-south line below the Gulf of Sirte, which divided western Libya—Tripolitania—from Cyrenaica in the east. Hitler had other conquests in mind than Africa. Rommel's job was to prevent an Italian collapse.

Yet even if army Enigma had been an open book, knowing those orders would have been little help to Churchill, the war cabinet, or General Wavell at the Middle East Command, because Rommel had no intention of letting orders get in his way.

By the time Rommel landed in Tripoli, the British forces in Libya led by General O'Connor had swept into Benghazi. Rommel had a passion for small planes. He took a six-hundred-mile flight out across the desert to look down at the meager Italian forces at the coastal village of Sirte. He started sending German forces forward as soon as they got off their ships. Without a stronger defense, Rommel believed, the British army would soon be on the outskirts of Tripoli.[24]

Wavell had no idea of what Rommel was up to, but Rommel was also mistaken about British plans.

Churchill and Wavell were anxiously expecting a German intervention on an Italian front—in Greece. Britain had pledged in 1939 to defend Greece, and had signed a mutual assistance treaty with Turkey. If it didn't help Greece now, Turkey would see that British promises were worthless. And if Turkey decided that the least harmful gambit was to allow German forces to pass through its territory, a German army would be in Vichy-ruled Syria, ready to push through Palestine and on to the Suez. Greece was the northern gateway to the Middle East, and Germany was preparing a battering ram.[25]

"It is estimated by British intelligence that in Rumania the Germans have 515 combat . . . airplanes, including 100 dive bombers recently arrived, as well as 23 divisions, including four armored ones," Fellers radioed the War Department in late February. "All African operation is overshadowed by the entire Balkan situation," Fellers reported. "The British are postponing the proposed advance into Tripoli."[26]

A week later, he sent an update. At a spot called Agheila, German armored cars had raided the forward British position in Libya. The British admitted that "these eight-wheeled armored cars are superior" to any they possess, Fellers said. But it was a skirmish; it didn't change the big picture. Meanwhile, he said, Australian, New Zealand, British, and Indian divisions were getting ready to embark for Greece.[27]

"Dan and his general flew in unexpectedly. General Neame is taking over command of Cyrenaica," Hermione Ranfurly wrote in her diary.[28] Philip Neame received a stripped-down force, barely more than a placeholder on the map: half of a newly arrived, inexperienced British armored division on the front line, and an equally raw Australian division, part of it holding Tobruk. Wavell wrote to Churchill, explaining his decisions: it was 471 miles from Tripoli to Agheila and another 175 miles from there to Benghazi; for most of the route there was no water; and the enemy was short on transport vehicles. The new German force might try to take Agheila, but wasn't likely to try for Benghazi till after the fierce heat of summer. Wavell said he was ready to take "considerable risk in Cyrenaica . . . to provide maximum support for Greece."[29]

Wavell could almost have read the minds of the German and Italian general staffs. Rommel flew to Berlin in March to report. Field Marshal Walther von Brauchitsch, commander in chief of the German army, denied his request for reinforcements. If Rommel wanted to move a bit forward, he should wait till the end of May, when his two divisions would be complete.

Rommel returned to Libya, and promptly sent a battalion to grab the British fort at Agheila. He radioed a request for the air force to send a squadron of bombers to Tripoli to help him. The answer was no, "on the grounds that center of operations lay elsewhere." Since this was an air force message, it went out in a key of Enigma that could be read at Bletchley Park. Hut 3 finally had a direct teleprinter line to General Headquarters Middle East for "special intelligence"—cover name for Enigma material—and sent word to Wavell.[30]

"Elsewhere" clearly meant Greece. Special intelligence confirmed Wavell's evaluation.

Rommel, however, was undeterred. He gave orders to seize the next British position in the desert. When he saw the British forces retreating, he decided he'd rush forward and "make a bid to seize the whole of Cyrenaica at one stroke."

General Italo Gariboldi, who'd just replaced Graziani as the Italian commander in chief in Libya, "berated me violently" for ignoring direct orders from Rome and warned that "the supply situation was far too insecure," Rommel would recall.[31] Gariboldi was right: food, ammunition, arms, and fuel all had to be brought by truck from Tripoli, after coming by ship across the Mediterranean from Italy. Even water had to come by truck. A division required 350 tons of supplies a day. The German army was using two-ton trucks. The further Rommel went, the further the trucks had to come to reach him, and that took even more fuel. The German general staff had estimated that in Operation Sunflower—Rommel's mission in Libya—it would take ten times as many trucks to supply a division as in a bigger operation planned for Europe.[32]

Yet when Rommel exercised his option to appeal to Berlin, he received approval to go ahead.[33] This message would have gone in an army Enigma key. Hut 6 could not read it. It made little difference. Neame had already ordered his meager forces to retreat. By April 4, the Germans were in Benghazi. The Arab and Jewish townspeople who'd welcomed the British as liberators were again under Axis rule.[34]

"There's a horrid rumor that Germans have arrived in North Africa," Hermione Ranfurly wrote. "Thank God Dan has a staff job." A few days later, home sick from work, she heard a knock on the door. It was Lady MacMichael, wife of the high commissioner of Palestine, who was staying with General O'Connor's wife while he was in the desert advising Neame. MacMichael asked about her health, "talked about the weather, fidgeted around the room and looked out the window." Suddenly she turned and said, "Your Dan is missing." So were O'Connor and Neame. They'd been together, and might have been taken prisoner. "She went on talking but I did not really listen. After a while I thanked her for coming to tell me, gave her a hug and closed the door gently behind her."[35]

Rommel launched an attack across the hump of Cyrenaica, just as O'Connor had done but in the opposite direction. It stalled when one unit ran out of fuel to move its artillery. He rounded up thirty-five cans of gasoline and delivered them himself. Another unit went missing in the desert. He took off in a light plane to look for it, nearly landed by mistake among British forces he mistook for his own, and got shot at by Italians who didn't recognize his German aircraft. Nonetheless, he pushed onward to the Egyptian border, down Halfaya Pass, and took Sollum. "Probably never before in modern warfare had such a completely unprepared offensive as this raid through Cyrenaica been attempted," he would write afterward. He'd shown again that will power and commanding from the front, not the calculations of desk officers, brought victory. He believed he had "an excellent springboard . . . for a possible summer offensive against Alexandria."[36]

At General Headquarters Middle East in Cairo, Wavell expected that offensive. He told Fellers that "he did not, repeat not, believe the German forces could get closer than one hundred miles from Cairo within the next two months."[37] This was phrased as an optimistic estimation. Fellers no longer needed to send his dispatches through the Cairo embassy's civilian code room in State Department codes; he'd finally received the military attaché code and cipher tables, William Friedman's clever invention.[38]

Rommel's position at the edge of Egypt was real, but his success was part desert mirage. He'd defeated a British force that, from the start of his campaign, was much weaker than he'd known. And far behind his front line, the Australians still held Tobruk. He needed that port for supplies in order to advance; Benghazi was 250 miles further away from his forward position at Sollum. His attacks on Tobruk failed. He found himself in an old kind of battle, the kind he recalled from the previous war and always sought to avoid, against men dug into fixed positions. He wanted to move, to race forward. At Tobruk, too many of his men were wounded or killed. The fault for that wasn't his, he wrote. "The high casualties suffered by my assault forces," he explained, "were primarily caused by their lack of training."[39]

General Franz Halder, chief of staff of the German army, wrote in his notebook that Rommel "was in no way up to his operational task," that the engines of Rommel's tanks needed replacing, that it was impossible to meet Rommel's demand to be resupplied by air since planes landing in North Africa "find no fuel for the return flight." He mused about how to rein in "this soldier gone stark mad." Nazi propaganda chief Joseph Goebbels, meanwhile, promoted Rommel publicly as the incarnation of German victory.[40]

HUT 3 SENT the word early on April 5: German air force units in Romania had received orders to start hostilities at 5:30 a.m., Greenwich Mean Time, the next day. Zero hour for the German Twelfth Army, poised in Bulgaria on the borders of Yugoslavia and Greece, was the same.[41]

From British commanders in Greece came a stream of "sitreps"—situation reports—for Wavell. The words "lost" and "retreat" and "in enemy hands" and "evacuation" repeated. The Germans were advancing on Salonika, Greece's second city, in the northeast. The last train from Salonika was leaving. The New Zealand division was dropping back to the passes at Mt. Olympus. The Yugoslav Second Army was asking the Germans to end hostilities. Enemy air action was spotted at Mt. Olympus. (The sitrep did not say whether Zeus, Hera, and Aphrodite had joined the refugees on the roads south.) The Germans demanded complete Yugoslav surrender, "otherwise ceaseless bombing of towns will follow." The Greek military command had broken down, and all Greek forces were in "complete disorganization."[42]

The decoded sitreps were typed up in only six or nine copies and marked "most secret," equivalent to "top secret" in the United States. Copies reached Fellers's desk. He told the War Department that General Henry Maitland Wilson, in command in Greece, "is retiring to Thermopylae, where he can hold out a week."[43] (Thermopylae, just north of Athens, was the pass where the Spartan king Leonidas and his few hundred men nearly stopped the army of Persia twenty-four hundred years earlier.) Before Wilson's week was out, Greece had surrendered and the Royal Navy was evacuating what was left of Wilson's army. Yugoslavia had already surrendered. One scrap of Europe remained in Allied hands, the Greek island of Crete, a dolphin-shaped piece of land stretched out in the Mediterranean almost halfway from Athens to Tobruk. Crete's location showed how artificial the sharp distinction between Europe and the Middle East actually was.

"KIND BONNER FELLERS has wired the American legation in Rome asking for help," Ranfurly wrote. The young countess was trying to find out if her husband was in fact alive in Italian hands. She met Fellers for lunch and found that "he is sad because his friend, Colonel Brower, has been killed while flying an aeroplane up from Takoradi."

Gerald Brower was an American air officer assigned as an observer to the Royal Air Force in Cairo. He'd flown to Takoradi, in the British colony of the Gold Coast in West Africa, because Britain was shipping warplanes that it received from America there. In Takoradi, they were assembled, then flown by RAF pilots in hops across the continent to Khartoum and on to Egypt. Brower wanted to check whether American pilots could deliver planes to the Middle East directly by flying them from Brazil to Takoradi, the shortest route across the Atlantic.

As a favor to the RAF, Brower flew back an American P-40 fighter plane. Taking off in Sudan, he made a tight turn at slow speed, went into a spin, and hit the ground. Thrown from the cockpit, he was killed instantly. "You'll have to stop scolding us Americans for being neutral," Fellers told Ranfurly, "when my friends are getting killed flying planes up to you British."

She liked Fellers. She did not say anything about her friend Toby, or about how many soldiers were dying in Greece and the Western Desert.

"We reckon this is one of your worst emergencies—the whole Mediterranean is threatened," Fellers said over their next lunch. "America must declare war soon." It was as if he'd never thought differently. Afterward he phoned one evening to say he had word from the American legation in Rome: "General O'Connor says Ranfurly captured. Last seen in good health."

With her husband in captivity, the Wavells invited her to stay with them. The general exuded serenity. One night after dinner, she played backgammon with him. "I must win one battle today, Hermione," he said, grinning. "You seem to be the only enemy I can be sure of defeating these days."[44]

Jacqueline Lampson, the young, half-Italian wife of Miles Lampson, invited Ranfurly to a dinner with the newly arrived American ambassador, Alexander Kirk. "You are the very man I want to meet, because your country still has a legation in Rome," she said when introduced to Kirk, with the kind of teasing that only half hides pain. "If you can get me a job there, I could visit my husband on my day off and talk to him through the bars."

"Lady Ranfurly, you must remember there is a war on," Kirk said.

"*That* from an American," she answered and walked away. She thought to herself that possibly her sense of humor had gone missing, but certainly her husband had gone missing.

After dinner, out on the lawn, Jacqueline Lampson came up to her. "When I ask you to dinner, I don't expect you to be rude to my most important guest. Mr. Kirk is very pro-British."

"I always say what I think," Hermione Ranfurly said, "whether it be to neutrals or Italians."[45]

MENZIES HAD TO talk Winston Churchill out of reading every single decrypted Enigma message. The prime minister wouldn't have time left for anything else, said the man called "C." He avoided saying that a prime minister reading raw intelligence—an old man with a boy's enthusiasm for spy stories—might jump to rash conclusions. Instead, "C" selected material and hand-delivered it daily, sometimes several times a day. In the spring of 1941, someone started an office file for those messages, with their dark red "most secret" stamps.

The first one in the file came from railway Enigma at the end of March. It contained orders for moving armored divisions, troops, and SS divisions in the weeks ahead to the Cracow area.[46] Cracow was in Poland, under firm Nazi control. For forces suited for blitzkrieg, it could only be a staging ground for an offensive eastward.

Churchill wrote a brief, veiled message for his ambassador in Moscow to hand-deliver to Soviet leader Joseph Stalin. Churchill wrote that a "trusted agent" had given him "sure information" on the troop movements. "Your Excellency will surely appreciate the significance of these facts," he wrote.[47]

The next message in the file contained a precise outline of the German plan for invading Crete. It had come in an air force key of Enigma, because Germany was about to do something unheard of. It would conquer an island from the air. Paratroopers would land and seize airfields. Planes would land with troops who would conquer the harbors. Only then would ships arrive with antiaircraft guns and supplies.[48]

GENERAL WAVELL HAD reason to feel that his realm was shrinking. Greece was lost. In Cairo, King Farouk was "believed likely to go to the German camp" if he thought Egypt was likely to fall.[49]

In Iraq, four pro-German colonels staged a coup in April 1941 and restored former prime minister Rashid Ali al-Gailani to power. The regent who ruled in place of the country's six-year-old king, Faisal II, fled to Transjordan, while the child king's mother smuggled him out of Baghdad.

The Foreign Office in London had already seen Gailani as Ali Maher's Iraqi twin—unreliable and most likely an Axis asset. The British embassy in Iraq said the four colonels, known as the Golden Square, were "in close and constant touch" with Hajj Amin el-Husseini, the exiled ex-mufti of Jerusalem. For the moment, Husseini's magnetism moved people more in Baghdad than in Palestine. The plotters had met in his home to plan the coup. He handled the link between the coup leaders and his German contacts, even as Berlin never quite made the promise he sought: support for full Arab independence in Palestine, Iraq, Syria, Egypt, and beyond. Iraq's government radio station broadcast Nazi propaganda. On Baghdad's streets, members of the pro-Nazi paramilitary Youth Phalanxes movement arrested random Jews and dragged them to police stations—or occasionally murdered them on the spot.

At the end of April, Iraqi troops surrounded the big RAF base at Habbaniya west of Baghdad and threatened to down any planes that took off. Practically speaking, Gailani had declared war.[50]

Hut 3 at Bletchley Park sent a stream of messages: From Athens and Rhodes, the German air force was to send bombers, fighters, and transport planes eastward, "with Iraq markings or no markings at all." Air crews would remove the German insignia from their uniforms and carry no identification. Ships arriving at Rhodes were carrying machine-gun rounds, antiaircraft shells, and bombs for Iraq. At Palmyra in Syria, a way station on the route, a German air force headquarters was being set up. On the map of the Middle East, two question marks could be erased. Both Iraq and the Vichy-ruled territories of Syria and Lebanon were fully aligned with the Axis.[51]

THE PLANS OF Fliegerkorps XI, the German 11th Air Corps paratroop force, might as well have been sent directly to Bernard Freyberg, the New Zealand general in command of forty thousand soldiers in Crete—though they actually had to be deciphered first from the air force keys of Enigma in Hut 6, passed to Hut 3, and then translated in the nicotine haze of the second hut before Freyberg got them.

Freyberg knew that zero hour had been postponed from May 17 to May 20. His men, from Britain, New Zealand, Australia, Greece, Cyprus, and Palestine, were tired. Almost all had been evacuated from mainland Greece, leaving much of their weaponry behind. But they were waiting for the parachutes to open that morning. In some places, the air was so thick with men dangling from white clouds of cloth that a single British machine-gun nest could kill them all before they touched the ground. But the paratroops kept coming, and after them airplanes pulling trains of gliders and releasing them so they could land more troops, or often carry them to their deaths when the glider pilots failed to find flat land on an island of sharp mountains, narrow valleys, and olive groves.

In Hut 3, you watched the battle through German eyes. "Malame aerodrome serviceable," read a decoded Enigma scrap on the second morning of the invasion. Enough of the German paratroopers and glider pilots had survived to capture the runways, so that transport planes with more men and guns could come down.

After a week, Freyberg knew Crete was lost. Some of his units were already surrounded. Those that weren't retreated to the port of Heraklion, or through the mountains to the tiny harbor of Sfakia on the south side of the island. The Royal Navy managed to evacuate less than half of his original troops.[52]

Seen from London and Cairo, the aerial invasion was another terrifying Nazi innovation. At Bletchley Park, it was reason for the kind of doubts that you had to erase to keep on working. Never before had a general been granted so much information about the enemy's plans and condition so quickly. Despite the victory over Enigma on the battlefield of the mind, out in the world the battle had been lost.[53]

At a general staff meeting in Berlin, Franz Halder jotted in his notebook a list of German battalions shattered, airplanes lost, officers and men killed. Crete was the kind of victory that a general did not want to repeat. "British were expecting airborne landing . . . and made effective preparations for defense," he recorded. "This explains our heavy losses." Had these words been radioed in the Red key of Enigma, they could have provided some consolation in Bletchley Park.[54]

"THESE DAYS NO fear is an exaggeration," Meir Yaari said. Yaari was a leader of a left-wing kibbutz movement; he was speaking at a meeting of Jewish labor leaders in Palestine. Another speaker described the mood among Palestine's Jews as "immense panic . . . fatalism . . . and total paralysis." Very suddenly it seemed that the Nazis could come from the west through Egypt, or the north through Syria, or from the air. A thousand Jewish soldiers from Palestine had been taken captive in Greece. By sheer bureaucratic coincidence, the British army picked that moment to send questionnaires to soldiers in Palestine, including local Jews, asking to list family members for possible evacuation. By another coincidence, a "wanted" poster appeared in police stations for

Fawzi al-Qawuqji, a leader of the late 1930s Arab revolt, which set fire to rumors that he'd returned from exile to start a new rebellion.

"A Nazi invasion of the Land of Israel isn't like the German invasion of Poland, even [as it affected] the Jews of Poland," said Moshe Shertok, for practical purposes the foreign minister of Palestine's Jews, at another emergency meeting. "It's possible there will be atrocities here."[55] The comment showed how little was known about what was happening in Poland. On that, intelligence was entirely lacking.

A WHITE CROSS made of bed sheets was supposed to be spread out in the desert southwest of Cairo. Captain Laszlo Almasy looked down from the German bomber. There was no cross.

The Hungarian explorer's plane and its escort had taken off from Derna, between Benghazi and Tobruk on the Libyan coast. They left late in the day so they would enter darkness and hostile territory at the same time. It was June 7, 1941.

Major Nikolaus Ritter, the Abwehr officer who had brought Almasy back to Africa, had managed to get the German air force to lend him the planes and their crews only after the fall of Crete. Ritter was certain that the deposed chief of staff of the Egyptian army, Aziz el-Masri, would be waiting that night, and would mark the landing spot. As Ritter would tell things, he had received word, via a contraband wireless set hidden in a church in Cairo, that Masri had confirmed he was coming. Almasy's plane would land and pick him up. Once in Axis territory, Masri would work to foment a revolution in Egypt.

The German planes had enough fuel to circle just above the desert for half an hour before turning back. The general never showed up. On the runway in Derna, Captain Almasy had to tell Ritter that he had nothing to show for the long flight over enemy territory.[56]

Masri, it would turn out, had tried to leave Cairo—three weeks earlier, on the night of May 16, in an Egyptian air force plane commandeered by two Egyptian airmen. Their destination was Beirut in Vichy-ruled Lebanon. Beforehand, Masri had told an SOE colonel in charge of British propaganda in the Middle East, Cudbert Thornhill, that he wanted to fly to Baghdad to propose a compromise to the

Gailani regime to end the crisis. The colonel did not approve the idea, but apparently he did not report the meeting either.

It's most likely that the old pro-German general's real intent was to join the Iraqi rebellion against Britain. But Masri's poorly trained Egyptian pilot panicked and made an emergency landing ten miles after takeoff. Masri went into hiding in Cairo and may well have confirmed the rendezvous with Almasy in the desert as his plan B—but Egyptian police arrested him the day before his intended escape. Afraid that Masri's meeting with the Special Operations Executive colonel would come out, Ambassador Lampson urged the Egyptian government to let the case fade away.[57]

The irony is that if Masri had made it to Baghdad, he might have ended up in Berlin after all.

Wavell, pressed by London to stretch his forces to yet another front, had rushed a relief force from Palestine to the RAF base at Habbaniya in Iraq. By the end of May, the Iraqi army crumbled, and the British force was approaching Baghdad. Gailani and Husseini fled to Iran, then traveled to Turkey and onward to Germany. From there they would try to create a German-Arab alliance: just the role that Masri was meant to play.

THE REGENT OF Iraq returned to Baghdad on June 1. The British troops stayed outside the city, in the hope that his return would not look like their doing.

It was the first day of the two-day Jewish holiday of Shavuot. Baghdad was one-sixth Jewish, and for Jews the fall of the Nazi-shaded military regime doubled the cause for celebration. A crowd in holiday clothes met the regent on the west bank of the Tigris River. As the Jews returned home, soldiers attacked them with knives and fists. Police watched and did nothing. Outside a hospital where the wounded were taken, a mob of people demanded that the Jewish doctors and nurses be delivered to them so they could be killed. Teens from the Youth Phalanxes joined the rioting. The supporters of Gailani and the Mufti had found someone to blame for their defeat. On the second day, the looting and bloodshed spread until the regent finally ordered the police to use live fire to disperse the mobs.

"A large number of Jewish shops and homes were looted, and several hundred Jews were brutally murdered," the British ambassador reported. "There is no doubt that a large number of [Jews] would emigrate . . . if only they could find a country to take them." The dead of the Farhood, as Iraq's Jews called those two days in June, may have been the least known, least acknowledged victims of Nazism. Jews had lived by the rivers of Babylon for twenty-six hundred years. At the beginning of the twentieth century, the community's greatest religious teacher, Rabbi Yosef Haim, had taught how to calculate the times for Jewish prayer according to the call of the muezzin from Baghdad's mosques, and based religious practices on the fact that it was safe to walk Baghdad's streets at night. Months after the Farhood, a "most secret" message from British military headquarters said that poor Iraqi Jews, some of whom had lost their shops in the looting, were paying truck drivers to smuggle them into Palestine.[58]

ROOSEVELT WROTE TO Churchill, saying that in both Britain and America, the public understood that Britain would win the war "even if you have to withdraw further in the Eastern Mediterranean."

Churchill did not like this. He composed a letter back. Spain, Vichy France, Turkey, and Japan might all decide whether to join the war based on what happened in the Middle East, he wrote. After thought, he added several lines. "The one decisive counterweight I can see to balance the growing pessimism" about Britain's chances among still-neutral bystanders "would be if the United States were immediately to range herself with us as a belligerent power." This was more direct than Churchill usually allowed himself. Stop cheering from the sideline, he said.

Roosevelt did not answer that plea directly. He sent back a long list of what he was shipping to the Middle East, including two hundred tanks fresh from American factories and seven hundred ten-ton trucks to carry supplies in the desert. The message meant: I believe you can hold on there, and this is the most that I can do.[59]

Barely, Britain held on. Crete was lost, but Iraq was safe for now. Wavell's hurried attempt to push Rommel back into Libya in June failed. But the Free French, British, and Australian forces he reluctantly sent out of Palestine against the Vichy army in Syria and Lebanon slowly pushed forward. Turkey stayed neutral. Persia was shaky. The leaders of both countries, Fellers radioed from Cairo, "have a great fear of the U.S.S.R., less of Britain, none of Italy, and a very remote fear and a great respect for Germany."[60] His sources for that anxious reading were almost certainly British.

RITTER AND ALMASY had failed to get the old Egyptian general out of Cairo. But they had another operation planned: to fly two German agents in. One had lived in Suez before the war, the other in Alexandria. The same two planes would go. One would land sixty miles from Cairo on a stretch of hard, gravel-strewn ground known to Almasy. It would drop off the spies, along with a motorcycle that they would ride into the city. The other plane would be the escort.

At take-off time, a mechanic told Ritter that the plane meant to carry the spies had a bad tire and couldn't land on gravel. Ritter decided to go with his two spies in the other, though its pilot was less experienced. "The front lines were waiting for information regarding enemy activities," Ritter would explain. "I had to take a chance."

Almasy, who'd come to the airfield, stayed on the ground. If the risk-enamored Hungarian argued with Ritter on the tarmac and refused to go, as gossip said afterward, Ritter must truly have been desperate for a success.

Hours later, Ritter's pilot descended—and suddenly pulled up. In Ritter's telling, the long shadows of sunset made the pilot think the gravel was a field of boulders, and he refused to touch down. Hours later, back over the Libyan coast, with their fuel running out, the radio man shouted, "No landing in Derna. Enemy air raid!" The pilot put the plane down at sea off the coast. One of the would-be spies was killed. Ritter's arm was badly broken. After a rescue squadron found the survivors, Ritter was flown out to Athens for treatment. His African adventure was over.

Almasy, on the other hand, stayed. He had a new plan for smuggling German spies into Cairo.[61]

WHEN HE DEFEATED Wavell's June offensive, Rommel would write, the German high command promised him new armored divisions. He could have done great things with those reinforcements, but they never came, he lamented.[62]

Churchill's attempt to share a secret with Joseph Stalin, one that had been sent in railway Enigma, did not go well. Instead of handing the message to Stalin himself, the British ambassador in Moscow had to give it to one of Stalin's top officials, Andrey Vyshinsky, formerly a prosecutor in the purge trials of the dictator's purported enemies.

The intelligence was accurate. But it had value only if the recipient trusted the messenger. It could make a difference only if he was willing to bend his certainties.

In Stalin's mind, it seems, even the movements of the clouds in the sky hinted at conspiracies against him. The attempts afterward to decipher Stalin's response to Churchill's warning—if, that is, Vyshinsky dared to give it to him—and to similar warnings would be endless. The most convincing reading is that he saw all of the intelligence as signs of a plot to draw him into war with Germany.[63]

There was such a plot. It was Hitler's. He had never made a secret of his desire to colonize the Slavic lands to Germany's east. Along with his war against the Jews, this was basic to his dark dream.[64]

5

THE LADY WHO SPIED ON SPIES

Summer-Autumn 1941. Cairo-Ukraine-Bletchley Park-Derna.

"THE GERMANS BELIEVE it will all be over in eight weeks," Galeazzo Ciano scribbled in his diary. There were more and more clues that it would start soon, he wrote.

The German envoy in Rome, Otto von Bismarck—grandson of his namesake, the first chancellor of united Germany—woke Ciano at 3 a.m. the next morning with a letter from Hitler to Mussolini, telling him that Germany was invading the Soviet Union. It was June 22, 1941. Operation Barbarossa had begun.

Bismarck told him that "German military circles" expected to take five million prisoners, Ciano wrote. Then Ciano corrected himself: "five million slaves" were the words that Otto had used.[1]

ONE NIGHT IN Cairo, Hermione Ranfurly would go to a dinner party that she did not want to attend, where everyone had been invited "for their name" and everyone had "a title or a million," where dinner had not been served by 10 p.m. because no one could eat until King Farouk did, and Farouk—thought Ranfurly—would not be hungry because he ate six pounds of chocolate a day. She found herself with the king, who began "a clumsy sort of flirting." She asked him why he never brought his beautiful queen to parties. "It would be fun," she said.

"Yes, for other people," he said, and let loose with a bellowing laugh.

He called the countess "Ramsbottom" and ignored her deliberate rudeness in response. She managed to get away from him. Not everyone did. Farouk was the best-known philanderer in his kingdom.[2]

In the spring and summer of 1941, though, Farouk was seeking a much more serious liaison. His go-between was his father-in-law, Youssef Zulficar, who was also his envoy to Iran. Zulficar belonged to the old Turkish aristocracy of Egypt. A photo from the time of his daughter's wedding to Farouk shows a pale-haired, thin-lipped, unsmiling man with a sharp chin and hooded eyes. In April, as Rommel overran Cyrenaica and appeared poised for a drive into Egypt, Zulficar asked for an urgent meeting with Erwin Ettel, the German ambassador in Tehran. Farouk, Zulficar said, had ordered him to ask for the meeting. The king had told him to express his "strong admiration for the Führer." Farouk expected the arrival of German troops "as liberators from the unbearably brutal English yoke," Zulficar said.

Ettel, an SS brigadier general, noted approvingly in a cable to Berlin that Zulficar was "strikingly Nordic in appearance."[3]

From Berlin came a reply in Hitler's name. Germany, it promised, wanted to create "a new order of things" that included the "independence of Egypt and the entire Arab world." Lest Farouk worry about Italy, Hitler assured him, this was also the Duce's view.[4]

So far, these were sweet nothings. At the end of June, Farouk took the relationship much further. Zulficar met again with Ettel, bearing information from the king: The British general staff was preparing to invade Iran. Preparations would take about two months, the conquest itself three weeks. By sharing this, Farouk's father-in-law stressed, the king meant to demonstrate his "candor and faith toward Germany."[5] Hitler did nothing with this information. His armies were busy along the eighteen-hundred-mile Soviet front.

Two months later, the invasion of Iran began. In three weeks, British and Soviet troops were in Tehran, the shah had abdicated and been replaced with his twenty-two-year-old son, and the new allies held a route by which American Lend-Lease aid could be shipped from Persian Gulf ports to the Red Army.

Farouk's tip had not been entirely accurate. Most importantly, it didn't include the Soviet forces that would come from the north. Ettel's letter to Berlin contains no clues as to how Farouk learned of the plan. What appears certain is that, as of June 1941, strategic information from the highest rank of the British command in Cairo reached the palace and that Farouk passed it on as proof of his support for Germany.

BEFORE SHE LEFT the office of the Special Operations Executive each evening and locked up, Ranfurly slipped the day's most revealing new documents into her bra. Around the corner, at the apartment of SOE officer Bill Stirling, she typed copies for him to deliver to the agreed contact. Then she went home. In the morning, she stuffed the originals back into her bra, opened the office, and returned them.

The agreed contact was General Arthur Smith, Wavell's chief of staff.

(Stirling shared the apartment with another disgruntled SOE man, Peter Fleming, the author and adventurer, whose younger brother, Ian, would yet make a name for himself. Stirling and Fleming had little respect for the flat's Egyptian owners and were apparently inebriated often. Once they brought a donkey up three flights into the flat. Another time, they held revolver practice in the drawing room, perforating the wall and quite nearly the Sudanese servant.)

Back when she'd started at the SOE, she loved the job, and not just because it kept her in Cairo and paid very nicely. Most of the staff were known by numbers rather than names. They reported in from the Balkans, Persia, Somaliland, and Palestine. "We sent little boats up the Danube to lay mines; we sent gentlemen forth with wirelesses in suitcases and instructions to blow up certain bridges," she wrote. The office had a room full of guns and ammunition and a safe full of gold bars.

Then she started seeing other things. The gold, it seemed to her, was "spent more on women than on war." Security was so bad that a house cleaner skillful with a straight pin could have stolen plans. Ranfurly was "astonished to find my office giving . . . extra aid to the Jewish

Agency, the Zionist headquarters in Jerusalem." Stirling told her the SOE was smuggling illegal Jewish immigrants into Palestine. "The Arab world under the statesmanship of King Ibn Saud had maintained peace" and allowed Britain to use the ports of Aden, Suez, and Haifa, she believed, but the SOE was endangering this.

Her employers were "double-crossing everyone except their mistresses," she concluded.

One night at the Wavells' home, the general inquired about her work. She told him. After that, Arthur Smith asked her and Stirling for evidence of what was happening in the maverick agency. Smith wanted to show it to the British cabinet's representative, Oliver Lyttelton, who was coming to Cairo to coordinate the war effort. Thus commenced Ranfurly's career "spying on a spy organization." It ended in late June, when she got a letter at the office from Smith saying she could accept an offer to become assistant private secretary to Harold MacMichael, the high commissioner of Palestine, "as soon you have finished your work for me in the SOE office." She found it on her desk, the envelope opened, and she stormed into the office of George Pollock, the director, and quit before she could be fired.[6]

An SOE file from later that summer on the troubles in the Cairo office reads like several men with very proper vocabularies shouting accusations at each other in a small room. The nature of the SOE's work attracted daring people who thought little of rules and who were better at blowing things up than keeping records. Whatever paper trail did exist was mostly burned later, and the remaining scraps redacted. So it is hard to know how much money was legitimately spent on bribes, false papers, boats, and bombs and how much was spent on liquor, silk stockings, and "cabaret girls." A couple of fantastical schemes for blocking ship traffic on the Danube came to nothing. The SOE did not bring Jews illegally to Palestine. But operatives of the Jewish Agency's secret organization for bringing Jews from Europe, the Mossad Le'aliyah Bet, once did so with a ship that it had already sold to the SOE. The Jewish organization's emissaries in Istanbul, it turned out, had only learned of the sale after they'd loaded the ship with refugees in Romania. That incident caused the one serious crisis between the Special Operations Executive and Palestinian Jews.[7]

King Abdulaziz Ibn Saud lacked the influence that Ranfurly attributed to him, and he depended on a British subsidy to keep his impoverished desert realm solvent.[8] But the British Empire's earlier support for a Jewish home in Palestine was indeed one cause of Arab rancor, and perhaps the easiest one for the empire's generals and diplomats to talk about. In London and Cairo, officials worried that alliances with the Zionists now would cost Britain dearly later, especially after the war. Ranfurly was mistaken in details, but it appears that she accurately wrote the anxiety.

SOE operatives lived inside other worries: not what governments might do later, but which local people could be trusted right now. "Our organization in the Balkans and the Middle East has . . . been receiving a very substantial measure of assistance from certain representatives in Palestine and elsewhere in the Near East of the Jewish Agency for Palestine," an SOE memo from early 1941 said. What the agency could "achieve in the Middle East will depend to a large extent on the continuance of good relations with these Jews."[9]

Wavell ordered the SOE to stop training Jewish saboteurs, an order that George Pollock, Ranfurly's boss, treated with "neglect." But in the bad days of May, when Wavell was preparing to invade Vichy-ruled Lebanon and Syria and needed guides to lead Australian units into Lebanon, he turned to the SOE to recruit Palestinian Jews.[10]

The leaders of the Haganah, the underground Zionist militia, had just decided to create their own small, full-time military group, the "strike force," or Palmah. The first few dozen men became the SOE's scouts. They were given all of a week to slip into southern Lebanon and map roads, bridges, and French positions and, just before the operation began, to cut telephone lines.

In a village called Iskanderoun on the Lebanese coast, on the first morning of the operation, six Australians and four Palestinian Jews managed to take a French machine-gun position, but came under fire from a nearby orchard. "I aimed the French machine gun at them . . . and looked through a telescope to see exactly where they were," the leader of the Jewish group reported afterward. "At that moment a bullet hit my hand and my eye and put me out of action."[11] He lived, but had to wear a patch over the shattered eye socket the rest of his life.

His name was Moshe Dayan. Another of the Jewish bands was led by Dayan's rival, Yigal Allon, and included Allon's friend, nineteen-year-old Yitzhak Rabin.

Damascus fell on June 21, 1941, Beirut on July 10. The Vichy forces surrendered the next day.[12] In a letter from Pollock to Wavell on the Syria operation, the role of the Jewish scouts accounts for four brief paragraphs. In the British story of war in the Middle East, this is less than a footnote.[13] In Zionist history, it became a legend: the first action of the Jewish army-to-be, led by the original warriors. Both accounts are accurate.

Ranfurly moved to Jerusalem to work for the high commissioner. Pollock was sent home that summer. Terence Maxwell, his replacement, was soon working with "the Friends," as the Zionists were called in the SOE.

THE GERMAN POLICE unit reported by radio that it had executed 1,153 Jewish "plunderers" near Slonim, a town in Belorussia.

The message was dated July 18, 1941, and came from a militarized wing of the police that worked with the SS. The German police did not have Enigma machines. They used a cipher method known as transposition: rearranging the letters of the original text, according to a pattern that shifted daily. At Bletchley Park, John Tiltman headed a section that had been breaking the police cipher since the start of the war. The main problem was intercepting messages, which were hard to pick up in Britain. This one was intercepted.

Others followed. In early August, an SS brigade radioed that it had killed 3,274 partisans and "Jewish Bolshevists." On August 7, it presented its total since the start of Barbarossa: 7,819 people executed. The same day a summary for the entire central sector of the front said the police had shot thirty thousand people, most of them Jews, in that time. The SS reports sometimes came in the police cipher, sometimes in an SS key of Enigma that Hut 6 labeled Orange and broke irregularly.[14]

The reports, with their cold, precise numbers, kept coming. "The Commanding Officer of Police for South Russia says . . . Police Regiment South Battalion shot 367 Jews," said one message, which was included in the daily packet for Churchill. The number is circled in red, the color ink that Churchill used.[15]

The numbers did not tell the young translators in their huts on the lawn in the English countryside names or ages. They did not portray faces, or tell how these human beings had been rounded up, or whether they had known what would happen to them. Still, the messages indicated something new was happening: just behind the advancing German divisions, the SS and the police were slaughtering Jews, methodically, keeping count to show they were doing their job. Since many messages were not intercepted, or not deciphered, the statistics indicated part of an unknown whole.

Churchill gave a radio speech on August 24.[16] He had just returned from a secret journey across the Atlantic in a battleship, risking attack by German U-boats, to meet Franklin Roosevelt in person off the coast of Newfoundland. Now he could talk about the meeting, though he did not reveal the location, or that he had asked Roosevelt again, repeatedly, to declare war, or that the president had said the time was not yet ripe.[17] Instead Churchill said in his speech that if the negotiations between America and Japan broke down, "we shall, of course, range ourselves unhesitatingly at the side of the United States." Then he talked about Hitler's attack on Russia. "As his armies advance, whole districts are being exterminated. Scores of thousands, literally scores of thousands of executions in cold blood are being perpetrated by the German police troops upon the Russian patriots who defend their native soil . . . We are in the presence of a crime without a name."[18]

In a GCHQ dossier on breaches of security, someone wrote down "30,000 Jews killed." Churchill hadn't actually mentioned that the Nazi machinery of murder was targeting Jews, but he had referred to the police as perpetrators. Using information from intercepts to stir public opinion was risky. Three weeks later the German police switched to a different method of transposition, in which the letters were rearranged twice. Tiltman's codebreakers, however, had an even easier time with the new cipher method, and the numbers kept coming. Nothing more was said publicly.[19]

In Berlin, at the Reich Security Main Office—the Reichssicherheitshauptamt, or RSHA—Walther Rauff did not have to worry about codebreaking or interception. Rauff, the once disgraced navy officer become SS bureaucrat, received all of the reports from the field.

The RSHA, under Reinhard Heydrich, was the main office of Nazi terror. The SS, the Gestapo, and the police all came under its roof. It directed the *Einsatzgruppen*, the Special Operations Units carrying out the slaughter in the east. Rauff headed the RSHA's technical arm. He was responsible for transportation, weapons, radio communication—all the physical machinery that served the murderers.

In September 1941, Heydrich assigned him to work on a new way to kill large numbers of Jews. The business of shooting people was wearing down the SS and police troops. Heydrich favored using trucks that would transport and kill at the same time, using the exhaust from the engine.

Rauff's job was to complete the most lethal, efficient design possible and produce the machines. He worked diligently. He contracted with a tram company to build the chambers to mount on truck chassis. By November, he had a prototype. In the first test, in Berlin, it efficiently extinguished the lives of thirty Soviet prisoners of war. He ordered more and sent them out to the *Einsatzgruppen*. He'd taken a further step in his career, from bureaucrat to engineer of death. From then on, "his signature, his initials or his name" would appear "on almost every piece of paper" regarding the mobile gas chambers. As many as half a million people would be murdered in them.[20]

In Tobruk, the Australians lived in trenches. There were twenty-five thousand of them. Royal Navy destroyers brought in supplies at night, slipping into the harbor through a pathway between sunken ships. The town was a "maze of broken tottering buildings, though they gleamed white and clear in the sun," Alan Moorehead wrote. Rommel could not risk advancing as long as the British might attack behind his front line. Tobruk was like the jagged butt of a broken bottle, poised an inch from his back.

Beyond the Tobruk perimeter, the war had wandered off someplace else that summer. "Possibly because of the Russian campaign, U-boats and German raiders were less active," Moorehead suggested, so more convoys were arriving safely. The British had driven the Italians out of Ethiopia, and Vichy out of Beirut and Damascus.

In Egypt, the troops ate well, better than people in England living on rations—and much better than the vast majority of Egyptians. In Monufia province, north of Cairo, the half million *fellaheen* (peasants) were living on less than one piaster a day each, one-hundredth of an Egyptian pound and the equivalent of four US cents. So the US commercial attaché wrote. The war at sea had cut the supply of fertilizer from Chile for Egypt's fields; the spring wheat harvest had fallen one-sixth short of the average. Egyptian bakers were ordered to mix rice or corn flour into their dough. Prime Minister Hussein Sirry warned British ambassador Miles Lampson that the bread shortage was "liable to give rise to disturbances."[21] People hoarded kerosene and sugar.

Soldiers did not see this. They did not wander into villages or understand anger spoken in Arabic. When they got leave in Cairo, Moorehead wrote, they "luxuriated in hot baths and cold beer." Even when they recalled or looked forward to battles, they could think of the desert war as "the most dangerous game on earth . . . No civilian populations were being destroyed . . . If Benghazi fell, then it was just a manoeuvre of war." Writing this, Moorehead forgot that civilians had lived in Benghazi, and the futility he'd felt watching the fires in Tobruk the first day Wavell's men got there.[22]

Archibald Wavell was gone. The loss of Cyrenaica and his failed counterattack had cost him Churchill's confidence. (A photo of Wavell's farewell party in Cairo shows the one-eyed general in conversation, smiling, with Bonner Fellers, the omnipresent genial American.) The prime minister replaced Wavell with Claude Auchinleck, the general who'd been in command in India, and sent Wavell to Delhi.

Auchinleck was a tall man with blue eyes, a long, narrow face, and a cleft chin. He had thick red hair; he did not look fifty-eight years old. He left his much younger wife in Delhi because officers of lower rank than his couldn't bring their wives to Cairo. He did not like to make speeches. He did not like large groups. He did not enjoy team sports, which made him nearly un-British. He worked. He was thorough.[23]

From the day he took over, he and Churchill argued by radiogram. Churchill wanted him to retake Cyrenaica, quickly. In April, Wavell had said he had six trained armored regiments waiting for tanks, Churchill wrote. The tanks were coming, from Britain and America; by the end of July, Auchinleck would have five hundred. "Our intelligence shows considerable Italian reinforcements of Libya, but little or no German. However, a Russian collapse might soon alter this to your detriment," Churchill said.

Auchinleck wrote back: His forces needed to retrain to work better together as teams. Those American tanks had new features and armament. His regiments needed to learn how to use them.

"If we do not use the lull accorded us by the German entanglement in Russia . . . the opportunity may never recur," Churchill said, in a message that showed his voice could rise even in a telegram. "It would seem justifiable to fight a hard and decisive battle in the Western Desert . . . and to run those major risks without which victory has rarely been gained."

"To launch an offensive with the inadequate means at present at our disposal is not, in my opinion, a justifiable act of war . . . To gain results risks must be taken," Auchinleck answered, "and I am ready to run them if they are reasonably justifiable."

Auchinleck was not willing to lose an army on a Churchillian whim. Churchill was disappointed with generals, all of them, who preferred "certainty to hazard." He wanted a general who could seize the moment. Churchill longed for a general like Rommel.[24]

"There are endless swarms of flies," Rommel wrote to his wife in one letter, and in the next, "The heat's frightful, nighttime as well as daytime." At first he blamed the Italian navy for not bringing him more supplies. Then he lamented to his wife that "with things as they are in the Mediterranean it's not easy to get anything across," and "for the moment we're only stepchildren" while the fighting lasted in Russia.[25]

Rommel's supply problems were not just due to Barbarossa. He could not know that the summer before at Bletchley Park, behind the old stable yard, in the cottage where Dilly Knox ran his research group, Mavis Lever had solved a message sent by the Italian navy's version of Enigma. The Italian machine did not have a plugboard, which cut the number of possible settings down to a mere couple of billion. Lever, just nineteen years old, had cut that down to one with a series of intuitive flashes about what might be in the message. (Knox's staff consisted entirely of "girls," who became known as "Dilly's Fillies." There is no evidence that he sexually exploited them. It does appear, though, that the codebreaker with the unkempt black hair and volcanic temper found women less of a threat to his ego.) Lever's break unlocked Italian naval traffic. From the Mediterranean, it neatly complemented German air force messages.[26]

"Fuel crisis of German Africa Corps likely to be extremely grave should British attacks continue successful," said a message on August 1, 1941. The "German Africa Corps" meant Rommel's forces. A tanker called the *Bellona* would therefore be leaving Naples for Bardia in Libya. The message gave the ship's precise route, along with instructions for German air force units to provide cover. From Bletchley Park, this information went to RAF headquarters in Cairo, followed by confirmation that the ship had sailed. Somewhere along its route, the crewmen would have seen an RAF reconnaissance plane overhead. The Italians would not have known that the British pilot had been told where to look for the tanker, or that he'd been sent from Alexandria to cover up the true source of information. "On seventh August at 0630 hours steamship Bellona . . . ordered to turn for Suda Bay because . . . British destroyers had been sighted," the naval section in Hut 4 at Bletchley Park reported. Suda Bay was the main naval base in Crete. The fuel had not reached Africa.[27]

Moorehead, likewise, did not know a key reason that more convoys from America bearing Lend-Lease supplies were making it to Egypt. Between March and June, the Royal Navy had succeeded in capturing three German ships and a U-boat and seizing Enigma settings, manuals, and codebooks from them. Those were the pinches that Alan Turing and Peter Twinn had so desperately wanted. Hut 8 was now reading naval Enigma, and convoys were routed to avoid U-boats.[28]

In the summer and again in the fall, German naval intelligence did conduct investigations into whether Britain might have found a way to crack Enigma. Both times the investigators posited other reasons for British naval successes. The British had found U-boats by locating the source of their radio signals, the German investigators suggested, and the Atlantic ports of Europe were full of British spies. It was statistically impossible to break Enigma.[29]

As Heinrich Sandstede saw things, his choice at age twenty-seven came down to volunteering to be a spy for German military intelligence, the Abwehr, in Africa or being assigned to active army duty, learning to march in formation and goose-step, and getting sent to fight in Russia. Marching in formation didn't suit Sandstede. Sandy, as friends called him, had dropped out of school in Germany when he was sixteen, worked on farms in South Africa and Mozambique, prospected for gold in Tanganyika, picked up Swahili, and learned to speak English well enough to pass as an Englishman.

Only the war had forced him to leave the British colonies in East Africa. Back home he'd been drafted. His years of wandering got him a job in the military high command's topographical department, marking maps with the roads, tracks, and bridges that he remembered from East Africa. He made friends there with Johann Eppler, another fellow who didn't march in step. Eppler had been born in Alexandria to a German woman and an unknown father. Afterward, he got a new name, Hussein Gaafar, when his mother married an Egyptian man. In 1937, Eppler, or Gaafar, married a Danish woman and moved back to Europe. At the topographical department, he'd corrected maps of Egypt.

Their luck held. The Abwehr took them. There was a plan to put them in a German desert patrol that might work out of Kufra oasis; there was a plan to parachute them into Egypt as spies, which the two men considered much too dangerous. They learned how to use wireless sets. While they waited, they stayed in Berlin, with fine salaries and as many ration tickets for food as they liked. "We live like kings. Most of the money is wasted by the end of the month and then we have to live on collected dry peas and beans etc.," Sandstede wrote. "The bars in Berlin are expensive and the girls are even more expensive."

Sometime that summer, Eppler was sent to Vienna to meet Captain Laszlo Almasy.[30]

6

THE ORACLES SPEAK GIBBERISH

Autumn 1941-Spring 1942. Bletchley
Park-Washington-Benghazi-Cairo-Gilf
Kebir.

AT HUT 4 of Bletchley Park, in a large logbook, a clerk hand-copied the most secret telegrams between GCHQ and the code-breaking agencies of the United States. An outgoing entry from December 3, 1941, at 1404 hours, 2:04 p.m., reads:

"On 1st December Tokyo ordered Japanese Embassy in London to destroy their machine. On 2nd December Embassy reported they had done so."

The instructions to smash the Purple machine had come enciphered in Purple itself. With the machine taken apart and hammered into scrap, the embassy sent a single word in Japanese, "dispatched," without use of a cipher, as the sign that it had followed orders.

Before the diplomats smashed their machine, they'd received a second, more detailed message. It said that similar instructions had been sent to Hong Kong, Singapore, and Manila. The Japanese mission in Batavia—capital of the Dutch East Indies, under the rule of the Dutch government-in-exile—had already sent its cipher machine home. The

Japanese embassies in Canada and Panama and the consulate in Honolulu—apparently lacking Purple machines—were told to burn their codebooks.

The same messages, picked up by American antennae, were being decoded and translated in Washington. The improvised Purple machine that the American officers had brought to Bletchley Park made it possible for Stewart Menzies to hand those messages, decoded and translated, to Winston Churchill. If Churchill had any doubt about why an embassy needed to destroy its codes, they were dispelled by the telegrams from the Japanese ambassador in Berlin to Tokyo and the response. Menzies delivered these, too, to the prime minister.

In a message sent from Berlin on November 29 but decoded at Bletchley Park only on December 4, Ambassador Hiroshi Oshima said he'd been called to a late night meeting with Nazi foreign minister Joachim von Ribbentrop, who wanted to know the state of the negotiations between Japan and the United States. Washington was demanding that Japan end its invasion of China. Tokyo insisted on a free hand in China and an end to a US embargo that was starving it of oil. The Japanese government had set the 29th as its deadline for reaching an agreement. Oshima told Ribbentrop he hadn't yet heard the outcome.

"Ribbentrop said Japan must not lose this opportunity of achieving the establishment of a New Order in East Asia," Oshima wired home. "As the Fuehrer had said that day," Ribbentrop had added, "the existence of Japan and Germany on one hand and of America on the other was fundamentally incompatible." If Japan went to war, Ribbentrop promised, "Germany would, of course, join in immediately."

The next day, Oshima got an answer from his government: tell the Germans the negotiations have failed, the cable said, and that it was likely "we shall find ourselves in a state of war with Britain and America.

"You should add that this may happen sooner than expected."[1]

Yet the signs were at once urgent and vague, like the echo of a stranger's footsteps somewhere in a dark building. In another intercepted Purple message, the Japanese embassy in Washington was ordered to destroy one of its two machines, to douse the pieces in acid—and to keep the other. In the Bletchley Park logbook, a message from the US Navy's OP-20-G agency on December 5 states, "Purple system still in use here."[2]

Purple was for diplomats; it did not reveal military plans. Neither the British codebreakers nor the Americans had made much progress against the Japanese naval code. Perhaps the Japanese would first attack Hong Kong or the British protectorate of Malaya in Southeast Asia, or try to seize the oil fields of the Dutch East Indies, and wait to see if America stayed out once more.

Nonetheless, the top US Navy and Army commanders in the Pacific received warnings of a possible Japanese attack. On the West Coast, in Panama, and in the Philippines, they put their forces on war footing. At Pearl Harbor in Honolulu, Admiral Husband Kimmel and General Walter Short did not. They did not believe the Japanese could possibly strike America's strongest naval base. The Philippines were the most likely target.

The final fateful Purple messages to the Japanese embassy in Washington were intercepted by the US Army's listening station near Seattle overnight between December 6 and 7. One was a text in English to be delivered to Secretary of State Cordell Hull. "Obviously it is the intention of the American government to conspire with Great Britain . . . to obstruct Japan's efforts toward . . . the creation of a New Order in East Asia," it said, and concluded that "it is impossible to reach an agreement through further negotiations." The second specified that the message should be delivered to Hull precisely at 1 p.m. Washington time. The third ordered the destruction of the last Purple machine in the embassy.

Together they announced the precise time of the coming Japanese attack—but not the place. OP-20-G and its army counterpart, the SIS, deciphered them more quickly than the Japanese embassy's own code clerks. On the morning of December 7, Roosevelt got copies and knew war was about to break out. Army Chief of Staff George Marshall ordered that a warning be sent to Pacific commanders, with priority on getting it to Manila in the Philippines. By a tragedy of errors, the coded message went to Admiral Kimmel and General Short in Hawaii as a commercial radiogram. It reached RCA's Honolulu office just after 7:30 a.m. local time, 1 p.m. in Washington. A motorcycle messenger set out to deliver it as Japanese planes began their bombing runs at Pearl Harbor.[3]

MANY YEARS LATER, Bonner Fellers would write a letter to Husband Kimmel, the admiral who was dismissed from his command after the Pearl Harbor attack. On the morning of December 6, 1941, Fellers would say, he visited RAF headquarters in Cairo and met the commanding officer, Air Marshal Arthur Longmore. "Bonner, you will be at war in 24 hours . . . We have a secret signal Japan will strike the U.S. in 24 hours," Fellers would quote Longmore as saying.

"I decided that if the British knew of the attack, we also knew of it," Fellers would write, so there had been no reason to send a cable about the conversation. Nonetheless, he would castigate himself for not having "alerted Washington, Panama, Pearl Harbor and the Philippine[s]." Even more, he would castigate the president: "How treasonous of FDR—my God." His implication is that Roosevelt knew and kept his commanders in the dark to ensure that America would enter the war.[4]

The letter is testimony to how treacherous the memory of human beings can be. A detail: Arthur Longmore had left Cairo six months before Pearl Harbor and been replaced by Air Marshal Arthur Tedder.

More essential: At the bottom of GCHQ's translations of Japanese orders to destroy Purple machines, a notation says the information was not sent to Cairo. Secrets are best shared only with those who need to know them, and the commanders in Egypt did not have a need to know. As for the final messages that heralded war within hours, it appears that only the Americans intercepted them.

Memory can shuffle dates, or squeeze several tumultuous days into a single hour. Memory makes us see a moment years ago through all the events that happened since, as if looking through a thousand distorting lenses. It tricks us into thinking that we knew then what we would know later. The meaning of an omen is obvious only in memory. In the lived moment, the oracles speak gibberish. People of the past had no more idea of the next paragraph of their stories than we have now.

It's possible that Fellers indeed met Tedder, not Longmore, on the morning of December 8 in Cairo, barely twelve hours *after* the attack on Pearl Harbor, before Roosevelt spoke to Congress. In that moment, Tedder might have said something close to "You will be at war in 24 hours." By then, Tedder would have also known about the Japanese landings in British Malaya, which began an hour and a half before the air attack on Hawaii.

It's also possible, though much less likely, that word of impending war somehow did reach Tedder by December 6 and that he shared the secret with the genial American. Everyone, after all, liked to talk to Bonner. Even then, Tedder would not have known that Pearl Harbor was a target. No one in Britain or America, including Roosevelt, knew of the Japanese aircraft carriers speeding toward Hawaii in radio silence.

Kimmel did, however, get broad warnings of approaching war. The intelligence did not help him. Kimmel was betrayed not by his president, but by his preconceptions.[5]

Fellers did send radiograms on those days in December 1941. None referred to Japan. He had just returned from his second trip in three weeks to Libya, driving to the battlefields in a camouflaged van with a bed in the back. He called it his hearse. The war had woken up again. Fellers wanted to see everything, learn everything.[6]

The first shots were planned for a minute before midnight at a house in Libya's Green Mountains, far to the west of Tobruk. Two nights earlier, a submarine had surfaced off the coast in stormy weather. On the shore, dressed as a Beduin, was Captain John Haselden, a British intelligence officer brought through enemy territory by the Long Range Desert Group.

Guided by Haselden's flashlight, a small group of commandos landed. From the local Senussi, Haselden had learned which house Rommel was using. The commandos moved at night, hid in the day. At the designated moment, while a dozen men took positions around the house, their commander and two others shot the sentry at the door and burst inside. The commander opened the door to a room; a shot from inside mortally wounded him. The other two commandos sprayed the room with gunfire and tossed in a grenade. In their retreat, several of the British soldiers were taken captive.

Rommel was not there. He'd stopped using the house. Other officers had moved in and were killed.[7]

Laszlo Almasy, who had returned to Africa, penned an account—poetic, embellished, and enraged—of the attack. "Commandos!" he wrote. "Rush into a house behind front lines and shoot indiscriminately into the room. Like the gangsters did in America during the Prohibition." Rommel, he claimed, arrived shortly afterward and gave orders: "The commandos were in uniform, therefore they are to be treated as prisoners of war." The British had behaved criminally, Almasy was certain, and Rommel held the moral high ground.[8]

The raid had an operational lesson: the submarine was superfluous; the Long Range Desert Group could have delivered the commandos.[9] Ralph Bagnold, forty-five years old, had finally surrendered to two decades of accumulated heat fatigue and left his beloved desert to become the LRDG's staff officer in Cairo. His younger comrade in desert expeditions, Guy Prendergast, now commanded the "mosquito army" in the field. Prendergast and his men slipped in and out of Libya, noticed by the Germans and Italians only when they bit and drew blood.[10]

The commando raid was also a message to Rommel. The British considered him so valuable, so extraordinarily savvy, that they had targeted him personally. "Rommel" had become the name of the enemy. It was a commendation to add to his recent promotion to full general and the renaming of his command as the Panzergruppe Afrika, the Africa Armored Group.

While Rommel was possibly busy sparing the captives, he was unaware of the tanks of the British Eighth Army—the upgraded Western Desert Force—deep in the Libyan desert. Rare rainstorms had turned German runways into mud and grounded reconnaissance planes. Lieutenant Alfred Seebohm, commander of the Panzergruppe's frontline listening company, reported on November 18, "Almost complete wireless silence of the English units." Seebohm was a master of radio intelligence. Even when his company couldn't decode British battlefield talk, it located units and figured out how armies were organized by tracking how many signals were coming from what direction.[11]

Rommel didn't notice that wireless silence spoke much louder than chatter. He was preparing, despite low supplies, for another attempt to take Tobruk. It took till the second day of Operation Crusader, the offensive that Claude Auchinleck, the single-minded general in Cairo, had spent months preparing, for Rommel to understand that hundreds of tanks had crossed into Libya, south of his forward forces. Half the British tanks quickly turned toward the coast. Half followed a long arc in the desert. To the surprise of Auchinleck's commander in the field, General Alan Cunningham, they did not find a waiting German and Italian line as they headed north toward Tobruk.

Late on the second afternoon, war correspondent Alan Moorehead drove into a British divisional headquarters in the desert and saw Bonner Fellers and his hearse.

"What's happening?" Moorehead asked.

"Damned if I know," Fellers replied. Just then the heavy gunfire began. The armies had begun to find each other.[12]

The Germans had an antiaircraft gun that fired 88-mm shells—three and a half inches in diameter—which they instead pointed at tanks, Fellers reported. Its range was much longer than that of the guns on the British- and American-built tanks; it destroyed them before they could get near. The RAF controlled the sky, Fellers would report, but couldn't bomb German tanks because, from above, pilots could not tell them from British ones. No one had thought of marking them on top.[13]

There was no front line; there was chaos. "Field dressing stations and hospitals were taking in British and German and Italian wounded impartially and as the battle flowed back and forth the hospitals would sometimes be under British command, sometimes under German," Moorehead wrote. He found places where the quickly dug graves of British and German tank crews were scattered among each other, next to tanks showing their insides "like the entrails of some wounded animal."[14]

Rommel chose the tactic on which he had gambled in the past, all the way back when he'd been a young infantry officer: a dash forward. He took one of his tank divisions and charged through the British forces to reach his cut-off garrisons at the Egyptian border. He expected to cause panic.

He did. Cunningham radioed Auchinleck that "it would be necessary to withdraw the entire army into Egypt to replace losses"—so Fellers reported from a reliable source. This was "the immediate cause" for Auchinleck to fly to Libya, replace Cunningham with General Neil Ritchie, and give orders to move west, not east—to advance, not retreat.[15] (The reliable, pained source was almost certainly Cunningham's older brother Andrew, commander of the Mediterranean fleet.[16])

Auchinleck had his own very reliable source. From Bletchley Park came a stream of deciphered messages that the Luftwaffe in Libya was desperately short of fuel. It was running out of tires for its fighters' landing gear. "British air superiority is overwhelming," said a German air force report. German truck convoys moved only at night because they were such easy targets for the RAF in daytime. They might cease altogether. "Germans thought shortage of fuel likely to immobilise their diesel-burning transport columns," said a report from Hut 3. This may have come from an Italian navy message, as the Italians were responsible for shipping fuel across the Mediterranean. After the first days of the battle, Hut 6 was unable to break the army Enigma keys, so it could not decipher messages telling how many shells or tons of tank fuel the Panzergruppe Afrika had left. Auchinleck had only indirect clues, which fit his preconception that Rommel could not keep going. In this case, the intelligence bolstered a preconception that was right.[17]

"Dearest Lu," Rommel wrote to his wife on their twenty-fifth anniversary, at the end of November, after his dash to the Egyptian border and his rapid return, "I've just spent four days in a desert counterattack with nothing to wash with. We had a splendid success."[18]

This may have been faithful to his mood after his adventure, leading from the front, out of radio contact with the rest of his army. Yet he'd had to turn back without saving his isolated garrisons. He'd left the rest of his army in confusion. While the world heard the news from Pearl Harbor, Rommel ordered a retreat—first to a line west of Tobruk, ending the siege of the town, then all the way out of Cyrenaica, back to Agheila, where he'd started out the spring before. "Dearest Lu," he wrote home on December 20, "We're pulling out. There was simply nothing else for it . . . Christmas is going to be completely messed up."[19]

Fellers drove back to Libya. Auchinleck's success, the first British victory against a German army, underwhelmed him. The Eighth Army had thrown away the chance to finish off the Axis army, he reported.

British field intelligence was intercepting Rommel's battlefield messages in low-level codes and knew his "plans, intent, [and] disposition." But "the miserable use which the British have made of this valuable information would eliminate German suspicion that their codes were compromised," Fellers wrote. Although the British "would win in the end, they are paying dearly," Fellers said.[20]

Moorehead and a fellow correspondent drove into Benghazi on Christmas 1941, arguing about where to stay, the Grand Hotel d'Italia or the Berenice, on the waterfront. "The Arabs were friendly" but the shops shuttered. Benghazi had changed hands three times that year. The RAF had bombed it night after night. The front of the Hotel d'Italia "bulged outward sickeningly," apparently from a blast within. The Berenice was burned out. They found an abandoned flat where they could cook two turkeys, which they'd somehow procured in the previous town, and celebrate the holiday.[21]

"Maybe better times are coming," Rommel wrote to his wife, mounting a defense against melancholy, "in spite of everything."[22]

"AN EGYPTIAN, WHO is close to King Farouk" also liked to talk to Fellers. They met in Cairo when Fellers was between visits to the front. The Egyptian wanted to tell about his journey to Istanbul and his conversation with Franz von Papen, the German ambassador to Turkey. Papen assured him that Germany's plan for the Middle East included "the independence of Egypt" as part of an Arab federation. The Palestine problem would be solved, Papen said, by letting the Jews become citizens of Arab states. "Italy's demand for expansion would be ignored completely," he'd told the Egyptian. The implication was that Farouk needn't be bothered by Mussolini's ranting about a new Roman Empire. Fellers did not say whether Farouk or his emissary believed Papen.

"My impression," Fellers wrote to the Military Intelligence Division in Washington, "is that the British do not know of this meeting."[23]

Fellers did not name the Egyptian. In all likelihood, it was Sami Zulficar, mentioned in one of Papen's cables to Berlin as coming to him in the autumn of 1941 "by order of his king" and asking "what fate Germany envisaged for Egypt." Zulficar's brother Youssef was the king's father-in-law, through whom Farouk had sent his warning the previous summer that Britain would occupy Iran.

Soon after, the Spanish chargé d'affaires from Cairo came to Papen, also bearing word from Farouk. "The king renewed his desire to bring about a complete understanding with the Axis," Papen told Berlin. If Farouk wasn't showing this openly, it was because "his position was of utmost difficulty, he is under surveillance even in his own house. He asked that this might be taken into consideration." It does not appear that the British ambassador to Egypt, Miles Lampson, knew about this meeting either.[24]

CHURCHILL SPENT CHRISTMAS in the White House. He arrived like a summer hurricane in midwinter, checked the beds in the guest rooms before choosing the one where he'd feel most comfortable working as well as taking his midday nap, and instructed Roosevelt's butler on the sherry he required before breakfast, the scotch and soda before lunch, and the brandy at night.[25]

Churchill had invited himself and his top generals as soon as he heard about Pearl Harbor and the invasion of Malaya, even before Congress declared war on Japan. Roosevelt worried that he might face a lack of political support for declaring war on Germany and Italy as well, but he needn't have. Hitler believed he'd acquired a navy by proxy, one that would defeat America at sea while Germany finished off the Soviet Union.

"Ribbentrop . . . is jumping with joy about the Japanese attack on the United States," Galeazzo Ciano wrote, after a phone call from the German foreign minister. "One thing is now certain," Ciano added. "America will now enter the conflict, and the conflict itself will last long enough to allow all her potential strength to come into play." His doubts, if he expressed them to his father-in-law, had no effect. The Duce had returned to euphoria. On December 11 Germany and Italy declared war on the United States, which immediately reciprocated.[26]

Roosevelt governed with a web of friendships and intrigues and with meetings in which no notes were taken. Churchill ruled with roared arguments. The two men liked each other. For their generals, Pearl Harbor brought an arranged marriage, followed by a difficult courtship.

The British military men thought the Americans had no idea how to run a government or a war because they did not do as done in London. "The president . . . has no proper private office, and no real private secretary . . . they have a hell of a lot to learn," one of them wrote. At a meeting in the Oval Office, there was no conference table. Except for the president, behind the desk that hid his wheelchair, everyone sat in a semicircle, "perched on chairs and sofas." Not only that, Roosevelt's dog attended and started barking. It was a peculiar complaint: Churchill called generals to meet him in his bedroom, where they would find him in bed, wearing his red-and-gold dragon-festooned dressing gown, a cigar jutting sideways from his mouth, the bed covered in papers. His gray Persian cat, Smokey, sometimes sat beside him. One morning the prime minister's toes wiggled under the blanket as he spoke on the phone with General Alan Brooke, now chief of the Imperial General Staff. Churchill's secretary saw Smokey's tail twitch. The cat leapt and sank his fangs into the toe. "Get off, you fool," Churchill roared into the phone. The general, uncertain what he'd done to enrage the prime minister this time, hung up.[27]

Churchill and his entourage stayed in Washington for three weeks. Despite the culture clash, they and their American hosts came to agreements. They would create a joint command based in Washington. (Brooke, who'd stayed in London to mind the war, saw this as Britain having "sold the birthright for a plate of porridge.") Their joint efforts would concentrate on defeating Germany first.

They did not agree about where to start. Churchill, like his generals, wanted to seize the Vichy colonies of Morocco and Algeria. From there and from Libya, American and British armies would close a vise on the Axis, drive it from Africa, and prepare the way to invade Italy or the Balkans. The Mediterranean would be safe, which would cut the time needed for ships to take troops, trucks, and arms to India and Egypt and to the Persian Gulf ports from which roads led to Russia. If each ship could make more trips, it would be like having many more ships.

The Americans did not like this idea. They wanted to take the most direct route into Germany, which meant landing divisions in France or Belgium as quickly as possible—by 1943, or even late in 1942. The way to defeat the enemy was to drive a stake into its heart. This was the "proper and orthodox" way to fight, as Secretary of War Henry Stimson would say. Brigadier General Dwight Eisenhower, the deputy chief of war planning, wrote a note for himself: "We've got to go to Europe and fight" and stop wasting time elsewhere. An adviser to Army Chief of Staff George Marshall said the British had "political [more] than strategic purposes" for invading the Vichy colonies. The Americans suspected the North Africa plan was designed to use US troops to save the British Empire.

The Americans' "orthodox" insistence on striking directly at the enemy's strongest forces has been attributed to the teachings of Carl von Clausewitz, the nineteenth-century master theoretician of war. The British strategy has been explained as resting on the teachings of the ancient Chinese theorist Sun Tzu: the way to weaken a powerful enemy begins with blows at the periphery of his forces.

Theory is not explanation enough. The British generals had read Clausewitz. But they had spent two brutal years fighting the Germans and losing, and they thought the supremely confident Yanks had no idea what they were facing. When Brooke eventually met Marshall, he described the American chief of staff as "a pleasant and easy man to get on with, rather over-filled with his own importance. But I should not put him down as a great man." Just as the dog in the Oval Office stood for American amateurism, Marshall stood for the naiveté of the upstart nation. The strategic meetings in Washington, ironically named Arcadia, ended. The question of a target—Africa or France—waited for a decision.[28]

CHURCHILL CAME HOME knowing that he had something he still had to tell his friend. He asked Stewart Menzies to write the note, decided the tone was too formal, and wrote a more personal version.

"One night when we talked late, you spoke of the importance of our cipher people getting in close contact with yours," he started. The two navies were already sharing ciphers, Churchill wrote. "But diplomatic and military ciphers are of equal importance and we appear to know nothing officially of your versions of these."

Then came the admission, delicately, and the warning. "Some time ago, however, our experts claimed to have discovered the system and constructed some tables used by your diplomatic corps. From the moment we became allies, I gave instructions that this work should cease. However, danger of our enemies having achieved a measure of success cannot, I am advised, be dismissed." That is: We've been reading your diplomatic mail, old boy. We've stopped. But change your codes.

"If possible, burn this letter when you have read it," Churchill added. He sent the note by hand with the US ambassador, who was making a home visit. At the end, to soften the jolt, he added by hand,

> *With every good wish & my kindest regards.*
> *Believe me,*
> *Your sincere friend,*
> *Winston Churchill.*[29]

MILES LAMPSON MADE time for the correspondent from the *Times* of London, James Holburn. "A decent little fellow but not very impressive," Lampson dictated to his diary typist. It was January 24, 1942. "I didn't know until he told me this morning that he had been shot up last time he went up to the front. They were in a passenger plane somewhere near Sollum when they were attacked by three Messerschmidts. He got hit in the eye by splinters—but they made a crash landing." It took more than this to impress the British ambassador, especially if you were not tall enough.[30]

After that, Lampson got to the news of the day: "Rommel is hitting back, apparently with unpleasant efficiency . . . It looks to me once more that we have made the mistake of underestimating German reinforcements in the West and being in a bit of a hurry in sending our stuff away to the East." Just that week, in a meeting with Auchinleck, Admiral Cunningham, and Air Marshal Tedder, he'd warned about repeating "the painful experience of last summer, when we had almost lost Egypt in the abortive attempt to save Greece."[31]

He had a point. Having rushed after Rommel's retreating forces, the Eighth Army was spread thinly along the coastal rim of Libya. Auchinleck had just replaced a battered armored division with a fresh and inexperienced one. Another division, on its way to Egypt, had been diverted to Malaya to fight the Japanese, who were quickly advancing toward Singapore.

"The RAF is sending fighters to the Far East," Fellers had reported on January 17. Unofficially, he'd said, the number was 250. He'd earlier written that the British had 450 fighters in operating shape in North Africa—and that the Germans had brought hundreds of warplanes to the Mediterranean from the Soviet front "on the assumption that the German army would be in Moscow by Christmas." That assumption had proven wrong. But in a world war, the Germans' need to get supplies to Libya helped the Red Army in the Russian winter, while the Japanese threat to Singapore robbed Air Marshal Tedder in Cairo of planes. "This reduction of fighter strength seriously jeopardizes British air position," Fellers wrote, "at a time when only those guilty of wishful thinking can believe an Axis Mediterranean offensive is not probable."[32]

Neither the German nor the Italian high command had considered an offensive probable or prudent. Rommel did not inform them of his intentions. The Italians, he believed, couldn't keep a secret safe. The British intercepted and read everything that Italian headquarters in Libya radioed to Rome, he was certain. It was a good justification not to tell his nominal superior, the Italian commander in Libya, General Ettore Bastico, whom Rommel liked to call "Bombastico." But he didn't tell Berlin either. "I'm full of plans that I daren't say anything about round here. They'd think me crazy. But I'm not; I simply see a bit farther than they do," Rommel wrote to his wife.[33]

Whether because he did see farther, or because he calculated that the eighty or so tanks brought by recent convoys gave him a momentary advantage that would evaporate when the British got new shipments, or because his instinct was that war must be fought by hurtling forward, or because the rush of action cured despondency, he attacked. This time it worked. Even faster than the British units had advanced, they now crumbled and fell back.[34]

"An English tank that took a direct hit is lying close to the highway," Laszlo Almasy wrote. "The German armor-piercing cannon shot clean through its 14 centimeter armor. The inside of the tank is repulsive, full of shreds of clothing and puddles of blood." He'd been ordered to drive a staff officer from Tripoli all the way to Rommel's headquarters and found himself chasing the general across Cyrenaica. "The officers tell us that Rommel has practically not rested since the big battle began four days ago . . . He expects a lot from his soldiers but the most from himself," Almasy wrote. For the general's men, he'd become half a god. An antitank gunner told Almasy that Rommel "neither eats nor drinks and never sleeps."

Almasy caught up with Rommel in Benghazi. The town had just been conquered, again. Almasy drove past the ruins of the Grand Hotel d'Italia and recalled his last stay there. At night British bombers had come, and Almasy had run to a bomb shelter. In the morning his room was intact, except that the stairs to it were gone and a wall had been sheared off. An Italian soldier had found a ladder and brought him his pajamas and slippers.

Outside town, Almasy noticed an intact, captured British truck. It was just what he needed.[35]

For Lampson, the reversal in the desert came at a most inconvenient time. Egypt's wheat shortage was getting worse, warned Colonel Raymond Maunsell, head of Security Intelligence Middle East. At the Suez port, "native laborers went on strike, complaining of the impossibility of buying flour," said an SIME intelligence roundup, adding that the poor blamed the British forces for buying up supplies. Hunger made people susceptible to enemy propaganda, Maunsell warned.[36] So did military failures. When Lampson told Prime Minister Hussein Sirry about the fall of Benghazi, Sirry "observed that the moral effect on the Egyptian public was certainly going to be bad."[37]

On top of this, there was Farouk.[38]

In early January, Egypt's foreign minister, Salib Sami, phoned Lampson to say that the cabinet was about to break diplomatic ties with Vichy. London had demanded this for months. The French government under Marshal Petain was an Axis satellite. Farouk was away, enjoying himself on the Red Sea coast, and had asked not to be "troubled with telegrams or state affairs."

Lampson was pleased. He'd been under pressure to somehow get the Wafd back in power. The Wafd stood for Egyptian nationalism. It was the only party with wide public support, and its leader, Mustafa

el-Nahas, was reliably antifascist, which in the view of Lampson's crit-
ics made it worth putting up with Nahas having a mind of his own.
Maunsell had been saying this in ornate offices behind Lampson's
back. For Lampson, the break with Vichy was proof of his wisdom
in exerting British influence quietly through Sirry's minority government. "Sirry and his crowd are giving us, almost without exception,
everything we want in . . . prosecution of the war," he wrote.

Two weeks later, Farouk got back to Cairo, erupted in curses at the
foreign minister, and demanded that he resign.

Lampson phoned Ahmed Hassanein, the former explorer whose
official position was now head of the royal cabinet and whose unofficial position for years had been indulgent father figure to the king.
They had to meet, Lampson said, that evening, it couldn't wait. Hassa-
nein came to the grand compound of the British Residency facing the
Nile at 10 p.m. The constitution, Hassanein told Lampson, required
the king's consent to break relations. When Farouk had returned to
Cairo, a memo had been waiting for him from deposed prime minister
Ali Maher and his henchmen, saying that the "royal prerogative had
been ignored." This was "His Majesty's softest spot," Hassanein said.
Maher's goal was to replace Sirry with someone less compliant with
British demands.

"I did not mince my words," Lampson dictated at midnight to the
secretary who kept his diary. The Egyptian cabinet had met a legitimate war-related request from its British ally. For Farouk to pick a
fight over this was "reckless irresponsibility on the part of a young and
headstrong sovereign" influenced by "evil counsellors." Sirry had to
stay, and Farouk had to finally sweep his Italian advisers and Maher's
cronies out of the palace.

Three different fights were tangled together. One was over who
ruled Egypt. One was over Farouk's loyalties in the war, and Lampson's
suspicion that the king leaned toward the side that had invaded his
country, not the side that was defending it. And one was over prestige,
which was also Lampson's soft spot.

In Cairo you could read, even in the censored press, that everywhere the British Empire was cracking. The top headline on January 25 in *Al Aharam* said the war was getting closer to Singapore,
as the Japanese pushed south on the Malayan Peninsula.[39] The next

morning, Lampson talked to Prime Minister Sirry. Since he'd taken office, Sirry said, he'd labored to save Farouk from "the charge of treachery." He'd closed the "palace channels of communication with the enemy . . . until only the Vichy Legation remained." Sirry said he would resign if the king dismissed his foreign minister. Lampson told him to hold on.

All this comes from Lampson's account. It's harder to know what Farouk was thinking during those days just before his twenty-second birthday, though his messages to German emissaries in Turkey and Tehran offer clues. He said that despite being in a "position of utmost difficulty," his heart lay with the Führer. Whether he feared the arrival of a German army or eagerly looked forward to it, Farouk may have guessed that letting his prime minister expel the Vichy representative signaled that he was useless to Hitler as a potential partner. Farouk's father had given him a car when he was eleven but never taught him the game of diplomacy. It was not like the poker games at the Royal Automobile Club, where the king reputedly kept everyone in the room till dawn so he could try to win back what he had lost.[40] He did not want to lose his kingdom, and could not expect new hands to be dealt.

February 1 was a Sunday. Lampson had left Cairo to go hunting; he looked forward to shooting ducks by moonlight. A messenger reached him before sunset with word that he had to return immediately. The crisis had leaked out into the streets. That night he went to Sirry's house. The prime minister came downstairs from a dinner party to talk. There'd been disturbances at Al-Azhar, the great seminary of Islamic studies, fomented by the rector "in concert with Ali Maher and other evil elements," Sirry said. Then demonstrations began at the university. Years before, student protests had been the first sign of larger anti-British upheavals. Sirry said he had asked Hassanein for the king's support in quashing the protests. The courtier had brought Farouk's reply: do as you please, but it's not my business.

Sirry understood: the king was done with him. I'm resigning, he told the ambassador. Lampson asked who should succeed him.

"Send for the Wafd," Sirry said.

Really, Lampson decided, "it was more evident than ever" that a government that wanted to uphold Egypt's side of the alliance with

Britain would have to "fight the Palace." Only a government supported by the majority of Egyptians could do that. This meant the Wafd. He wrote this as if he had never thought differently.

LAMPSON WROTE CABLES to London, lining up Foreign Office support. He went to Abdin Palace and told Farouk who the next prime minister had to be. He did not meet overtly with Nahas, but with an intermediary. The Wafd leader had been waiting since the rigged election four years earlier had denied him power. He was ready to rule, on his terms: there'd be no coalition with other parties, and there would be new elections.

On the morning of February 4, Lampson met with Auchinleck, Cunningham, Tedder, and Oliver Lyttelton, the British cabinet minister resident in Cairo. They agreed on the message that Lampson would give Hassanein: "Unless I hear by 6 p.m. today that Nahas has been asked to form a government, His Majesty King Farouk must accept the consequences." Hassanein came to the embassy, listened, and went.

By chance, the man who'd written the abdication letter for King Edward VIII of Britain in 1938 was now serving Lyttelton as head of the British propaganda department in Cairo.[41] He prepared a letter for Farouk to sign. Since Farouk had only daughters, the next in line for the throne was his much older first cousin, Prince Muhammad Ali. Conveniently, the prince was the rare Anglophile in the royal clan. That left the question of how to dispose of a slightly used king, still young. Admiral Cunningham suggested to Lampson putting Farouk on a ship, without saying where it would go. Ceylon was a possible destination. In London, the Foreign Office tried checking to see if Canada would take him. Bonner Fellers heard from a "reliable source" that a plane was waiting to take Farouk to South Africa.[42]

Just before lunch, Lampson recorded in his diary, he received a report that students were demonstrating at the university. They were shouting, "Long live Rommel," "Long live Farouk," and "Down with the English." There were no chants about Hitler or Mussolini. It was easier to think of Rommel as liberator.

Farouk called the leaders of Egypt's political parties to Abdin Palace. At 6 p.m. Hassanein traveled the mile and a third from the palace to the British embassy, bearing a message. It listed the politicians, including Nahas, and said they all agreed "the British ultimatum is a great infringement . . . of the independence of the country," and that Farouk therefore rejected it. Lampson answered, "I shall be arriving at the palace at 9 p.m."

Nahas's man showed up while Lampson was sitting with General Robert Stone, commander of the British garrison responsible for internal order. Ignore Nahas's name on that list, Nahas's man said. Lampson could count on the Wafd leader.

The usual wartime blackout was in effect; Cairo's nighttime streets were dark. Tanks appeared around Abdin Palace at 7:30, Fellers told Washington. "A tank drove through the closed iron gate and infantry followed into the court," Fellers wrote.[43]

Lampson came with General Stone and with what the ambassador proudly described as "an impressive array of specially picked stalwart military officers armed to the teeth." Hassanein and the king were in the royal reception room. "In rising indignation," Lampson wrote afterward, he read out a prepared statement. He had held himself in diplomatic restraint for years; it evaporated. The king's advisers were assisting the enemy, Lampson declared. The king had refused to entrust government to the party with "the commanding general support of the country." Thus, "Your Majesty is no longer fit to occupy the throne." Lampson handed him the letter of abdication.

Hassanein spoke to Farouk in Arabic. Lampson did not understand the language. Farouk "looked up and asked almost pathetically" for another chance. He would call for Nahas, he said. Lampson agreed, though he had his heart set on abdication. He left through "passages filled with British officers and court chamberlains, the latter a crowd of scared hens."

Back at the embassy, he had the "comic relief" of a phone message from Hassanein asking that he remove the troops because they weren't letting Nahas in. From the palace, the new prime minister came to the embassy. Lampson told him that "my desire, as ever, was to remain as much as possible behind the scenes." Diana Cooper, the aristocrat and actress, was staying with her politician husband at Lampson's residence. After 11, she found the embassy hall crowded. Lampson "came out of his den, dressed in a pearl-grey *frac*, arm in arm with Nahas Pasha, both grinning themselves in two."[44]

Lampson wrote a long cable that night. Its tone suggests that the ambassador's blood was still pounding pleasurably in his ears. "So much for the events of the evening, which I confess I could not have more enjoyed," he concluded.

Several days after, Second Lieutenant Khaled Mohi El Din of the Egyptian Cavalry Corps heard from a colleague about a meeting at the Officers Club in Cairo. When he got there, he found "about three or four hundred" men, top brass and junior officers like himself, some "crying in bitterness, rage and humiliation, others shouting." Whatever they thought of Farouk personally, the king represented the nation. Someone proposed a protest march to the palace. Someone more senior said that military discipline barred political demonstrations. In the midst of the meeting, a phone call came from the palace with word that Farouk "appreciated the expression of loyalty" but asked them to return peacefully to their duties. Everyone left. The king embodied the nation less than he had, and so did the Wafd.[45]

February 4, 1942, was the day when "Mustafa el-Nahas Pasha lost our respect," Anwar al-Sadat wrote much later. In his version of what followed, "officers assembled in Cairo and marched out to Abidin [*sic*] Palace to salute the king, and he came out to return their salute." The description is in third person. Sadat does not claim to have been present as a young signals officer. It's not clear whether someone else misinformed him or he invented the heroic march to the palace and the salute. Either way, it was a more honorable past, at least in Sadat's eyes, than the real one.[46]

WORD OF THE coup d'état was sure to seep out, Fellers radioed. "British prestige among Egyptians, at a time when the military situation is critical, is lower than at any time since my arrival sixteen months ago."[47] Lampson had made sure Egypt had a government opposed to Rome and Berlin. In the battle for esteem, however, he too had lost.

Only Rommel had gained prestige. He was part of everyone's calculations: he had inspired demonstrations, inflamed Farouk's hope or fear, and helped convince Lampson that confrontation was essential. In Rome, Ciano wrote, Mussolini summed up a meeting of his ministers with his "usual attack" on Italian generals and then praised Rommel, "who is always in his tank leading the attacking columns." The soldiers of the Bersaglieri, elite Italian infantry units, "are enthusiastic about him . . . carrying him in triumph on their shoulders, shouting that with him they are sure they can reach Alexandria."[48]

Yet Rommel's advance stopped just as the coup was taking place in Cairo. His tanks were out of fuel and shells; he'd again outrun his supplies. The British built their new defenses on a line running into the desert from a village called Gazala on the Libyan coast.[49] The Eighth Army was 125 miles west of where it had started in November. Tobruk was no longer besieged. In a dispassionate accounting, this made the last two and a half months of fighting a British victory, albeit costly. Yet memory is often shaped by the end of a story. Because Rommel regained much of the ground he initially lost, the battle was easily remembered as his victory and Auchinleck's loss.

Lampson was right, though, that Britain paid dearly for taking warplanes and troops from the African front to the Far East. That decision had made Rommel's counterattack possible. Yet Singapore fell to Japan on February 15, and seventy thousand British, Indian, and Australian soldiers, including newly arrived reinforcements, went into captivity.[50] In the clarity of retrospect, the message telling Japanese diplomats in London to destroy their Purple machine heralded the surrender of Singapore, Auchinleck's failure to take Tripoli, and tanks surrounding Abdin Palace in Cairo.

"COUNT ALMASY IS a splendid fellow, quiet and considerate, and knows all about the desert," Heinrich Sandstede wrote. He and his friend Johann Eppler were overjoyed when they were assigned to the Hungarian explorer's tiny unit. Almasy's German uniform showed the insignia of a *hauptmann*, a captain. But he didn't make them shout "*Jawohl, Herr Hauptmann*." Just "yes" was enough. Even better, Almasy said they wouldn't need to jump out of an airplane; he would drive them into Egypt. Sandstede had the idea this would be less dangerous. He had not traveled before with Laszlo Almasy.[51]

In February, they took a train to Napoli, then flew across the Mediterranean to Tripoli. With them, they brought their suitcase-sized wireless sets. Other supplies caught up with them there—packages listed as "tobacco" in Abwehr radio messages, which really meant British banknotes for Eppler and Sandstede to use in Egypt, and copies of an English novel. Abwehr agents used a cipher in which the letters of the original text were rearranged in a complex pattern. The pattern shifted daily, based on words on prearranged pages of a published novel, in a language fitting the agents' false identities. In Egypt, Eppler would revert to being Hussein Gaafar, an Egyptian, but Sandstede would carry British papers in the name "Peter Muncaster." In Abwehr messages, their codenames were Max and Moritz, the boy pranksters from a classic German children's book. Almasy was "Salam," a near-anagram of his name and the Arabic word for "peace."

Two radiograms to Salam told him to dock Max and Moritz's pay for bills they'd left unpaid on their Berlin apartment. The messages were translated two weeks later in Hut 3. GCHQ had cracked the ciphers used by Abwehr agents in the summer of 1940. In December 1941, Dilly Knox's section in the cottage at Bletchley Park had figured out how to read messages sent between main Abwehr stations with the agency's special model of the Enigma machine. Knox, dying of cancer, gave credit to Mavis Lever and another woman in his group, Margaret Rock, for solving the puzzle. The value of Abwehr traffic was that it led to spies.[52] Messages to Tripoli about delinquent utility bills got low priority for translation.

Almasy delivered two of his men to Rommel's frontline headquarters, where they would be responsible for relaying wireless messages. Then he returned to Tripoli and set out to Cyrenaica with the rest of his small crew. He'd succeeded in getting three captured British trucks and three Ford command cars. Just past Agheila, they turned off the paved coastal highway onto a track south into the desert. Through a sandstorm they drove 150 miles to an oasis called Jalo, home to less than three thousand people, as well as fifty thousand date palms and an Italian garrison.

Almasy planned to drive six hundred miles almost due east from Jalo to Assiut, the largest town in Upper Egypt. He hadn't explored this area before. He was counting on Italian maps that showed flat, gravelly desert, near-perfect driving terrain, for most of the journey.

The maps, it turned out, were wrong. They were based on imagination or laziness. Eighty miles east of Jalo was a sand sea: wave after wave of soft dunes.

Almasy tried anyway. They got stuck, dug themselves out, got stuck again. It did not help that the men had no desert experience, or that they were out of shape. It did not help that Almasy had ignored Bagnold's method of stripping every unneeded piece of metal from the trucks to lighten them. Handing out amphetamines did not help. They drank too much water, except for Sandstede, who had brought schnapps. They got diarrhea. Almasy said that turning back "would question the whole enterprise and embarrass me immensely"—so Sandstede would remember. They tried radioing for a plane to drop supplies but the big Italian transmitters at the oasis blocked reception.

They turned back to Jalo and started again. They left behind everything possible. The only extra set of clothes were the civvies that Eppler and Sandstede would wear if they ever got to Egypt. They searched for a path in the dunes. The gearbox on Almasy's station wagon cracked. They had to abandon the car in the dunes.

Almasy had shown that he either did not fear death or did not believe it would happen to him. He did fear shame. He stayed up through the night calculating a new route, and announced it in the morning. They would go south, almost to Kufra oasis, and gamble on slipping past the British garrison there. He sent one truck back to Jalo with the two men who were in the worst shape. That left six men, and two trucks and two cars, and no fuel to spare because he was adding at least three hundred miles in each direction. The trucks would be left at points along the way, so their fuel could be used for the way back.

Their luck got better. They found a track that the Italian trucks had used to supply Kufra before the war. They got around the oasis without the British spotting them, and found another track, now used by the Sudanese convoys that came to Kufra from Wadi Halfa. It led to the edge of Gilf Kebir. Almasy wrote in his diary, "In May 1932 I discovered this mighty plateau," though he knew that Prince Kemal el Din, Farouk's cousin, had been there before him.

He showed the men the prehistoric drawings at the Cave of the Swimmers, as if he were just an explorer guiding aristocratic adventurer-tourists. He found a cache of water he'd left in 1933, four full tins, still good. They managed to get through by wireless to their men at Rommel's headquarters and report their position.

After two days of searching, Almasy found the pass through the plateau that he and the English pilot Hugh Penderel had spotted nearly a decade earlier, and that he'd drawn on a map for an Italian intelligence officer all those years before. It was "the secret gateway for breaking into Egypt," Almasy wrote in his diary. For part of the way, he was able to follow tire tracks he'd left himself. His greatest problem was the men, especially Eppler and Sandstede. Sandstede "drives as usual like a wild man," he wrote.

On the far side of the plateau, short of fuel, Almasy decided to drive right through the oasis village of Kharga. When two Egyptian sentries stopped him and told him in Arabic to check in at the government house, he said his commander was behind him and would do that. The sentries did not notice their German uniforms. From there Almasy followed an old Roman road and then Darb el Arbain, the slave caravan route.

At two in the afternoon, the two remaining cars stopped on a plateau above Assiut and the Nile. Eppler and Sandstede got out. "A few handshakes, a short farewell" and Almasy and the other driver turned back. The journey, so far, had taken nine days since Almasy had changed the route. The escapade may have been the counterfeit count's greatest feat, and he could tell almost no one about it.

Eppler and Sandstede continued on foot, lugging their two wireless sets in suitcases. They decided to bury one of them, along with their uniforms. They split their cash, put on their civvies, and descended into the town to catch a train for Cairo. Up to now, they had been supporting actors in Operation Salam, the journey. Now they constituted Operation Condor.

At Hut 3, Jean Alington got an Abwehr message to translate. Alington was twenty-four years old. Her path to Bletchley Park had begun with studying opera in Germany and Austria before the war.[53] The message had been sent from Tripoli to Berlin. It was short, and a couple of days old. It said, "Salam reports arrival at Gilf Kebir." Alington had read Ralph Bagnold's book *Libyan Sands: Travel in a Dead World*. She knew where Gilf Kebir was. The message meant that the Abwehr had someone operating out there, in the dead sands.[54]

Act III

A PARTICULARLY
RELIABLE SOURCE

1

THE WOMAN OF DAUNTING INTELLIGENCE

April-May 1942. Bletchley Park-Cairo-Rome-Mishmar Ha'emek.

A British intercept operator heard the dots and dashes and took down the stream of letters before the sun rose on April 24, 1942.[1] By late that afternoon, the whirling wheels of one of the twenty or so bombes now operating at Bletchley Park and at a couple of outstations, operated by the land-bound sailors of the Women's Royal Naval Service, had produced a break for the Red key of Enigma. Hut 6 transformed the predawn message from Field Marshal Albert Kesselring of the Luftwaffe into a string of five-letter groups that, once properly divided into words, would be German.

A square wooden duct, just wide enough for a wooden tray to pass through, connected Huts 6 and 3. Someone put freshly decoded messages on the tray and shouted into the duct. If there was no response, she banged the inside of the duct with a broom handle left next to it for this purpose. On the Hut 3 end, someone else pulled a string attached to the tray and reeled in the fresh material.

The Watch Room of Hut 3 was laid out like the newsroom of a small newspaper, in this case one with an extremely small, elite readership. In the middle was a horseshoe-shaped table, like a newspaper's copy desk. The Number One of the watch, sitting inside the horseshoe, read the decoded Kesselring message, decided it was urgent, and handed it to one of the translators facing him on the outside of the horseshoe for immediate attention. A few minutes later, Number One was reviewing the translation.

"Reports from a particularly reliable source," it said, revealed that "the British high command intends" to use "heavy American bombers from the Egyptian area" to attack German aerodromes in Sicily, and to send commandos to Sicily to sabotage German warplanes on the ground.

Most importantly, Kesselring's message quoted the particularly reliable source as confirming that the British were planning an offensive in Libya in order to push the Axis forces westward, back beyond Benghazi. Once the Royal Air Force could operate from the Cyrenaica coast, it would be able to provide air cover for convoys to the besieged island of Malta.

A sentence pregnant with uncertain meaning followed, referring to the planned British offensive: "As the last named operation is not possible before June, it will come too late."

Number One approved the text. Since this was mainly air war material, he handed it on to the air advisers—two RAF officers who sat at another table, along with the army and naval advisers. The RAF man added commentary and wrote up a paraphrase to send to MI6; to army, air force, and naval intelligence in London; and to the commanders in chief in Cairo. He passed his work through a window to the next room, where the duty officer sat.

The buck stopped with the duty officer. He had to make sure that the paraphrase told enough, and was accurate, and did not give away anything unnecessary, especially about where this information came from. Among the elect who knew about breaking Enigma, the constant fear was that the secret would spread to one person too many and get back to the Germans.

"The Enigma code as now used by the German Air Force and German Army is, as far as known at present, theoretically unbreakable," but German carelessness made all the difference, Gordon Welchman had written to Commander Edward Travis. "Our methods . . . are based on taking advantage of the enemy's mistakes." It was only "a little short of miraculous," Welchman wrote, that the Germans kept using stock phrases—the cribs that Hut 6 used to set up the bombes and break the keys.

There were crazier German mistakes: Whoever created the key settings was getting tired of writing endless lists of which wheels to use each day, how to set the rings, how to set up the plugboards. The anonymous code-meister had begun to recycle: He would take the wheel orders from January's list for one key, the ring settings for another key, and combine them to use for a third key for February.

A Hut 6 staffer named Reg Parker had, on his own, started keeping a record of all the settings of all the keys ever broken. At the beginning of each month, he would look for repetitions of settings seen earlier in other keys. They started appearing. A few days of recycled ring settings or wheel orders meant that they were almost sure to keep repeating. In a moment, a large piece of the solution for the key for the whole month was ready. If the Germans ever found out that Enigma was being read, all they had to do to foil the British was to start being more careful.

Edward Travis was now in charge at Bletchley Park. Alastair Denniston, who'd created GCHQ, and would have much preferred to read other gentlemen's mail than demand bigger budgets, was sent back to London together with the department that broke diplomatic codes, for which there was no longer room at Bletchley Park. Denniston was like a master weaver after the invention of steam looms, out of place in the industrial age.[2]

Travis was "of the bulldog breed," Welchman would say. He had a thick neck, a wide nose, and round black-rimmed spectacles that emphasized his eyes.[3] He could be friendly; he could also write "BALLS" in the brown ink that was his trademark across a proposal he disliked.[4] He sent out a memo on security to everyone at Bletchley Park. "Do not talk at meals," it said; the waiters and waitresses had ears. Do not talk on the train home, or by your parents' fireside. If a friend or old aunt asks what you are doing in the war, answer, "Working for the Foreign Office," or the navy, or whatever. If asked, "But what do you *do*?" do not say it is secret. Answer, "Oh—work."[5] A woman who'd been study-ing German at Cardiff University when a strange man approached her in the library and asked her if she'd like a job he couldn't explain with the Foreign Office and who now decoded messages in Hut 6 was billeted with a nearby family. The master of the house pestered her with questions and told her that she talked in her sleep. She stopped sleeping, fainted at work, and woke up in the sick bay with influenza. It was a Bletchley Park form of war wound.[6] Nervous breakdowns were another form. When a doctor started using hypnosis to help one of-ficer who collapsed under the strain, MI5 was told to interrogate the physician to find out what the patient might have revealed.[7]

To Kesselring's message citing his particularly reliable source, either the duty officer or the air adviser added a note: The sentence saying that the British operation in Africa "will come too late" could mean that the Germans intended to act in Africa before June 1. Or it could mean that it would "be 'too late' to have any influence on supplying Malta because of German intentions against Malta."

Implicitly, though, the entire message was about Malta. The island, smaller than the New York City borough of Brooklyn, was a hunk of rock between Tunisia and Sicily. Even more than Crete, it rendered the distinction between Europe and the Middle East meaningless. The quarter million people who lived there spoke a North African dialect of Arabic written in Latin characters, practiced Catholicism, and, in April 1942, lived under the most intensive bombing on earth.

Every ship from Italy to Tripoli had to pass near Malta. It was the choke point on Erwin Rommel's supply line. From the island, British warships and planes had attacked the Italian convoys. For both the Axis and the British, Malta was the key to North Africa and the Middle East. Kesselring, commander of all German forces in the Mediterra-nean, had six hundred warplanes based in Sicily, half an hour's flight from Malta, and more planes in Libya, and they were coming day and night to bomb. The Luftwaffe was flying as many sorties over the tiny island daily as it had over all Britain in the summer of 1940.[8]

Malta's fishermen could not go to sea; they would be machine-gunned from the air. Since the war began, there'd been no pasta from Italy. Potatoes could be had only on the black market. Farmers lacked feed for their pigs. The last British convoy had set out in March from

Alexandria with twenty-six thousand tons of food, fuel, and ammunition. Only a fifth of that made it off the two ships that got through to the deep cleft in the rock island that was Malta's Grand Harbor. Churchill wrote a letter to Roosevelt, who sent an American aircraft carrier to the Mediterranean. From its deck, British Spitfires flew to Malta to reinforce the RAF. The fighters could not bring food. The Maltese cut tunnels into the rock for shelter and grew hungrier.[9]

Stewart Menzies delivered the Kesselring message to Churchill late that night. Churchill drew a red line next to the paragraph that said a June offensive would "come too late." This fit his concerns. He was again pushing Auchinleck to attack. The general in Cairo was insisting that he "would not have reasonable numerical superiority until June 1."[10]

Earlier in April, Churchill had received a decoded German message that said the RAF headquarters in Cairo was informing "all subordinate units that the HQ of the German air force is . . . six miles east of Benghazi." This alarmed him. In red, he scribbled an order to Menzies: "Please report on this. How did they know that we had told the army in Egypt where it was?" The order set off an investigation of RAF code and radio security in Egypt.[11]

This time, the problem slipped past Churchill's tired eyes. The prime minister did not ask Menzies to find out what particularly reliable source had handed Field Marshal Kesselring an intelligence jewel: what "the British high command intends," and how much time Kesselring had before Auchinleck's planned attack.

THE BRITISH FOURTH Armored Brigade "has most excellent morale," wrote infantry Lieutenant Colonel James Fry of the US Army when he returned to Cairo from the Western Desert. "Both officers and men are extremely enthusiastic about the new army equipment," which included American tanks. That was where his good news ended.

Fry's report showed that Auchinleck had more to worry about than achieving numerical superiority. The Eighth Army had been compelled to issue an order that in training, US tanks should not be driven more than one hundred miles a month. It was hard to keep them in running order, especially because the air cleaners were "in a most inaccessible place" and kept clogging. The tank engines weren't designed for the otherworldly conditions of deserts.

Besides that, the men needed training, but Fry said, "I never found an officer actively conducting any instruction . . . I did see officers enjoying their tea during the hours you would normally expect training." A couple of times, he found officers in bed at 8 a.m., being served tea by their orderlies. "This is fairly hard to understand from an American viewpoint," Fry wrote.[12]

Colonel Fellers, his superior, forwarded Fry's report to the Military Intelligence Division in Washington. A year and a half before, Bonner Fellers had come to Cairo alone. Now he was in command of two dozen American officers and civilians at the military attaché's office in Garden City. He had an assistant attaché for air war, and one for armored forces, and several more, along with battlefield observers. He had his chief code clerk, Marie Broach, and her two assistants, whom he shared with General Russell Maxwell, whose office was in the same mansion on El Nabatat Street.[13] Maxwell headed the US military supply mission in North Africa, in charge of bringing the tanks and trucks that kept coming by ship around the Cape and the warplanes that flew from America, to Brazil, to Takoradi in West Africa, to Egypt.[14] The American technicians who came with the machines were his responsibility.

Five months after the United States declared war, Fellers and Maxwell were the American commanders closest to fighting on the ground against Germany and Italy. Washington and London were still debating where and when US troops would first land—France, or North Africa, or perhaps Norway. Fellers's office grew because the War Department was ravenous for information about how well its weapons worked, how its forces should prepare, and how its ally was performing.

In a meeting with Auchinleck, Fellers said the War Department wanted information on Malta. The tall red-headed general with the pale eyes said that his own weekly situation report went to Field Marshal John Dill, former chief of the Imperial General Staff and now Britain's military representative in Washington. Dill was surely sharing his reports with the War Department, Auchinleck said. He added that "he was concerned lest General Dill and [Fellers] might present divergent views on the situation in the Middle East." Even worse for Auchinleck, the War Department often got Fellers's criticism a day earlier than Auchinleck's upbeat assessments, which at times were channeled through London.

"Our government desires its own intelligence agency," just as Britain would, Fellers answered Auchinleck.[15]

Auchinleck knew this was reasonable. But he also knew that Britain had been fighting alone, and its army was now being criticized by American officers who had yet to make decisions while under German fire. If Lieutenant Colonel Fry's comments about the Eighth Army's flaws got back to him, Auchinleck might well have whispered Countess Ranfurly's words: "*That* from an American."

Yet Auchinleck would have liked some of Fellers's telegrams—had he seen them—much more than the attaché's commanders did. In April Fellers radioed a long proposal for sending a major force of American heavy bombers to the Middle East. In Fellers's plan, they would strike the Romanian oil fields on which Germany depended for fuel and would bomb Axis airbases around the Mediterranean. To protect that force and prevent a German invasion of the Mideast via Turkey, he urged sending four ground divisions, some sixty thousand American soldiers. He did not get a response. He repeated the recommendation. He warned that Japan could reach Persia via the Indian Ocean and cut the Allied supply route to Russia through that country. He proposed an American invasion of the Balkans, thereby hitting the German armies in Russia from behind and preventing collapse of the Soviet Union.[16]

His faith in airplanes as the key to victory showed the influence of his old friend, Charles Lindbergh. His view of the Middle East as key to the war showed the growing influence of the British officers with whom he spoke. More than that, it showed the influence of where he was physically. From Cairo you could see that the Middle East was the arena where German armies from Russia and Libya might meet, where the Japanese could meet the Germans. You could see that the Middle East was the middle of the world.

People are best deciphered by their contradictions. To the British, Fellers was a harsh ally, an intensely supportive adversary.

He did not make friends in Washington. Secretary of War Henry Stimson, army chief of staff George Marshall, and Major General Dwight Eisenhower, now head of the army's Operations Division, in charge of planning, all agreed: America must invade France and strike toward Germany as soon as possible. It must not give in to British wheedling to fight Germany elsewhere.[17] It did not help Fellers's case that Eisenhower and Fellers had served together under Douglas MacArthur in the Philippines in the 1930s. Fellers worshipped MacArthur. Eisenhower left despising him, with some venom left over for his acolyte.[18]

"Middle East is the responsibility of the British," Marshall finally, tersely answered Fellers. "At the present time accepted strategy precludes the diversion of materiel, personnel and shipping to the Middle East."[19]

UNLIKE CHURCHILL, MARGARET Storey did pay close attention to Kesselring's April 24 message. But it is not clear whether it got to her desk in Hut 4 by the next day, or if she only found it later, searching for more pieces of a puzzle.

Storey, the slight young woman in dark cardigans with the smoky voice who could speak many languages, had moved to Hut 4, home of the Naval Section of Enigma intelligence, in February. Her promotion may have partly been a consequence of Travis's advancement. Travis's personal assistant, Russell Dudley-Smith, the thin tall man with the rumpled uniform and horn-rimmed glasses, now had more administrative work and less time for making sure that British codes and ciphers were secure. Yet Bletchley Park's successes at breaking Axis ciphers were seeping into its commanders' nightmares, in which Germans and Italians were breaking British codes. If this was indeed happening, the echoes of decoded British information would show up in deciphered Axis signals. Someone had to look for echoes.

Storey, it seems, had shown a quickness that was wasted in the mechanical repetitiveness of her earlier job. (The few people who would remember her long afterward would describe her as "self-effacing," as "introspective," as "very intelligent," as having "daunting intelligence," "absolutely formidable intelligence," as having a "rat-trap of a mind" that retained everything she read or heard, as smoking incessantly, as "shy, very shy," as "the brain."[20]) Her new job title was "research specialist," responsible for sifting through decoded enemy naval messages for hints of Axis signal intelligence. Storey's mentor was Dudley-Smith, who would teach her how British code systems worked so that she could more easily spot evidence they had been compromised.

Storey took to the work. She was given more responsibility, or simply took it. By the spring she was dissecting all decoded messages, not just naval ones, for signs of enemy espionage. She analyzed whether the enemy source was a human agent, or a broken code, or traffic analysis, or something else. It's possible that she got her start working on army and air force Enigma messages when a Hut 3 air adviser or duty officer spotted Kesselring's message and asked her or Dudley-Smith to attack the problem.[21]

Or perhaps it was another message—one that an intercept operator took down and sent to Bletchley Park on the same day, but was only decrypted five days later, on April 29. It came from the German army headquarters in Europe and was addressed to the intelligence officer of the Panzerarmee Afrika—the Africa Armored Army, as Erwin Rommel's again-upgraded command was now named.

As part of an assessment of the situation in Malta, it said, "It is reported from a good source that the British will not be strong enough to justify an offensive before 1 June with the limited objective of taking Benghazi."[22]

In Hut 3, an army adviser or the duty officer added commentary before sending out a paraphrase under the brand-new label for Enigma intelligence, "Ultra."[23] This and Kesselring's message were apparently based on the same intelligence report, the comment said. But this one referred to the source as being "good" rather than "particularly reliable." The implicit question was: Why the difference?

There was one clue, handwritten at the bottom on an internal copy saved in Bletchley Park, absent from the copy given to Churchill and the paraphrase sent to Cairo. The notation was an abbreviation for "Chaffinch II." Chaffinch was Hut 6's name for three Enigma keys that the German army used in the Mediterranean region. The name, Welchman would recall, came from a "reddish-brown pencil that bore some resemblance to the color of a chaffinch's chest" and was used to mark the discriminants, the daily call letters, for the key. As the supply of new colors ran out, zoological names for keys became the rule. Chaffinch II linked the German army headquarters in Europe with Rommel's headquarters.[24]

For the first months of 1942, Hut 6 had no luck with Chaffinch.[25] Then someone figured out that messages sent in a German air force key for Africa, nicknamed Gadfly, were apparently being resent in Chaffinch keys. One day a piece of a short Gadfly message was decoded as "WEGEN SANDSTURMES AUF PANZERFRONT, "Because of sandstorms on the armored front . . . " The bombes were set up to test Chaffinch messages for these words. The test failed. Then someone in the Crib Room of Hut 6, the place where people strained their minds to think of what a message *might* say, suggested that the German code clerk had made a slip. Maybe it was *GANZER FRONT*, "the whole front."

The wheels turned, and the bombes found a Chaffinch key for that day, which produced more cribs, which unlocked it for more days. In April, the Chaffinch problem received just under a quarter of all the hours that the bombes ran, and they ran night and day. This was a sign that breaking Chaffinch was still tough, that most suggested cribs still failed, and that information flowing to and from Rommel was a top priority.

The week when the assessment from "a good source" was decoded, the Chaffinch II key was broken for only three days, two of them from previous weeks. Hence the message was decoded belatedly.[26]

The intelligence services of the German army and air force had both received the information, and they agreed that it was essential. But in the air force's message sent in Red, the source was called "particularly reliable"; in the army's message sent in Chaffinch, the source was "good."

Slowly, with prodigious effort, Gordon Welchman's team was beginning to read mail to and from Rommel's headquarters. In that mail came hints that Rommel was getting mail, indirectly, from Cairo.

GENERAL UMBERTO PIATTI owned a large estate in Cyrenaica. In one of those moments when Axis tanks were retreating and the British had not yet taken control, Berber nomads chopped down all his olive trees, turning the colonial groves back into grazing land. The *riconquista* hadn't stamped out all the embers of insurrection in Libya. They roared into flames when the chance came. Arabs and Berbers raided farms and drove out, or sometimes killed, Italian settlers.

Then the Italians came back. Piatti was not just a landowner; he was in charge of internal order in rear areas of Libya. He combined personal and professional vengeance. His methods included bombing nomads' herds and machine-gunning encampments. The Fascist Party's police force and the paramilitary Carabinieri carried out mass arrests and executions. For natives found guilty of helping the British raiders who came out of the desert, the method of punishment was to put steel butcher's hooks through victims' jaws, "hang them up, and leave them to die of shock."

After leaving Africa, Rommel would write a memoir called *War Without Hate*. In one place, he criticized "excesses" by Italian soldiers against local Arabs and rejected the use of mass reprisals against civilians.[27] In the winter of 1942, though, Italian Fascist officials in Libya were in touch with Rommel's headquarters about signs of Arab rebellion behind the lines. Speaking for Rommel, his officers told the Italians to crack down harder. One aide wrote that "the most drastic measures" were needed. Perhaps Rommel did not know or care about the specifics; perhaps his motivation was not hate but dispassionate efficiency. The distinctions would have escaped the men hanging from hooks.[28]

Mussolini concluded that the town-dwelling Jews of Libya were behind the attacks on colonial farmers in the countryside. He aimed his rage not just at Jews in Cyrenaica, who'd greeted the British as liberators from the race laws, but at all the Jews in Libya. Through the Ministry of Italian Africa, he issued a decree on February 7, 1942, to expel them to a concentration camp in the desert.[29]

It took time to organize. The Italian colonial authorities started with the Jews of small towns in Cyrenaica. In Barce, fifteen-year-old Rahamim Bukra heard rumors at the end of March, before the holiday of Passover. Bukra was from Benghazi, but when British bombing of the city had grown worse in 1941, his family had fled sixty miles east to Barce. There were a few hundred Jews in the town. After rumors came lists posted in the synagogue, every two weeks, of who would be next. Survivors would remember that forty people were packed onto each open truck, that there were eight or ten trucks in a convoy, that they traveled five days in the sun and slept outside in the desert cold at night, and that at the end they came to the camp at Giado in the desert highland 120 miles southeast of Tripoli.

Barbed wire surrounded the camp. Inside were long huts. Three hundred or more people were put in each hut—men, women, and children together. The water supply was meager. The inmates received between 100 and 150 grams of bread a day, and rarely any other food. Giado was not a death camp like those the Germans were beginning to operate in Europe. It was not built to exterminate its inmates. Neither, though, was it built to keep them alive.

In early May, the German consul in Tripoli wrote to the German ambassador in Rome. "Up to now, only 700 Jews have been concentrated in Giado," he reported. The process was slow because trucks were in short supply, he said. Implicit in that statement was the fact that amid Rommel's supply problems, trucks were sometimes being used, and drivers and fuel, to transport Jews to a concentration camp.

Transporting the Jews of Tripolitania was to come later, after Cyrenaica was emptied. But those with French citizenship or French colonial papers were already being expelled to Tunisia. Those with British papers were sent by ship to internment camps in Italy. Foreign citizenship had once been a form of protection for Jews in Libya. Now it was only a ticket to a different destination.

JOHN TILTMAN TRAVELED to America on an American troopship, squeezed into a cabin with eight large mail sacks full of Bletchley Park codebreaking materials—gifts to the US Navy's OP-20-G and the army's SIS, the Signal Intelligence Service. Part of his mission was to convince the two American agencies to merge, copying Britain's model. He gave up on this quickly. "The dislike of Jews prevalent in the U.S. Navy is a factor to be considered, as nearly all the leading Army cryptographers are Jews," he wrote. He was also supposed to convince the Americans that they should do all the work on Japanese codes and leave Enigma to Britain. His hosts accepted the part about a US monopoly on Japan. Post–Pearl Harbor, they were going all out to break the Japanese naval code they'd labeled JN-25. The navy people, though, were fiercely suspicious that Tiltman was keeping them in the dark about Enigma. An alliance did not translate into instant trust.

Tiltman stayed for a month with William Friedman and his wife, Elizabeth. Friedman had recovered enough from his Purple-induced breakdown to serve as an adviser, the old wise man, to SIS. In the evening, Tiltman and Friedman apparently took their minds off code-breaking by discussing ancient Hittite hieroglyphics. Tiltman's trip home was quicker. He got a lift on a B-24 Liberator bomber, which made a crash landing at full speed at an aerodrome in Scotland.[30] He survived. Henceforth, the channel between Bletchley Park and SIS ran between Tiltman and Friedman.

In early May, Denniston got a radiogram from Bletchley Park's outstation at Heliopolis, outside Cairo. At Heliopolis intercept operators listened for Axis radio signals too weak to reach Britain, and a codebreaking section solved the simpler, low-grade ciphers used by German and Italian units. The Heliopolis station forwarded any Enigma material picked up in the Middle East to Bletchley Park. It sent intercepted diplomatic traffic to Denniston's operation in London. Another intercept station operated in Palestine, at the British base at Sarafand southeast of Jaffa.

Sarafand, said the radiogram from Egypt, had intercepted conversations in cipher between the American embassies in Tehran and Jeddah, the diplomatic capital of Saudi Arabia. "Do you want any American traffic at all?" asked the director of the Heliopolis station, Colonel Freddie Jacob.

"We are not interested in American traffic," Denniston answered, "and do not want it at all."[31] Churchill had promised to stop eavesdropping on America. Denniston was very definite that the promise was real.

ELIAHU GOTTLIEB TALKED his way into the British army in February 1942, at a recruitment office in Haifa, on his third attempt. His story that time was that he was nineteen years old, that he had reached Palestine in 1938 on an illegal immigration boat, and that he'd had to leave his parents behind in Germany.

The part about being from Germany was true. He was seventeen. He'd been born in Berlin, where his name was Ernst. His parents had brought him to Palestine in November 1933. He'd tried signing up the first time in Jerusalem when the war broke out, soon after his fifteenth birthday. By his third try, he was better prepared. He brought a letter from the association of Jewish immigrants from Germany certifying his false biography.

That spring Gottlieb was in a training course for truck drivers at Sarafand when an officer came to recruit native German speakers for a new commando unit. Gottlieb and one other soldier signed up.[32] The officer was almost certainly Herbert Cecil Buck.

Captain Buck was twenty-four and had studied German at Oxford. At the end of 1941, near Gazala in Libya, he'd been taken prisoner. He escaped, stole a dead German officer's uniform, talked his way through encounters with Axis soldiers, and made it to British-held territory. His adventure demonstrated how easily one could move behind enemy lines with borrowed clothes and fluent German.[33]

By April, Buck was building the Special Interrogation Group, the SIG, a name falsely suggesting that the unit would question captured German soldiers. The recruits were "fluent German linguists . . . mainly Palestinians of German origin." (The writer used the common meaning of the word "Palestinians," which meant Jews when no further identification was given.) Some, like Maurice Tiefenbrunner, a twenty-six-year-old who had in fact reached Palestine on an illegal ship weeks before the war broke out, had already fought as commandos against Italy in East Africa. There weren't many of them. One captured German command car and two German three-quarter-ton trucks were requisitioned to take the entire SIG, otherwise known as Captain Buck's Group, into Libya.

Intelligence officer John Haselden, now at headquarters in Cairo, wrote to the head of an existing commando force. "For our various nefarious schemes," Haselden said, "we are particularly anxious to build up a stock of German and Italian accessories . . . such things as matches, notebooks, rations, etc." Collect them and bring them in from the desert, he asked. Two German prisoners of war who'd once been in the French Foreign Legion and professed to be anti-Nazis were recruited. At a base in Egypt, they trained the Jewish commandos to goose-step, sing German songs, drive captured German trucks, speak Panzerarmee Afrika slang, and rattle off their invented German identification.

Eliahu Gottlieb, fictional nineteen-year-old, was now a fictional Aryan soldier, with German matches and a photograph of a blonde girlfriend—actually a British woman soldier—in his pocket.

"Axis may attack Syria either by passage through Turkey or by seaborne invasion," said the report from Colonel Fellers, as paraphrased for President Roosevelt's war room. British intelligence sources told Fellers they did "not believe either of these operations probable."

Fellers disagreed. The Turks might indeed agree to let a German army through their territory. Moreover, "Brit prestige in Moslem Turkey has been lowered since the episode in Abdine [*sic*] Palace"[34]—that is, Lampson's coup.

Despite the optimism of his intelligence officers, Auchinleck also worried about his northern front, meaning Syria. In the face of Churchill's exasperated telegrams, Auchinleck would not move troops from Syria to Libya. If he attacked in the Western Desert, he considered, he might suddenly need to move planes from there to Syria. If he came to London to justify his near insubordination in person, it might be just at the moment when he needed to shift forces to the north. He believed he should be at his post, not off explaining himself.[35]

If German armored columns did come from the north, British planners had concluded, the most that could be done in the northern stretches of Syria would be to slow them down. Their goal would be the Suez Canal. To get there, they'd have to get through the mountains of southern Syria, Lebanon, and Palestine to the coast. Mountains favored fixed positions and foot soldiers. Tanks might be new, but the shape of the land was the same as when the Babylonians and Assyrians had come with chariots. On Mt. Carmel above Haifa, by April of 1942, rows of iron rails stuck upward at an angle from the hard earth to block tanks. Trenches zigzagged through the rocks. On high points where tourists might come in peace to look across the hilltops all the way to the sea, the earth had been flattened in semicircles for artillery pieces.

"Large areas of the defenses are tank-proof," a British defensive plan said. The exceptions included passes leading to the Jezreel Valley, as at Megiddo on the southern end of the Carmel range, on a route taken by the armies of empires since the time of the pharaohs. The plan's maps showed heavy fortifications around Megiddo—or Armageddon, as the name appears in New Testament Greek.

The British defensive plan was called Final Fortress of Palestine.[36] The apocalyptic tone may have been at least half intentional. "The Land of Israel [Palestine] . . . according to the prophetic vision, which the Christians believe even more than the Jews do, will one day be the final battlefield on which [the Devil] will be defeated. On the plain of Megiddo—precisely there!—the battle must take place," the Jewish Agency's Moshe Shertok said at a conference of Haganah militia commanders. "I have met [British] officers who believe this with a perfect faith," Shertok said.

Personally, Shertok added, he didn't claim that the current war would be decided in Palestine. But he did believe Britain's defense of the country would decide the fate of its Jews. He was pushing for Palestinian Jews to enlist in the British army.[37] The opposing view was strongest among the hard-left faction in the kibbutzim: Jews needed to build up their own independent military because "our interests and those of the [British colonial] regime are not the same. The regime might abandon us." So wrote Yisrael Galili, a leader of the Haganah and of the United Kibbutz Movement.[38] Behind this position lay both intense yearning for an army of one's own and a fierce inner battle about the British: they were the people fighting the Nazis; they were also the people who'd closed Palestine to Jews fleeing the Nazis.[39]

Galili had found his own British ally, though: Major General B. T. Wilson, the Special Operation Executive's "number one for Palestine." Wilson's job was to make sure that if the Nazis did conquer Palestine, a trained resistance would destroy roads and railway lines and ambush soldiers. High Commissioner Harold MacMichael's office had placed "a ban on any mention" to Arabs that the British were worried they might lose the country. So Wilson only worked with the SOE's established "Friends," the Palestinian Jews.

"The plan has been authorized by the gentiles," Galili wrote to his wife in late March. "A report says that there was a negative recommendation from police circles—casting doubt on the loyalty of the Jews. Nonetheless, even the high commissioner had to give his seal of approval." Wilson would fund the project, a detail that in typical SOE fashion he forgot to tell his Cairo office. The Palmah, the tiny full-time military force of the Jewish community in Palestine, created the year before, would provide the recruits. Wilson's money would allow it to double its strength to one thousand members. Galili was pleased that they would not wear uniforms, be sworn into the British army, or serve outside Palestine.[40]

The training camp opened at the end of April at Kibbutz Mishmar Ha'emek, less than five miles from Megiddo. From Nicholas Hammond, a Cambridge classics scholar who'd gone from hiking in prewar Greece to being the SOE's expert in detonating German ammunition dumps there, they learned sabotage. From the SOE's small-arms expert, Hector Grant-Taylor, they learned how to hold a pistol low, next to the belly, and to shoot so that what you saw, you hit. (Palmah fighters knew for a fact that Grant-Taylor had worked for the FBI against gangsters in the 1930s, and had led a commando raid in France in which he'd assassinated German officers. All this was false, but his ability to teach people to kill was real.) For the young Palmah recruits, the atmosphere was a near-erotic mixture of youth movement and underground, which alchemized into lifelong nostalgia the moment they left.[41]

According to one SOE document, 160 saboteurs were trained; according to another, 400.[42] According to Lieutenant Aubrey Eban, or Abba Eban as he was called in Hebrew, "The camp actually trained all of the Palmah's members." Eban had been a Cambridge fellow in Middle Eastern languages and an aide to Zionist leader Chaim Weizmann before he went into uniform. The army had sent him to Cairo for the mind-numbing work of censoring Arabic letters and newspapers. In early 1942, he wrote to Moshe Shertok, begging him to find a way to bring him out of Egypt. Very quickly, an SOE major called Eban into the organization's Cairo office. Eban was needed for delicate diplomacy: The SOE and Palmah more or less trusted each other. High Commissioner MacMichael's office and the Jewish Agency did not trust each other at all. Nor did the high commissioner trust the SOE. It was a medical disagreement: MacMichael was concerned with the long-term health of the British Empire, to which Jews trained in sabotage would not contribute. The SOE saw the empire as being on its deathbed; Jewish saboteurs were indicated as urgent treatment.

Among the Jews, the argument was nearly reversed: Galili was fixed on the long-term goal of Jewish independence, Shertok on coping with the immediate threat of extinction.

Eban was sent to Jerusalem, given a house on Bethlehem Road amid the well-off Arab burghers, and became the four-way liaison. Whatever number of Palmah irregulars were officially supposed to be trained at Mishmar Ha'emek, Eban "interpreted" this—as he put it—as the number who could be present at one moment. Everyone in the Palmah rotated through for explosives and pistol training. Mandatory police regularly arrested young Jewish men in civilian dress carrying guns; Eban got them out. Judging from the rest of his long diplomatic career, the British police were overwhelmed by the same upper-crust Eban mannerisms that infuriated the Hebrew-speaking socialists he was springing from jail.[43]

Besides cooperation with the SOE, Galili was promoting another proposal that spring: turning a "region around Haifa" into "a kind of Tobruk." Just as Tobruk had held out for months the year before while Rommel reconquered the rest of Libya, "Haifa-Tobruk" would hold out against a German invasion. Jewish fighters would defend it, as long as the British supplied the port from the sea. He suggested alternate names: "Haifa–Musa Dagh" and "Haifa-Masada." Musa Dagh was a mountain 240 miles north of Haifa on the Mediterranean coast, where thousands of Armenians had held out against Turkish forces during the 1915 genocide, until they were finally rescued by Allied ships. Masada was the mountain fortress in the Judean Desert where Jewish rebels resisted during the Great Revolt against the Roman Empire in the first century CE, finally committing mass suicide rather than surrender. Rediscovered, Masada had become the destination of dangerous pilgrimages by Zionist youth groups in the 1930s.[44]

The names marked a range of expectations for what Jews with guns could do against the Axis armies—from defiant hope of holding out, to a tragedy in which the only choice was how to die. Many of the leaders of the Haganah and Palmah would quickly remember the proposal as the community's concrete plan of action. The half million Jews of Palestine, or at least the hundred thousand of the Haifa area, would take refuge in the Carmel to determine their own fate. Memory transmogrified the British defenses of the Final Fortress into the groundwork for Masada on the Carmel. Yet, to be carried out, the plan depended on support that Britain never offered or considered giving. The memory was a defense of the mind against the horror of being defenseless.[45]

"ACCORDING TO A report from a good source," the German message said, the British Seventh Armored Brigade in Egypt was "apparently being reconstituted," meaning that for the moment it was out of action. The radiogram was sent to Rommel's headquarters, and intercepted by a British operator, on the morning of May 2.

Another message to Rommel, later that day, gave an "unconfirmed, general picture" of the location of troops who'd shipped out from Britain since December. At the end, if the reader was paying close attention, came two items with more solid confirmation. "According to a report from a good source," the British Tenth Armored Brigade in the Middle East was "presumably not in fighting condition," and Lieutenant General W. H. E. Gott was the new commander of the Thirtieth Armored Corps.[46]

The volume of Ultra intelligence from Hut 3 to Auchinleck's headquarters was rising. If anyone at the Grey Pillars complex in Cairo's Garden City noticed that the material from "a good source" was more accurate than the usual German reports on the location and condition of British units, there's no known evidence that word got back to Bletchley Park. The report, or the Hut 3 translation of it, did mistakenly identify William Gott's new command: it was the Thirteenth Corps, not the Thirtieth.[47]

A week passed. On May 9, Rommel's intelligence officer received a long radio message that began with two-month-old information: "A good source reports on March 2, 1942: Axis air force recently suffered from fuel shortage. The Germans have nine battalions [of] infantry . . . Rommel needs a further month's rest." The information appeared drawn from at least one detailed British intelligence document from Cairo.

The same message to Rommel said that the "good source" had reported on April 4 that the British had put down "continuous minefields" from the Libyan coast to Bir Hakeim, in the desert thirty miles southeast of Tobruk, and that British positions were "in part blasted out of the rock." Following that came the map coordinates of a series of British units and battle headquarters in Libya.[48]

The German message came in the Chaffinch II key, with which Hut 6 still struggled. It took two days to decode. On the third day, a paraphrase was encoded on Britain's own TypeX cipher machine and sent to Cairo. Strangely, despite the provocative questions the message raised, Stewart Menzies did not put it in one of the thin packets of Ultra material and decoded diplomatic cables that he delivered at least once a day to Winston Churchill. Judging from his behavior on later occasions, the most likely reason was that the MI6 chief understood that the Germans' good source represented a problem, and he preferred presenting problems to the prime minister along with their solutions.[49]

The message did, however, go immediately to the Naval Section in Hut 4, where Margaret Storey and Russell Dudley-Smith dissected Enigma messages looking for Axis espionage. It went in a file that—later, at least—was labeled "Bluebird." For the moment, all they could do was wait for more bluebirds to land, perhaps bearing evidence of where they had come from.[50]

2

MARE INCOGNITUM

May 1942. Bletchley Park-Cyrenaica-
Rome-Cairo-Gilf Kebir.

JUNE 1 WOULD be too late to save Malta. So Air Marshal Kesselring
had said.

What did he mean, though?

It was a riddle known to a very few people at Bletchley Park and in
Cairo and at the Joint Intelligence Committee in London, the experts
who were supposed to make sense daily for the chiefs of staff of all available secrets about the enemy. They received many clues from Ultra—
and yet not enough clues, because the most important decisions that
Hitler, Mussolini, and their generals made in conference rooms were
not sent by radio and because the decisions were evasive and ambiguous.

"No attempted air borne invasion of Malta is impending," an
anonymous analyst at Bletchley Park wrote early in May 1942. The
Germans had planned to take the island early in the year, the writer
deduced, but they'd had to keep more planes in Russia than they had
expected. They were likely to attack in Libya late in May. If they took
Tobruk, they would be able to route supply convoys from Greece to
Cyrenaica, keeping their ships out of range of planes from Malta. Then
they would prepare to invade Egypt the next winter.[1]

Kesselring had moved his battle headquarters to Derna in Libya, a Joint Intelligence Committee report noted. Artillery was being shipped to Rommel. The German air force was moving a unit of transport planes to Africa for dropping paratroops and pulling gliders. This signaled an airborne attack on Tobruk, the committee's experts concluded. All the signs of a German offensive had begun after April 24, the day of Kesselring's report from the "particularly reliable source" about an expected British operation. Ergo, the source's information had set off "hasty planning and preparation" for Rommel to move before Auchinleck could.[2]

From Cairo, Air Marshal Arthur Tedder sent a semi-dissent. The demands of the Russian front would prevent a German invasion of Egypt this summer, the Royal Air Force commander in the Middle East estimated. But Hitler wanted a "headline success" in the Mediterranean. He believed Rommel would indeed attack in Cyrenaica—as the prelude for landings from the air and sea to take Malta.

The situation on the island was desperate, and British commanders in Egypt were evaluating a plan to send a supply convoy from Alexandria, Tedder wrote. "It is not my habit to be alarmist," he added, but the attempt would involve "certainty of very heavy losses with only slender chances of affecting anything useful for Malta."[3]

On May 26, the Hut 3 research room tried once more to make sense of the hints. The expected Axis operation had not yet begun. But Enigma messages showed that it would include Italian marines. A flotilla of landing craft was being assembled at Tripoli. General Ugo Cavallero, head of the Italian Supreme Command, had asked for two German ferries, of a type that had been part of the aborted plan to invade Britain. Hut 3's analysts expected an amphibious attack "behind our lines in Libya or even Egypt." The Axis codename for the operation was "Hercules." The codename, suggested the analysts, could allude to Hercules's mythical "exploits in Egypt."[4]

THIS IS WHAT intercepted radio messages did not reveal:

Rommel had come to Hitler's eastern front headquarters in March to ask for more forces. General Franz Halder, the army chief of staff, turned him down and did not bother to note Rommel's visit in his diary. Halder filled his notebooks with details about the battles in the Soviet Union. By his listing, over a million German soldiers had been killed, wounded, or captured since Barbarossa began.[5]

Erwin Rommel did not forgive being slighted. With "a few more divisions" he could win "victories in the Near East, which in their strategic and economic value" would surpass conquests in southern Russia, he believed.[6] Nonetheless, Rommel made plans to attack in Cyrenaica, hoping to take Tobruk. He would make his move in June—after the invasion of Malta. Cavallero and Kesselring were planning the airborne and seaborne landings on the island. It was to be mainly an Italian effort, with German help. The codename: Operation Hercules.

On April 22, Galeazzo Ciano wrote that Hitler had given Kesselring approval for Hercules. Two days later Kesselring sent his message that June would be "too late" for Britain to save the island.

The Italian Supreme Command produced plans, and doubts, and demands for help on a scale the Germans rejected. Delays resulted. Cavallero "hopes to derive a great deal of personal glory from this operation," Ciano wrote. "But I believe he will never go through with it."[7]

Yet decisions had to be made, quickly. The "particularly reliable source" had informed German intelligence that the British would attack in Libya in June. By summer, a large part of the German air force in the Mediterranean would be moved to the eastern front for the new offensive there. Rommel wanted to move up his attack in Cyrenaica; Cavallero wanted to delay Hercules.

Mussolini went to Salzburg at the end of April to meet Hitler. "Hitler talks, talks, talks," Ciano wrote. "Mussolini suffers, since he is in the habit of talking and, instead, practically has to keep quiet."

Still, they came to a decision: Rommel would attack late in May to preempt Auchinleck. His goal would be to take Tobruk and to push the British back to the Egyptian border. After that would come Hercules. Then Rommel could prepare to take Egypt.

Hitler promised support for Hercules, and immediately had doubts. He remembered the cost of taking Crete. Kesselring received a phone call telling him not to do any more to plan for Hercules. He ignored those instructions. Axis radio messages confused British experts because they accurately reflected confusion and conflict within the Axis high command.[8]

"Every war is rich in particular facts," master theoretician Carl von Clausewitz wrote in his *On War*, "while at the same time each is an unexplored sea, full of rocks which the general may have suspicion of, but which he has never seen with his eye."[9] Each Enigma message marked more rocks in the sea of Axis plans and disputes. And still, it was *mare incognitum*.

JUST BEFORE HE left for Salzburg, Ciano got a letter from Rashid Ali al-Gailani and Hajj Amin el-Husseini.[10]

Gailani, the deposed prime minister of Iraq, and Husseini, the former mufti of Jerusalem, had escaped Baghdad a year before, then fled Iran when Britain occupied that country. By November 1941, both were in Berlin, where they became rival leaders in the small circle of Arab expatriates. Husseini grandiosely claimed to speak for the "entire Arab people," who wanted, all of them, "to enter into the struggle on the side of the Axis powers," as he wrote to Nazi foreign minister Joachim von Ribbentrop. Gailani, by some accounts, was slightly more modest, claiming only to speak for the country he no longer led. They trafficked in delusions; they also seemed to have convinced themselves that Berlin and Rome were interested in liberating nations.

Husseini had quickly managed to get an audience with Hitler, at which he asked the Führer to declare publicly his backing for "the independence and unity of Palestine, Syria and Iraq." Such a promise, Husseini said, would ease his "work of secretly organizing the Arabs" for rebellion at the right moment.

Hitler responded that both the capitalists of Britain and the communists of the Soviet Union were serving the goals of the Jews, so the war was in essence "a battle between National Socialism and the Jews." He promised Husseini only that this battle included "the struggle against the Jewish national home in Palestine" and that once the German armies in Russia pushed south through the Caucasus mountains into the Middle East, "Germany's objective would then be solely the destruction of the Jewish element residing in the Arab sphere under the protection of British power."[11]

Myths would be created about this meeting. In reality, Hitler gave nothing but a pledge to do what he was already doing—murdering

Jews in whatever territory came under Nazi control—and a preview of Germany's strategy of reaching the Middle East via Russia and Iran.

The regime did, however, treat Husseini as a useful collaborator and radio propagandist. It gave him a large living allowance and an office. The SS assigned him a liaison and security officer, a thirty-year-old *obersturmführer* (first lieutenant) named Hans-Joachim Weise.

Husseini and Gailani found an ally of sorts in the Japanese government. "The Japanese have proposed a tripartite declaration on the independence of India and Arabia," Ciano wrote in his diary in mid-April. "Initial reactions in Berlin are unfavorable."[12] Japan's strategy for overrunning the southern rim of Asia even while fighting America depended in part on stirring local national movements to rebel. Promising to drive out European colonial empires, Japan would build its own.[13]

So Husseini and Gailani saw the Hitler-Mussolini meeting in April 1942 as an opening to press their demand. "We request the Italian government to render all possible assistance to the Arab countries which are at present under the tyranny of Britain" and "to recognize the sovereign rights and independence of these countries," Husseini and Gailani's letter to Ciano said. The German foreign minister, Ribbentrop, got a parallel letter addressed to his government. The Japanese ambassador in Rome radioed the text to Tokyo—which meant that Menzies was able to hand Churchill a decoded and translated copy.

Ciano wrote back to the exiled Palestinian and Iraqi in early May that "the freedom and independence of the above-mentioned Arab nations are aims of the Italian government." Yet he also said that the letter had to remain secret. This was not what the two exiled Arabs had sought.

Japan's ambassador in Rome explained to his foreign ministry in Tokyo—and, unknowingly, to Churchill: The Duce and the Führer had discussed the subject at Salzburg. They'd agreed that it was the wrong time for a public declaration because "it would run the risk of not arousing any particular reactions" in the Arab world. Put differently, they did not have confidence in Husseini's claim that the Arab world was soaked in inflammable pro-Axis emotion; they did not believe that their promise of independence would ignite rebellions.

The Arabs would remain passive, which would be a victory for British propaganda. Perhaps later, when the Axis armies were near enough to the Arab heartland to support uprisings, it would be time to say something.[14]

Amid the disagreements about Axis strategy in the Middle East, the SS put its confidence in Rommel: that he would soon reach Cairo and Alexandria, and then Palestine. In May, Obersturmführer Hans-Joachim Weise got new orders: He was to set up an *Einsatz-kommando*—an SS special operations command for mass murder—for Rommel's army.[15]

IN THE THIRD week of May, Gordon Welchman's team was still straining to crack Chaffinch II, the Enigma key used between Rommel's headquarters and the German high command. For nearly a third of the hours that the bombe wheels spun that week, they were testing possible cribs for that one key. The successes added up to the Chaffinch II settings for one day of that week and for four days in earlier weeks.[16] A message intercepted on May 12 was decoded only on May 17. It came from the high command for Rommel's intelligence officer and described the proportion of tracer shells that the British used in their antitank and antiaircraft guns. The information, it said, came from "a good source."[17]

On May 19, Welchman's team belatedly found the Chaffinch II settings for April 30. Among the nearly three-week-old messages that could now be deciphered was another one from the high command for Rommel's intelligence officer. It opened with the words "Good source reports." Then came a string of dates, each with its own packet of intelligence.

On February 19, the good source had said that among the British forces in the Middle East, there was a "need of tools" for American tanks, and such a "critical" shortage of spare parts that four US-made tanks had been taken apart to provide parts for others. American tanks carried eighty-one rounds of 75-mm ammunition and eighty-four rounds of 37-mm ammo, the source had reported in March. To make room for more shells, the machine gun that the tanks normally carried had been removed.

On March 28, the source gave the "assumed" positions of four Axis divisions in Libya. It did not say who was assuming this; the implication was that these were high-level British assessments.

"There are not enough British troops in North Africa to guarantee its safety," the source had reported on March 29—information that would presumably have pleased Rommel were it not for an update from April 24: "If the German troops are not reinforced, the British are strong enough to prevent the capture of the Nile Delta."[18] These points, too, looked like assessments from somewhere within General Headquarters in Cairo.

The intercepted message containing all these reports was a grab bag: nuts-and-bolts information from tank workshops together with strategic assessments. The obvious question was the identity of the source. A subtler riddle was why all this had come at the same time. An even deeper mystery was what else might have come from this source but not been intercepted by British wireless operators or decoded at Bletchley Park.

Menzies avoided such queries from Churchill; the message did not go into his packet for the prime minister.

It did go into the Bluebird file in Hut 4. It gave Margaret Storey and Russell Dudley-Smith more clues and more questions. Most of all, it shouted the need to find answers, quickly.[19]

In Egypt, Colonel Bill Liardet's regiment had fifty American tanks when he took command on May 15. Twenty were the older model that the British had named Stuarts, after a Confederate general of the Civil War; thirty were the newer Grant tanks, designed in a rush when the United States belatedly started preparing for war, manufactured in equal haste, and freshly delivered.

The regiment "was in a pretty untrained state, rather dirty and undisciplined," Liardet would later write to his wife. The men had no experience with US tanks. Liardet "set about the most intensive training" and tightening of discipline. But he had to "teach them an entirely new technique, of which I was none too certain myself," and had only till June 1, when they were supposed to move from their base near the Nile to the front in the Western Desert.[20]

Lance Corporal Ron Hurlock wrote to his father from the Western Desert on May 25. He was a signalman, which meant that when the time came he'd go forward in a wireless van with three other men. "I chose this, as I thought Jerry would hardly waste an expensive bomb on [a van], whereas a tank is a good prize" for the enemy. He told his father he'd finally received a letter from his wife, sent over two months before. "It's short, and not terribly loving, and if there is anything to drive a man scatty out here, it's that," he wrote. "Jerry, the sand, the sun, diseases, insects, cannot scare me half as much as she."[21]

E. H. Wilmott's truck was dug into the sand near Bir Hakeim at the southern end of the British line in Libya. Bir Hakeim itself was held by General Pierre Koenig's Free French brigade of about four thousand men, including recruits from France's sub-Saharan African colonies and soldiers of the Foreign Legion.

Wilmott was in the Twenty-Second Armored Brigade. On May 26, he was due to get a week's leave, but his place on the truck out was taken by another man who was being sent for a training course with the Grant tank. "I wasn't worried," he wrote in his diary. No one said anything to make him expect leaves would be canceled; he assumed he'd get his soon.[22]

ON MAY 21, at Bletchley Park, a message came into Hut 6 in an Enigma key nicknamed Primrose, only recently broken. Luftwaffe supply units used it. If any trucks belonging to four supply groups were still in Tripoli, it said, they must "be loaded and sent off immediately, even during the night." They had to reach Derna, on the far side of Libya, near the front. "Latest permissible time of arrival [is] evening of 25th May," the message said. Hut 3 sent the information to Cairo on the night of May 22.[23]

Another German message, deciphered on May 24, said that one thousand armor-piercing shells, 75-mm caliber, would be "delivered to Derna in five or six aircraft as from 26th May." In the Watch Room at Hut 3, an air or army adviser added a comment: this was "strong evidence" that German tanks were being outfitted with a new gun. The adviser did not note the urgency involved in sending ammunition by air; this was obvious.[24]

A message in Chaffinch II came in on May 22 but took four days to decipher. The Italian Supreme Command, it said, argued that three infantry battalions newly arrived in Africa needed several weeks' training before they went into battle. Rommel answered "that for the known projected operation, not one single man can be dispensed with, let alone three battalions." Hut 3 sent the information to Cairo on May 26.[25]

Hundreds of items of intelligence now flowed weekly from Bletchley Park to the British commanders in chief in Egypt. Most dealt with Italian naval convoys or the daily reports of the German air force. The few that came from the German army did not tell when the "known projected operation" would begin, or where, or what the plan was. They would shine brilliantly with meaning—when seen in hindsight.

"GROPPI'S ICE CREAM is only ONE in Egypt made by the American process. It is pasteurised," said a full-page ad for Cairo's most famous cafe in the new guidebook, which was just the right size for a soldier's uniform pocket. The Fleurent restaurant advertised its American bar; La Taverne Française claimed that *it* was Cairo's most "famous American bar and grill room." The Metro advertised that it was "Cairo's only air conditioned cinema." The Marconi Radiotelegraph Company provided a map of downtown so you could find its building.

The guidebook included pages of useful phrases in Egyptian Arabic so that the swarms of soldiers on leave and the countless staff officers stationed in the city could learn to say "Do you understand?" and "Go away," and "You, boy, go and get me a cab," and "Barman, beer." A section titled "The Casino," which meant any nightclub, included the Arabic for "blonde" and "brunette" and for "Waiter, are these girls Egyptian?" and "What's your name?" and "What a beautiful name!"[26]

On the evening of May 23, two men arrived in the city on the train from Assiut in Upper Egypt.[27] Both had light hair and pale eyes. The short one with the slight build wore a moustache. That was Johann Eppler. The tall one, Heinrich Sandstede, known as Sandy, was clean-shaven. Only that morning they'd awoken in the desert. At mid-day they had said farewell to Almasy. They had a suitcase with a wireless set in it and the clothes they wore, as well as six hundred Egyptian pounds and three thousand British pounds. Combined, this was the equivalent of what Hermione Ranfurly would have received as twelve years' salary at the SOE's generous rates or thirty years' salary for newly commissioned cipher officer June Watkins. Despite his Egyptian connections, though, Eppler was apparently unaware that British banknotes were not legal tender in Egypt and would have to be exchanged on the black market.

They needed to find a room. Either because the hotels were packed or because it suited their tastes, they ended up at the Pension Nadia, a brothel. They stayed there three nights while hunting for lodging.

(Far away to the southwest, Laszlo Almasy and the three men still with him drove their captured Fords back through the pass across Gilf Kebir. On the far side, they met a convoy of the Sudan Defense Force, the colony's small military, on its way to Kufra with ammunition and other supplies for the garrison there. Unable to evade the Sudanese, Almasy drove right past them, saluting as he went, as if leading an unexpected British patrol. The Sudanese saluted in return, and Almasy disappeared into the desert and headed back for Jalo oasis.[28])

A real estate agent helped Eppler and Sandy find rooms with a Frenchwoman named Madame Therese, for which they paid seventy-five pounds as three months' rent. Sandstede listed another fifty pounds in his diary as a signing fee, but that was just to cover up their other spending. The flat didn't work out: it turned out that Therese was a prostitute; both clients and police kept turning up. Among the visitors was a man named Albert Wahda, unreliably reported to be Therese's pimp, who recognized Eppler as Hussein Gaafar, his classmate from the lycée, the French-language high school, in Cairo.[29]

Sandy bought a radio set and a roof antenna. The radio was needed as a cover story for his need for the antenna, which he hooked up to his wireless transmitter. He began regularly sending out his call letters, "HGS," and waiting to hear back "WBW" from Waldemar Weber, the Abwehr wireless man whom Almasy had left at Rommel's headquarters in the desert.

No one answered. Sandy concluded that the high buildings around their flat were blocking reception. They'd have to find another place to live.

"WE HAVE INFORMATION that [an] enemy intelligence unit may shortly be established in area [of] Gilf Kebir," said the "most secret" cable from General Headquarters Middle East in Cairo to the British general in command of the Sudan Defense Force.

The information came from the Abwehr message that had caught translator Jean Alington's eye at Bletchley Park. She'd read it two days after it was sent from Tripoli, which was two days after Almasy reported his position at the desert plateau on his way into Egypt. After Alington translated the four-day-old intelligence, it took another three days for the information to get to Cairo, possibly because the MI6 officer in charge of distributing decoded Abwehr material did not like to share it with anyone outside his own agency.

The "most secret" cable to Khartoum was sent on May 25. It said that the Sudanese forces should organize a search and try to capture the enemy unit. By then, Eppler and Sandy were staying at the Pension Nadia; Almasy was crossing back through Gilf Kebir on his way to Jalo. Several days later, an RAF pilot left Cairo for Khartoum in a small reconnaissance plane. His assignment was to help comb the desert for an Axis intelligence group.[30]

THE AXIS COLUMNS rolled forward just where Auchinleck had expected: on the coastal road toward Tobruk, and further south at the center of the British line stretching into the desert. It was the afternoon of May 26.

Those were feints.

The British had laid down one million landmines along their front; they had dug into the rocks. But it was impossible to build fortifications all the way across the desert when, as Ralph Bagnold had written, it was an emptiness as large as India.[31] Their line ended, and beyond that was open country.

The moon was two-thirds full that night. To the south, past Bir Hakeim, beyond the far end of the British line, Rommel rode forward at the front of his tanks and the columns of trucks carrying men and supplies. Rather than batter his way through the British wall, he'd again chosen to go around. The tactic was a gamble; it created a long, vulnerable supply route. But in the morning, the weight of his army was plunging northward behind the British line.[32]

"The British were completely surprised," Lieutenant Colonel James Fry reported from the desert. Bonner Fellers's assistant attaché said British officers told him they had less than half an hour's warning before their units came under fire. "As a result the Third Indian Brigade was practically destroyed, the Seventh Armored Division . . . was completely overrun, and the Fourth Armored Brigade lost 50% of its tanks."[33]

Rommel also slammed into surprises. He had never faced Grants before. Even for a tank, the machine was ugly—lopsided, too tall, too visible. The US Army had wanted a 75-mm gun able to shoot armor-piercing shells at long range, but American factories weren't ready to build a turret for a gun that big, so the gun was stuck on a platform on the right front of the hull, and the whole tank had to turn toward the target. On top, off center, was a rotating turret with a smaller gun. Seen from the front, the Grant resembled a cubist sculpture in steel of a rhinoceros, with its menacing big horn and the smaller horn above it. But it was fast and deadly.

"Our plan to overrun the British forces behind the Gazala line had not succeeded," Rommel wrote of the battle's first day. "The principal cause was our underestimate of the strength of the British armored divisions. The advent of the new American tank had torn great holes in our ranks." What prevented a rout, Rommel would write, was that General Ritchie, commander of the Eighth Army, sent his tank units into battle in small numbers, never in a united action. That prevented them from overwhelming Rommel's reduced forces.

Meanwhile, the Free French ranged out from Bir Hakeim, attacking his truck convoys. Rommel's main forces, including his surviving tanks, were on the east of the British minefields. His stores of fuel and ammunition were on the west side. In the first day's confusion, Rommel got separated from most of his own staff. By the second day of fighting, his immediate goal was to open a supply route.[34]

On the fourth day, the Axis forces had opened two gaps in the minefields. So Ritchie wrote in his daily situation report, sent in cipher to Auchinleck. "Seems definite," the Eighth Army commander added, "that enemy intends withdrawing west through these gaps."

He was mistaken. Rommel intended to widen the gaps, bring fuel and ammunition through them, and keep fighting.[35]

In the midst of this chaos, British troops captured two Germans in a van with an antenna north of Bir Hakeim on May 27. One of the men was Waldemar Weber, the wireless operator assigned to relay Eppler and Sandy's messages as part of Operation Condor. The other man was his driver. The two had apparently gotten separated from Rommel's staff.

Before he was taken prisoner, Weber managed to discard his notebook, two letters, and the plan for a communications network listing six wireless addresses. They included his own, as well as "Salam" for Almasy and "Condor" for Eppler and Sandstede. The letters, from the German consul in Tripoli, were to be sent by radio to Almasy. A Long Range Desert Group patrol found Weber's papers a couple days later.

The LRDG patrol returned to its base at Kufra oasis a week later with the papers of the enemy communications net. Weber and his driver, though identified as Abwehr men, were held for three weeks before they were interrogated.[36] The puzzle pieces were too scattered to create a picture of what Almasy was up to. In Sudan, the search for him continued.

The arrangements for Operation Condor had assigned Weber alone to answering Sandy and Eppler.[37] By the time they rented their flat, there was no one in the desert to respond to Condor's call letters from Cairo.

A LEGEND WOULD grow up around Operation Condor and about Johann Eppler as an adventurer, ladies' man, and "spy of exceptional daring and competence." In that legend, neither Weber nor his driver spoke a word of English, but they were carrying an English-language copy of the best-selling novel *Rebecca* by Daphne du Maurier when they were captured. The discovery of this incongruity would be essential to the legend.[38]

In reality, Weber and his driver had both been born into the sizeable German community of Palestine and had grown up under British rule. Weber spoke some English; the driver was fluent in the language. For the latter to have had a book in English would have been unremarkable.

There's a seed of fact in the legend: Weber should indeed have had a novel in English, meant to serve him, Sandstede, and Eppler as the shared key to their Abwehr cipher. But no mention of it appears in the British document describing Weber's capture or in the reports on the papers found in the desert.[39] Either Weber managed to dispose of it separately, or it did not attract his captors' attention. The book that sparked the hunt for Condor was not *Rebecca*. But the people who wove the Condor legend knew nothing about Enigma, or Bletchley Park, or Jean Alington having read Bagnold's *Libyan Sands*.

HANS-JOACHIM WEISE HAD served only briefly as head of the nascent *Einsatzkommando* for the Middle East when he got word that a higher-ranking SS officer was to command the unit: Walther Rauff. Weise would serve under him, recruiting Arab collaborators.

Rauff had been working in Prague. His patron, Reich Security Main Office chief Reinhard Heydrich, had been given the additional post of Nazi viceroy of the Protectorate of Moravia and Bohemia. Rauff went with him to institute a reign of terror in the protectorate, the remainder of Czechoslovakia. On May 27, two SOE-trained Czechs hurled a bomb into Heydrich's car in Prague and mortally wounded him.

Rauff was unexpectedly available. The engineer of the gas wagons would take charge of murdering Jews in the lands that Rommel would conquer.[40]

"THE RAF IN Egypt is making no use of the technical courses established by the Americans" on how to repair US airplanes, the message said. Because the RAF crews lacked training, they were unable to locate or fix problems in instruments from the Sperry Corporation, or in the engines, or anywhere else in the Kittyhawk fighters that the United States had sent to Egypt. "The result is a dreadful waste of equipment materials." There were requisitions on an "abnormal scale" for spare parts. Until they arrived, "the Kittyhawk is grounded."

All of this and more, the message said, had come from a report on April 16 by "a particularly reliable source."

The message was sent in the Red key of Enigma. The intelligence officer at Luftwaffe headquarters in Libya, to which it was addressed on May 29, was undoubtedly pleased by the news.

Intercepted in England, decoded in Hut 6, translated the next afternoon in Hut 3, hand-delivered by Stewart Menzies, it made Winston Churchill much less happy. "What action?" he wrote in red at the bottom and handed it back to the MI6 chief.[41]

As Menzies understood it, the prime minister's question was whether the report was true and what was being done about it. How the Germans knew was a secondary issue.

For Russell Dudley-Smith and Margaret Storey, German intelligence was the main issue. The message fit the Bluebird pattern.[42] The report was lengthy and specific, including the name of the manufacturer of the aircraft instruments. It was precisely dated. The Germans, it seemed, again regarded their source not just as "good," but as "particularly reliable." Or perhaps they were talking about more than one source. Yet they'd waited six weeks to forward the information. Why?

3

SPIES, EVERYWHERE

June 1-9, 1942. Bletchley Park-Cairo-Bir Hakeim-Rome.

FIELD MARSHAL ALBERT Kesselring sent word on the last day of May: the rail line that the British were building would reach to within fifteen miles of Tobruk by June 1. "The British supply position in North Africa" on the eve of the renewed battle "was considerably better than in November," when the previous British offensive had begun.

This intelligence was two weeks old, according to Kesselring's message, having come from a "particularly reliable source" on May 17. Still, it had immediate value, especially the final words: "German air attacks on locomotives caused considerable damage." A railroad was the most efficient means to move massive supplies. The message confirmed that air attacks against it were effective. The day after Kesselring sent this, Auchinleck had the text in English, as did Churchill.[1]

Evidence soon followed that the Germans were starting to get much fresher information. "A good source" reported that at noon on May 30, General Koenig's Free French held an area that extended at least twelve miles north of Bir Hakeim. The location was given in coordinates taken from a British military map. The British had 360 tanks left, the source said. An addendum from the German high command

noted, "The British seem to believe firmly in the withdrawal of the
Axis forces."

The message was sent in the German army's Chaffinch II key of
Enigma on June 1. By June 2, the key was broken, the intelligence
passed on.[2] The translator and army adviser in the Watch Room at Hut
3 did not have a basis to judge just how good the source actually was.
They received no information from the front but what came through
Enigma. This prevented any unconscious bending of what they read
from the German messages to fit what they knew from British sources.[3]
Dudley-Smith and Storey probably worked under the same constraint.

In Cairo, Claude Auchinleck or his intelligence chief may have
noted that the map location for the Free French precisely matched
General Neil Ritchie's situation report on the afternoon of May 30,
the same one in which he assessed that the enemy intended to withdraw westward.[4]

More likely, both were under too much pressure to line up a snippet of information from Ritchie with another from Hut 3, especially as
they were getting ever more material from the latter source. Bletchley
Park was reaching a pace of deciphering over eleven hundred Enigma
messages daily.[5] A large portion were from North Africa and the Mediterranean. Hut 6 was beginning to break a key it called Phoenix, used
between Rommel and the divisions and corps under his command.
A German officer who methodically sent a message every two hours
saying, "No change," followed by his code name, provided a crib for
Phoenix that worked again and again.[6]

Reg Parker, the Hut 6 staffer who watched out for recycled keys,
made an astounding find: the German maker of the keys was entirely
reusing each month's settings for the minor air force key called Primrose. The next month they became the settings for the key called Scorpion. The only change that the anonymous key meister made was to
shuffle the days, so that the Primrose setting for May 10 might be the
Scorpion setting for June 1, or June 22, or some other day. When the
first Scorpion message of the day came into Hut 6, it took just a few
minutes to figure out which day's Primrose settings from the previous
month would unlock it.

Scorpion was used by the German air force officers who served
as liaisons to army units. One way in which the German military was

years ahead of the British was in the tight coordination between the German army and air force. The liaison officers sent the air force constant updates on the condition and plans of army units. The remarkable reuse of old Primrose keys for Scorpion meant that their updates could be read as soon as they arrived in Bletchley Park.

Scorpion "gives hour by hour current information about Axis front lines . . . and intentions of ground forces," along with air force plans, an early June memo said. The real problem with Scorpion, and even more so with Phoenix and Chaffinch, was that the transmitters sending them were meant for short distances. Intercept operators in Alexandria managed to hear Scorpion. To eavesdrop on Phoenix, operators had to be deployed at Eighth Army battle headquarters in Cyrenaica, or near Mersa Matruh in Egypt. They took down what they heard on paper. Light planes carried the paper to Heliopolis east of Cairo, where the messages were typed into Britain's own cipher machine, TypeX, to be radioed to Bletchley Park. Messages that could be cracked in an hour were taking two days to reach Bletchley Park. If they could be moved faster, Auchinleck and Ritchie would practically be sitting in Rommel's tent.[7]

The Germans could easily have noticed their own security mistakes if they'd had less faith in the statistical impossibility of cracking Enigma, Gordon Welchman would write.

He concluded, "We were lucky."[8]

THE GERMANS ALSO had luck with their enemy's codes. Margaret Storey began to list as much of it as she could find in the deciphered messages, week by week. The title at the top of her first effort, at the start of June, indicated that she'd been assigned only to look for signs of success by the Germany navy's signal intelligence agency, the B-Dienst. After all, she worked in Hut 4, the Naval Section.

But the limitation made no sense. So Storey listed every hint of enemy intelligence she could find. She noted the work of a German station that tracked how much wireless traffic there was between British ships. She noted a report from Lieutenant Seebohm's battlefield listening station in Cyrenaica that mapped out the relations between British units based on their chatter. She pointed to the intelligence apparently coming from a German undercover agent in Gibraltar who had seen an aircraft carrier that he surmised was taking fighter planes to Malta.

Storey's reports say nothing about how she gathered her material or evaluated the sources of the information. Her knowledge of languages and occasional corrections of translations suggest that she combed through large numbers of deciphered messages, at least some of them in the original languages.

She left no letters or diaries telling how she felt. If she left any hidden message of her state of mind in her reports, the code has yet to be broken. If we can judge at all from the memories of others who worked at Bletchley Park's most analytical tasks, the jobs that demanded reason and intuition, she felt driven, exhausted, excited, aware that much depended on her and not nearly aware just how much, and—as Gordon Welchman described his feelings—was having the greatest fun that life would ever offer.

In the category "German agents," Storey listed the message about the British railway to Tobruk and the bombing of locomotives. The message about the Free French position and the British view that Rommel was trying to withdraw she likewise attributed to an agent.

This was a reading of clues, not a certainty. But the clues did in fact point toward an agent. The information came from someone who could compare the British supply situations in November and May, and who knew how many tanks the Eighth Army still had after four days of battle. It came from someone who was privy to commanders' private assessments of the enemy, the kind they gave in conversations in closed offices and did not necessarily feel certain enough to send to London. The information had the fingerprints of someone highly placed or very well connected in British headquarters in Cairo.[9]

ALBERT WAHDA DIDN'T know that his old school friend Hussein Gaafar had been in Germany. Hussein said he'd returned to Cairo after living for five years on a farm near Assiut. Nor did Albert know that Hussein was also Johann Eppler, Abwehr agent. He did know that Hussein and his British friend Peter, or Sandy, enjoyed spending freely on themselves and others at Cairo's nightspots.[10]

Albert took Hussein and Sandy to the rooftop garden at the Continental Hotel. The accountant there agreed to change some of their British cash for them on the black market. He gave them forty-seven piasters for a British pound; the official exchange rate was ninety-seven piasters. They asked the headwaiter to introduce them to a girl. After the evening's show, he brought the belly dancer, Hekmet. She lived in one of the tony houseboats moored along the Nile, and invited them to stay there for a night. Later they would insist that none of them had slept with her. She had a lover, a British officer, who was away from town. He'd left a suitcase on the houseboat. Inside, it would later emerge, was a map of the defenses of Tobruk.

Eppler would later be overheard telling Sandy he'd never thought to open the suitcase, as "that was a bit dangerous." Sandy's later claim to have seen the map was almost certainly fiction. In any case, the map would have been of little use to Rommel. It showed the Italian defenses from before the first British conquest of the town early the year before.

They liked the houseboat, though, and found one to rent for themselves with two decks, well appointed with chintz furniture, woodwork painted pale green, and Egyptian wall hangings. It was moored near the Kit-Kat Club, another nightspot they liked, and facing Gezira Island, where the city's best sporting club was. They were spending twenty Egyptian pounds a night. As they would explain the expenses, they were lubricating British officers with liquor so that they would say more than they should.

Eppler and Sandy also had names provided by Almasy of well-connected contacts. At the top of the list was Prince Abbas Halim, a cousin and rival of Farouk. Abbas Halim shared Almasy's injured aristocratic pride and his love of airplanes. In the previous war he'd first fought for Germany, then become a pilot for the Ottoman air force. Pro-Axis but in conflict with the king, he was an unlikely candidate for access to any military secrets. Eppler and Sandy were, however, risk-averse spies. They picked up in Cairo conversations that the prince was "too suspect" to risk contacting. This was true; the prince's name had only recently appeared in the "most secret" weekly security report put out by Security Intelligence Middle East.[11]

Sandy hid his wireless set underneath a gramophone turntable in a cabinet on the houseboat. He sent out his call letters and got no answer, though reception was no longer blocked by buildings. The transmitter still did not work, he concluded. They continued to spend their evenings and money at the Continental and the Kit-Kat Club.

IN GARDEN CITY, on the other side of the river and a mile or two from where the houseboat was moored, Auchinleck's intelligence chief composed a "most secret" update on the search for the enemy intelligence unit operating around Gilf Kebir. He read the evidence through the lens that was familiar to him: his own army's Long Range Desert Group. "Hauptman Graf Laszlo von Almasy," he wrote, "was in charge of a German unit equivalent to the LRDG." (The German *Graf* was equivalent to the aristocratic title "count"; Almasy would have been pleased by this recognition.) The papers captured near Bir Hakeim, with the list of six codenames for wireless stations, suggested that Almasy's commando unit had "six sections or columns." Entries in a notebook found with the list suggested that "English money was used for certain of the Commando's transactions." The unit might be connected to two prisoners of war, also captured near Bir Hakeim, who belonged to an Abwehr sabotage force.

"The possibility of sabotage activities in Upper Egypt cannot be overlooked and the passing of agents into Egypt along this route appears to be a definite possibility," he wrote. Far to the south, between Gilf Kebir and Wadi Halfa on the Nile, the search for Almasy's commandos continued.[12]

"IN THE NAZI attitude toward them as a race the Egyptians find neither hope nor tolerance. Those who have read *Mein Kampf* realize the German theory of racial superiority advocates glorification of some races, subordination of others . . . Fascists dream of Roman Empire revival, Mediterranean domination, African colonies," Bonner Fellers wrote.

Nonetheless, he said, deep anti-Axis feeling "fails to turn Egypt to Great Britain." In time of war, the Anglo-Egyptian treaty "has failed to serve the best interests of Egyptians, has contributed neither to their dignity or national aspirations. The treaty guarantee of independence has been deliberately, consistently violated."

The obvious example was Farouk being forced "to appoint a prime minister of British selection." Besides that, citizens had been imprisoned without charges "for the security of the state." When Prime Minister Mustafa el-Nahas had held elections in March, "certain opposition candidates were told to withdraw . . . opposition voters were thrown into jail."

The British maintained "their 19th century tradition" of colonial rule by force, Fellers said. Only a few patriotic Egyptians showed leadership, preventing a rebellion by relying on Islam's rationalist tradition and its prohibition of treason. When the war ended, Egypt would demand that Britain leave and give up control of the Suez Canal Zone. "Should these demands be rejected fighting will begin," he concluded.[13]

The report sounded credible, certainly as a description of an educated political class that could read *Mein Kampf*. It suggested that Fellers—the cosmopolitan isolationist, the conservative anticolonialist—was developing an affection for Egypt like the feeling he'd once nurtured for Japan. The report also sounded omniscient, without attribution to informants. The SIME security records give clues. "It is reported that [Abdul Rahman] Azzam and others are planning to form a new party, Al Hizb al Islami," to unite Muslim associations in support of the palace, SIME's intelligence roundup said in mid-April. The next roundup said that "the king proposes to win the favor of the U.S. authorities in the Middle East, presumably driving a wedge between them and ourselves."[14]

Azzam, a prominent political figure, was one of Fellers's first contacts in Egypt. The two would remain friends for years. In Fellers's description, Azzam despised the Italians. He was the logical person to decry Britain's colonial obtuseness—and to tell Fellers that the account would come due once Britain had won the war. Fellers was a receptive audience for an argument both anti-Axis and harshly critical of Britain.[15]

INSTEAD OF AIR, there was sand and dust. At noon, "visibility was fifty yards," Alan Moorehead scratched in his reporter's notebook when he reached the fighting in Cyrenaica. "At 1400 hours it was twenty yards; at 1600 for a good part of the time it was nil." Men fired machine guns uselessly into air that changed colors with the thickness of the sand, from pink to orange to gray. He reached a brigadier's dugout at the British strongpoint called Knightsbridge. Officers swept sand off maps with their hands and gave orders through field telephones to artillery gunners who fired with no idea of what was out there or if they had hit anything.[16]

The wind dropped, sand fell, chaos remained: the two armies were entangled. Part of Rommel's army coalesced in an area the British named the Cauldron, on what had been the British side of the mine-fields and fortifications stretching from Gazala south to Bir Hakeim.

Colonel Bill Liardet's half-trained regiment, rushed from Egypt to Libya with their American tanks, was sent to a spot near Knightsbridge and repeatedly ordered to attack German positions in the Cauldron. He lost five tanks and "a number of chaps" in one useless attack, a few more in the next. "I did not like seeing my tanks burning on the sky-line" in "this frittering [away] of our armor," he wrote.[17]

The Axis was holding on to the Cauldron, Fellers radioed Washington on June 6. "From the information available to this office," he said, echoing Liardet's complaint, the British did not appear to be using their divisions "as tactical units." Two hours later Fellers sent another message. One of his assistant attachés, the one responsible for keeping a situation map of the battle, had come back from General Headquarters Middle East. He'd learned that the Operations Branch "does not know exact composition or location of its 2 armored divisions." The "personal belief" of his informant at headquarters was that "the Germans have not abandoned original plans . . . of taking Tobruk."[18]

To get there, Rommel decided, he first had to take the desert fortress of Bir Hakeim, which sat on his supply route. The Free French brigade at Bir Hakeim included Frenchmen who'd escaped their country, Czechs and Poles, Spanish Republicans, recruits from the French colonies of Senegal and Cameroon, Tahiti and Madagascar, Foreign Legionnaires from dozens more countries, and one Englishwoman— Susan Travers, driver and mistress of General Pierre Koenig, the commander. Koenig himself had been proclaimed a traitor by France's government in Vichy. "The French fought in a skilfully planned system of field positions and . . . slit trenches, small pillboxes, machine gun and anti-tank gun nests," Rommel wrote. They fought as if it were the last redoubt on earth. The Luftwaffe's Stuka dive-bombers came in swarms, and the RAF hunted the dive bombers. Rommel sent in a German infantry division and an Italian one, outnumbering the Free French defenders by at least five to one. Both Axis divisions were beaten back.

Ritchie twice managed to get supply trucks through to the fortress; then Rommel surrounded it completely and again sent his divisions against the lone French brigade. Ritchie did not manage, despite Auchinleck's urging, to launch a major offensive against Rommel's ring from the outside. Bir Hakeim was alone.[19]

"ACCORDING TO A secret service report, there is famine in Malta," said a radio message from Kesselring to the Luftwaffe commander in North Africa, intercepted by a British wireless operator on June 4. "The morale of the civil population and the military has been weakened by continuous air attacks." On the smaller island of Gozo next to Malta and the islet of Comino between them, it said, "there is a shortage of drinking water."[20]

For Margaret Storey, "secret service" suggested a human source— one who knew about the local mood and conditions, even on Comino, where only a handful of people lived. It appeared there was a German agent on the island.[21]

The more Enigma messages Storey got from Hut 3, the more German spying showed up, tantalizing, dangerous, and anonymous.

IF THERE WAS a spot in the world lonelier than Bir Hakeim, it was Midway: two patches of land in the mid-Pacific, thirteen hundred miles northwest of Hawaii, twenty-five hundred miles from Tokyo. Together, the islands were barely twice the size of New York's Central Park.

On June 4, 1942, Japanese bombers appeared above Midway's American airfield. Japan's naval commander, Admiral Isoroku Yamamoto, had brought a fleet spearheaded by four of Japan's eight intact aircraft carriers to conquer the US outpost. Yamamoto's strategy said that taking Midway would protect Japan from US air raids and provide a launching station for invading Hawaii.

Yamamoto's planning did not account for the belated, desperate, and successful effort of the US Navy's OP-20-G to crack the main Japanese naval code after the Pearl Harbor debacle. His plan did not include the contingency that his order to proceed would be overheard in Hawaii or that US admiral Chester Nimitz would trust the intelligence and send his own carriers toward Midway.

Before the Japanese could launch their second wave of bombers against Midway, American dive-bombers came from the east to hurl their explosives down at Yamamoto's ships. By the next day, all four Japanese carriers had sunk. The shattered remains of Japan's fleet retreated.[22]

For America, all the pieces necessary for an intelligence victory had come together: the code broken, the unambiguous message deciphered, the commander receptive and daring, the necessary forces available.

"U.S. Navy Knew in Advance All About Jap Fleet," read a headline on the front of the *Washington Times Herald* the day after the battle. The article, by a *Chicago Tribune* correspondent in the Pacific, cited "reliable sources in the Naval Intelligence" as saying that "advance information enabled the American Navy" to strike the Japanese fleet. Bletchley Park's liaison to OP-20-G sent a copy of the news story from Washington to Britain's naval intelligence director, Rear Admiral John Godfrey, and called it "a very unpleasant article." (Read in the proper accent, this was very close to a burst of obscenities.) He described the compounding acts of carelessness that led to the journalist getting the story. Somehow, the news did not lead the Japanese navy to change its code.

For Godfrey and his colleagues, Midway was not just evidence of what "special intelligence"—information pulled from the enemy's highest-grade ciphers and codes—could accomplish. It confirmed their heartfelt fear that in the art of guarding special intelligence, their American allies were amateurs.[23]

FROM THE GARDENS of Government House, the British high commissioner's residence in Jerusalem, Hermione Ranfurly could look beyond the lavender hedges and fig trees to the Old City walls and the Dome of the Rock. As High Commissioner MacMichael's assistant private secretary, the young countess had a desk at the end of the residence's billiard room and her own bedroom. From the newspapers, she knew that the war in the desert had flared back into flame. "It is terrifying to think that nearly all our friends are down there fighting," she wrote in her diary.

At Government House, "each morning an Arab gardener arranges flowers in the cool arched rooms; the red leather boxes go back and forth to the Secretariat," she wrote. "Lady MacMichael and I visit hospitals." Ranfurly got a letter from her husband that took only five weeks to reach her from the POW camp in Italy. "The evening sun turns the hills gilt color," she wrote. "We change for dinner and afterwards, if there are no visitors, we all read." The 9 p.m. broadcast from London made little sense of the battles in Libya. "Around ten o'clock we take ourselves and our anxieties to bed."[24] At Government House, the war was both disturbing and far away to the west.

The SOE camp at Kibbutz Mishmar Ha'emek closed in early June, six weeks after it opened. All 150, or 400, or most likely 1,000 Palmah fighters, depending on which account of events one trusts, had completed their training to resist Nazi occupation of Palestine. "I do not know what the enemy will think of them, but by God they frighten me," an SOE officer said of them, paraphrasing what either King George II or the Duke of Wellington had supposedly said of his generals. Major General B. T. Wilson, the SOE's number one in Palestine, "had made a very good impression with the Jews in Palestine and they were collaborating with him successfully," the SOE's war diary said.

Wilson was forthwith dismissed.

According to the British military commander in Palestine, Wilson "was endangering security in Palestine by giving too much latitude to the 'Friends,'" meaning Jews. Palestine high commissioner MacMichael concurred. The SOE investigated and concluded that the accusations were "exaggerated and somewhat vitriolic" but that SOE cooperation with the authorities in Palestine depended on Wilson leaving.[25]

In February, with troops and tanks at Abdin Palace, both Lampson and the British generals had made a statement that immediate war needs took precedence over avoiding a revolt in Egypt in some hard-to-imagine time after the war. In Jerusalem, MacMichael and the generals were still more in the habit of worrying about Jewish rebels in the future than about an Axis invasion much sooner.

The SOE, though, maintained its plan for a network of four hundred Jewish resistance fighters in Palestine. The Cairo office asked London for the funding that Wilson had promised the Jewish Agency for the project. The London office did not want to pay.[26]

"THE INFORMATION RECEIVED by the enemy on 16 April" about Royal Air Force technicians failing to maintain American airplanes bore a "striking resemblance" to a signal from Washington to General Russell Maxwell's US supply mission in Egypt. So wrote Air Marshal Tedder, the RAF chief of staff in the Middle East, who then transmitted the text of the American message.

Tedder was answering the RAF commander in chief, who needed a reply for Stewart Menzies, who had to tell Churchill whether the Germans' "particularly reliable source" was right about the "dreadful waste" of US aircraft and spare parts. Tedder had quietly been in touch with Maxwell's staff, who told him that the information from Washington was utterly false, tantamount to "fifth column propaganda." The complaints had come from "disgruntled . . . representatives" of the American manufacturers, who'd been in Egypt and had been sent home.

"Dope given in German report suggests information was obtained in Washington," Tedder added, since the message had only been decoded in Cairo on April 17, a day after the Germans got it. In other words, the most likely explanation was a German source in the War Department.[27] If one took a globe and stuck red pins where German spies appeared to be successfully at work, one more pin had to be inserted at Washington.

ON MALTA, BREAD was scarce. For a month, everyone had been living on siege rations. "Troops and civil population accepting reduced rations and discomfort cheerfully," wrote General Auchinleck in early June.[28] Auchinleck's weekly reports to General Alan Brooke, chief of the Imperial General Staff, spoke in a resolutely positive tone. Still, food was running out on Malta. So was fuel for the planes that fought off German bombers.

In Alexandria and at Gibraltar, ships gathered. From each end of the Mediterranean, convoys would strive for the Grand Harbor of Valetta in Malta. The one from Egypt was named Operation Vigorous. Auchinleck's contribution was supposed to have been an offensive at the start of June to take the coast of Cyrenaica, so that the RAF could take off from airfields there to protect Vigorous from Italian ships and German planes. Just as Kesselring's particularly reliable source had predicted, June was "too late." Rommel had preempted Auchinleck, and the Luftwaffe would rise from the Cyrenaica aerodromes to attack the convoy.

General Headquarters in Cairo produced a new plan. The Long Range Desert Group would cross the sands far to the south of Bir Hakeim and the battles on the Gazala line, then head through Axis territory toward Derna in the east and Benghazi further west. It would deliver commandos who would attack six Luftwaffe fields, destroying planes on the ground. Other commandos would reach Crete by submarine to sabotage planes there.

Most of the commandos for the Libya raids came from the Special Air Service, the SAS. The name was misleading: parachuting proved to be a disastrous way to deliver men behind enemy lines. Instead, the SAS traveled with the experienced navigators of the LRDG. This time, they were joined by the Special Interrogation Group, Captain Buck's contingent of German-speaking Palestinian Jews in Nazi uniforms. On June 8, Buck and fourteen of his men, including seventeen-year-old Eliahu Gottlieb, left Siwa Oasis at the edge of the Sand Sea and crossed into Libya to try their luck at piracy on the high desert.[29]

THE MESSAGE FROM the intelligence officer of the German high command to his opposite number at Rommel's headquarters explicitly cited an "army source" with information from General Headquarters Middle East in Cairo. Sent in the Chaffinch II key on June 7, translated in Hut 3 two days later, it said that the British Fourth Armored Brigade was at the spot called Eluet et-Tamar, northeast of the

Cauldron, and that the "200 Guards Brigade and support group of the First Armored Division [are] established at 386-412," coordinates on British war maps, placing them due east of the Cauldron. Rommel could not have asked for information more precise.

Auchinleck's chief of operations "does not know the exact constitution and location of his two armored divisions," the message added. "In the view of an agent, the Germans have not given up their original plan of . . . taking Tobruk." The paraphrased version of this, sent from Hut 3 to the army command, referred explicitly to a "British agent."[30]

Later that evening, another message to Rommel's intelligence chief was belatedly deciphered and translated. On June 4, it said, there had been "no news of any important [*sic*] from Good Source." Enigma messages did not have upper- and lowercase letters. But the message made clear that "Good Source" was no longer a descriptive phrase, an evaluation applicable to any number of sources. It was a name. And a day when Good Source had no important news was so unusual it needed to be noted.[31] In that case, British intercept operators had overheard only a small piece of what had been sent.

THE KEYS TO the Swiss legation in Rome were most likely provided by the servant called Peppino, later named as working for Manfredi Talamo's Sezione Prelevamento, or P Squad. It's possible, though, that Talamo had additional agents on the Swiss staff whose names have been lost to memory. Following his standard method of operation, Talamo presumably entered the building himself, opened the safe, took documents to the Servizio Informazioni Militari photo studio, brought them back, and put them precisely in their original place.

It was a fruitful operation. Talamo, now also in command of SIM's counterintelligence section, had suspected that the Swiss were cooperating with Allied intelligence services. To test the thesis, he fed a double agent—a Soviet spy actually working for Italy—a report that an anti-Communist army was being formed in Italy. The fictional army included an imaginary "Divisione Buon Servezi." In the Swiss safe, Talamo found messages from Berne asking the Swiss military attaché for information about the anti-Bolshevik army and the Buon Servezi division. Ergo, the double agent's fake intelligence had found its way from Moscow to Berne and back to Rome.

The stolen papers also revealed that the Swiss military attaché had an agent in the German embassy in Rome.

"Dr. Sauer, a cultural attache, has already been arrested and has confessed," Foreign Minister Ciano wrote in his diary on June 9. "He made it clear that he did not act for money but out of hatred for Nazism and Fascism." German envoy Otto von Bismarck dismissed that explanation, Ciano wrote. "He says that Sauer is a pederast and that he has been induced by his vice to commit this serious offense."

Herbert Kappler, officially the police liaison at the German embassy, actually the Gestapo's man in Rome, was not pleased. Kurt Sauer was Kappler's friend. Not only that, but an Italian had exposed a German spy that the Gestapo had missed. Kappler looked bad.

Talamo was promoted from major to lieutenant colonel. But Kappler remembered, and did not forgive.[32]

Act IV

"THE MATTER BECOMES OF EXTREME URGENCY"

1

COMPROMISED

June 10-16, 1942. Bir Hakeim-Bletchley Park-Washington.

"At noon June 10th left Libya," Colonel Fellers wrote that same evening from Cairo. The battle had turned into a stalemate, he radioed Washington. "The present situation will continue for some time," he believed. "Rommel has obviously failed in his mission," largely because the German general had underestimated the American Grant tank. Bir Hakeim was of no real strategic value in itself, Fellers said, but politically the British "cannot allow the destruction of the Free French."

He wrote in the quiet of El Nabatat Street in Garden City with his mind still in the rush of the battle, alive to a thousand details, at once detached, despondent, and furious. He mixed strategic lessons with positions of British units and "costly mistakes" by the British.

Fellers had listened to many British commanders. The German air force acted like a flying artillery, striking British ground units. The RAF gave no support. Eighth Army commander Neil Ritchie had sent an Indian brigade to block the gap in the minefields through which Rommel brought supplies. The brigade had "insufficient antitank guns and artillery." While Rommel's tanks were firing at the Indians on their west, British armored units on the east had been silent. The

Indian brigade was destroyed. "Tank losses on both sides have been heavy," Fellers said, but the British had lost more.[1]

Lance Corporal Ron Hurlock was in a tank that exploded in flames that day. There is no record of why he'd been shifted to a tank from the wireless van on which he'd hoped a German gunner would not waste a shell. His letter worrying about his wife's coolness was his last.[2]

For the eavesdroppers at Hut 3, relations between the Luftwaffe and Rommel's ground forces did not sound so harmonious.

"I am grieved," Field Marshal Kesselring radioed Rommel on that same June evening, that successful dive-bomber strikes on Bir Hakeim weren't matched by a "commensurate infantry and tank attack." Kesselring demanded "most urgently to establish temporarily a tank concentration" against the fortress.

Rommel thought it was "completely out of the question" to use tanks against minefields and dug-in strongpoints. Tanks were for mobile battles and rapid movement. He was relying on infantry to take Bir Hakeim.

Rommel demanded heavier air strikes. Kesselring's subordinate, the commander of the Fliegerkorps X—the 10th Air Corps in North Africa—radioed a rejection. To the Luftwaffe liaison officer at Rommel's headquarters, the 10th Air Corps chief sent word that he would be visiting. He suggested they "take leave together until Hakeim has been cleaned up." In the Watch Room at Hut 3, the air adviser added a comment to the decoded message that the "suggestion [was] thought to be result of irritation and not intended seriously."[3]

That night Rommel reported that his forces had pushed forward against "fanatical resistance." Everywhere in the Eighth Army, war correspondent Alan Moorehead wrote, soldiers were "full of glowing pride" in the French. The "little tricolor"—the French flag—still aloft at Bir Hakeim was erasing "all the bitter accusations against the French soldier after the fall of France," Moorehead said, though he knew most of the soldiers around that flag were not French.[4]

"The value of [Bir Hakeim] . . . though still great, is less than when battle started," Auchinleck decided at General Headquarters Middle

East in Cairo. His reasons for this judgment are unclear, but Ritchie gave General Koenig permission to pull out.

Rommel's morning report on June 11 said that overnight the Free French had "attempted . . . to break out to the southwest. The attempt was almost completely defeated." Rommel was mistaken. Koenig had found the gap in the German siege line. In a car driven by Susan Travers, he led most of his surviving men out. Travers would eventually receive the Croix de Guerre, the War Cross, with a citation for her "bravery in the face of several barrages of intense artillery fire, numerous bullet strikes of her vehicle and pitch blackness." At Bir Hakeim, only the wounded stayed behind. Germans records show that the prisoners included forty-four nationalities.[5]

Later that day, a British wireless operator managed to take down a few words of a German message. Its evaluation of the strategic importance of the battle differed ominously from Auchinleck's.

At 8 a.m., it said, Bir Hakeim, "the southern bastion of the fortress of Tobruk," had fallen.[6]

"A Good Source" reported that he had visited the headquarters of the British Thirteenth and Thirtieth Corps and the Fourth Armored Brigade a month earlier. So said the deciphered text that Menzies handed Winston Churchill on June 10.

"Battle morale of officers and men excellent," the source had conveyed, and also, "Training inferior according to American ideas."

That reframed everything.

The source had measured British training by "American ideas." It fit together with a previous clue: German intelligence having the full text of the complaint from Washington about RAF technicians failing at upkeep of American-made warplanes.

As usual, Menzies had clipped a narrow slip of paper to the front of the "special intelligence" material, with a one-sentence typed summary. This time, under the typed words, the MI6 chief added a handwritten note in green ink.

"Prime Minister," it said, "I am satisfied that the American cyphers in Cairo are compromised. I am taking action."[7]

Menzies no longer suggested that the Germans had a spy in Washington, or in Egypt. Rather, he said, they were reading a code used between the two places. This evaluation came from Bletchley Park, where the cipher security officer was Russell Dudley-Smith and the research specialist on enemy intelligence was Margaret Storey.[8]

The evaluation would be asserted, and cast again into doubt, on the top-secret telegraph channel between Washington and Bletchley Park.

Sometime that night, while Koenig and his soldiers were breaking out of Bir Hakeim, John Tiltman wired William Friedman at the Signal Intelligence Service. There was a leak in communications between Cairo and Washington, he said.[9]

"What system is being read?" Friedman replied. This meant: What kind of code or cipher was used for the leaked messages? Friedman listed the methods used by Americans in Cairo. The military mission—General Maxwell's supply operation—used a "secret cipher machine." The military attaché used an enciphered code. The US Navy used a device known as a strip cipher; the State Department's people also used a strip cipher, along with "several codes, all enciphered."

"Must have some definite information before action can be taken," Friedman wrote, and then added another question: "With whom [on the] British staff should our army authority in Cairo confer? Most urgent reply requested."[10]

Friedman had made a faux pas, or an accusation. The note implied that Tiltman also knew how the words were encrypted. This was something that you would know from intercepting the original, encoded American message. Friedman's cable thereby hinted that the British themselves were intercepting American traffic and had broken their ally's code or cipher.

The suggestion from Washington was most undiplomatic. Tiltman ignored it.

Instead, Tiltman referred to content. His answer was cosigned by Solomon Kullback, one of Friedman's original protégés, still a senior American codebreaker, who was visiting Bletchley Park. "Leakage includes a particular message of April 16th . . . for Maxwell," they wrote, pointing to the certain evidence of the complaint about RAF negligence. "[We] have seen the German messages as well as the original American message." They matched.

British authorities, they said, "beg no communication with Cairo." This meant: No, you must not ask your army people there to talk to ours. If your men clumsily radio home, the eavesdropping Germans will hear—and may figure out that we are listening to *them*. If anything was more dangerous than the leak itself, it was a leak about an investigation.[11] It could endanger everything Bletchley Park had accomplished.

The cables were marked for urgent handling. Yet the conversation was terrifyingly slow, delayed by differences in time zones and when people were awake, by coding and decoding of the messages, by the need to make very quiet inquiries in Washington. They were written in hurried telegraphic language, meant to be precise, yet often ambiguous. Brief texts sent by electric pulses were a method of miscommunication.

Only the next evening did Friedman answer. The message to Maxwell, he said, had been sent "in the Military Intelligence Code, which is [a] large two-part code enciphered with tables changed every two months. New table became effective on 1st May." Moreover, the code was no longer in use between Cairo and Washington, Friedman said. On June 3, it had been replaced with an American electric cipher machine. In other words, even if the Germans had succeeded in reading a message in April, the code would have become illegible again in May and vanished in June.[12]

A few hours later, another cable arrived from the War Department. The "facts here," Friedman said, lead us to believe that the "alleged compromise" was due not to cryptanalysis, codebreaking, but to the activity of "enemy agents."[13] Kullback, at the English end of the telegraph line, was sympathetic to this view. Back in the 1930s, when the whole staff of the Signal Intelligence Service could meet in one room, he'd helped Friedman create that code. He didn't readily believe that someone had cracked it.[14] And according to Friedman's information on the changes in the cipher system, if the leak was continuing, as it was, the Germans' source had to be a spy, one who had access to messages going from and to Cairo.

BY NOW IT was June 12. In the evening, Menzies gave Churchill a packet intended to answer the prime minister's questions about the

RAF repair crews in Egypt. It contained Air Marshal Tedder's note from Cairo and a cover letter from Chief of Air Staff Charles Portal, commander of the RAF. The cipher security experts had confirmed "that the Germans are reading an American cypher in use between Washington and Egypt," Portal said. "Action has already been taken to rectify this."

That was vague for Churchill's tastes. He scribbled a note for Menzies. "Report what steps you have taken about the cipher," it said in bright red.[15]

The next thing Menzies did was to send a note to Portal, saying he'd passed on his letter to the prime minister. "In point of fact," Menzies told Portal, "as a result of my communications with the American Crypto-Analyst Bureau," he had doubts about the Germans reading a US cipher. (By "my communications," he apparently meant Tiltman's; by Crypto-Analyst Bureau, he meant the SIS.) Instead, "there is a possibility that a traitor is providing the Germans with the contents of certain messages."

Menzies said he was still investigating. (This meant: Tiltman, Dudley-Smith, and Storey were still investigating.) In the meantime, he was sure Portal would agree that it was best not to bother Churchill with "this alternative form of leakage."[16]

DESPITE HIS FRIENDSHIP with Friedman, Tiltman stepped aside in favor of the "bulldog." Bletchley Park director Edward Travis wrote the next cables to Friedman. "Our source is the highest German security system," Travis said, meaning Enigma. The German message from "a particularly reliable source" about maintaining US planes so precisely followed the American text that one could see where the German translator misunderstood the English.

Besides that, he said, the German War Office had recently been sending messages to the Panzer Army, all referring to "a Good Source." At first, Bletchley Park hadn't connected them with intelligence attributed to a "secret service report." But then a detail had clicked into place: a single German message on April 30 had quoted "Good Source" reports from five dates over more than two months. They wouldn't have all been forwarded to Rommel at the same time,

Travis said, if an agent had been steadily sending them. Instead, "it was possible that [the] cypher first became compromised about the end of April." Then the German codebreakers would have gone back and begun decoding earlier messages.

Travis sent snippets of three more Good Source reports so that Friedman's people could look for the American messages on which they were based. The most recent of these cited information from the Good Source on June 7. Travis didn't mention that the Germans had sent this on June 9 and Hut 6 had deciphered it on June 11.[17] Nor did he mention that every German text citing a Good Source had come in Chaffinch, an army key of Enigma. The other appellations, such as "particularly reliable source," came from air force messages. Travis was keeping his telegram condensed.

But the pattern seemed clear. Bletchley Park was picking up messages from two different branches of the German military that depended on the same source. As breaking Chaffinch got quicker and more frequent, more "Good Source" reports showed up. They showed that the Germans were also getting faster at sending these reports—a sign of steady improvement at codebreaking. And despite Friedman's assertion about changing the code, the Germans were apparently still reading it.

A personal message from Kullback to Friedman followed. He didn't think the Germans had worked out the American codebook. When you do that, you figure out the code equivalent for one word at a time, and part of the codebook remains unknown. The Germans had translated every word of the message about the incompetent technicians. That indicated they could have an intact copy of the codebook, and perhaps of the cipher tables. The alternative was that a spy in Cairo had obtained the American messages. But in that case, Kullback asked, why send the intelligence to Berlin instead of radioing it directly to Rommel in Libya?[18]

THE MEMO FOR Auchinleck's intelligence chief came from the blandly named Inter-Services Liaison Department—in fact, the MI6 station in Cairo. It cited a report from "Triangle"—the local codeword for decrypted messages from Bletchley Park—which said that Almasy had returned to his starting point in Libya by May 28. We missed him, MI6's man said. The search in Sudan was being called off.[19]

In Cairo, Eppler and Sandy were unnoticed, unpursued, invisible.

THE MORNING AFTER Bir Hakeim fell, Churchill cabled Auchinleck. The battle had lasted two grinding weeks. It looked like the Eighth Army was holding on, which meant bleeding more slowly than Rommel's forces. Auchinleck had told the prime minister that Ritchie's forces had lost 10,000 men, "of whom 8,000 may be prisoners." But 25,000 reinforcements had arrived, and more were on ships that had already passed the Cape on their way to Suez. The Eighth Army still had just over 300 tanks; it had lost 350.

It would be best to win with a masterstroke, Churchill told Auchinleck in response to this information. But, he added, "we have no reason to fear a prolonged *betaille d'usure*," a battle of attrition. "Please give my compliments to Ritchie," Churchill wrote, "and tell how much his dogged and resolute fighting is admired by the vast audience which follows every move."

Thank you for your encouragement, Auchinleck wrote back. "Our losses have been heavy . . . but as you say, our resources are greater than his"—Rommel's—"and his situation is not enviable."

Churchill and Auchinleck may have meant what they said.[20] Or each may have been working to keep the other's confidence up, and his own. Sometimes seeing through brief words to the mood behind them is like looking through a sandstorm to see whether there are tanks on the horizon.

A German commander gave an order that every truck that took troops forward had to bring back empty water containers, so they could be refilled and taken back. An Italian commander complained that his corps was desperately short of trucks for supplies. These shards of information from the Libyan desert came in messages deciphered in the distant chill of Bletchley Park. Rommel had given orders not to fire artillery against tank attacks since "the ammunition situation is strained." Only antitank guns should be used, he ordered. Aircraft fuel was running low, the Luftwaffe's quartermaster in Africa said.[21]

Rommel got word from Rome: Kesselring had met with Mussolini and Cavallero, the Italian commander in chief. They'd agreed that Rommel's next goal should be taking Gazala, at the northeast end of the British defensive line. Kesselring did not see besieging Tobruk as a "binding" objective, but only as a possibility to be weighed later. He was concerned about "the supply problem" and not leaving "our troops completely exhausted."[22]

By the time those instructions reached him, Rommel had already sent his divisions northwest from Bir Hakeim—not toward Gazala, but deep behind the British line, toward the Knightsbridge strongpoint and the fortifications at a place called El Adem, on the way to Tobruk. He'd been delayed two weeks. He had not changed his plan. His answer to quartermasters, and to staff-college-trained generals who listened to them, was to move fast and win before supplies ran out. While he led an armored division toward El Adem, his column was hit with bombs that German dive-bombers had ditched to gain speed as the RAF pursued them. Rommel "escaped once again without a scratch," he'd recall. Yet again, he'd shown that the odds didn't apply to him.

At Knightsbridge, his forces struck the British from three sides, while the wind turned the air into a cloud of sand. "The slaughter of British tanks went on," he'd write. By the night of June 13, the Eighth Army was down to seventy tanks.

"Garrison of Knightsbridge withdrawn night 13/14 June," Ritchie radioed Auchinleck. In the morning, "the enemy started his expected thrust" northward, toward the coast, Ritchie said.

"Dear Lu," Rommel wrote to his wife. "The battle has been won and the enemy is breaking up . . . I needn't tell you how delighted I am . . . Perhaps we will now see each other in July after all."[23]

WITH CHURCHILL IMPATIENT for him to report on having shut down the leak, Menzies concluded he had to admit to having a problem. "There are at least three American cyphers in use between Cairo and Washington," he told the prime minister on June 14, "and until the Americans inform me which cypher was used for the message in question, it is impossible to determine whether the Germans have broken a cypher, or whether there is a traitor who is betraying information and transmitting it to the enemy by secret channel."[24]

At first glance, Menzies's note was strange. Friedman had already said that the "message in question"—to Maxwell, about the aircraft technicians—had moved in the Military Intelligence Code. Yet Friedman had also said that code had gone out of use on the Washington-Cairo link. Menzies apparently understood that a different system might have been compromised—or that there was in fact a spy in the mansion on El Nabatat Street. The only thing certain is that nothing was yet certain, and the leak continued.

Travis lost patience. "Further information from 'Good Source' reveals our future plans," he cabled Friedman the same day, "and matter becomes of extreme urgency." The source was sending information that would cost British lives.

To help trace the leak, Travis sent Friedman two examples of Good Source messages conveying particularly dangerous intelligence. One example was the first line of a much longer message. It said, "Good Source reports on 10th June: British made costly mistakes resulting in extraordinary losses."[25] The rest of that message had included the location of a long list of Eighth Army units—thereby giving Rommel a map of British positions just before he began his successful drive toward Knightsbridge and El Adem.

Travis did send the full text of the second German message. "Good Source reports on June 11th: It is intended simultaneously to attack aircraft on 9 Axis aerodromes, on the night of 12th–13th June with sabotage units. Attack to be carried out by parachutists and patrols of the Long Range Desert Group, using sticker bombs."[26]

The Bletchley Park log does not record what happened next in Washington. But it could not have taken more than an immediate, discreet visit by an SIS staffer to the British Empire Section of the Military Intelligence Division to learn within minutes that the first text was from Bonner Fellers's Cable 1118, Part 2, of June 10.[27] The second came nearly verbatim from his Cable 1119, radioed the following morning, though a translator had garbled it a bit: Fellers had written that the raids would be on the "nights of June 12th June 13th"—meaning two consecutive nights.

This should have produced shouts of "Eureka!" at the SIS. There could be no doubt: the British were relaying the texts of Fellers's radiograms.

And yet, amid their lingering distrust of the British and their reluctance to believe their own code had been compromised, the Americans balked at the implication: The Germans were intercepting and reading encoded mail between Cairo and the War Department—mail with explosive implications.

FELLERS'S MOTIVE FOR sending the cable about the commando raids had been to recommend the tactic. "This method of attack offers tremendous possibility for destruction, risks is [*sic*] slight compared with possible gains," he'd written.[28] The German's Good Source message, naturally, did not quote this commentary.

The Good Source report, sent in the Chaffinch key, was actually the third warning, and not the last, based on Fellers's message and deciphered at Bletchley Park. One came on June 12 in an Italian naval code and cited a "reliable source." Another came the same day in the Primrose key of Enigma, used by Luftwaffe supply units. It gave no source at all but told airfields to be on high alert from 5 p.m. till dawn. Ammunition dumps and fuel depots should be searched "with a view to discovering bombs and incendiary matter with time fuses" and then constantly guarded, airbase commanders were ordered. Yet another air force warning, to airfields in the Aegean, was also sent that day but deciphered at Hut 6 only the following week.[29]

All around the Mediterranean, Axis radio networks carried the word: expect commandos.

By the afternoon of June 12, Hut 3 had sent General Headquarters in Cairo a paraphrase of the orders to boost security at German airfields.[30] Even if it reached someone who was in on the secret of the commando raids, even if that person had figured out a way to radio a warning to the Long Range Desert Group patrols without committing the cardinal sin of hinting at the Enigma break, it was too late.[31]

The night before, the LRDG's desert buccaneers had dropped off bands of Special Air Service saboteurs, including a team of Free

French, near Benghazi. The SAS men would make the final approach to four Axis landing fields on their own. Further east, on the other side of the hump of Cyrenaica, Captain Buck's team from the Special Interrogation Group parted from its LRDG guides. Buck's group consisted of fourteen of his German-speaking Palestinian Jews and their two professedly anti-Nazi German instructors, all in German uniform, along with fourteen Free French paratroopers and their commander. They rode in captured German trucks. At checkpoints, the German instructors did the talking and identified the French as prisoners of war. The raiders split into two groups. Their targets were an airfield at Derna and another at nearby Martuba.

What happened after that will remain indistinct, the subject of two sets of stories, British and Axis, with disputes within each set.

Major David Stirling, commander of the Special Air Service group, reported that his Free French contingent destroyed or damaged fourteen planes at one of the fields, at Berca. The French commander claimed only eleven. At another landing ground, Stirling wrote, his men destroyed five planes and up to thirty new engines and left hangars burning behind them. At yet another, they got only one plane. At the Barce airfield, the planes were too well guarded to approach.

Across Cyrenaica, at the Derna landing ground, a truck arrived late at night, driven by one of SIG's professedly anti-Nazi German trainers. With him were Eliahu Gottlieb and another Palestinian Jew, Czech-born Petr Haas. In the back, in the guise of prisoners or perhaps hidden under a tarp, were the French fighters.

The French commander later made it back on foot, alone, to the point set for the rendezvous with LRDG. His story, as passed on with multiple variations by those who heard him, was that the German driver went into the guard booth and betrayed the group. German soldiers came out, surrounded the truck, and demanded surrender. A Special Interrogation Group man would recount afterward that Gottlieb and Haas responded with gunfire and grenades. (He could have only known this, or misheard it, from the French officer.) In another telling, one of the two Jews blew up their own supply of explosives, killing some of the Germans in the process. Except for the lone French officer, the French were either killed or captured. The closest thing to a certainty is that Haas and Gottlieb died as they fought Nazi soldiers. Gottlieb was two months short of his eighteenth birthday.[32]

The second SIG team headed into the night toward Martuba. What happened next is mostly mystery. A few days after the raids, the LRDG's intelligence officer, Bill Kennedy-Shaw, wrote from Siwa Oasis to a superior at General Headquarters. Captain Buck, he relayed, believed that the men he'd sent to Martuba airfield had "done their stuff." Explosions had been seen there. But after the raiders' cover was blown, Buck had been forced to leave the rendezvous point without waiting for the Martuba team. Buck "thinks they may have got 15–20 aircraft" at Martuba, Kennedy-Shaw said. As for the fate of the Martuba raiders, he could only say that there was "a chance" that some might have escaped capture and were hiding in the Green Mountains.[33]

Altogether, in the British reports, the raiders destroyed as many as forty warplanes, along with spare engines, and damaged more.

Seen from inside the Axis bases, the action looked very different. A German pilot who'd been at the Derna landing ground, and who was shot down and taken prisoner soon after, knew of an attempted raid but had heard nothing of a betrayal by the driver. His account was that the truck pulled up to the sentry's booth, "a melee ensued . . . and all the occupants were shot on the spot," apparently including the driver. As for Martuba, a German pilot from there, also taken prisoner, "stated that he knew nothing about a raiding party" on his field that night.[34]

The two captured German pilots agreed on this: there'd been warnings in advance to expect British raiding parties, dressed in German uniforms. According to the Derna pilot, the commanding officer banned any movement of trucks in and around the field after sundown.[35]

It's possible the German driver indeed betrayed the party at Derna. It's very possible, though, that he had nothing to do with the sentries' response to the truck they'd been told to expect and suspect.

A German report from the morning after the raids lists a total of ten planes destroyed and one more lightly damaged, a hangar ignited, and several pilots killed—far less damage than in the British accounts. The German report says nothing of an attack at Martuba. At Derna, "one van with explosive material" was seized and "a saboteur . . . in German uniform was captured."[36] The information is telegraphic, the drama at Derna absent.

Airfield commanders may have had reason to understate what happened. But they could count the wreckage when the sun came up. Stirling and Buck could only listen for explosions and look back for flames as they fled.

Two stories were born that night. In British memory and histories woven from it, the raids were a success of audacious daring, albeit marred by disaster at Derna.[37] The most succinct Axis account comes from General Cesare Amè, head of Italy's Servizio Informazioni Militari, the SIM. The raids, Amè would later write, "failed almost completely" due to the last-minute intelligence from Cairo. The British plan to cripple Axis air strength came to naught, Amè would write.[38] The credit, he said, belonged to his SIM.

Two HUNDRED MILES north from Derna, off the shore of Crete, a submarine had surfaced with a band of commandos—one English officer, four Frenchmen, and one Greek—from the British unit known as the Special Boat Section. They came ashore on June 11 in rubber boats and hiked into the mountains, burdened with explosives. On the night of June 13, a German patrol discovered them while they cut the fence around the airfield at Heraklion. Fortunately, the English officer would recount, the Germans "were quite unprepared for the presence of British or Allied troops . . . A happy snore from one of the Free French satisfied them that we were a party of German drunks!" The only thing that interfered with their subsequent work of sticking explosives with time-delay fuses on German planes was an RAF air raid. Failure to coordinate the commando mission and the air attack saved the Germans at least ten planes.[39]

Here, unusually, the British and Axis accounts line up almost precisely. Kesselring ordered an investigation of what happened on Crete. The commander at Heraklion had received general warnings of impending commando actions, which came from "overheard radio messages, agent reports and interrogations of prisoners and deserters."

The information from Cairo brought those warnings into sudden, sharp focus, with the nearly precise date of the raid. Yet the Heraklion commander said that the critical orders on June 12 and 13 to boost security at the airfield never reached him. The intruders arrived unnoticed and managed to place "17 to 18 explosive devices on 13 planes." Some of the aircraft would take days or weeks to rebuild; some were total losses.

What happened to the base commander is unclear. The day after the attack, the German report states, "fifty hostages from guilty elements of the local population were shot."[40]

"THE ALEXANDRIA-MALTA RUN is perhaps the most dangerous in the world," wrote a Royal Navy telegraphist of his thoughts on being assigned to Operation Vigorous. The convoy of supply ships and their escort sailed from Egypt on the afternoon of June 13, hours before the commandos approached the Cyrenaica airfields. "Malta convoys were known as suicide runs," another anxious sailor wrote.[41]

Clear weather and the long June days made it easier for German planes to find them. On board the cruiser HMS *Newcastle*, the navigating officer scribbled changes of course, minute by minute, in a notebook the size of his palm.

At 4:32 p.m. on the second day, he noted the approach of a Ju-88, a German bomber.

"Eight more," he wrote at 4:35.

"Eighteen Stukas attacked again from astern," he recorded at 5:44. "One direct hit on [the] Bhutan," a supply ship that came to a standstill and began to sink. Rescue ships were picking survivors out of the water, his next notation said.[42]

Night, when it came at last, was moonless. The convoy commander gave orders not to return fire so that German pilots would not be able to find the ships. "The policy was quite unsuccessful because aircraft were searching for the darkened convoy with flares," a destroyer's commander wrote. "Any ship within range was caught in a pool of light against which she became an isolated target for bombers gliding out of the darkness with no other evidence of their passage than the explosion of their bombs."[43]

The telegraphist was in the wireless office of his destroyer, the *Airedale*, the next afternoon when a wave of Stukas appeared. Three bombs hit the ship. He was unhurt, but "bodies were strewn all over the deck and one had been flung high and became entangled halfway up the funnel." He jumped overboard. He and another man shared a plank and "drifted through masses of thick, black cloggy oil." A ship steamed away; they despaired. At last the crew of another spotted them. On board, "I found myself on my head with my legs [held] high in the air by two friendly sailors who were pumping oil and seawater out of my body."[44]

At the outset, the greatest expected danger to the convoy was an Italian fleet that sailed out to meet it. British submarine attacks and bombers from Malta slowed the Italians. Yet the convoy turned back toward Alexandria. In the constant fighting with German planes, the warships had used too much of their antiaircraft ammunition. Not enough was left for a dash to the island.[45]

General Amè would argue that the intelligence that defeated the commando attacks also foiled the convoy.[46] It's impossible to test this claim—to know if the ships would have gotten through, or if the men killed on the *Airedale* would have lived, had Stirling's and Buck's men wrecked a hundred planes. But they did not destroy anywhere near that number, even according to their commanders' own optimistic estimates. The advance warning from Cairo certainly put most of the targeted bases on alert, which in turn saved Axis planes from destruction. The convoy from Alexandria did not reach Malta.

Operation Vigorous did have this success: it diverted enough Axis attention that the second convoy, from Gibraltar, managed to bring two of its six supply-laden ships to Malta. They carried enough food to allow the island to withstand the siege for a couple more months.[47] Whether it could withstand invasion was a separate question.

"TONIGHT," FELLERS RADIOED from Cairo, "British will withdraw 1st South African and 50th divisions" from the Gazala line, or the last remnant of it. It was June 14.[48] The South Africans had dug in all spring, preparing to stop Rommel's forces in the worst case, to push forward toward Benghazi in the best. Then Rommel had come behind them.

They had to leave before his forces reached the sea and cut them off. They took what they could quickly put on trucks and blew up the rest. Already Axis artillery was bombarding the coastal road. The South African truck drivers found themselves in a traffic jam with shells falling on them. The lucky ones reached Tobruk. The British Fiftieth Division, further inland, already had its obvious escape route blocked. It turned westward, smashed through surprised Italian forces, then took a long loop through the desert around Bir Hakeim and headed across the border into Egyptian territory. Ritchie was pulling most of his army out of Libya.[49]

"Presume there is no question of giving up Tobruk," Churchill cabled Auchinleck. "As long as Tobruk is held no serious advance into Egypt is possible." The generals disagreed with Churchill's judgment of Tobruk's military value. What Churchill left unsaid was that Tobruk had become a symbol of British resilience during the long siege of 1941. Generals lead armies. The prime minister led a nation, whose morale he had to maintain. A symbol was a strategic asset.

Auchinleck answered that he'd ordered Ritchie to keep Rommel from crossing a line running from the coast west of Tobruk to El Adem south of the town. But Auchinleck was in Cairo. In the desert, Ritchie thought Auchinleck's plan wouldn't work. He hoped to hold El Adem. He hoped to hold the coastal road from the Egyptian border to Tobruk. At worst, if he lost the road, the garrison at Tobruk would have to hold out for a month or two till he could counterattack. Tobruk had survived one siege. Ritchie gambled that it would survive another.[50]

MARGARET STOREY COULD not list all of the reports that German or Italian intelligence received from Cairo, because not all of them were repeated in Axis radio messages. Of those that were radioed, not all were heard by British intercept operators, and not all those that were intercepted could be decoded.

The entire Enigma-cracking effort was a peephole in a shut door to a large room. Most of what happened in that room was at the wrong angle to spot through the peephole. The Cairo source had turned into a fountain, a gusher. Some of the information it provided would be found soon after the war in captured enemy documents; some would only be found decades later.

So no one at Bletchley Park would see the memo to the Luftwaffe's intelligence staff, passing on a radiogram from General Russell Maxwell's office on El Nabatat Street to General Henry Arnold, commander of the US Army Air Forces. The RAF, Maxwell said, wanted to know when the United States would take over the Sheikh Othman airfield in Aden, the British colony at the southern tip of the Arabian Peninsula. The base would serve as a stopover on the American air ferry that brought warplanes and other weaponry across Africa, then onward to India and China or to Persia and then to Baku in the Soviet Union. Aden provided an alternative to flying via Egypt and Iraq. Rommel didn't need to know about this; it was strategic information above his pay grade. For the Luftwaffe high command, it was high-value intelligence: it meant that even if Egypt fell, the American supply route from sub-Saharan Africa to Asia would remain open.[51]

The leak was more dangerous than Churchill, Menzies, or anyone at Bletchley Park knew. But what Bletchley Park could see through its peephole was frightening enough. The day after Travis sent Friedman his examples of what the Good Source was revealing, Menzies gave Churchill copies of both deciphered messages—the commando-raid warning and the criticism of "costly mistakes" by the British accompanied by the positions of British units.[52] Churchill said to cable Washington that unless Menzies received "a report on the leakage within twenty-four hours," Churchill would wire Roosevelt personally.[53]

At the Signal Intelligence Service in Washington, the suspicion persisted that the British were themselves reading American messages from Cairo. To this another suspicion was added: the story of the leak was a subterfuge for getting Fellers out of Cairo. One US colonel would later go so far as to suggest that MI6 had deliberately fed Fellers the information about the raids "for the purpose of bringing matters to a head or even for the purpose of stamping Fellers as a dangerous person to have around."[54]

Most plausibly, the dark view of British motives was born when the SIS checked the texts sent by Travis with Fellers's superiors in military intelligence. They would have known about the Fellers paradox: Auchinleck and other top British commanders resented his independent reports and his blunt judgments—yet Fellers and his assistants had no trouble opening office doors and officers' mouths in General Headquarters Middle East.

Nonetheless, the threat of involving Roosevelt finally produced results at the SIS. "Washington informs that it is now clear that the cypher of the American military attaché in Cairo is compromised," Menzies informed Churchill the next day, June 16. Menzies had told the Americans that the code and cipher had to be replaced immediately with a more secure one. They were not to give Fellers any reason for the change.

"In my opinion," Menzies added, "the Germans have succeeded in photographing the American cypher book, but as this is held at a number of stations abroad, it is impossible to determine where the treachery occurred." (What Menzies called "my opinion" matched Kullback's hunch, likely passed on by Travis or Tiltman.) The spy could even be in Washington.

And yet, Menzies indicated, neither he nor his contacts in Washington were really so certain. Switching the cipher was a test. If the leak continued, Menzies wrote, "we shall then know for certain that there is a traitor in Cairo."[55]

2

INSIDE INFORMATION

Late June, 1942. Tobruk-Washington-Cairo.

A SENIOR BRITISH officer, privy to the talk in generals' offices, "most reliable," spoke to a friendly man, one who was always willing to listen—the American colonel, Bonner Fellers.

"General Auchinleck blames the Libyan reverses largely on the battalion commanders, their laxness in supervision of training, their lack of ability to handle armored units," Fellers wrote afterward. One commander had led tanks into his own mine field, Auchinleck was complaining. General Ritchie blamed the tank crews, who carelessly drove straight toward the Germans' brutal 88-mm antitank guns. Ritchie also thought the Free French had pictured the attack at Bir Hakeim as "much heavier than it actually developed," while "the Free French claim the British let them down."

Fellers couldn't understand how the commanders could shift responsibility to their subordinates. Writing, he was not friendly. The Eighth Army ignored "personal welfare of the private soldier and was lenient toward inefficient senior officers." Commanders had responded slowly to swift changes in the battle. They had consistently underestimated the enemy, Fellers wrote. The Middle East was in greater danger than it had been at any time since the German invasion of the Soviet Union a year earlier, he said. British reinforcements—an armored division and an infantry division—were still on the long sea journey around Africa and would arrive only in late July.

The Middle East was too important to rely solely on the British to defend it, he told the War Department. The only American help that could arrive in time would be heavy bombers. Send them, he urged the generals in Washington.[1]

It was June 17. In Ritchie's reports to Cairo, the word "withdrawing" repeated. The Eighth Army had just given up El Adem, south of Tobruk. It gave up Sidi Rezegh, further east. The RAF pulled out of a nearby airfield. The coastal road from Tobruk to Egypt was lost.[2]

"Believe Tobruk can be captured in a very short time," Fellers radioed the next day. "British morale is low; their losses heavy."[3]

"Tobruk is temporarily isolated" but more strongly held than during the previous siege, Auchinleck wrote in his weekly report to General Brooke, chief of the Imperial General Staff. He'd just visited the Eighth Army's advanced headquarters at Sollum, on the Egyptian side of the border. "I . . . found morale high and an excellent spirit prevailing."[4]

GENERAL BROOKE READ Auchinleck's cable in Washington. The chief of the Imperial General Staff was wearing the lightweight uniform his London tailor had sewn in a rush. Churchill had told Brooke that Roosevelt was "getting a bit off the rails," and they must go speak to him. Wearing a London uniform in Washington in June would be hell. Brooke's new uniform lacked the field of ribbons on his chest because the tailor hadn't had enough time to sew them on. The tailor delivered the uniform at the railway station as Brooke was leaving. Churchill and Brooke took the prime minister's special train to Loch Ryan in Scotland, then a motorboat to the Boeing flying boat, "beautifully fitted up with bunks to sleep in, dining saloon, lavatories, etc.," Brooke noted.

It took off, northwest toward the solstice sunrise, just before midnight. An hour later, there was light on the horizon. Twenty-six and a half hours later, the big plane put down on the Potomac.[5]

Churchill had at least two reasons to worry. One was Midway: the victory might push American public opinion toward a Japan-first strategy. The other worry contradicted this one: Stalin's foreign minister, Vyacheslav Molotov, had secretly visited the White House. The Soviet Union desperately needed America and Britain to invade France this year, to pull away German divisions before the Red Army collapsed, Molotov had told the president. Afterward, publicly, a joint US-Soviet statement announced agreement on the "urgent tasks of creating a Second Front in Europe in 1942."

Churchill often disagreed with his generals. Brooke considered one of his essential tasks to be keeping Churchill from going off the rails. "Winston never had the slightest doubt that he had inherited all the military genius from his great ancestor Marlborough!" Brooke would write, referring to the legendary seventeenth-century English general. Churchill's "military ideas varied from the most brilliant conceptions at one end to the wildest and most dangerous ideas at the other," Brooke believed. But they agreed that a head-on cross-channel invasion this early would be suicidal. For Churchill the idea raised the very painful memory of his mistake at Gallipoli.[6]

Churchill took another plane to Roosevelt's estate at Hyde Park on the Hudson. Brooke stayed in Washington to meet with George Marshall and the other American generals. Brooke and the Americans agreed that the focus of joint strategy should be invading France, hopefully in 1943. They agreed that invading the Vichy-held French colonies of North Africa was a distraction. They shared great worry about what Churchill and Roosevelt were discussing, unsupervised.

Roosevelt, like Churchill, had to think about leading a nation, not just an army. Japan, not Germany, had attacked America. Public ardor for fighting Germany could wear off if getting Americans into battle in or near Europe was delayed too long. Delay past election day in November could bring more isolationists and Republicans into Congress. Churchill had a solution: open the second front in French North Africa.[7]

Brooke expected a quiet Sunday on June 21. Then Churchill phoned. He and Roosevelt were back in Washington. Brooke and Marshall went to the Oval Office to meet the two leaders. It was a very hot day. Roosevelt put Brooke at ease by inviting him to take his uniform coat off. They broke for lunch, then resumed discussing alternatives: France, North Africa, the Middle East.[8]

Someone came in with a pink slip of paper, an incoming telegram. It was from Colonel Bonner Fellers in Cairo. Roosevelt read it and handed it to Churchill.

"Night of June 20th June 21st Rommel took Tobruk Port," it said.

Besides the loss of the port and the thousands of men taken prisoner, two months' supplies had been lost. The Eighth Army was now defending Sollum, on the Egyptian side of the border. "British troops very tired, dazed, morale low," Fellers wrote. Their best hope was to fall back further, over 130 miles to Mersa Matruh, and there make their stand.[9]

"What can we do to help?" Roosevelt said. Churchill and Brooke thought no words were ever better chosen.[10]

"NEITHER WINSTON NOR I had contemplated such an eventuality and it was a staggering blow," Brooke would recall. Tobruk had held out the year before.

The year before, "there had been no doubt in the minds of the men defending Tobruk," Moorehead wrote. They'd dug the trenches themselves. They were well organized and proud. This time around, they were men who'd just retreated in confusion into Tobruk, men who were exhausted, hungry, and defeated.

The South African general in command had two fresh South African brigades that he had put on the southwest. The year before, that's where Rommel had attacked. But the year before, Rommel had figured out too late that the weakest point was on the southeast. This time around, he attacked there instead. Tanks broke through the perimeter, infantry leapfrogged past, the tanks moved up. They reached the harbor. The fresh South African troops got orders to surrender before they started to fight. This time around, Rommel took Tobruk in twenty-five hours.[11]

"A GOOD SOURCE reports on 20 June," the deciphered message began. What followed were the estimates of "the British intelligence service" of the strength of the German and Italian forces, including captured British guns. Sent in the evening in the German army's Chaffinch key of Enigma, it was deciphered and translated by the next morning.[12]

It was just the kind of message that looked like a report from a very highly placed agent, one who knew British commanders' assessments of the enemy. Now, though, Margaret Storey told her superiors that "Good Source" reports came from the Germans deciphering American messages. The information indeed came from someone highly placed, but who had no idea that he was a good source, or that the enemy was reading his mail.[13]

For Menzies, the one thing that removed certainty from this conclusion was that the Americans had promised to change their code, and the Germans were still hearing from Cairo.

AFTER HE SENT word of Tobruk, Fellers got back to the long radiogram he'd been writing. Captured Axis documents showed that when Rommel started his offensive in late May, he "expected to take Tobruk in four days," Fellers wrote. It had taken close to four weeks, and Rommel "has used more ammunition and fuel, has suffered greater losses than he calculated."

But the Eighth Army's own losses were staggering. It was down to two South African brigades "of low combat efficiency," an Indian division, a British division, some Free French, and a "fresh and complete New Zealand" division. An Australian division was still in Palestine and Syria. Fellers's British sources wouldn't tell him how many tanks they had left. A "most optimistic estimate" was one hundred, only a few American, the rest "mostly worthless" British tanks. Up to half the British artillery had been lost.

His frustration rose as he wrote. "With numerically superior forces, tanks, aircraft, artillery . . . the British army has twice failed to defeat the Axis in Libya." There had to be an explanation. His was failure at the top. "Under their present command, the British cannot be given enough lend-lease equipment to win a victory," he said. "Eighth Army failed to maintain morale of its troops. Its tactical conceptions were consistently faulty . . . German Air Force has complete control of the Eastern Mediterranean. The Royal Navy is impotent."

"If Rommel intends to take the [Nile] Delta," Fellers wrote, "now is an opportune time."[14]

"According to some intercepted cables from the American observer at Cairo, Fellers, we learn that the English have been beaten, and that if Rommel continues his action he has a good chance of reaching as far as the Canal Zone," Galeazzo Ciano wrote in his diary.

The one problem was that Hitler, ecstatic, had rewarded Rommel for taking Tobruk by promoting him to field marshal. The Italian generals who were theoretically Rommel's commanders would have to get the same rank. "Bastico's promotion will make people laugh; Cavallero's will make them indignant," Ciano told Mussolini.[15]

Kesselring ordered his planes back to Sicily to prepare for Operation Hercules, the invasion of Malta. Cavallero ordered a halt of the Axis ground forces at the Egyptian border. Bastico, the Italian commander in Libya, sent a liaison officer to tell Rommel to stop.

Rommel told Bastico's man that he would not follow this "advice." He went over Bastico's head, sent a message to Mussolini, and asked for approval to plunge "deep into Egypt." Mussolini asked Hitler. Hitler answered that the Eighth Army was "as good as destroyed." In southern Russia, advancing German armies would swing down through the Caucasus region into the Middle East. Rommel would provide the other side of a pincer movement that would bring "the collapse of the entire eastern part of the British Empire," Hitler said. "The goddess of victory only approaches a leader once," Hitler told Mussolini. "He who does not seize the opportunity will never have it again."[16]

Before dawn on June 24, Rommel received word from Rome: "Duce agrees to Panzer Army's intention to pursue the enemy into Egypt." Rommel had not waited. "We're on the move and hope to land the next big punch very soon. Speed is the main thing now. The events of the past week lie before me like a dream," he had written to his wife the day before, and had sent his forces to clear a gap in the minefield along the border. When approval came from Rome, they were already rushing into Egypt. Lack of fuel slowed down the advance. His armored force was down to forty-four tanks.[17]

Rommel could have made this decision without a message from Cairo. He was euphoric. He had defied his commanders after the fall of Bir Hakeim, and his wager had paid off.

But by June 23, and possibly by the day before, Rommel had what any general would value: detailed information, from a source that had proven accurate, a source on which he already depended, that his enemy was crumbling, that if he wanted to reach the Nile, this was the moment.[18] He had what a compulsive gambler could only prize: an inside tip that the gamble that felt right in his bones, despite the odds, was a sure bet. If he waited, the Australian division might already be in Egypt. American reinforcements could arrive.

Rommel wagered all he had gained, all that was left of his army, and plunged toward the Delta.

AT THE WHITE House, on the afternoon of June 23, Roosevelt and Churchill and the generals met again. The agenda included possible answers to Roosevelt's question: How could America help in the Middle East?

Marshall's first impulse when he heard about the fall of Tobruk was to send an American armored division to Egypt. The idea was out of character. It showed how deeply the news shocked him. Still gearing up for war, the US Army had only a couple of armored divisions ready. Marshall was entirely committed to building up forces in Britain to invade Europe. The Middle East, as he'd told Fellers, was Britain's responsibility.

Before the meeting, Roosevelt read Fellers's long telegram. The day began earlier where Rommel was. It's likely that Rommel read the telegram before Roosevelt.

Along with Fellers's criticism of the British, the attaché recommended sending "great quantities" of American bombers, tanks, and artillery to the British in Egypt. Even that wasn't enough, he said. He urged creating an American armored corps in the Middle East, of much greater strength than Marshall had suggested. Send two armored divisions, an infantry division, and two antitank brigades, Fellers wrote. At the meeting, the president brought up Fellers's ideas.

Roosevelt did not know how much Fellers disliked him politically. It would not have mattered to him. He was intellectually omnivorous. The attaché's ideas fit his appetite. They would quickly have Americans fighting Germans.

"Fellers is a very valuable observer," Marshall wrote to the president that evening, "but his responsibilities are not those of a strategist and his views are in opposition to mine and those of the entire Operations Division."

Brooke took a train with Marshall to watch army training exercises in South Carolina. He was underwhelmed; he did not think that his allies "have yet realized the standard of training required." In Washington, the Operations Division wrote an analysis showing that shipping a US division to Egypt would cripple the buildup in Britain.

Marshall could now retreat from the idea. He proposed an alternative: the United States would ship three hundred tanks and one hundred howitzers to the Eighth Army. The tanks would be the newest ones, which the British named Shermans, after the Civil War general. They were an improved version of the Grants, which British headquarters in Cairo said were the only Allied tanks "capable of meeting German tanks on anything approaching equal terms." The Shermans, fresh from the factory, had been intended for an American division that was waiting for them in North Ireland.

It was a compromise. On one side was Marshall's own strategy, shared with all his military planners, which said that nothing should be diverted from preparations to invade France. On the other side was British desperation and Roosevelt's desire to help, reinforced by the formerly isolationist military attaché in Cairo.

Roosevelt and Churchill embraced the compromise. Churchill and Brooke took a train to Baltimore; in the harbor they boarded their flying boat for the trip home. The big question, of whether to invade France or French North Africa, was still open, subject to argument, intrigue, and confusion.[19]

Secret agents Johann Eppler and Heinrich Sandstede liked to go to Hollywood Hairdressers on Emad el Dine Street for their morning shave. In the afternoon they often went to the cinema. Evenings they spent at Groppi's, or the Continental rooftop garden, or Madame Bardia's casino, or the Kit-Kat Club. Eventually, to make this all easier, they hired a driver. They hired two servants for their houseboat. Sandstede had a girlfriend named Sandra. Eppler's constant companion was named Edith. She knew him only as Hussein Gaafar. The girls went home at night, not to Eppler and Sandstede's houseboat, one servant would later testify. Nonetheless, Edith had the attraction of forbidden fruit for a German spy: she was Jewish.

Regularly, Sandstede would try sending out his call letters from their wireless set. He got no response. This did not matter terribly, because with all the drinks they'd bought, they'd yet to get any officers to reveal any information.

Rommel's sudden advance in late June worried them. In their diaries, they began recording imaginary espionage activities. Sandy wrote that Eppler had visited Suez and Port Said, at the south and north ends of the Canal, to recruit agents who would report on shipping and troop movements. On June 25, Sandy wrote that Hekmet, the belly dancer, had "rendered us valuable services. Today I received the plans of the dug-outs and fortifications of Tobruk." Then he crossed out "Tobruk" and wrote "Mersa Matruh." He later admitted that he had trouble remembering the difference between the two harbors, one in Libya, the other in Egypt. But the newspapers would have reminded him that Rommel had already taken Tobruk, and was now advancing toward Mersa Matruh. He wrote that after he studied the map, he destroyed it, because it would be too dangerous to keep it. Sandy, it appears, did not know that Hekmet's British lover really had left an old map of Tobruk on her houseboat. His fiction happened to have a slight overlap with the truth.

They figured that when Rommel got to Cairo, the diaries would be their evidence that they had accomplished something as spies.[20]

The Abwehr was getting nothing from its Condor team. But Rommel had plenty of information from Cairo. Before he attacked Tobruk, he received reports that the British had lost most of their tanks to German 88-mm guns, that British commanders were blaming the officers under them and their tank crews for their defeats, that Eighth Army morale was shattered, that British troop movements to prevent collapse in Libya had left Syria and the Persian Gulf unprotected.

After taking the town, he got updates. Only 30 percent of the British warplanes in the Middle East were in shape for combat, and the British had at most one hundred tanks. All of his judgments of how inferior British tactics were to his own, and British generals to himself, were confirmed by the source in Cairo. He knew that British soldiers were getting insufficient rations consisting mainly of canned meat. He did not know that in reporting what forces General Ritchie had left, the source had reduced a South African division to two brigades and that a mistranslation from English to Italian had cut it to one brigade. The Italians did not bother with the word "source." They sent translated documents, including the name at the bottom, "Fellers."

Rommel learned from Fellers that his enemy's best remaining division was New Zealanders under General Bernard Freyberg. A crucial piece of information repeated: the Eighth Army would mount its defense of Egypt at Mersa Matruh.

Some of this was overheard by British wireless operators and decoded at Hut 6. Much more was not.[21]

THE ROAD EAST, from Sollum at the border to Mersa Matruh and beyond, was a slow river of trucks, bumper to bumper. They carried men; they carried supplies that had taken months to move forward, whatever could be loaded up and saved, rations and artillery shells, the machinery of tank repair workshops, bullets, blankets, aircraft fuel, and clothing, with ambulances carrying the wounded stuck between the trucks. The military units were mixed up, like houses lifted by a flood and broken apart and dragged onward. Their great good fortune was that Rommel had moved too quickly for Kesselring's air force, which was short on planes and fuel and was busy attacking Malta so that British ships and planes there could not attack Italian supply ships crossing to Libya. The chaos that was called the Eighth Army moved eastward under mostly clear skies.[22]

At General Headquarters in Cairo, an officer from the Operations Section came to talk to Colonel Ralph Bagnold about the Qattara Depression. More than two years had passed since Bagnold had given a tour of the desert to the general who was then his division commander, and shown him the cliffs overlooking the vast Qattara lowlands and salt marshes. The general had been reprimanded for leaving his headquarters. Now the strategists were interested in topography. Bagnold said that the cliffs were impassable for vehicles except in two spots, that only one track through the lowlands might be useable by light tanks, that in some areas vehicles would likely get bogged down in sand and elsewhere in standing water. Telling what would be passable from the air was impossible.[23]

Bagnold had driven through territory that no one else had dared cross. Politely, he was saying that it would be easier to drive tanks across a sea than across the Qattara Depression.

On June 25, four days after Tobruk fell, two days after Rommel invaded Egypt, a two-engine RAF bomber landed at the spot in the desert east of Mersa Matruh where General Ritchie had set up his headquarters. On board were Auchinleck and his old comrade in arms Major General Eric Dorman-Smith. From the plane, the two drove to Ritchie's tent.

Auchinleck stepped inside and told Ritchie that he was no longer in command of the Eighth Army. Auchinleck was taking over in the field himself. He'd left a deputy in Cairo to manage the entire Middle East Command.

The flight from Cairo could not have lasted more than an hour. Auchinleck and Dorman-Smith had sat on the floor of the bomber and tried to figure out how to stop Rommel's army before it reached Alexandria and Cairo. Since the beginning of the war, plans had designated Mersa Matruh as the final point of defense. The public knew this.

Auchinleck chose a new plan. He would leave General Freyberg's New Zealand division and other forces at Mersa Matruh. If the small town and port fell, people would believe Egypt was lost.

Nonetheless, most of the Eighth Army would retreat over a hundred miles more, to a line starting at the rail station known as El Alamein. By pulling further back, Auchinleck would be leaving only sixty miles between his chosen battlefield and Alexandria. But he would stretch the Axis supply line even further and shorten his own.

Most important, El Alamein marked where the coastline and the Qattara Depression came closest, leaving a corridor of passable desert only forty miles wide. Rommel might fight his way through Auchinleck's line. But he could not go around it.[24]

DESPITE WARTIME CENSORSHIP, newspapers were constantly referring to the "ability and personality of Rommel," Security Intelligence Middle East complained in a roundup on the public mood. "An Axis-inspired whispering campaign" had exploited this and "exalted him to an almost legendary figure of invincibility," SIME said. The British agency's informants reported a tidal wave of rumors: that "pro-British Egyptian politicians had received anonymous warnings that they would be publicly hanged by Rommel's orders on 3 July," that Britain was "trying to force the Egyptian army into the war," that "the Egyptian army was preparing to join the Germans," and that Churchill visited Washington in an "act of despair" in order to discuss what peace terms to offer Germany.

There were also optimistic rumors, SIME said, but they were harmful, too, because they'd lead to disappointment: that American troops had landed in Tunisia, that sixty-five thousand Americans had arrived in Egypt, that eighty thousand were on their way from South Africa, and that General Wavell had returned to Egypt. In the Cairo streets, Wavell had graduated to the rank of savior, and was about to have a second coming.[25]

At Panzer Army headquarters, Konstantin von Neurath received a cable from Berlin with a calmer evaluation of the mood in Egypt. Neurath was the German Foreign Office's liaison to Rommel, and was in charge of propaganda warfare. "King Farouk is extremely well disposed towards Germany," said the cable. "We are at the moment anxious to get a message to the king that he should conceal himself from the British at the proper moment, as his person is of great importance to us." Untangled, that meant: We're afraid the British will take Farouk when they retreat, and we'd like him as a puppet. "The German watchword" must be that the Axis has come "not to conquer Egypt, but to free her from British imperialism," the cable said.

As for the Egyptian army, Neurath was told, it would neither help nor hinder the invasion. The junior officers had "great sympathy" for Germany, but the British had taken all of the army's effective weaponry, leaving it powerless.[26]

Mussolini was happy about the victories but upset that Rommel was getting all the credit, stealing Italy's glory. So Ciano wrote in his diary. Italian officials were busy preparing "a declaration of independence for Egypt, changes in government, etc.," Ciano said. Lest there be a question of what "independence" meant, he noted that Mussolini hoped Italy could establish its "commissariat," its governing office, in Alexandria within half a month.[27]

"The rumor was that Egypt would be given to Italy," Anwar al-Sadat would recall. He got together with his friends among the junior officers and came up with a plan: they would send someone to the German side of the lines and offer to "recruit an entire army" to fight on the Axis side; they would provide aerial photos of British positions, in return for full independence. Sadat's memory often glorified his actions. In this case, though, the plan was real—and shows that it was only at this moment that the officers fully realized that an Axis victory might mean trading British domination for Italian or German rule.[28]

At the Reich Security Main Office, the RSHA, in Berlin, preparations accelerated to send Walther Rauff's *Einsatzkommando* to Africa. Rauff's assignment would be to carry out "executive measures"—the SS bureaucracy's term for mass murder—against the seventy-five thousand Jews in Egypt. Once Rommel advanced further, so would Rauff and his men. Its future targets would include Palestine, where at least half a million Jews lived; the twenty-five thousand Jews of Syria and Lebanon; and if Rommel realized his "Oriental strategy" of conquering the entire Middle East, close to one hundred thousand Jews in Iraq.[29]

THE MESSAGE WAS from the Good Source. It described the tactics of German tanks attacking British positions. Translated into German, it was sent to Rommel's intelligence officer on June 23. It took another three days for Hut 6 to find the settings for the Chaffinch key of Enigma. On June 26, Menzies gave the decoded message to Churchill.

"Is this still happening?" Churchill scrawled, outraged, in his red ink.

Menzies checked, and answered. The Americans had, at last, changed their cipher on the 25th, he said. He did not explain what had taken so long, because he had no idea. "If leakage continues, then there must be a traitor with access to American telegrams in Cairo, transmitting by secret wireless from Egypt, but available evidence does not support this likelihood."[30]

Since several days could pass between when the Good Source in Cairo sent a message and when it showed up at Bletchley Park in decoded Enigma texts, it was too early to know if the Americans had finally plugged the leak. In the meantime, Rommel was spurring his sleepless, victorious troops toward the Nile.

CECIL BEATON, CELEBRITY fashion photographer turned war photographer, was in the Syrian desert snapping an armor and artillery exercise when he heard about Tobruk. In Tehran he'd done a portrait of Fawzia, queen of Persia, King Farouk's sister, her hair covered, her arms bare, her face incandescent, her eyes looking for something lost and distant beyond the palace walls; in Baghdad, he photographed King Faisal II, age seven, wearing shorts and looking lost on an immense throne. Beaton had left much of his luggage in Cairo. The night after he heard about the defeat, he dreamed that the "Germans had arrived in Cairo, and had discovered my excessively indiscreet diaries left at Shepheard's Hotel, which were now getting a very mixed reception among my friends, relayed over the air to England by Lord Haw-Haw," the Englishman turned Nazi radio propagandist. War creates many fears. Like Almasy, it seems, Beaton feared shame most of all.[31]

ROMMEL'S TANKS CROSSED the minefield south of Mersa Matruh. Inexplicably, the mines did not explode. On British wireless networks, reports turned the last thirty tanks of the Panzer Army into a force of a hundred. General Freyberg was wounded. His New Zealanders were surrounded. They broke through the German forces and escaped. An Indian division and a British one were mauled as they retreated.[32]

"Now the battle of Mersa Matruh has also been won and our leading units are only 125 miles from Alexandria," Rommel wrote to his wife on June 29. He'd already advanced three hundred miles from Tobruk in a week. The British had left the roads and railway in "first-class order" for him to use, he exulted. "There'll be a few more battles to fight before we reach our goal," Rommel wrote, "but I think the worst is well behind us." He was winning his wager.[33]

Act V

LINE IN THE SAND

1

EL ALAMEIN

July 1942. El Alamein-Cairo-Bletchley
Park-Washington.

SMOKE ROSE FROM the grand British embassy facing the Nile. Smoke
rose a few hundred yards down the river, too, from the mansions of
Garden City that war had transformed into British General Headquarters. General Tom Corbett, left in charge in Cairo by Auchinleck,
was on his own, out of touch with the front. He ordered officers to
wear their pistols at all times, imposed a curfew, and ordered the burning of all secret documents.[1]

In British offices, secretaries told war photographer Cecil Beaton that everything was "a flap," a very polite way not to say "panic."
Beaton had just flown back to Cairo. A RAF squadron leader showed
him a map with a pencil line marking the El Alamein positions. They
looked "perilously near to Alexandria," Beaton thought. Outside, on
the crowded streets, "black charred pieces of papers drifted down from
the chimneys—a storm of black cinders, a hail of funereal confetti." It
was July 1, 1942. The German radio station promised that Rommel's
forces "would be in Alexandria on the 6th and in Cairo on the 9th."
People expected them sooner. At Groppi's garden cafe, cipher officer

June Watkins looked out the window of the ladies' room and saw waiters painting welcome signs in German for Rommel's officers.[2]

Alexander Kirk, the US ambassador, came to see Miles Lampson. Kirk had instructions to stay in Cairo if Lampson did. Lampson said he intended to keep his entire staff in Cairo. The British embassy had a "special position" in Egypt, Lampson said. He did not need to spell out that the ambassador embodied the empire. Leaving would have a "lamentable effect" on morale, Lampson said.

Kirk "argued vehemently against this position." A diplomatic mission caught in a conquered city, he said, was "an embarrassment to its government . . . besides being treated by the enemies as objects of contempt and ridicule."

Lampson had his own fears. He did not admit them to an American.[3]

AUCHINLECK KNEW THE positions of the German units as they pushed forward from Mersa Matruh, and that German antiaircraft batteries urgently needed both diesel fuel and shells. He knew that Rommel had intended to attack the British line at El Alamein on June 30 but his "troops did not reach the areas ordered" on time, so the attack would come early the next day. Auchinleck knew that Rommel's plan was to launch a feint toward the south. So the Eighth Army could ignore the German division traveling loudly and visibly southward on June 30; Auchinleck knew it would turn back to the north and join the real attacks. He knew within one kilometer the points on the map where the attacks were aimed.

The close coordination between Rommel's ground forces and the Luftwaffe, one of the Germans' strengths in battle, had become their hidden weakness. Luftwaffe liaison officers at Rommel's headquarters used the Enigma key that Hut 6 had named Scorpion. The German code clerks had no idea that when they set up their machines at midnight, the wheel order, ring settings, and plugboard pairs that they'd been assigned were all copied from a previous month's setting for a different key. Hut 6 was now breaking Scorpion so quickly that a liaison message about German army plans for the next day reached Auchinleck in as little as seven and a half hours.[4]

The German army's Chaffinch key was still a harder problem. Sometimes it took several days to break; sometimes a day's messages were never decoded. On July 1, Margaret Storey had not seen a report from the Good Source for six days. This was promising. She couldn't yet be certain.

But Rommel was sure. The Good Source was silent, at least for now. "Unfortunately, we can no longer count on the reliable messages for the foreseeable future, which we have used till this point and which gave us immediate insight into enemy operations," said an intelligence evaluation from army headquarters in Germany. It was dated June 29.[5]

Rommel had seen this happen before. All through the winter before, he had depended on those "reliable messages" from Cairo. Before Christmas, in the worst moments of his retreat, he'd received a gift, upsetting but valuable: word that the British were intercepting all his communications and knew what orders he was giving.[6] In January, after he'd lost half of Libya, the intercepted letters from Fellers told him that the RAF was sending 250 warplanes to the Far East, "undermining the position of British aviation in the Middle East," and that five thousand British soldiers had embarked from Suez for the Pacific, half of them from field artillery.

He had not needed to read the minds of British commanders. He had not needed supernatural intuition. He was a gambler, but one who could read the other player's cards.

As he went on the offensive, he knew the British thought he had "insufficient air and armored forces for a major counter-attack." In the days that followed, the intercepted mail from Cairo had told him how many tanks the British had, and that British workshops would take months to restore damaged tanks to combat condition. It had told him that an Indian division was short of motor transport, that a South African division was "badly depleted," that the British expected to be pushed back almost to Tobruk. He had proved them right.[7]

In early February, out of fuel and ammunition, harassed by commanders in Rome and Berlin who thought he was irresponsible and dangerous, he had stopped.[8] A few days later, the mail from Cairo also ceased.

In April the Good Source had miraculously reappeared, overflowing with information. So on June 29, his experience said that conceivably, in two months or three, it could start again. But right now he was driving forward, and the source failed him.

Recognition that the silence wasn't momentary, that it would last, had come slowly. The last message to or from Cairo that he received was sent on June 25 at the latest.[9] Before that, Washington had informed either Colonel Fellers or General Maxwell that an American armored division would be shipped to Egypt. Cavallero, head of the Italian Supreme Command, received word. Rommel almost certainly did. They did not see Marshall's order, late on June 25 Washington time, cancelling the plan.[10]

Much more important for his hour-to-hour decisions, Rommel saw Fellers's cables saying that Mersa Matruh was where the Eighth Army would turn, fight, and try to save Egypt. No cable from Fellers told him of Auchinleck's decision late on the 25th to make his stand at El Alamein.[11]

After Rommel took Mersa Matruh, the Luftwaffe's aerial reconnaissance and Captain Alfred Seebohm's battlefield listening group, Strategical Intercept Company 621, could tell him that the British were building positions at El Alamein. But Rommel's intelligence officers knew that there was "no comparison" between the quality of the "good source" and what Seebohm could supply.[12] He had every reason to believe that he had already won the crucial battle and that El Alamein would be a mere epilogue.[13]

WILLIAM FRIEDMAN HAD been mistaken in his second cable to John Tiltman about the leak: the cipher tables of the Military Intelligence Code had not been replaced on May 1. The code room on El Nabatat Street in Cairo had not stopped using the code on June 3. Friedman knew what instructions had been sent. Someone had not gotten around to carrying them out. The proof was that the leak did not stop on either of those dates.

The mystery was why it took another two weeks before the code was replaced. At least a week passed between Churchill's threat to call Roosevelt and the leak stopping. What were the Americans up to?

One possibility was that Friedman and his colleagues discovered that the new cipher machine for the Cairo office was still in Washington, and had it sent by air—on the ferry route south to Brazil, across the Atlantic to Takoradi, thence to Khartoum and Egypt. If that was the case, neither the Signal Intelligence Service nor the Military Intelligence Division ordered Fellers to stop using the old code while the new machine was on the way.

An American intelligence officer visiting Bletchley Park a year after these events had a different explanation: a radiogram to Cairo gave the order to change the code as of June 17. "But for some incomprehensible reason," RCA, the commercial radio firm, "failed to send the message."[14]

There was no scheming traitor in Washington or Cairo. The treachery was carelessness.

In the week that slip of paper with the text for Cairo allegedly sat in the RCA office, Tobruk fell and thirty-five thousand men were taken prisoner.[15] In that week, Rommel learned from a source hitherto absolutely reliable that this was the moment to conquer the Nile Delta, and he seized the moment. And then the source went silent—this time, never to resume.

A DOZEN PLANES landed at Derna. The last one crashed coming in. A single passenger was killed—Mussolini's barber, who had been brought to shave him each morning.

Waiting to enter Egypt as its new Roman emperor, the dictator stayed in the Green Mountains, at the town of Beda Littoria. His presence was a secret, so all the Italian war correspondents knew. Sandbags surrounded his villa, and soldiers set up a checkpoint on the main road outside. One day they stopped two trucks carrying British prisoners. Mussolini, with a tommy gun hanging from his shoulder, came out to look and to talk to the guards. "You must hate the enemy," he told them. "Be on the lookout and shoot at the first sign of revolt."[16]

Hatred came in different degrees. The Italian army segregated POWs. Indian and South African black soldiers were kept in worse camps and got less food than white prisoners.[17] Even greater hatred was reserved for Italy's Libyan Jewish subjects. By the end of June, the regime had trucked most of Cyrenaica's Jews to the camp at Giado. Men in the camp were subject to forced labor that included carrying rocks or bags of gravel back and forth. The prisoners understood that the only purpose of the Sisyphean task was to degrade them. When some of the inmates worked up the courage to complain about the lack of food, the camp authorities told them, "The purpose of bringing you here is not to feed you but to starve you to death."[18]

From a Nazi perspective, the Italians were dilettantes.

On June 30, an item appeared in the *New York Times* under the headline "1,000,000 Jews Slain by Nazis, Report Says." It described this as something that World Jewish Congress spokesmen had "charged" at a London press conference. They cited the underground information smuggled out to Poland's government-in-exile, which said that seven hundred thousand Jews had been murdered in that country. To that they added the slaughter of Jews in Romania, Nazi-occupied Russia, and elsewhere in Europe. The *Times* story did not include such details as the murder of thirty-five thousand Jews in Lodz in gas vans. The article was six paragraphs long, on page seven of the paper. One had to be cautious in reporting such things; they might be propaganda or rumor.[19]

The next day, Walter Schellenberg, head of the SS foreign intelligence service, met SS chief Heinrich Himmler to lay out his completed proposal for Egypt. The same afternoon, Himmler met with Hitler and got approval to attach Walther Rauff's *Einsatzkommando* to Rommel's army. The engineer of the gas vans could get to work as soon as Rommel conquered Egypt.[20]

To THE NORTH of the railway stop at El Alamein, a couple hundred yards away, was blue sea. If you looked to the east, west, or south, you saw a flat land of yellow-brown sand and scattered dots of scrub in a shade closer to gray than green. Sometimes the wind caught sand and threw it upward in careless beige brushstrokes. The battle map showed the ground rising to hilltops a hundred feet higher than the sea. The slopes were gentle; an old man carrying a load wouldn't have been tired by them. Inland were two ridges running east to west, wrinkles in the land. The southern one was Ruweisat Ridge.

Axis commanders expected to pass through quickly. "When the Nile Delta is reached," the Panzer Army's chief medical officer told his subordinates on June 30, they needed to take precautions against smallpox and plague, and to prevent soldiers from drinking unboiled water or buying ice cream from street vendors. Kesselring wrote that there was "evidence of sympathy for Rommel" in Egypt, which "would come over to the German side" if propaganda was skillfully handled. Rommel's orders at noon on July 1 assigned units to "mop up" the British strongpoint on the coast at El Alamein, to open the road to Alexandria, and to "pursue [the] British to the east."[21]

Hut 6 relayed a translation of those orders to the Eighth Army's field headquarters. When Auchinleck read them later in the day, the tired general had reason to smile for a moment.

In Rommel's plan, two Panzer Army tank divisions were supposed to speed between British positions and cross Ruweisat Ridge, then encircle the British from behind. When they started up the ridge, artillery shells rained down on them. The shells were fired by an Indian brigade that had just arrived from Persia. The Indians were inexperienced, short of ammunition—and a complete surprise to the Germans, who spent the day dislodging them. At dusk, white-turbaned Sikh soldiers retreated. But the German divisions were stuck on the ridge, their advance blocked.

A German infantry division was supposed to pass north of the ridge, closer to El Alamein, and turn toward the coast. The plan did not account for a South African division, whose presence and very existence was unknown to Rommel. The South Africans opened up with "machine guns, anti-tank guns, mortars and artillery." Some of the German infantrymen turned and ran.[22]

Rommel had stuck his fists into a thornbush and they were caught.

A Luftwaffe liaison officer with the army begged the German air force overnight for fighter protection of a division hammered by RAF bombers. Another liaison officer conveyed an urgent early-morning request from Rommel to bomb the El Alamein strongpoint "as progress there is difficult." A Luftwaffe commander replied that sandstorms made this impossible. "Enemy resisted obstinately with artillery and tanks," a liaison officer reported in the Scorpion key at the end of the second day. "No movements of retreat observed," another German air force man radioed.

Auchinleck received these unintended words of encouragement within hours. The messages from German supply networks could take a bit longer. They told of truck shortages, of the Italian high command demanding the return of one hundred trucks lent to the Luftwaffe, of a German armored division that had "water for two days, food for one day." From his own army, he knew that artillery units were at last coordinating their fire, concentrating on one point instead of fighting separately.[23]

On the third night, Rommel admitted to the German high command that "the strength of the enemy, our own decreasing fighting strength and the most precarious supply situation, compel us to discontinue our major attack for the time being." Rommel's gamble had presumed that the Eighth Army would indeed crumble, that taking Alexandria would give him a new port, that the quick conquest of the Levant would eliminate the threat from RAF bases there and make shipping to Alexandria safe. Instead, a planned convoy to bring Italian reinforcements via Alexandria was shelved.

The battle wasn't over. Auchinleck needed fresh forces to hold on and push back. Rommel needed more fuel than he had to retreat to Libya. His only direction toward sufficient supplies was forward.[24]

ANYWHERE BEYOND THE desert, the details of the battle were lost. Rommel was delayed, as a train might be. He would still arrive. "At the High Command in Rome they are optimistic, and convinced that the lull is altogether temporary," Ciano told his diary.[25]

"Arabs, receive the good news and spread it throughout Arabian lands," Germany's Arabic-language station broadcast on the morning of July 3. "In this solemn moment, when Axis forces are advancing victoriously into Egypt, the governments of the Reich and Italy declare Egypt independent . . . These Axis war activities in the Near East are carried out for the sole purpose of freeing the Arabs from the British rule. The Axis policy towards Egypt is one and only one, namely: Egypt for the Egyptians."[26] Two months earlier, Rashid Ali al-Gailani and Hajj Amin el-Husseini, the exiled pretenders to Iraqi and Palestinian Arab leadership, had begged for such a declaration. Hitler and Mussolini had decided against it, for fear that it would not inspire Arab insurrections against British rule, and Axis claims to wide Arab support would look empty. Now they decided the odds were in their favor. Rommel's victories would inspire a rebellion in Egypt, in turn speeding his conquest of the Nile.

The Japanese ambassador in Berlin met with Foreign Minister Ribbentrop. Germany's just-launched offensive in the Soviet Union included a thrust southeast. Once Stalingrad fell, the way would be open to cross the Caucasus into Persia. With Russia defeated, "while Rommel on the other side is pressing forward through Egypt into the Near East, then the war will have been won," Ribbentrop said. "In the last four weeks we have come closer to this goal than the German leadership, even in its greatest optimism, could ever have hoped to achieve."[27]

In Alexandria, you could "hear the endless firing of guns all day and night," a Greek woman wrote to a friend in England, in a letter stopped by the censor. Her Italian neighbor "was singing at the top of her lungs and whenever I heard her I felt I could murder her."[28] The Turkish ambassador in Cairo cabled Ankara. "The number of Egyptian Jews who desire . . . visas for Turkey is increasing every day," he said, and asked how he should respond.[29]

On the road from the coast of Palestine to the pass at Megiddo, a team of Palmah fighters scouted where to place explosives to block the expected Axis advance from the south. A long line of trucks came from the opposite direction. They carried the men of the Ninth Australian Division from Syria. A truck stopped. To the Jewish fighters, the men who climbed out "to drink beer and piss" looked like happy giants.

"Why do you look so sad?" an Australian asked the Jews, as one of the latter would recall many years later.

"Rommel is coming," a Jew answered.

"Wait for the news," an Australian said. They climbed back into their truck and headed toward El Alamein.[30]

Two thousand miles from the sandstorms of El Alamein, in a sunless room with a nicotine-stained ceiling, Margaret Storey wrote up her listing of enemy intelligence for the first days of July.

For her very select group of readers, the report had welcome news, conveyed by silence. The Good Source in Cairo had vanished. He had appeared two months earlier. His reports, each containing a splinter of a hint of who he was, had piled up on her desk, next to the ashtray full of her cigarette butts, until Good Source became a name. At first, she'd listed him as an Axis agent. As the fragments of clues began fitting together, the source had shifted shape: not one man but several, in Cairo and Washington; not traitors, but using a compromised code. Now, despite the lethargy and disbelief in Washington, the source had been eliminated.[31]

Still, Storey and Russell Dudley-Smith could not close the Bluebird file. They had no idea of how the Germans had acquired the Americans' code.

The first memo about sharing information with the United States had passed between British staff officers at General Headquarters Middle East in January 1942. "We ought to tighten things up now that the Americans are in the war," it said. Rules were needed about what secrets could be shared. Orders from London said that "future operations should be divulged . . . to Americans only when their cooperation is required." Complicating matters, General Maxwell was the highest-ranking US officer in Cairo, but he was a logistics man, not a combat officer. Fellers seemed to represent George Marshall, the US Army chief of staff, the American who mattered. The memo sat on desks for months before anyone took action.

Bonner Fellers, meanwhile, sent unhappy cables to Washington, saying he had to depend on friendships to get information because the War Department hadn't named him liaison to the British command. Indirectly, this was testimony to how many friendships he had developed.

When, at last, he officially got the title of liaison officer, a British lieutenant colonel wrote up orders on what Fellers could be told. The American was not to get secrets such as the dates of planned operations, or the location of forces to be used. A short list of officers could give him information. Auchinleck personally had to approve telling him how many tanks, in what condition, British forces had. Air Marshal Tedder had to sign off on telling him how many planes the RAF could get in the air. The final version went out to General Ritchie at his Eighth Army battle headquarters in the desert and to other top officers in mid-May.[32]

And then, it appears, everyone went right on talking to the congenial American. Someone, for instance, told him that commandos were about to attack Axis airbases in Libya and the Aegean. In his radiograms, Fellers assiduously went on demonstrating that he knew just what was happening on the battlefield, and even what would happen.

Now, at the beginning of July, Fellers added another title to his list of jobs. Maxwell's supply mission had just been upgraded to the US Army Forces in the Middle East. Fellers became the acting chief of staff. And then, very quickly, Maxwell decided that Fellers should go home. "Due to unfortunate disclosures, Colonel Fellers finds it most difficult, if not impossible, to gain access" to useful information from the British, Maxwell reported to the War Department.[33]

Orders followed for Fellers to fly to Washington "for temporary duty," after which he'd return to Cairo. Whether he knew it or not when he boarded a military plane southward for the first leg of his long journey, the temporary duty would be permanent.[34]

Before leaving, he had an uncomfortable meeting with his direct commander. Colonel Louis Compton, head of the British Empire Section in US military intelligence, had been sent to the Middle East to report on the political mood in the shadow of Rommel's advance. At British military offices, he met a mix of suspicion, hostility, and silence. "With difficulty," he got permission to visit Auchinleck's battle headquarters. He asked to go to the front and got turned down.[35]

Compton gave Fellers disturbing news. "Some time during the spring someone, either the British or the German, or both, cracked our secret code, and the British were getting all my complementary messages which were coming to Washington," Fellers wrote to his former chief code clerk, Marie Broach, who'd just returned to America.

Compton was investigating the leak, and Fellers wanted Broach to send a statement about how strict security had been—for instance, that "the cipher table [and] the code books were kept in separate safes" and that when one clerk married an RAF sergeant, she was switched to different work. "Beyond a doubt, the code was either lifted in Maxwell's office or cracked by intercept radio," Fellers wrote.[36]

He was right about this much: he'd become persona non grata in Cairo because of the content of his cables—not because of the leak itself. The Germans had read Maxwell's radiograms, but he did not have to go home. They'd read Marshall's cables to both men. Fellers's messages, though, revealed not just his "complementary" views but also his unsettling success at learning British plans, which he'd sent to Washington even before operations were carried out.

Fellers's assignment as attaché in Cairo was constructed out of contradictions: he was an overt spy, gathering intelligence for an ally. He'd been very successful at it. He'd had no idea that he'd been turned into an Axis spy as well, and no idea how it happened.

Fellers was mistaken about the British cracking his code. They'd accidentally spied on his spying by cracking Enigma. His insinuation about his rival and friend Maxwell was also wrong: Maxwell had not left the codebooks unprotected, allowing someone to steal them. As for Compton, nothing he could learn in Cairo explained the gaping breach in US cipher security.

"EGYPTIAN POPULATION HAS remained surprisingly steady. Curious feature has been almost complete absence of Egyptian fifth column." So Colonel Maunsell of SIME and another intelligence officer responsible for Arab affairs, Iltyd Clayton, reported to their superiors in London. Prime Minister Nahas helped maintain that calm by arresting "over 300 undesirables . . . since the German advance" and shutting the Royal Automobile Club, a "centre of well-to-do enemy sympathisers," according to SIME. Ali Maher, the pro-Axis former prime minister, had been under house arrest since March.

"Many Egyptian elements previously hostile have offered cooperation and support," Maunsell and Clayton added. "Azzam for example has spoken out most openly for us and against Axis."[37] Fellers was likely less surprised at Abdul Rahman Azzam's behavior. He knew that his Egyptian friend hated the Axis even more than he wanted to be rid of the British.

Mussolini and Hitler had lost their bet: Rommel reaching El Ala-mein did not set off an insurrection in Egypt. The day after Clayton and Maunsell sent their cable, though, an Egyptian air force officer took off for a training flight and did not return. The next day, an-other pilot vanished with his plane. Evidence accumulated that both had headed east, toward Axis-held territory. At least one was trying to deliver the offer of Egyptian junior officers to support the Axis. The Axis promise of independence had not even reassured the rebellious young officers; they believed they needed to provide a quid pro quo to avoid Italian rule.

In Anwar al-Sadat's telling, the Germans shot down one of the British-made planes and killed the pilot. Germany's Arabic-language radio, on the other hand, claimed that three (not two) Egyptian pilots had successfully defected to the Axis. Erwin Ettel, the SS colonel and former German ambassador to Iran, told Ribbentrop that King Fa-rouk had claimed credit for sending the airmen "with plans and maps for Rommel" as proof of the king's "readiness to work with the Axis."[38]

Ettel's report would eventually fall into British hands, to Farouk's embarrassment. It was almost certainly false. The junior officers had a prominent mentor, but it was not the king. They'd lost faith in him in February, when he surrendered to Lampson.

A more accurate assessment of Farouk's mood came from a long-time friend of his late father, who told Lampson that he'd met the king and found him "extremely frightened." Farouk wanted to hold onto his throne and could not make up his mind whether that meant leaving with the British if they left Cairo, or staying under Axis occupation. His way of coping was to dine at Shepheard's Hotel with one of his Italian cronies and throw parties from eleven at night to four in the morning at his country estate.[39]

"We can't give the invader a pretext to annihilate us," Werner Senator insisted. Senator was speaking at an emergency meeting of the Jewish Agency Executive, the top Zionist body in Palestine. A Hebrew University administrator and a man of moderate politics, he was arguing against engaging in partisan warfare if the Axis conquered the country. Moshe Haim Shapiro, a religious Zionist leader, backed him up. "If

someone told us that an invasion of the Land of Israel means anni-
hilation of the Jewish community," he said, then it would make sense
to say, "Let me die with the Philistines"—that is, emulate the biblical
Samson, who chose death in order to kill his enemies. But, Shapiro
said, "if there is another possibility, of living in a ghetto in the Land of
Israel, then there's hope, albeit meager . . . that some will survive." Like
the anonymous editor at the *New York Times*, it seems, Shapiro did not
believe the news item that the Nazis were exterminating Jews.

Another member of the executive, Yitzhak Gruenbaum, answered
with fierce despair. "If the Germans in Poland had met violent resistance from Jews, our situation there wouldn't be worse, because it
couldn't possibly be worse than it is now," he said. "There's no hope
of saving any of what we've created from the German invader, if he
conquers this land . . . At least we can make sure to leave a legend of
Masada after us."[40]

High Commissioner MacMichael had a guest for a night in Jerusalem, Hermione Ranfurly wrote in her diary. General Henry Maitland
Wilson, commander of the Ninth Army in Syria and Palestine, was
returning from the Sinai to Beirut. He'd received orders to prepare
defenses facing south, in case Rommel pushed past the Suez Canal.
Until now, he had steadfastly maintained that the danger of a Nazi
invasion came from the north.[41] (At the beginning of the war, as head
of the British forces in Egypt, Wilson had already demonstrated his
blinkered vision by berating the division commander who left Mersa
Matruh to reconnoiter the desert with Ralph Bagnold.)

The Palmah deployed two companies to kibbutzim in southern
Palestine to face the invasion. They had no guns. The weapons with
which they'd trained at Mishmar Ha'emek belonged to the British.
After a week and a half, rifles arrived from the Haganah militia's illegal
stores. The deployment was a tragic gesture. Two companies of briefly
trained irregulars were not going to stop the Panzer Army. They were
there to die and leave a legend.[42]

EXCEPT FOR THE eager Australians, Auchinleck's army consisted of battered divisions that had retreated from Libya. The New Zealanders were
exceptions only in that they'd been battered at Mersa Matruh inside

Egypt. One of Auchinleck's successes was getting artillery units to focus their fire to block enemy attacks and support his own infantry. (Each of his successes underlined his error in waiting so long to relieve Ritchie and take over in the field himself.) And yet, having lost vast ammunition dumps everywhere from Bir Hakeim back to Mersa Matruh, Auchinleck was using up his artillery shells before new supplies could arrive by sea.[43]

Auchinleck knew that his enemy was in worse shape. A precise stream of deciphered Italian naval messages on Mediterranean convoys allowed the RAF to target tankers bringing fuel to Africa. Deciphered Enigma messages revealed that Rommel needed reinforcements to be brought quickly, by air. But aircraft fuel was so scarce in Axis-held Africa—so said a Luftwaffe supply message decoded in Hut 6—that transport planes bringing troops had to land at Tobruk, a short enough hop from Crete that they could return without refueling. The Luftwaffe was short on escort planes to protect the troop planes, said another deciphered message. From Tobruk, trucks had to bring the soldiers hundreds of miles to El Alamein. Trucks were in short supply, so men got stuck in Libya. Airplane fuel wasn't the only kind desperately needed. Tanks and trucks also had to run on something. The Panzer Army's "most urgent need is fuel and ammunition," said yet another decoded message.[44]

Auchinleck knew as well that Rommel intended to send what remained of three of his divisions on July 7 to overrun the New Zealanders' position at Bab el Qattara, the Gate of Qattara, on the southern end of the front. The New Zealand division quietly pulled out. Rommel spent three days—and badly needed fuel and ammunition—capturing the empty fortifications at Bab el Qattara.

Rommel had left weaker Italian forces to hold the line near the sea. Auchinleck knew this too. In the predawn darkness of July 10, the Australians attacked on the coast. Rommel was twenty miles away in the desert. He found out about the Australian attack from the roar of artillery that carried across the sands and yanked him from his sleep.

With first light, a brigade of Australians pushing forward on a rise of white sand spotted a clump of trucks and antennae. As the Australians closed in, they came under machine-gun fire. When they got close enough, they realized the enemy gunners were German, not Italian. After an hour and a half of fighting, the Australians had seventy-three prisoners, including the wounded commander, Captain Alfred Seebohm.

No advanced intelligence had revealed that the forward sections of Strategical Intercept Company 621 would be in that spot or that Seebohm himself would be visiting that day. The capture of the unit was a gift of fortune.

The men themselves, "well trained, intelligent . . . of strong Nazi conviction and full of German propaganda cliches," revealed very little under interrogation, except that Seebohm was the "pivot on which the whole company turned." The deputy commander, not yet digesting that he would not soon see his superiors, feared that he and Seebohm would be court-martialed for deploying the intercept team where it had only Italian infantry to protect it. Seebohm himself died before he could be questioned.

The stacks of documents in the trucks, on the other hand, revealed that Company 621 knew the British code for map locations and the radio call signs for Eighth Army units. It possessed a wealth of captured British codebooks. Often it did not need to decode anything because British officers communicated freely in plain language. On the other hand, the Urdu spoken by Indian officers and the Afrikaans of the South Africans might as well have been unbreakable ciphers. None of Seebohm's men knew those languages.

Seebohm's personal papers included his unit's monthly reports. In one, the anonymous author examined intercepted messages for evidence of British intelligence successes. Without knowing her name, he had tried to emulate Margaret Storey. Seebohm's man concluded confidently that the British had not broken Enigma.

A German intelligence document written later in the war said that the capture of Company 621 was "for us the equivalent of a lost battle." It took months to replace Seebohm and the men he'd trained. In the meantime, according to the Italian intelligence chief in North Africa, battlefield intelligence was "very poor."[45]

Throughout May and June, Rommel could see the Eighth Army's plans, positions, and perceptions, its strengths and weaknesses. He had two good eyes. Just as he burst into Egypt, Rommel lost one eye, the stronger one. The last thing he'd seen with that eye was a vision of conquering the Nile and then the entire Middle East.

In those same weeks, with each new success at reading Enigma keys, the cataracts were removed from the eyes of the British.

Before the battle began at El Alamein, another battle had nearly been decided. The struggle began with Rejewski, Turing, and Welchman; it continued with Herivel and his brainstorm about the psyche of the tired Enigma clerk, with Reg Parker and his patient expectation of repeated keys, with Storey and Dudley-Smith's sifting of clues. They had defeated whoever it was, as yet unknown, who had given Rommel his secrets.

This victory was not enough, by itself, to save Cairo and Suez, Jerusalem and Damascus from the fate of Warsaw and Paris. Men from Punjab, from New Zealand sheep farms and Welsh mines still had to fight in the desert. They could not know that there were phantoms on the field with them, that a struggle of minds came before the struggle with steel.

With the capture of Strategical Intercept Company 621, Rommel lost his other eye. His knowledge of the enemy was now even weaker than his supply lines.

If the myths of secret agents were true, if Rommel had only had a spy in Cairo, if the Abwehr had planted someone there years before who'd recruited a clerk or a cleaner at General Headquarters or even at the American office on El Nabatat Street to steal documents, then he might still have seen into the mind of his enemy.

Instead, Rommel had Eppler and Sandstede. They were busy gathering information about the cabarets of Cairo.

VICTOR HAUER, BORN in Vienna, was thirty-seven. Before the war he had worked at the Austrian embassy, then at the German embassy in Cairo. When other German men in Egypt were interned, he managed to stay free by getting a job at the Swedish embassy, handling the interests of German internees and their families.[46]

One day in July 1942, a young Egyptian friend named Hassan Gaafar showed up at Hauer's office and asked if he'd be willing to help two German spies. They spoke in German; it was Hassan's mother's language.

A couple weeks before, Hassan had received a brief note telling him, "Meet me at the Americaine Bar." He'd recognized the hand-writing of his older half brother, Hussein Gaafar, alias Johann Eppler. From then on, he'd say afterward, he was so excited at his brother's return, he didn't think about the meaning of what he was doing.

Hauer agreed to help the spies. Late that night, as Hassan in-structed him, he came to Madame Bardia's casino. The next stop was Eppler and Sandy's houseboat. The spies provided whiskey and told Hauer that they had "been directing Rommel's advance" with infor-mation they'd gained from inebriated British officers and from agents they'd placed in Suez and Port Said. But their transmitter had stopped working, they said, and Rommel might think they'd been caught. Ep-pler was good at telling stories. This one sounded better than saying that the transmitter had never seemed to work, or that they had man-aged to run through most of £3,600 in a month and a half and wanted more money. Hauer had a solution: in a complicated rendezvous, he delivered an American wireless transmitter that German diplomats had stored in the basement of the Swedish embassy.

At their next meeting, Eppler told Hauer that they couldn't get the American transmitter to work. The last orders he'd received before his own radio failed, Eppler said, were to report to Rommel's headquarters, and then to the Führer. (Eppler told Hauer more stories: that his money had been delivered by parachute, that ten German would-be spies had been shot one night while trying to parachute into Egypt, that the Ger-man navy now had submarines powered by bottles of a lightweight atomic fuel.)

Hauer again had a solution. He'd just met a Viennese doctor mar-ried to an Egyptian. Now called Fatma Ammar, she wanted to help Germany, and knew Egyptian officers with the same goal. Hauer took Eppler to her house. From there, a "tall, dark, young Egyptian" took him to meet an Egyptian pilot in a nearby coffee shop. When Eppler returned to her house, another guest was there: Aziz el-Masri. They talked deep into the night. The deposed Egyptian chief of staff, who as a young man had taken a surname that meant "the Egyptian," ex-plained that he "was an Aryan, a Circassian, and talked about the great future of the Aryan races" and his plans for "his country, Egypt, after the final German victory."

On the night of July 23, at 9:30, a dark brown car pulled up at a bus stop on the road to Heliopolis. Eppler, who'd been told to wait there, got in. Masri was driving. With him was the pilot, whose name was Hassan Ezzet, and a signals officer introduced as Anwar. They wanted proof that Eppler was really a German agent. Ezzet explained that "his man," a pilot named Seoudi, had taken a plane and flown to German lines earlier in the month, but they hadn't heard from him. Seoudi had carried a letter of introduction from Masri and aerial photos of targets for the Luftwaffe, Ezzet said.

To try to prove his bona fides, Eppler took Ezzet and Anwar back to the houseboat at midnight to meet Sandy. Anwar took a look at the American wireless set they'd received from Hauer, and talked them out of tossing it in the Nile as a piece of junk. In the morning, he came again, and took the wireless to see if he could get it working. He left a phone number and his first name. He did not write his full name: Anwar al-Sadat.

At 5 a.m. the next day Egyptian police arrived at the houseboat. With them were soldiers from Field Security, a relatively visible intelligence unit responsible for preventing subversion and sabotage in occupied areas. Eppler and Sandstede's inept espionage career was over.

The other suspects, including Ezzet, Masri, and Sadat, were rounded up afterward. Masri was last. In Sadat's possession police found a diary that indicated he'd been sending information to the enemy. When Ambassador Lampson received a report of this, he wrote at the bottom, "I hope that man will be shot . . . Please let me know what is done with him."[47]

There are three accounts of how Eppler and Sandstede were captured. The first, published in several variations, says that they paid for everything from groceries to girls with British banknotes, the larger ones counterfeit. Major Alfred Sansom, the head of Field Security in Cairo, the typecast shrewd and debonair spy hunter, followed the trail of their cash. When a German "mobile field radio monitoring unit" was captured in the desert, a British intelligence agent noticed that two soldiers who spoke no English had a copy of *Rebecca* in English. The final clue came from a French cabaret dancer named Natalie, or perhaps Yvette, actually a Jew from Palestine working underground for the Jewish Agency, who slept with Eppler "to serve my cause" and

found a copy of *Rebecca* on the houseboat—or perhaps Eppler was
given away by his Jewish girlfriend Edith, who was working for both
the tiny Jewish extremist group that the British called the Stern Gang
and for Sansom's Field Security. This story contains several facts, some
misunderstandings and anachronisms, and quite a bit of what can most
kindly be considered mistaken memory. It became part of the Operation Condor myth.[48]

The second account is in Lampson's files, and comes from Colonel
G. J. Jenkins, the district security officer, which is to say the MI5 chief,
in Cairo. Informing the British embassy of the arrests, Jenkins said he
had been working on the case "for months." To Lampson, he could not
explain that the first clues came from intercepted Abwehr messages
about Laszlo Almasy operating near Gilf Kebir. The breakthrough,
Jenkins told the embassy soon afterward, came with the arrest of an escaped German internee, who gave a statement about Hauer knowing
of something suspicious at a particular houseboat. Arrests followed.
Hauer had "unfortunately" vanished, Jenkins told Lampson.[49]

The third account is in Jenkins's letter to MI5 director David
Petrie and in a pair of interrogation reports Jenkins sent to London.
When Hassan Gaafar asked for help, Hauer had decided to "safeguard
himself" whichever way the war went, and began "playing the double
agent." He went to talk to a German Jewish gynecologist, Dr. Radinger,
whom he knew to be an agent for British intelligence. Radinger told
him to meet the spies but to keep reporting back.

Jenkins concluded that Hauer knew more than he was telling the
doctor. But MI5 did not have authority to arrest people, and Jenkins
was not ready to involve Egyptian authorities. As he calmly informed
Petrie, "I therefore decided to kidnap Hauer."

"Picked up on coming out of the Metro Cinema at 11:45 p.m." on
July 21, Hauer was soon in a cell at SIME's interrogation center for
POWs. He "was made to understand that his reprieve from shooting"
depended on telling what he knew, after which his surname would become Muller and his identity that of a German prisoner of war. He
talked and was sent to a POW camp in Palestine.

"Both my own police and the Egyptians are still hunting for Hauer,
whose disappearance was reported by the Swedish legation," Jenkins
concluded.[50]

Sadat and Ezzet were not shot. Rather than being court-martialed, they were dismissed from the Egyptian military and interned for the rest of the war, as was Masri. Abbas Halim, the Egyptian prince whose name had been given to Eppler as a contact, was placed under house arrest away from Cairo, as were two other prominent pro-Axis royals.[51] By breaking up Operation Condor, MI5's Jenkins had not denied Rommel any intelligence, since the spies were providing none.

But the end of Condor completed the British victory in the covert political battle in Egypt: it removed the mentor and two leaders of the pro-Axis junior officers, crippling subversion in the army, and it sidelined more pro-Axis aristocrats, increasing Farouk's isolation.

To avoid turning Eppler and Sandy over to Egyptian authorities, they were treated as prisoners of war. To get more information out of them, they were moved from a cell to a tent at the interrogation center. They did not believe that a tent could be bugged. They were mistaken; a microphone had been inserted in the tent pole. The transcript of their conversations includes Eppler saying to Sandstede that he hoped their girlfriends Edith and Sandra would be quickly released.

"Those poor girls did not know anything about us and they never did anything wrong," Eppler said. The two women were in fact released. Had Eppler been a more successful spy, his Jewish girlfriend's fate might have been different.[52]

WALTHER RAUFF'S EINSATZKOMMANDO Egypt received its official orders for "executive measures against the civilian population" on July 13. Now an SS *obersturmbannführer*, a lieutenant colonel, Rauff commanded twenty-three men. At least four of the six other officers had joined the Nazi Party before it came to power, a badge of ideological fervor. Hans-Joachim Weise, Hajj Amin el-Husseini's former liaison officer, and Wilhelm Beisner were SS experts on the Middle East.

The unit's size testified to confidence that it would be able to recruit local collaborators in Egypt, Palestine, and the rest of the Middle East. That presumption rested in part on the Arab-Jewish conflict over Palestine, and in part on intelligence reports that glowingly described enthusiasm for Nazism, Hitler, and Rommel in Arab countries—reports reinforced by Husseini's boasts.[53] The German intelligence reports cannot be assumed to be more reliable in reading the public mood than British reports of that summer, which said that pro-Axis feeling in Egypt, Syria, and Palestine faded as the danger of living under actual German occupation grew. The reaction to Rommel's approach, said one SIME analysis, had "discredited those alarmists who saw a 'Fifth Columnist' in every Muslim, every speaker of the Arabic language."[54]

Most of all, though, the confidence of Rauff's commanders rested on experience nearly everywhere in conquered lands. (The glaring exceptions were Denmark and the only Muslim country in Europe, Albania, but in both cases the resistance to the Nazi roundup of Jews became apparent later in the war.[55]) Universal support for the Nazi regime was unnecessary. Most of the population would be scared and passive. Some people would resist. Some would willingly join victorious Nazis in the murder of Jews.

On July 20, Rauff flew from Crete to Tobruk, then onward to Rommel's battle headquarters to meet Rommel's chief of staff. Lieutenant Colonel Siegfried Westphal told Rauff that the conquest of the Nile was being held up by logistics problems. Bringing the full *Einsatzkommando* to El Alamein immediately wasn't practical. Instead, they agreed that the unit would move from Germany to Athens to wait for Rommel's victory.[56]

Even that decision indicates that Westphal wasn't feeling as bleak as Rommel had in a letter to his wife three days before. "Things are going downright badly for me at the moment," he wrote. "The enemy is using his superiority, especially in infantry, to destroy the Italian formations one by one, and the German formations are much too weak to stand alone. It's enough to make one weep."[57]

The same day that Rauff came to El Alamein, Mussolini flew home from Derna. His pretense at optimism lasted for two days, Ciano wrote. Then he began raging at Cavallero, at his other generals, at the Germans.[58]

THE MEN OF the British Twenty-Third Armored Brigade and their tanks disembarked at Suez in early July. The men had trained in England, and had never been in the desert. The tanks, immobile and exposed to sea air for two months on the journey around Africa, were rushed in and out of workshops. Their wireless sets were not refitted with the batteries and tubes needed for the furious Egyptian heat.

At dawn on July 22, the Twenty-Third went into action—"these fresh-faced boys from England . . . full of confidence and courage for this, their first real action," as Moorehead saw them. Operation Splendour, which according to battle orders would "destroy the enemy's army," had begun hours earlier. The infantry went first, in the darkness, when the German and Italian artillery and tank gunners were blind. That part of the operation succeeded, but with first light the infantrymen were exposed. Tanks were supposed to join and protect them.

Ten minutes before the tanks of the Twenty-Third Brigade moved forward, its divisional headquarters radioed word that a minefield hadn't been cleared, and that the tanks should skirt it to the south. No one heard that order. In the middle of the minefield, the brigade came under antitank fire. Out of 106 tanks, 6 survived.[59]

Operation Splendour failed. So did Auchinleck's next attempt at a counterattack.

After Tobruk, the British Ministry of Information had received an urgent cable from its man in Washington, asking how to explain the defeat. "We have had to build up these tank forces from scratch during the war years," the first draft of an answer said, "and we are still to a considerable extent matching amateurs against professionals."

The generals deleted the uncomfortable part about "amateurs."[60] But it fit what Moorehead reported from Egypt. German armored forces "had been trained to the nth degree," so that dive-bombers, tanks, recovery crews, fuel trucks, and antitank gunners worked together like a machine. "We are simply not trained to it and they had years of practice," Moorehead wrote.[61] Those were the years in which Nazi Germany had prepared for war and Britain had ignored the threat.

FELLERS WAS ON his way to Washington, said the cable from Alexander Kirk in Cairo to the undersecretary of state, Sumner Welles. Fellers "knows more about military developments in this area than any of us" and should see the president, the ambassador wrote. Welles forwarded the cable. "I want to see Colonel Fellers," Roosevelt wrote across the corner for the naval officer who managed his war room.[62]

Fellers, we can guess, had warring emotions when he came to the White House on July 30. He would personally brief the president of the United States—who was Franklin Roosevelt, of whom he was ever ready to believe the worst.

He came at a moment of decision.

All through July, the dispute had continued in Washington and London, and most of all between them, over where America and Britain should take the war. Marshall and other American military planners pressed for a plan code-named Sledgehammer: six divisions, or perhaps nine, would land that autumn in northwest France near Cherbourg to establish a beachhead and to force Germany to pull forces from the eastern front. General Brooke, Marshall's British counterpart, believed that this would mean the useless sacrifice of six divisions, and that Marshall's rigid strategy ignored the "different standard of training of German divisions as opposed to the raw American divisions and to most of our new divisions." The British war cabinet rejected Sledgehammer.

Roosevelt sent his closest adviser, Henry Hopkins, to London with Marshall and navy commander in chief Admiral Ernest King to reach agreement on Sledgehammer—or an alternative plan for US ground troops to be fighting in Europe or Africa before the year's end. Roosevelt's instructions to them included a list of strategic reasons that the Middle East must "be held as strongly as possible." It could have been cribbed from the cables that Fellers had sent in the spring and that Marshall had brushed aside.

Marshall, defeated, returned from London with a plan called Operation Torch: the United States and Britain would invade Morocco and Algeria "to drive in against the backdoor of Rommel's armies." When Fellers came to the White House, all that was still needed was an explicit, final order from the president.[63] Fellers pressed the case for helping the British in the Middle East. He was "very pessimistic as to the ability of the British to hold the Nile Delta," and "estimated that General Rommel would penetrate the British positions by the last of August," according to Roosevelt's brief notes.[64]

That evening Roosevelt called the military commanders to the White House and issued his order: Torch should "be undertaken at the earliest possible date."[65] Fellers's final message from Egypt, delivered in person, may have only confirmed what Roosevelt had already resolved, or it may have been the conclusive, deciding factor. The man whom the British wanted out of Cairo had backed Churchill's position against Marshall's.

Fellers was right about the strategic value of the Middle East, just as Brooke was right about how unready American troops were. But by the time Fellers spoke to Roosevelt, his portrait of the war in Africa was a month old, and an eon out of date.

On July 27, quiet had come to the front. On the map, the Panzer Army had advanced nearly four hundred miles since the start of its offensive two months earlier. Yet Rommel had lost his gamble, and the battle. He had not reached the harbor at Alexandria. Rommel's army was virtually marooned in the desert, in far greater danger than if he had stopped at the Egyptian border.

Tobruk's small port, 340 miles away, could handle only one-fifth of the fuel, food, ammunition, and other supplies he needed. It was known as the "cemetery of the Italian navy" because of RAF bombing of the port and the convoys heading for it. Benghazi and Tripoli were safer—but were eight hundred and fourteen hundred miles from El Alamein. Trucks devoured the fuel that Rommel's hungry tanks needed—and the RAF bombed the truck convoys too.[66] Rommel was in the position of a man who had climbed down an immense cliff, only to find that his rope ran out while he was dangling sixty feet in the air.

Militarily, the rational decision would have been for Rommel to retreat at least to the Libyan border to prepare for the inevitable British offensive. But he did not serve a rational master. Going to war had not been rational; invading the Soviet Union and pulling America into the war had not been rational. Hitler's hubris did not make retreat a possibility.

It would take two more battles before Churchill would declare, "It is not even the beginning of the end, but it is, perhaps, the end of the beginning."[67]

Looking back, with greater calm than was possible that summer, July 1942 was really the end of the beginning of the war. On the western front in its widest sense, this was when the Axis armies could go no further, when the Nazi and Fascist empires had reached their outermost border. At El Alamein, the Eighth Army truly drew a line in the sand.

The battle between Rommel's exhausted professionals and Auchinleck's amateurs could have tipped either way. Each factor was insufficient in itself, and essential to the outcome—Auchinleck's choice of El Alamein, the courage of his unready men, and the intelligence victory that preceded the battle.

Precise intelligence had not saved Crete, because General Freyberg's forces had been too weak. Intelligence warnings did not prevent the surprise of Barbarossa, because Stalin would not listen to them.

The siren song of a seemingly perfect source drew Rommel to El Alamein and abandoned him. After that, Auchinleck acknowledged, the "most secret sources" overheard at Bletchley Park gave him the decisive advantage.[68] Mussolini would not ride his white charger through Cairo; Rauff would not bring his gas vans to Jerusalem; Rommel would never fulfill his dream of meeting German forces from the Caucasus in Persia.

AN ITALIAN INTELLIGENCE official whispered it to a friend in the Vatican: the Axis had deciphered a message from "the American consul in Cairo" on the "weakness of British military equipment in Libya," and this was "one of the factors" that had led Rommel "to make as far an advance as he did."

The Vatican man passed the secret to another friend, the US chargé d'affaires at the Holy See, Harold Tittman, who sent the tip by diplomatic bag to the US ambassador in Switzerland, who cabled the State Department, which at the end of July radioed Ambassador Alexander Kirk in Cairo and asked if he could identify the message that the Axis had deciphered.

No one at the US legation in Egypt signed cables as "American consul," Kirk stiffly answered. He raised the "possibility that spurious intercepts may be produced for the purpose of compromising certain officials." And he pointed to the "probability that even the most confidential ciphers are being broken by both hostile and friendly governments." In diplomatese, Kirk was suggesting that the tip from Rome was somehow tied to the British either breaking Fellers's code—or entirely inventing the leak in order to rid themselves of the troublesome, brilliant colonel.[69]

The State Department also asked the Military Attaché Section at the War Department about the Vatican allegation. But the inquiry went no further. If anyone at the US Army's Signal Intelligence Service cabled Bletchley Park about it, the records are missing.[70]

Tittman's information would not become a cryptic hint in Russell Dudley-Smith's search for a solution to the Bluebird mystery. Some of the answers lay in as yet undeciphered Japanese messages. Some lay twelve hundred miles north and two years of hard fighting away from El Alamein. And some answers would be lost to the grave.

2

UNKNOWN SOLDIERS

August 1942-May 1945. El Alamein-
Tunisia-Rome-Bletchley Park.

AT SUNRISE ON August 3, 1942, an American Liberator bomber descended into Cairo. Sitting in the copilot's seat was a passenger, Winston Churchill. General Brooke, the chief of the Imperial General Staff, had landed earlier.

Churchill came to shake things up. Once in Egypt, he offered Brooke command of the Middle East in Auchinleck's place. Brooke was tempted but refused. His duty, he believed, was to keep the prime minister under control. Churchill chose to bring General Harold Alexander from Britain instead. To head the Eighth Army, he picked General William Gott, one of Auchinleck's field commanders. Gott boarded a plane to fly to Cairo for a brief leave—and was shot down and killed.

Churchill, stricken, accepted Brooke's suggestion: General Bernard Montgomery, who had to fly immediately from England.

Montgomery was supposed to take over on August 15. He arrived at Eighth Army headquarters two days earlier and announced he was in command. He found contingency plans for retreat, prepared by Auchinleck's hapless deputy in Cairo, General Tom Corbett.

Montgomery treated them as if they reflected Auchinleck's intentions and ordered them destroyed. He found Auchinleck's plans for an offensive and presented them as his own. He gave orders that every soldier must know "the name Montgomery by tonight." He went from unit to unit speaking to the troops. He courted press coverage. Instead of ordering his officers not to refer to the enemy as "Rommel," he hung a captured copy of the Nazi propaganda portrait of Rommel in the trailer he used as his quarters. He let it be known that he studied it to understand his enemy's mind.[1]

Churchill had still been looking for his own Rommel. Montgomery had never been in the desert or led armored forces. He was as cautious as Rommel was impetuous.

Montgomery shared this with Rommel, though: he understood that in a mass army, most soldiers knew a general at most as a name. He needed to be real to them, to be larger than real, to be the champion they would follow. A modern general needed to build an image, to manufacture a legend. Esprit de corps mattered more than historical truth or the reputation of his painfully self-effacing predecessor, Claude Auchinleck.[2]

Montgomery did know Rommel's thoughts, and his fears, but not from communing with his portrait. In July, a team from Bletchley Park arrived in Heliopolis, outside Cairo, and began deciphering the Scorpion and Phoenix keys of Enigma. Putting the team in Egypt eliminated having to send locally intercepted messages to England and wait for decrypted texts. The intelligence reached Montgomery many valuable hours sooner. At the end of July, Hut 6 solved the key used for air transportation of troops and supplies from Crete to Africa. It completed a set: Gordon Welchman's team was now cracking, at least on some days, every air force and army Enigma key that the Germans used in the battle for the Middle East.[3]

A British convoy finally reached Malta, so more planes from there could take off to target the tankers identified in deciphered Italian naval messages.[4] Montgomery received a stream of German messages on plans—most of them impossible to carry out—to bring fuel to the Panzer Army by airplane, submarine, or motorboat. He learned that the poor rations of Luftwaffe pilots in Africa caused stomach trouble that kept them from flying at high altitude. (The pressure of excess gases inside the stomach and intestines became unbearably painful as air pressure outside the body dropped.) Montgomery read the radioed message to the German high command on August 26, in which Rommel said that his own failing health had improved just enough that he could postpone "fairly long treatment in Germany" until after the "coming operations."[5]

Montgomery told his officers that the Axis attack would come in the south, when the moon was full at the end of August. The offensive in fact began on the last night of the full moon, just as officers began to doubt Montgomery's intuition. Rommel counted on surprise and on the fuel carried by two Italian tankers still at sea, possibly his most desperate wager yet. A British brigade found the German armored forces at midnight. The battered German columns took too many hours to advance through gaps in a minefield. They turned toward Alam Halfa ridge, and met waiting British antitank guns. The RAF sank one of the Italian ships and damaged the other so badly it was beached.

Rommel's bid to break the El Alamein line ran out of fuel.[6] He blamed a lack of intelligence; he blamed the Italian navy. It was always easiest to blame the Italians for his logistic crises. "With the failure of this offensive," he wrote afterward, "our last chance of gaining the Suez Canal had gone."[7] For the moment, the desert was quiet.

CHURCHILL EXPECTED ALEXANDER and Montgomery to launch their own attack quickly. Even more stubbornly than Auchinleck had, the two generals rejected haste. They would wait for the new Sherman tanks to reach Suez, along with a hundred American artillery pieces mounted on tank chassis; for over forty thousand new troops to arrive and be trained; for every unit in the Eighth Army to be pulled off the line and rehearse its part in the offensive. They'd wait to have all the fuel and spare parts they needed, for British radio-intercept teams to learn all of Seebohm's arts of battlefield intelligence. They waited for the full moon of October 23, which gave just enough light for the infantry to move up at night. At 9:40 p.m., nearly nine hundred guns of the British artillery opened fire. To the east, along the entire Axis front line, a curtain of flame rose.

Rommel was in Germany, being treated for his stomach troubles, low blood pressure, and fainting spells. Hitler ordered him back to Africa. On November 2, he sent a message to Hitler that after ten days of fighting, his army was on the verge of destruction and that he would have to retreat the next day. Hitler's answer proclaimed that the "stronger will" would triumph and that Rommel had "no other road but that to victory or death."

Rommel waited a day more. By then, the British had wiped out his Italian armored divisions. The Italian infantry was stranded without transport and surrendered. Rommel defied orders. With what was left of the German core of his army, he fled westward.[8]

Four days later, over one hundred thousand American and British troops invaded Algeria and Morocco. This time, secrets had been kept well. No deciphered message revealed Operation Torch. Even when German air reconnaissance discovered two Allied fleets steaming east of Gibraltar, Axis commanders had no idea where they were heading. The Allied commander was Dwight Eisenhower, who'd previously never led men in battle. The landings at Oran in Algeria were a "mix of anarchy and success," the anarchy largely due to the American forces being as unready as Brooke had believed while watching them train in June, the success attributable to surprise and the poor condition of Vichy troops. But by November 12, Allied forces controlled Algeria and Morocco and were preparing to turn eastward.[9]

Rommel abandoned Cyrenaica. The Eighth Army returned to Tobruk on November 13. Benghazi changed hands, for the fifth time in the war, a week afterward. Mussolini and Bastico, the Italian commander in Africa, gave Rommel permission to withdraw from the rest of Libya. The British entered Tripoli on January 23, 1943. A day later they liberated the Giado concentration camp. Of the three thousand Jews who'd been imprisoned there, nearly one in five had died of hunger or typhus.[10]

Reacting to the Torch landings, Hitler immediately scuttled the 1940 armistice with Vichy. Ten German and six Italian divisions invaded the hitherto unoccupied remnant of France. German fighter planes, then troop transports, landed in Tunisia. Fifty thousand German soldiers and nearly twenty thousand Italians were in the last Axis foothold in Africa by the end of 1942. Larger numbers followed.

Torch was not the second front that Stalin had hoped for, but every German division sent to France or Tunisia was one that could not be deployed on the eastern front. After Torch, Hitler sent hundreds of warplanes from the southern end of the Soviet front to the Mediterranean. Just days later, the Soviet counterattack at Stalingrad trapped the German army of a quarter million men in the city. The Germans had lost control of the sky, even as their troops depended on supplies brought by air.[11] The ninety thousand Germans still alive in Stalingrad surrendered on February 2, 1943. "Stalingrad" became the name for a much larger shift: Hitler's dream of Russian conquest had come undone. All along the eastern front, the Red Army was pushing forward. Seven months had passed since Rommel reached El Alamein, confidently expecting to burst through the Middle East and meet German armies coming south from Russia into Persia. The war had utterly changed shape.

ONE OF THE early flights from Germany to Tunisia brought the blond, pale SS commander Walther Rauff. Rauff's special operations command had pulled out of Athens after Rommel's failed attempt to break through at Alam Halfa. Now it had employment, and quadrupled in size. The SS, in its mix of cruelty and self-deceit, expected Rauff to recruit collaborators who would set off a rebellion in Morocco and Algeria, and then to murder the 270,000 Jews of those countries and the 66,000 Jews of Tunisia. The occupation of Tunisia, though, was as much a retreat as an invasion, the attempt of a defeated army to hold a shrinking redoubt in Africa. The plan for a revolt in Allied-held Morocco and Algeria came to nothing.

Constrained, Rauff nonetheless implemented as much of the Nazi program against Jews as he could. Field Marshal Kesselring wanted Jews as slave laborers, so Rauff took Jewish leaders hostage in order to round up five thousand Jews for forced labor in camps near the front lines. He imposed fines of tens of millions of francs on the Jewish community, on the pretext that the local Jews were part of "international Jewry," which was supposedly responsible for Allied bombing. Local Fascists conducted pogroms with German encouragement. German soldiers preyed on Jewish women. A few Jewish leaders were deported to death camps in Europe. Others went into hiding. Some of them, like some of the Jews who escaped labor camps, were hidden by Tunisian Arabs.

The larger SS plan was to deport all of Tunisia's Jews to the death factories in Europe. But with shipping to Europe under constant attack, Rauff could not carry out the intention. In Tunisia, the logistical breakdown and military collapse foiled the machinery of mass murder.[12]

In March, Rommel launched one more counterattack against Montgomery's army. Rommel planned on surprise; Montgomery knew the offensive was coming and defeated it. Rommel left Africa for sick leave. The Axis army in Tunisia gradually shrank to an enclave around the city of Tunis. Rauff and his men flew out on May 9. Four days later, a quarter million Axis soldiers surrendered.[13] Africa was liberated.

FOR TWO YEARS, Gustave Bertrand's underground Command Post Cadix had continued operating in the Vichy-ruled piece of France— intercepting German police, Abwehr, and SS messages, and secretly transmitting information to England. The code words "The harvest is good," sent from London to Bertrand on the eve of Operation Torch, were the signal to shut down.

Marian Rejewski and Henryk Zygalski fled the Nazis for the third time. (Polish mathematician Jerzy Rozycki, the other member of the codebreaking trio, had died in a shipwreck months before on his way back from Cadix's substation in Algeria.) Rejewski and Zygalski moved from safe house to safe house, then followed a smuggler across the Pyrenees to Spain. There they were jailed, along with many other escapees. Months later, freed by the efforts of the Polish Red Cross, they traveled to Portugal. From a tiny harbor, a fishing boat took them to a British warship.

In England, Rejewski and Zygalski were assigned to work for a Polish signals battalion, breaking relatively easy SS ciphers. The two Poles were told that their time in Vichy disqualified them to work at GCHQ. Dilly Knox had died; Denniston had been shunted out of Bletchley Park. Alan Turing was still there, but it's likely that a nameless official turned down Rejewski and Zygalski without ever checking if anyone at Bletchley Park knew their names. Once again, bureaucratic caution cost Britain the services of the quiet geniuses who first broke Enigma.[14]

WITH ROMMEL'S RETREAT from Egypt, the danger of a Nazi conquest of Palestine vanished. For the half million or more Jews in Palestine, the sense of relief lasted less than three weeks before being swept away by horror.

First came a statement from the Jewish Agency: "authoritative and reliable sources," it said, reported that the Nazi regime was engaged in the "systematic extermination" of the Jews of Poland and of other countries who had been deported there. Two days later, corroboration came from Washington. Rabbi Stephen S. Wise, chairman of the World Jewish Congress, announced that half the Jews in occupied Europe had already been murdered. The State Department, he said, had released documents confirming this.

No longer were the news items from Europe unsubstantiated rumor; no longer were they local atrocities. Denial was impossible.[15]

The Jewish community in Palestine had an immensely complicated relationship with European Jewry. Most Palestinian Jews were Zionists; they saw themselves as a vanguard building an independent Jewish life. In their own eyes, they had taken control of their fate, unlike Jews elsewhere. Now they were orphaned—as a community and, for a great many who'd left families behind in Europe, as individual sons and daughters. They were awash with guilt for surviving, and for not believing the earlier reports.

The fading of the Nazi threat to Palestine virtually ended the covert collaboration between the Palmah and the Special Operations Executive. The British organization did not need to build a resistance in a country that would not be occupied. In reality, far more Palestinian Jews enlisted in the British army than in the Palmah, despite British reluctance to send the recruits to combat units.[16]

It was the Eighth Army of the British Empire that saved Palestinian Jews from genocide, not for their sakes but as an incidental side effect of preventing an Axis conquest of the Middle East. Perhaps for that very reason, the legend of Masada on the Carmel and the Palmah's readiness for resistance lived on. Especially in the face of the news from Europe, it preserved the idea that a small group of people could carve out a role in their own history. It defied despair.

On the far side of the world, in Hollywood, German Jewish émigré filmmaker Billy Wilder directed a movie in early 1943 called *Five Graves to Cairo*. Pieces of desert in Arizona and California served as the scenery of the North African battlefield. The film takes place in June 1942. In it, Erwin Rommel, advancing into Egypt, stays for a night at a tiny desert hotel. A British soldier hiding there, John Bramble, overhears Rommel boasting to captured British officers that he will be in Cairo in six days. "I have my reservations at Shepheard's Hotel," Rommel says. Bramble learns that before the war, Rommel had come to Egypt in the guise of an archaeologist. His expedition hid military supplies at five supposed excavations on the way to the Nile. Bramble escapes with this information, and Rommel's supply dumps are destroyed just as he reaches El Alamein.[17]

The film succeeded because everyone who listened to radio news or saw newsreels knew the riddle on which it was based: Rommel was the mastermind of desert warfare, yet he'd been defeated at El Alamein because he'd stretched his supply line past the breaking point. Surely, Wilder suggested, there had to be some secret that explained Rommel's overconfidence, some secret that explained why he'd been mistaken.

Wilder's fantasy answer was wrong; the Germans had never expected to fight in North Africa, and Rommel had never paid enough attention to logistics. But there was a secret that explained Rommel's overconfidence and what went wrong: the overheard message from Cairo that Egypt was his for the taking, and the sudden silence of his superb source.

On July 10, 1943, the British Eighth Army and the US Seventh Army landed on the Italian island of Sicily. For the first time, the ground war had come to the soil of an Axis power. Germany had already begun moving divisions into Italy and Italian-occupied territories. Field Marshal Erwin Rommel commanded the operation.

In the gilded offices of Rome, a tangle of plots grew. At the Palazzo Venezia, overlooking the Altar of the Fatherland and the avenue leading to the Colosseum, the ruling body of the Fascist Party, the Grand Council, met on the night of July 24 for the first time since the war started. After midnight, the leaders of the party voted 19–7 to take the role of military commander in chief from Mussolini and give it back to King Vittorio Emanuele.

Galeazzo Ciano voted against his father-in-law. For years he had worshipped and doubted the Duce. Far too late, Ciano decided in favor of his doubt.

The next afternoon, Mussolini went for his usual biweekly meeting with the king. Vittorio Emanuele told Mussolini that he'd become the "most hated man in Italy," deposed him as the head of government, and appointed Pietro Badoglio in his place. When Mussolini stepped outside, he was arrested. Badoglio's government surrendered to the Allies on September 3, the same day Allied troops began landing at the southern tip of mainland Italy.

Badoglio and the king utterly mishandled the aftermath. Rommel's forces seized control of nearly all of Italy and took over four hundred thousand Italian soldiers prisoner. Badoglio and Vittorio Emanuele fled Rome for the Allied-held south. The SS began rounding up Italian Jews and sending them to Auschwitz. Libyan Jews who'd been held in Italy were sent to Bergen-Belsen. The Germans freed Mussolini and installed him as the head of a puppet republic in the German-occupied part of Italy.

Ciano was imprisoned and tried for treason. On January 11, outside the gates of Verona, he was tied to a chair, his back facing the firing squad to deny him any honor in death, and executed. He was forty years old. He'd once been seen as Mussolini's heir. His wife, Edda, smuggled his diaries to Switzerland.[18]

LASZLO ALMASY HAD left Africa in the summer of 1942. He'd come down with amoebic dysentery, possibly during the daring, futile expedition to take the inept Eppler and Sandstede to the Nile. After treatment in Athens, he returned to Budapest, where he wrote and published a memoir of his time with Rommel. Censorship removed details but left his poetic riffs about the desert. His lover of seven years, Hans Entholt, who'd been serving in North Africa, was killed by a land-mine during the retreat from El Alamein. After that news, he wrote, "everything has seemed banal, empty and sad." He was forty-seven years old.

In March 1944, to prevent Hungary from signing a separate peace with the Soviet Union, Germany occupied the country and installed a lackey as prime minister. Sometime during that autumn or winter, as the SS rounded up Hungarian Jews, Almasy provided hiding places for four of them. Two were the wife and son of a craftsman who'd been deported to Auschwitz; before the war the man had done some work for Almasy. Two were the wife and son of a Jew who'd won Olympic medals for Hungary in fencing decades earlier.[19]

The contradiction between Almasy's views and the exceptions he made for people he knew isn't unique: In the abstract, he supported a racist ideology. Looking at individual human beings, he ignored the ideology. As with everything else he did, though, Almasy performed the drama of his life on a tightrope, alone, above the crowd: he risked his life for the Nazis; he risked his life to save Jews.

BRITISH GENERALS HAD long since given up on getting Hermione Ran-furly out of the Middle East. Instead, they wanted her to run their offices. She flew to Baghdad, where Jumbo Wilson now commanded the Tenth Army, to become his secretary. When the "tall, immensely fat" general, who looked "exactly like an elephant . . . standing on its hind legs," got promoted to commander in chief, Middle East, Ran-furly moved back to Cairo with him. In November 1943, Air Marshal Tedder told her he'd received word: her husband Dan had escaped during the chaos in Italy and was now hiding in the mountains in the Nazi-occupied north of that country.

A few days after, General Eisenhower visited Cairo. His aide asked Ranfurly to join a dinner with the general and his staff. She was seated next to Eisenhower, who spent the whole evening speaking to the woman on his other side, his secretary, driver, and alleged mistress, Kay Summersby. When Eisenhower finally turned in Ranfurly's direction, the countess asked if he knew Bonner Fellers, "the American attaché we all liked."

Eisenhower answered, "Any friend of Bonner Fellers is no friend of mine," and turned his back.

The ex-attaché stamped himself in people's memories. Eisenhower had not forgotten his falling out with Fellers in the Philippines. Ranfurly hadn't forgotten his instinctive willingness to help find her missing husband. The man was a master at making friends, and enemies.

The next morning Eisenhower's aide called Ranfurly again. Eisenhower thought he'd been rude and invited her to dine with him that evening. Ranfurly declined, saying she already had plans. "An awful lie," she wrote. "I had no date tonight."

From Cairo, she followed Wilson to his next posting, in Algiers. She'd now been married for five years. For three of them, her husband had been in captivity or in hiding behind the lines. In May 1944 a cable came for Wilson from General Alexander at Allied headquarters in Italy. "Dan Ranfurly arrived here this afternoon," it said. Wilson left it for her on her desk, then came into her office and watched her read it over and over.

She stood on a runway late in the afternoon and watched a small two-engine plane touch down. Her eyes misted; she couldn't see him get off the plane. "Suddenly, his arms were around me," she wrote the next day. "Heaven—is being together."[20]

AFTER ITALY, ROMMEL's next assignment was in France. From January 1944, he was in command of preparing for the expected Allied landings on the northern coast. He had no idea where the Americans and British planned to land. "I know *nothing* for certain about the enemy," he was quoted as saying.

The Allies, on the other hand, knew a great deal about German defenses, and not just from German radio traffic. Japanese emissaries in Berlin were unknowingly generous. The Japanese ambassador, Hiroshi Oshima, visited the Atlantic Wall—the German defenses on the French coast—near the end of 1943. He radioed home a detailed description, enciphered in Purple, and deciphered in Washington.

The Japanese military attaché in Berlin, Colonel Ito Seiichi, also inspected the coastal defenses, and sent a thirty-two-part radiogram to Tokyo. Seiichi couldn't know that in 1942, John Tiltman had figured out how the code used by Japanese military attachés worked. The attachés' formal style had made his work easier. Each message contained the words "I have the honor to report to Your Excellency that . . ." Bletchley Park recruited some young classics scholars from Cambridge and gave them an intensive, five-month course in Japanese. They took over mastering the Japanese military attaché code, and in early 1944 decoded Seiichi's precise report.

Not to be left out, the Japanese naval attaché toured the Atlantic defenses in May 1944. A joint British-American effort had just broken his cipher. Rommel, he told Tokyo and the Allied eavesdroppers, planned to "destroy the enemy near the coast, without allowing them to penetrate any considerable distance inland."[21]

German intelligence was so poor that Rommel was at home, celebrating his wife's birthday, on D-Day, June 6. By the time his chief of staff phoned him, one hundred thousand Allied troops had already landed at Normandy. Eisenhower was in command of all Allied forces, Montgomery of the ground forces. Africa had been their training ground; they were no longer amateurs. Rommel's plans collapsed the first day. His confidence followed. In conversations, he talked about the need for a separate peace with Britain and the United States, even an alliance with them against the Soviet Union.

On July 17, while he was on an inspection tour of the front, a British warplane strafed his car. Rommel suffered a fractured skull. He was in a coma in a hospital on July 20, when the attempt by army officers to assassinate Hitler and take power failed.

Rommel slowly recuperated, first in hospitals, then at home. Meanwhile, the Gestapo rounded up and tortured suspects in the botched coup. On October 14, two generals came to Rommel's home. Conspirators had named him as part of the plot, they said. They gave him a choice: take poison they'd brought for the purpose, or stand trial and be executed. The choice was a product of the long-running propaganda promotion of Rommel. It would have looked bad for Hitler to admit that his most celebrated general had turned against him. Rommel said good-bye to his wife and son, and swallowed the poison.

A state funeral was held. Rommel's "heart attack," it was said, was a result of his injuries. After the war, the real cause of death would emerge. Historians would find evidence of Rommel's despair and his fantasy of a separate peace—but would cast doubt on his connection to the attempted coup. Yet the story of Rommel as part of the conspiracy to save Germany from Hitler would live on. It was the essential final chapter in the legend of Rommel as the chivalrous enemy on the playing field of war, who fought for Germany yet somehow was unstained by fighting for Hitler and Nazism.[22]

THE FIRST AMERICAN soldiers entered Rome late on the night of June 4, 1944. By morning, the last German troops abandoned the city. "The first of the Axis capitals is now in our hands," Franklin Roosevelt exulted in a national radio broadcast. "One up and two to go!" By the next day, Allied troops were fighting their way onto the beaches at Normandy, and the liberation of Rome slipped to the margins of news coverage.[23]

An MI6 agent known as "92,700" was in Rome soon after. At least one of his tasks was counterintelligence: tracking down Axis espionage successes, especially against Britain, so that leaks could be plugged and enemy intelligence efforts foiled. On July 22 he cabled his superiors: Italy's Servizio Informazioni Militari, SIM, had penetrated both the prewar British embassy and the legation to the Vatican and had made copies of British ciphers, he wrote. Copies of his cable went to Menzies and to Russell Dudley-Smith.

From London, Agent 92,700 received orders: We need to know the "exact means and degree" of the infiltrations. Extract more information from your SIM contacts.[24]

By mid-August, he and another MI6 agent, 32,000, had uncovered the responsible unit within SIM: Manfredi Talamo's P Squad. They interrogated four of Talamo's noncommissioned officers, as well as an Italian who'd worked for the British embassy to the Vatican and had been recruited to remove cipher books from the safe. Talamo had provided the key, taken the books, and returned them within an hour and a half, the man explained.

A cable from 32,000 naturally stressed the penetration of the British embassy and confirmed that all of Major Valentine Vivian's 1937 warnings had been meticulously ignored.[25] But two longer reports by the MI6 team gave a much fuller picture of the P Squad's operations against the diplomatic missions of nearly twenty countries. The real number was likely higher; the MI6 agents had found only four of Talamo's men, and their memories were incomplete. Still, the two reports are the best surviving account of Talamo's work, since the P Squad's own records were burned at the time of the Italian surrender and the German takeover of Rome in September 1943.

Usually, the P Squad men could tell their British interrogators little or nothing about the intelligence gained through their work or its effect on the war. There was one exception.[26]

TWO HANDSOME BUILDINGS stood just off Via Vittorio Veneto, the main avenue of Rome's Ludovisi district. Greek and Roman statues stood on the corners of their roofs, including a first-century figure of Artemis, Greek goddess of the hunt, on one building and a second-century figure of a satyr atop the other. Nearly two thousand years before, the area had been gardens owned by the emperors of Rome. Ludovico Ludovisi, a seventeenth-century cardinal, turned it into his estate, decorated partly with classical sculpture dug up on the grounds. His nineteenth-century heir sold off most of the estate for development, renovated the cardinal's palace, built two identical houses next to it for his two sons, and promptly went bankrupt. In 1941, the palace was an office of the Fascist Party. The two houses were the US embassy.[27]

In one of them, Colonel Norman Fiske, the US military attaché, had his office. Fiske lived around the corner at the Hotel Ambasciatori, which made it easier for the P Squad's noncommissioned officers and the four Italian employees of the embassy who were on Talamo's payroll to keep track of when he was leaving his residence for his office.[28]

Sometime in the last weeks before Pearl Harbor, before time ran out, Talamo found the moment of opportunity for another of his precisely planned operations. He or one of his men entered the building, climbed the wide marble staircase in the entry hall, unlocked Fiske's safe, and studied the placement of the volumes inside. Then he removed the codebook and the cipher tables for the Military Intelligence Code and for the Confidential Code.[29] (Attachés used the former for their most secret messages, the latter for lower-grade material.) The books were rushed to SIM's photo studio, photographed, and returned precisely to their places. Fiske never suspected.

"As a result . . . at the time of the Battle of El Alamein, the Italians were able to intercept all dispatches of the U.S. military observer of the Eighth Army, Feller [*sic*], who was then at Cairo," MI6's agents wrote, based on what Talamo's men told them.[30] This was not entirely accurate. The codebooks unlocked not only Fellers's messages but also General Maxwell's and the traffic from Washington to Cairo—all from *before* the first battle at El Alamein, not during it.

Nonetheless, the MI6 investigation sealed the case: As William Friedman and Solomon Kullback had suspected, codebreakers had not puzzled out the codebook. The code had been stolen intact. As no one in Washington or Bletchley Park had suspected, the Italians—not the Germans—had pinched it.

There were no traitors in the strictest sense of the word. The embassy employees recruited by Talamo were Italians, not Americans. If they were able to obtain the keys to the safe and the building, the fault lay with their employer.

The treachery, again, was carelessness. As far back as 1936, the US ambassador to France, William Bullitt, had sent a series of warnings to the State Department about abysmal code and cipher security: about the antiquated safes used to store secret documents at his embassy, about the code clerk hired only because he was an American in Paris, about the even poorer situation at the US embassies in London and Berlin.[31] The warnings had the same effect as Major Vivian's advice to the British Foreign Office: nothing was done.

In June 1941, the State Department launched its own study of its cryptographic security. Five experts, including Friedman, confirmed Bullitt's concerns and added more. Codes and ciphers, for instance, were sent to embassies abroad in diplomatic pouches. The bags were either closed with locks that could be "picked in a few minutes" or sewn closed, even though the stitches could be removed, the contents photographed, and the seams resewn "so as to show no signs of tampering." The means for storing codes and ciphers at most embassies abroad were "woefully inadequate," the experts said. "No system for secret communication," regardless of how well designed it was, how statistically unbreakable it might seem, "can be considered safe for use" if it could easily be stolen, they wrote, underlining every word in a plea for attention.

The State Department had to install safes with combination locks at all embassies, Friedman and his colleagues said. It had to make sure that "only suitably paid American citizens" were employed as guards at embassies, especially "when those offices are closed between office hours."[32]

If State applied those measures somewhere in the world, it wasn't Rome, the capital of a country that could soon be at war with the United States. In fact, at the end of 1943, Friedman and three colleagues conducted a follow-up study. The information they managed to get from overseas stations suggested that the "physical security" of codes was still "inadequate" at many posts abroad.[33]

A hint about Colonel Fiske's own regard for security appears in Ciano's diary, on October 31, 1941. He refers to Marchesa Fanny Patrizi—the American-born wife of an Italian aristocrat—as "the lover of the United States' military attaché." Ciano had heard insider gossip that SIM would arrest her on suspicion of spying for America.[34] So it is unlikely that Patrizi was also working for Talamo—though double-dealing is as possible in espionage as in romance. But an attaché's affair with a woman who'd become an Italian aristocrat hardly showed rigorous concern for the military secrets he was supposed to guard.

The photos of the codebooks and cipher tables were delivered to an eighteenth-century apartment building on a narrow, cobblestoned street in a working-class neighborhood near Rome's famous Trevi Fountain. The only sign on the building was the address, Via Poli 48. That was the location of SIM's Cryptographic Bureau.[35]

It would take time for wireless operators at SIM's intercept station at Fort Braschi, on a hill northwest of the Vatican, to identify messages in the purloined codes, and for the Cryptographic Bureau's meager staff to get the knack of using it. In the meantime, Colonel Fiske would stand in a crowd at Palazzo Venezia and listen to Mussolini declare war on the United States, after which Fiske returned to his office, took his codebooks from his safe, and destroyed them.[36]

By December 22, 1941, at the latest, SIM's codebreakers had succeeded in reading a message in the US Military Intelligence Code. It
had taken them four days to decipher Bonner Fellers's Cable 406 from
Cairo, in which he lamented that the British Eighth Army had failed
to destroy Rommel's forces in Cyrenaica despite having a three-to-one
advantage in tanks and despite the British successfully decoding Rommel's orders to his forces. Cavallero received the translation. He told
SIM's General Cesare Amè to warn Rommel immediately that "all his
communications are being intercepted by the English."[37]

Soon SIM was supplying the German command in Africa with verbatim translations of radiograms from Cairo. An SIM report, captured
intact in Rome by British or American agents, shows the Italian agency
boasting of its role in Rommel's counterattack in late January 1942. At
least one channel for passing the information was General Enno von
Rintelen, the German military attaché in Rome.[38]

Neither Talamo's men nor former staffers at the SIM Cryptographic
Bureau interrogated in Rome could say whether SIM shared the codebooks and cipher tables with the Germans, allowing the latter to decode American messages themselves. Tiltman's success in cracking the
code used by Japanese military attachés provided the answer.[39]

In the spring of 1941, Colonel Tashei Hayashi took a train across
the Soviet Union to reach Berlin. Hayashi was the head of the Japanese army's cryptological agency, and wanted to trade information on
American and British codes. Whatever information his hosts shared
did not include advance notice of Operation Barbarossa. The German invasion of the Soviet Union left Hayashi stranded in Berlin.[40]
As an occasional liaison on codebreaking, he used the Japanese military attaché code to radio Tokyo. Late in the war, Allied cryptologists
began going through old messages in the code, from before Tiltman
cracked it. Some of those messages filled in missing pieces of the
Bluebird story.

In early January 1942, Hayashi let his agency in Tokyo know about
the "U.S. military attachés' cipher" that had been "received" in Rome.
He got back a radiogram asking for more information.[41] In a lengthy
response, Hayashi gave a precise description of the Military Intelligence Code and the tables used to encipher it. Since Japan's Pacific

offensive had left no US military attachés within range of Japanese intercept stations, Hayashi saw no reason to send the code itself.[42]

Virtually at the same time, the German high command's own cryptography agency, OKW/Chi, sent an order to its intercept station at Lauf, near Nuremberg. Interception of messages between Cairo and Washington should be "as complete as possible," it said. Listen for messages addressed to MILID or AGWAR in Washington, and to the "military attaché" at the US embassy in Cairo, the order said. MILID stood for Military Intelligence Division, Fellers's usual addressee. AGWAR meant Adjutant General, War Department, the standard recipient of Maxwell's messages.[43]

The evidence is clear: by mid-January, SIM had shared all of the material it had taken from Fiske's safe with Japanese and German codebreakers. German intercept operators aggressively searched through the endless stream of encoded radio messages for the Cairo-Washington traffic. Rommel would get the information from both Rome and Berlin.

And not only Rommel. The Luftwaffe command received a summary of three cables on the negotiations between the United States and the Soviet Union on opening a route from India to Turkmenistan in Central Asia to deliver American warplanes. While described as coming from the "American military attaché in Cairo," they were almost certainly from Maxwell, the American responsible for the strategic supply route.[44] The SIM Cryptographic Bureau translated the first half of Fellers's chronicle of the February 4 coup at Abdin Palace in Cairo; the German ambassador in Rome forwarded it to Berlin.[45]

The United States had military attachés in more places, and obtaining their code gave the Axis agencies access to their radioed reports too. In February 1942, for instance, Ciano wrote that he'd given the German ambassador the text of a cable from the US attaché in the Soviet Union. It complained "about the failure to deliver arms promised by the United States, and says that if the USSR is not aided immediately and properly she will have to consider capitulating."[46]

But nowhere else did the American military's representatives have the kind of direct access to the battlefield that Fellers had, not to mention his dedication and his staff. The traffic from his code room also included Maxwell's constant updates on America's global effort to provide arms to its allies. Cairo was the richest vein for the Axis eavesdroppers.

At some point in the first half of February—possibly between when Fellers sent the first and second halves of his report on the coup—the messages from Cairo evidently became unreadable to the Germans and Italians.[47] The cipher tables had apparently changed—either as a matter of routine, or because Fellers himself had complained that code clerks at the War Department had become so careless in their use of the previous tables that they were endangering the code.[48]

Before receiving the codebooks and cipher tables photographed by Talamo, the chief codebreaker at OKW/Chi had considered the code used by US military attachés to be "unsolvable, and had laid it aside."[49] Now, though, German and Italian cryptologists had the codebook and knew how the cipher worked. They knew names that repeated in the Cairo cables, like "Rommel," "Malta," and "Tobruk," and phrases, such as "RAF intelligence" and "Seventh Indian Brigade," and they had a wealth of long messages with which to work. Once cracked, the code remained forever structurally weak. By April 24, after devoting a full week's work to it, OKW/Chi was able to read Fellers's cable saying that the British would not be able to attack in Cyrenaica until June, which would be too late to save the besieged island of Malta.[50]

The Germans got faster as they filled in the cipher tables. They went back and read old radiograms. They sent messages that too obviously depended on one "good source" in Cairo, but their messages were enciphered in Enigma, and they knew it was a mathematic certainty that Enigma could not be cracked. At some point, SIM's Cryptographic Bureau also got back into the Military Intelligence Code; another SIM report would boast of the agency's role in Rommel's march from Gazala toward the Nile.[51] The Italian signals based on Fellers's cables passed almost unnoticed at Bletchley Park.[52] The German ones finally pointed directly to the source. While Rommel's and Auchinleck's tanks clashed in the desert and men died, a silent war of minds was fought. On one side were Welchman, Storey, and Dudley Smith and the small army of Bletchley Park; on the other side were Axis codebreakers, who were only able to fight on this front because of Talamo's opening gambit. Welchman defeated Talamo, and then Auchinleck defeated Rommel.

ONE PIECE OF the Bluebird puzzle remained unsolved: exactly when Talamo raided the US embassy. Talamo, a man who cared about details, would have remembered. He was not available when MI6 agents 92,700 and 32,000 got to Rome.

In September 1943, when the king and Badoglio fled Rome and the Nazis seized control, two Italian resistance movements formed. One was mainly civilian, dominated by the Communists. The other, smaller organization was the royalist Fronte Militare Clandestino di Resistenza, the Clandestine Military Front.

Lieutenant Colonel Manfredi Talamo, loyal to king and country, joined the Military Front and went into hiding. The new commander of the SS forces and German police in Rome was Herbert Kappler, hitherto the Gestapo representative at the German embassy, whose friend Kurt Sauer had been executed as a spy based on Talamo's evidence. With the help of informants, the Gestapo arrested Talamo in October 1943. Kappler personally ordered excruciating tortures. Talamo gave away no information on the resistance.

On March 23, 1944, a cell of the civilian resistance detonated a bomb as a column of German military police marched down Via Rasella, another narrow cobblestoned street near the Trevi Fountain. Thirty uniformed Germans died immediately, three more by the next day. Kappler recommended killing ten male Italians for each soldier who had died. Field Marshal Kesselring, commander of the German forces in Italy, authorized the massacre.

Kappler's Security Police emptied jail cells of political prisoners and dozens of Jews. To fill out their quota, they pulled civilians off the street. Miscounting, they rounded up 335 people. Kappler decided to kill the extra five as well. The hostages were taken to the Ardeatine Caves, the remains of ancient Christian catacombs, just outside the city. In the last act of the failed bid to renew the Roman Empire, the catacombs would receive new martyrs. The Security Police shot the hostages, then blew up the entrance to the caves, creating a mass tomb.

When the SS men had entered the Regina Coeli prison to collect victims for the massacre, the first name they had called out was Manfredi Talamo.

Talamo had been a secret agent, though he was not smuggled into a foreign country and did not operate behind enemy lines. Most of his operations took place within walking distance of his office. His raid on the US embassy produced, for half a year, the best intelligence source the Axis had during the war. The evidence of his career suggests that his ideology was military loyalty to his country, not to Fascism, certainly not to Nazism. Yet his loyal service brought the Nazis close to conquering the Middle East.

Talamo's body was left in a mass grave, along with the bodies of the other victims: Jews, political prisoners, and men who'd simply been on the wrong street at the wrong moment. The last months of Talamo's life and the manner of his death transformed him in Italian memory into a hero of resistance to the Nazis. Yet the moral meaning of his career may be a cipher too complex ever to be solved. The memory of him as martyr erased the riddles of his life.[53]

THE ORDER WENT out on April 26, 1945, the day that American and Soviet troops met at the Elbe River. Victory over Germany was very near.

The order was addressed to all those who'd known about Ultra intelligence. It warned them that they must "maintain strict secrecy both now and after the war." They were bound by law and honor to avoid even "hinting at what they did in the war." Several reasons were given. There could still be fighting against German undergrounds. In the Pacific, fighting would last longer; the Japanese could be given no clue that their own codes were being broken.

Those were temporary concerns. The first and lasting reason to keep the secret was that "no possible excuse must be given to the Germans to explain away their complete defeat by force of arms . . . and the uncanny success of our intelligence would offer them just such an excuse."[54] Germans could not be given a pretext for thinking, as they had after 1918, that they had lost because of a fluke or a betrayal. They must not have hope for a third round.

For Gordon Welchman and Alan Turing, for Joan Clarke and Jean Alington, for John Herivel, Mavis Lever, Russell Dudley-Smith, and Margaret Storey, for all the people who had cracked Enigma, who had broken the keys day after day, who had translated the messages and made sense of them, the order meant this: You played an extraordinary role in this victory. For victory to last, your role must be forgotten. When friends tell battle stories, when you go on a date, when anyone asks what you did in the war, you must say, "Oh, worked," and change the subject. You made history. Now history must have no memory of you.

EPILOGUE

```
Washington-Bletchley Park-Cairo-
Jerusalem.
```

WAR TRANSFORMS SOME people who survive it. For others, it is an interlude. They shed revelations from the battlefield as easily as uniforms. Truths that they held beforehand and saw broken become whole again.

Bonner Fellers belonged to the interluders.

After a few months stateside, Fellers was reassigned in 1943 to the Pacific, to serve on the staff of his mentor and hero, Douglas MacArthur. In 1946 he retired from the army. Politics on the archconservative edge of the Republican Party had been his avocation before the war, when he still wore a uniform. Now it became his profession. In Cairo, contradictions to his isolationist views had sprouted in his mind. Back home, he uprooted them.

He worked for the Republican National Committee, backed prewar isolationist Robert Taft for president in 1952, and quit his party post when Dwight Eisenhower won the Republican nomination. Fellers became the executive director of For America, which listed "internationalism" even before fascism and socialism as ideologies it opposed. In 1956, For America kicked off its election-year program with a rally at Madison Square Garden in New York—headlined by Senator Joseph McCarthy. Fellers spoke, too, denouncing NATO.

Next, Fellers established the Citizens Foreign Aid Committee—in fact, the committee against foreign aid—and became a full-time lobbyist. Foreign aid, he said, served the Communist plot to destroy America's economy. He publicly endorsed the John Birch Society. The fundamental idea of that organization was that every event was the result of someone's intentional action, and that a web of conspiracy joined those actions. The only plausible explanation of Cold War setbacks abroad and political defeats for conservatives at home was treason—Communists within the ranks of American government who acted on behalf of the Kremlin.[1]

Fellers's embrace of such thinking was ironic, because the Good Source affair was devastating disproof of the conspiratorial view of human affairs. History does, indeed, contain stories hidden beneath stories. It is shaped by determined people, evil and good men and women, cowards and heroes—but very often, not as they intend.

An American officer writing reports in a mansion on El Nabatat Street had an effect on the war far more complicated than he could have planned or imagined. There was no conspiracy in Cairo to betray Britain's secrets. For that matter, there was no secret Allied plan to deceive Erwin Rommel, to draw him to El Alamein where his army would be shattered. Had any British general conceived of laying such a trap, the proposal would instantly have been dismissed as too dangerous. Yet Fellers drew Rommel to defeat.

The outcome of a battle or war can seem to have been inevitable from the start. Not so, Victor Hugo wrote in a long meditation in *Les Misérables* on the Battle of Waterloo. "If it hadn't rained during the night of June 17–18, 1815," Hugo said, "the future of Europe would have been different." That was the night before the battle. Napoleon planned to have his cannons in place at six in the morning. The rain muddied the ground, slowed the artillery carts, delayed the battle till half past eleven. By then the advance of a Prussian army, allied with the British against Napoleon, utterly changed the battlefield.

The rain was one disaster. The other was a road that ran just beyond the crest of a hill. Napoleon knew the road was there when he sent his cavalry charging up the escarpment toward the British line.

He did not know that road lay in a deep ditch, into which his horse-men plunged. A cloudburst and a rut in the earth forever changed the history of a continent.[2]

In June 1942, a message from the War Department to Cairo told Fellers to change his code. Had it been radioed on time, Rommel might not have flung his tired army into Egypt. Somehow, it seems, the slip of paper with the message got lost for a week in the Washington office of RCA before it was sent. Had the message lingered longer, Rommel might have known what awaited him at El Alamein and burst through to Alexandria, Suez, Palestine, and beyond.

A piece of paper apparently misplaced and then found on a desk changed the lives of millions and the future of the Middle East.

A FISSURE RAN through Winston Churchill's speech in November 1942, the one in which he declared that the final victory at El Alamein and the landings of Operation Torch marked the "end of the beginning" of the war. Churchill spoke, characteristically, against tyranny and for the "liberation of the peoples of Europe." He also declared that he had "not become the King's First Minister in order to preside over the liquidation of the British Empire." His words revealed the contradiction in the entire British imperial project, and in Churchill himself: the tectonic clash between democracy at home and colonial rule over hundreds of millions of people outside Europe.[3]

Churchill wanted to believe that the war would be a mere interlude and that the empire would endure. His words suggest he knew differently. The war could not preserve the empire. But in complex ways, it shaped what happened afterward, when the empire came undone.

In Palestine, the end of world war reignited the local conflict. Britain, weakened and bankrupt, had no solution for irreconcilable Arab and Jewish demands. Britain's postwar Labour government asked the United Nations to step in. The UN decision to partition Palestine set off civil war in the country.

In the last days before Britain pulled out in May 1948 and Israel declared independence, leaders of neighboring Arab countries dithered, listened to the chanting of protesters demanding war, and at last made up their minds to invade. In Cairo, pressure on the government came from both the street and the palace. Farouk hoped to seize at least part of the land that the United Nations had allocated to the Arab state in Palestine.[4]

"Morale, especially among the younger officers, was high" on the eve of the invasion, wrote Gamal Abdel Nasser, who went to war as a battalion staff officer. The Egyptian army would be fighting "volunteer groups . . . Zionist gangs," thought armored corps officer Khaled Mohi El Din. "The officers and men went to the war, brimming with patriotism . . . but were surprised to find themselves facing an experienced enemy stationed in bunkers and fortified emplacements."

The Egyptians were utterly unready. "We had entered a war without any preparation," Nasser wrote. "There was no concentration of forces, no accumulation of ammunition and equipment. There was no reconnaissance, no intelligence, no plans." Nasser, Mohi El Din, and other young nationalists in the military looked for reasons for Egypt's defeat. They blamed their generals. They blamed "weak minority governments that were submissive to the King and the British." Their last shred of loyalty to Farouk vanished.[5]

Yet one reason for Egyptian weakness was missing from their list: the Egyptian army had been absent from the harsh schooling of the world war.[6] In 1940, Egypt had chosen to treat the Italian invasion as a battle between Britain and the Axis that only incidentally took place on Egyptian soil. Farouk had played the starring role in that decision, but the young officers had been even less eager to fight on Britain's side. Abdul Rahman Azzam, in 1948 the first secretary-general of the Arab League and a key figure in Farouk's support for invading Palestine, had brokered the 1940 deal by which Egypt turned its artillery and tanks over to the British army rather than fighting.

Palestine's Jews, on the other hand, had overwhelmingly chosen to put aside their anger at Britain to fight a greater enemy. By 1945, over thirty thousand Palestinian Jews had enlisted in the British forces.[7] Other Jews in the new Israeli army had been trained in the Palmah or in the armies of other countries or had learned war as partisans in Europe. In the world war, the fate of Jews had been determined by where Britain and the Soviet Union had stopped the Nazi armies. The borders of genocide were the last line of British and Soviet retreat. In

1948, the fate of Jews was finally in their own hands, and they were indeed more experienced at war than the Egyptians.

Inside Egypt, World War II had diminished the power of all three forces that had wrestled for power beforehand: King Farouk, the Wafd party, and the British themselves. The defeat of 1948 added the military high command to the list. A vacuum was waiting for someone to fill it.

On July 23, 1952, at 7 a.m., a voice on Egyptian radio read a manifesto to the nation. Overnight, it said, "we have carried out a purge" of the "fools, traitors and incompetents" in command of the army. The "purge" was in fact a full-scale coup d'état by the Free Officers, the young men led by Nasser. The voice on the radio was that of the dismissed and reinstated officer Anwar al-Sadat.[8]

Farouk was in a palace in Alexandria, on the shore. The officers ordered him to abdicate. Unlike Lampson a decade earlier, they gave him no alternatives. He was allowed six hours to pack. At the age of thirty-two, Farouk boarded his yacht and sailed away from Egypt. The new regime confiscated his lands and his collections of guns, coins, stamps, cars, Koran manuscripts, and pornography. He took enough gold with him, and had enough wealth deposited overseas, to live comfortably in exile in Italy. In 1965, the forty-five-year-old ex-king died of a heart attack. President Nasser allowed him to be buried in Egypt, at the tomb of one of his ancestors.[9]

In 1967, a crisis mainly of Nasser's making led to another war with Israel, another military debacle for Egypt, and Israeli occupation of the Sinai Peninsula, along with Gaza, the West Bank, and the Golan Heights. Nasser, broken, died in 1970. Sadat succeeded Nasser as president, at last rebuilt the army, and together with Syria launched a surprise attack on Israel in 1973. The outcome was a military stalemate that Sadat successfully presented domestically as victory. Four years later he surprised the world even more by flying to Israel to offer peace in exchange for return of the Sinai. His initiative led to the first Arab-Israeli peace treaty.

In 1981, as Sadat reviewed a parade commemorating the 1973 "victory," Islamic revolutionaries shot and killed him.

Miles Lampson had died in 1964. The longtime ambassador was thus not available to comment on how the Middle East might have been different if Sadat had been executed in 1942, as Lampson had advised. Sadat's career can be read as an essay on how little the early chapters of a person's life foretell the later ones.

THE FIRST BOOK on Operation Condor was published in 1958 by Leonard Mosley, a former war correspondent. Mosley said he'd tracked down Eppler in Germany after the war and interviewed him repeatedly. This explains many, though not all, of the fictions in Mosley's account: that Eppler was recruited in Beirut in 1938 by a female Abwehr agent who used a Vietnamese beauty as bait; that he was personally interviewed by Abwehr chief Wilhelm Canaris on September 1, 1939; that Eppler devised the plan to fly Aziz el-Masri out of Egypt in 1941; that Eppler arrived in Cairo in 1942 with £50,000 in British banknotes; that the belly dancer Hekmet became his lover and also seduced British officers in his service. With Hekmet's help, Mosley wrote, Eppler got his hands on orders from Auchinleck for General Ritchie in mid-July (June and July blur in Mosley's account), but Major Sansom of Field Security closed the net before Eppler and his partner could radio this espionage treasure to Rommel. Instead, supposedly, British headquarters used Eppler's name and cipher to send false information to Rommel.[10]

Sansom wrote his own memoir of his spy-catching days in Cairo. In it, he claimed to tell the true story of the "brave and decent" German spies, Eppler and "Monkaster," alias Sandstede. Sansom wrote that Hekmet invited him, too, to her houseboat and tried to seduce him to protect the spies, but Sansom resisted her enticement, as it was "not quite British fair play to . . . make love to a woman when I might be responsible for her being executed as a spy."[11] Eppler published his own purported autobiography in 1974 in French, and afterward in English, granting himself an espionage career that began well before the war and making himself Almasy's partner in navigating the desert.[12] In a 1980 interview, Eppler boosted the amount of money he'd brought to Cairo to $5 million and the time he spent there before being caught to seven months.[13]

Almasy, who'd died in 1951, could not object. The reports of Colonel G. J. Jenkins, the MI5 man who actually caught Eppler, remained classified for over sixty years. Sansom's memoir referred only once to Jenkins, not by name but by his "lengthy nickname of 'keep it under your hat, old boy,' his favorite expression."[14] Jenkins wrote no memoir.

The myths published first were quoted, retold, embellished, and quoted again, until they looked like the rock-solid history of Rommel's man in Cairo.

WALTHER RAUFF NEVER gave an accounting of his life. He did leave a paper trail, much of it in intelligence agency reports, some reliable, some less so. At the end of the war, according to a later CIA document, he was the SS chief in Milan in northern Italy, where US officers captured him. Two years later he escaped, and was given refuge in a Catholic convent, or perhaps a series of them. He reached Syria, where he worked for one of the country's security agencies—possibly military intelligence, "which he reportedly attempted to reorganize along gestapo lines." After a 1949 coup, he was arrested and expelled, eventually reaching South America. By 1958, Rauff had settled in Chile.

Both Germany and Israel sought to extradite the man responsible for creating the mobile gas chambers in which half a million people were murdered. Chilean courts rejected the requests. In the late 1970s, Chilean political refugees claimed that Rauff was a "principal advisor" to the secret police of dictator Augusto Pinochet. In 1984, he died in Santiago of lung cancer. "It was God that made justice," a Nazi-hunter commented; human courts had failed.[15]

THE GOVERNMENT COMMUNICATIONS Headquarters produced a different kind of historical account: dozens of fat volumes, marked "Top Secret Ultra," intended for very few eyes, so that staffers of the future could learn from the successes and frustrations of the people who eavesdropped on the Axis. The history of Hut 4's work, naval intelligence, ran to fifteen volumes. There were only two women among the authors, a reflection of how few had held senior posts. Only one volume, on German and Italian signal intelligence, had a woman as sole author—the slight, shy woman who'd started at Bletchley Park in 1940 with the rank of "untrained clerk," Margaret Storey.[16]

GCHQ moved out of Bletchley Park, then moved again to the town of Cheltenham, in Gloucestershire, west of London. Storey moved with it. She had a very small circle of friends. She never spoke of her wartime work. Keeping things to herself came naturally, which is why the whisper of her one lover is impossible to track down. She had a nervous shake in her late years. In 1990, all her secrets inside her, she died.[17]

Like her, Russell Dudley-Smith had found his life's work at GCHQ. Like her, he smoked incessantly. When he visited Washington in the 1950s and stayed with John Tiltman's daughter, he had a hacking cough. Dudley-Smith's own daughter knew that he went to the office early and came home late but had no idea what he did there. He died in 1966, at age fifty-five. The obituary in the *Gloucestershire Echo* mentioned his interest in botany and Roman archaeology in Britain and that he headed a division at GCHQ, but could say nothing of what he'd done in the war.[18]

Marian Rejewski returned to Poland in 1946, a risky move because the new Communist regime was suspicious of anyone tied to the army-in-exile of the old regime. But his wife and children were there. He moved from one anonymous job as an accountant to another.[19]

Alan Turing left GCHQ at the war's end to work in the genesis of electronic computers. In 1952, he was arrested and convicted of "gross indecency," meaning consensual homosexual relations. Given a choice of prison or "chemical castration," hormonal treatment to suppress the libido, he chose the latter. Two years later he committed suicide, intentionally leaving evidence that he'd accidentally poisoned himself, so as to soften the blow to his mother.[20]

Edward Travis served as the director of GCHQ until his retirement in 1952. There was no place left for Alastair Denniston, the first head of the agency and the man who'd overseen the original, seemingly hopeless struggle to break Enigma. He was pushed out with a small pension in 1945, before victory over Japan, and became a French and Latin teacher at a prep school. He was anonymous when he died in 1961.[21]

In 1974, the first book in English about the breaking of Enigma appeared, F. W. Winterbotham's *The Ultra Secret*. As a Royal Air Force officer during the war, Winterbotham had been in charge of the secret Special Liaison Units that conveyed intelligence from Bletchley Park to commanders in the field. He knew virtually nothing about how Bletchley Park worked, and gave a picture of a far quicker, more complete success in breaking Enigma than happened in reality. Among other errors, he described Britain as supplying the United States with the solution to the "Japanese counterpart" of Enigma, thereby erasing the American breakthroughs against Purple and the Japanese naval systems.[22]

Winterbotham worked from memory, since he was allowed no access to wartime papers. Still, he received permission to publish. Winterbotham averred that his British publisher had made use of his personal friendship with Prime Minister Harold Wilson.[23] The real push may have been the publication two years before, in France, of the memoirs of Gustave Bertrand, the French intelligence officer who'd worked with the Poles before the war and who brought Alastair Denniston and Dilly Knox to Warsaw in 1939. Even earlier, a Polish colonel had discovered a wartime report in his country's archives and written a book on the work of Rejewski. Winterbotham's book shrank the Polish and French role and returned the glory to Britain.[24]

Gordon Welchman saw a review of *The Ultra Secret* during a visit home to Britain and began thinking of writing his own account of how Enigma had been broken. Welchman had left GCHQ after the war and moved to the United States three years later. By the time his book, *The Hut 6 Story*, appeared in 1982, he was a semiretired consultant for a defense research and development firm. He assumed that as a US citizen, he was no longer subject to the British Official Secrets Act, and besides, Winterbotham had already told the world about Britain's intelligence victory.

So it was a shock when three US government agents came to his house and told him that he had revealed information that was classified in the United States. A late-1940s agreement with Britain and a federal legal clause based on it made British codebreaking secrets into American secrets as well. He was at risk of being sentenced to ten years in prison and a $10,000 fine. A letter followed from the National Security Agency, heir to America's World War II codebreaking agencies, warning Welchman not to reveal anything more about Enigma or methods used "to successfully exploit code or cipher systems." The difference between earlier tell-alls and Welchman's was that they'd merely described the military value of the intelligence. Welchman had explained how the unbreakable cipher was broken.

Welchman was never prosecuted. He did endure more harassment from American and British authorities, including FBI interviews and agents sitting in unmarked cars outside his house, before his death in 1985 from pancreatic cancer.[25] It was a strange form of appreciation for the man who had transformed codebreaking from a craft into an assembly line, an industry that changed the shape of the war.

THE REASON THAT Welchman's book upset his heirs at the NSA and GCHQ, historian Nigel West argued, was that Welchman had stressed that in theory Enigma was "impregnable if it had been used properly." German mistakes and failure to follow simple security rules had created the openings Bletchley Park exploited. His book, therefore, was not just about how an archaic cipher from before the computer age was cracked. It was a warning to contemporary enemies to tighten security.[26] If they took note, their encryption could become unbreakable.

Yet Welchman was partly mistaken, and so were the agencies frightened by his book.

Welchman's error was in underestimating what Rejewski had achieved before the war. Welchman found it "hard to believe" that in 1938 Rejewski had figured out the wiring of the new Enigma wheels added by the Germans. But Rejewski had done so. A problem had appeared unsolvable to brilliant minds. Another brilliant mind turned it sideways, looked at it differently, and found a solution. The cipher was theoretically unbreakable, until it wasn't.

More than that, Welchman made his own early breakthroughs, sitting alone in an empty classroom at the edge of Bletchley Park, when a flash of light in his mind showed him that German security measures were actually back doors into Enigma.

The other mistake was in thinking that the rules could ever be followed perfectly. The cipher had to be used by people, often tired and under pressure. This is what John Herivel had realized the night he fell asleep in front of the fireplace and imagined an Enigma clerk woken at midnight to send a message in a hurry. The more complicated the procedures, the more certain it was that people would take shortcuts. Decades after Turing midwifed the age of computers, people would be asked to protect supposedly perfect encryption by using long, random passwords and changing them regularly. Some would write the passwords on pieces of paper and leave them on their desks.

The flaw in the machine was its human inventor who forgot that human beings would not behave like machines.

THE PERSECUTION OF Gordon Welchman was useless. The secret was out. More and more books appeared. In Poland, Rejewski had been belatedly recognized as a national hero and awarded two military decorations.[27] In Britain veterans of Bletchley Park began to enjoy acclaim—those who'd managed to stay alive long enough, those unlike Storey who could believe it was proper to talk about what they'd done. In 2013, Alan Turing received a posthumous royal pardon.[28] The ruined grounds of Bletchley Park were restored and turned into a museum where recorded ghostly voices spoke in empty rooms of the huts.

THE OLD MAN's living room in Jerusalem was half-lit, as if it were a space between memory and reality. The man was Haim Gouri, one of Israel's most famous poets. He was ninety-one years old. He had been nineteen in the summer of 1942 when his team from the Palmah was sent to scout the road to Megiddo in anticipation of Rommel's advance.

He told me about watching the endless line of trucks carrying Australian soldiers toward El Alamein, about the truck that stopped, about the huge, happy men who climbed out and drank beer and talked to the Jews who were preparing to fight as partisans after the

Nazi conquest. "Wait for the news," an Australian told them, and then the Australians rode onward to the battle that stopped Rommel.

"When I think of it," the old poet said, "where could I find them to say thank you?

"You owe your life to nameless people, and you don't know where to find them."[29]

Acknowledgments

WRITING THIS BOOK has been a wonderful intellectual journey, and has required many thousands of miles of actual travel. Both were made more productive and far more enjoyable by the extraordinary generosity of many people.

At the outset, Gerhard Weinberg drew on his unparalleled knowledge of World War II to suggest sources to consult and issues to consider. Benny Morris was a superb guide to archives and background material. Rob Rozett mapped out scholarly debates on German strategy and the Holocaust.

Gill Bennet, Christopher Andrew, Richard Aldrich, Calder Walton, and Stephen Budiansky shared their knowledge of intelligence history. I am especially grateful to David Alvarez, who was always willing to answer questions and point out new directions, and to Rebecca Ann Ratcliff, who shared not only her time and expertise, but also her archival notes.

I am incredibly appreciative of the openheartedness of people who have spent their lives studying closed, secret agencies. Searching for one document mentioned in a footnote, I cold-called Brian Sullivan. He responded by meeting me, advising me over many months, sharing his stacks of documents and writing on Italian intelligence history, and connecting me with more scholars. Ciro Paoletti gave me an in-depth and insightful tour of Fascist-era Rome and the secret locations of intelligence agencies. John Gooch and MacGregor Knox shared Italian intelligence documents that changed my understanding of this story. Maria Gabriella Pasqualini met with me in Rome, provided an in-depth explanation of Italian secret services, and shared with me crucial documents that she discovered and that give the clearest picture of Manfredi Talamo and his Sezione Prelevamento.

Ralph Erskine was always ready to share his expertise on Bletchley Park and to help with archival documents. Christos Triantafyllopoulos was a constant source of insight and material on codebreaking. Andreas Biermann happily provided access to documents he'd found in his research on Operation Crusader.

I was most fortunate to meet Patrick Bernhard at a small conference at Hebrew University. His presentation there, our conversation and correspondence, and his writings demonstrated over and over how false the myth of a "war without hate" in North Africa was.

Yoram Meital and Israel Gershoni gave me wonderful guidance on the politics of Egypt. Seth Anziska, Eugene Rogan, Walter Armbrust, Avi Shlaim, and Hazem Kandil were open with their time and Middle East expertise and added to my range of sources. Joshua Teitelbaum, as always, had the source I needed on Saudi Arabia.

Kuno Gross, Michael Rolke, and Andrés Zboray eagerly shared information from their exhaustive research on Laszlo Almasy.

For finding arcane archival and published material on American conservative politics in the postwar years, Rick Perlstein came through yet again.

Yacov Haggiag-Liluf shared with me his extensive files on Libyan Jewry during World War II, and Maurice Roumani provided me with additional avenues for research. Matti Friedman added to my sources on the Palmah. Louise Fischer gave me source material on Jewish politics in Palestine in 1942. Sarah Guthartz shared her historical expertise on wartime fashions.

Given the sometimes arcane filing system for World War II military records at the US National Archives at College Park, Maryland, I am particularly grateful for the guidance provided by archivist emeritus Tim Mulligan. Robert Hanyok gave me excellent suggestions based on his many years of research in those records, shared documents from his own files, and uncovered more in the archive in answer to my queries. I am truly indebted to them.

I HAD THE pleasure of working with several excellent research assistants. Sam Miner searched through captured German documents for me at College Park, translated other material from German, and shared his knowledge of German military history. Giulia Sbaffi and Annalisa Bernardi sifted through and translated Italian materials.

My son Yehonatan Gorenberg handled Arabic press reports. My daughter Shir-Raz Gorenberg lent a hand with a last-minute visit to a Jerusalem archive, and applied her artist's expertise to analyzing photographs. My daughter Yasmin Gorenberg applied her professional eye in helping to analyze Margaret Storey's reports and the deciphered messages on which they were based in order to understand Storey's reasoning.

ORIGINAL DOCUMENTS FROM the time of the events are the foundation of this book. Most came from archives. Some of the most important papers, though, came from the children and grandchildren of key figures in the story.

One of the most rewarding moments in my research was finding and making contact with Amy Lear, granddaughter of Bonner Fellers. In her attic were manila envelopes, patiently waiting for a historian, full of his documents. I am truly grateful for her permission to draw from these papers and from the much larger collection of Fellers's personal papers at the Hoover Institution Archives at Stanford University.

One of the published sources for this book is *To War with Whitaker*, the wartime diary of Countess Hermione Ranfurly, a remarkable observer and writer. However, some fragments of her writing were not included in the published version. I am most grateful to her daughter, Lady Caroline Simmonds, for inviting me to her home, enabling me to go through the manuscript fragments, and allowing me to quote from them.

Another long search brought me to the home of Lottie Milvain, daughter of Russell Dudley-Smith. Waiting for me on her table were cardboard folders filled with his writing and notes, virtually all from before he joined the Government Code and Cypher School. I am indebted to her for the opportunity to see this material, and for the additional family lore she shared in conversation with me, providing me with a window into the personality of a man whom I otherwise knew only from official documents. Through her, I was also able to contact John Tiltman's daughter, Tempe Denzer, in Hawaii and to learn more about both Tiltman and Dudley-Smith.

Margaret Storey did not leave personal papers. But at the Cheltenham Local History Society, Kath Boothman responded to my request and ran an ad in the society newsletter seeking people who knew her, and Joyce Cummings found records including Storey's last will and testament, allowing me to identify her heirs. I am indebted to both of them and to Dorelle Downes, Pauline Flemons, Nicholas Fenn Wiggin, Nikki Swinhoe, and James Hodsdon, who shared what they knew about Storey and enabled me to fill in the picture of this remarkable and forgotten woman.

I am also grateful to Jeffrey Maunsell, who has allowed me to draw from the memoir of his father, SIME chief Raymond Maunsell, and to Tori Rosen, who shared with me her father's flight log on the trans-Africa air ferry route.

The RICHEST ARCHIVAL source for this book was the UK National Archive in Kew. I lost track of all the remarkably friendly and helpful staffers who made my months of work there more pleasant. I am grateful to all of them and to the equally friendly staff at the Imperial War Museums archival departments.

I'm indebted to Guy Revell at the Bletchley Park archive; to Debbie Usher at the Middle East Centre Archive at St. Antony's College, Oxford; to Lianne Smith at the Liddell Hart Centre for Military Archives at King's College, London; and to Julia Schmidt at the Churchill Archives Centre at Churchill College, Cambridge.

At the National Cryptologic Museum Library at Fort Meade, Maryland, Rene Stein went far beyond the call of duty to render assistance to me. Her retirement is a loss for research on intelligence history. I'm grateful to the staff of the Hoover Institution Archives, especially to Lisa Miller, who located many megabytes of newly declassified papers for me, and to the staff of the Franklin D. Roosevelt Presidential Library, especially William Baehr, who helped make sense of the format of War Department cables and their telltale time stamps. At the US National Archives at College Park, Bill Cunliffe added information on the War Department cables, and Eric Van Slander spent much time guiding me through the filing system.

I would also like to thank Zvi Bernhardt at Yad Vashem in Jerusalem, Yuval Ron at Yad Tabenkin in Ramat Efal, Tamar Fuks at Yad Ben Zvi in Jerusalem, and Pnina Yeruchami at the Palmach Museum in Tel Aviv for their assistance.

THE MANY PUBLISHED works that I consulted are listed in the bibliography. But I must make special note of several that were truly essential. Gerhard Weinberg's magisterial *A World at Arms* provided the most integrated overview of World War II, the development of Hitler's strategy, and the central place of his war against the Jews in that strategy. Of the countless works on El Alamein, Niall Barr's *Pendulum of War: The Three Battles of El Alamein* gave the most precise and detailed account and incisive analysis.

Klaus-Michael Mallmann and Martin Cüppers's groundbreaking article "'Elimination of the Jewish National Home in Palestine': The Einsatzkommando of the Panzer Army Africa, 1942," their book *Nazi Palestine*, and Cüppers's subsequent biography of the *Einsatzkommando*'s commander, *Walther Rauff—In deutschen Diensten: Vom Naziverbrecher zum BND-Spion*, lay out what the consequences of an Axis victory at El Alamein would have been for the Jews of the Middle East.

FOR SOME PARTS of this book, the document I needed to read was the landscape. Yigal Greiver at the Haifa Historical Society gave me a tour of the World War II fortifications on Mt. Carmel. Hilary Olsin-Windecker of the US State Department connected me to the US embassy in Cairo, where Thomas Goldberger found information on the location of American diplomatic offices during the war, and to the US embassy in Rome, where Stephen Labensky and Carmela Cirami arranged for me to tour the majestic embassy compound. Amr Yosef at the Egyptian embassy in Tel Aviv was most helpful with arrangements for my visit to Egypt. My guide there, Mounir Mahmoud, was remarkably friendly, knowledgeable, and ready to assist in finding the landmarks on my idiosyncratic list. I am grateful to all of them.

MY RESEARCH REQUIRED long stays in London. I am grateful to Norm Guthartz and Lindsey Taylor-Guthartz, who treated me not as a guest but as a regularly returning member of their family, and to Julian Gilbey and Deborah Lee, who opened their home to me. Likewise, I am grateful to Dan and Rochel Rabinowitz, who welcomed me into their family each time I returned to the National Archives in Maryland.

The generosity of the Knapp Family Foundation and a collaboration of Columbia University's Graduate School of Journalism and Institute for Israel and Jewish Studies have made it possible for me to spend spring semesters at the university. The funding and the resources of a great university have been essential to the writing of this book. I'm grateful to them and to the talented students in my seminar on writing history at the School of Journalism, from whom I constantly learned.

It was a pleasure to work with cartographer and historian Mike Bechtold, who created the map for this book.

I am extremely thankful to my editor at PublicAffairs, Ben Adams, for his support and encouragement throughout this project, and to my wonderful agent, Lisa Bankoff, who is always there when I need her and who makes everything happen.

THE MOST IMPORTANT part of every journey is coming home. I am grateful for the help and encouragement of my children. Most of all, I am grateful beyond words to my wife, Myra Noveck, for her love and constant support, for lifting my spirits, and for her advice and wisdom in helping with each step in putting together this story.

Bibliography

ARCHIVES AND PRIVATE PAPERS

Archivio dell'Ufficio Storico dello Stato Maggiore dell'Esercito, Rome, Italy

Bletchley Park Archive, Milton Keynes, UK

Churchill Archive (digitalized papers of Winston Churchill), www.churchill archive.com

Churchill Archives Centre, Churchill College, Cambridge, UK

Columbia University Oral History Research Office, New York, USA

Dudley-Smith Papers: private papers of Russell Dudley-Smith, generously shared by his daughter, Lottie Milvain

Fellers Family Papers: private papers of Bonner Frank Fellers, generously made available by his family

Franklin D. Roosevelt Presidential Library, Hyde Park, New York, USA

Hoover Institution Archives, Stanford University, Stanford, California, USA

Imperial War Museums, London, UK

Knox Mellon Collection of material about the John Birch Society and other radical conservative organizations and causes, UCLA special collections, Los Angeles, California, USA

Liddell Hart Military Archives, King's College, London, UK

Middle East Center Archive, St. Antony's College, Oxford, UK

National Cryptological Museum Library, Fort Meade, Maryland, USA

Palmah Museum Archive, Tel Aviv, Israel

Qatar Digital Archive, www.qdl.qa/en

Ranfurly Personal Papers: private papers of Hermione Ranfurly, generously provided by her daughter, Lady Caroline Simmonds

United Kingdom National Archives, Kew, Richmond, UK
United States National Archive and Records Administration, College Park, Maryland, USA
Yad Tabenkin Archive, Ramat Efal, Israel
Yad Vashem Archive, Jerusalem, Israel

BOOKS AND ARTICLES

Abbasi, Mustafa. "Palestinians Fighting Against Nazis: The Story of Palestinian Volunteers in the Second World War." *War in History* 26, no. 2 (2019): 227–249. doi.org/10.1177/0968344517696527.

———. "Palestinim Nilhamim Benatzim: Sippuram Shel Hamitnadvim Hapalestinim Bemilhemet Ha'olam Hashniyah." *Katedra* 171 (Nissan 5779 [April–May 2019]): 125–147.

Abitbol, Michel. *The Jews of North Africa During the Second World War*. Translated by Catherine Tihanyi Zentelis. Detroit, MI: Wayne State University Press, 1989.

Aldrich, Richard. *GCHQ: The Uncensored Story of Britain's Most Secret Intelligence Agency*. London: Harpers, 2010.

Aldridge, James. *Cairo*. London: Macmillan, 1970.

Alexander, Martin S. "Safes and Houses: William C. Bullitt, Embassy Security and the Shortcomings of the US Foreign Service Before the Second World War." *Diplomacy and Statecraft* 2, no. 2 (1991): 194–203.

Almasy, Laszlo (under the name Count L. E. de Almasy). "By Motor Car from Wadi Halfa to Cairo." *Sudan Notes and Records* 13, no. 2 (1930): 269–278.

———. *The Unknown Sahara*. Translated by Andras Zboray. www.fjexpeditions.com, 2012 (originally published 1935).

———. *With Rommel's Army in Libya*. Translated by Gabriel Francis Horchler. Bloomington, IN: 1st Books Library, 2001.

Alvarez, David. "Axis Sigint Collaboration: A Limited Partnership." *Intelligence and National Security* 14, no. 1 (1999): 1–17.

———. *Secret Messages: Codebreaking and American Diplomacy, 1930–1945*. Lawrence: University of Kansas, 2000.

———. *Spies in the Vatican: Espionage and Intrigue from Napoleon to the Holocaust*. Lawrence: University of Kansas, 2002.

Alvarez, David, and Robert A. Graham. *Nothing Sacred: Nazi Espionage Against the Vatican, 1939–1945*. Portland, OR: F. Cass, 1997.

Amè, Cesare. *Guerra segreta in Italia, 1940–1943*. Rome: Gherardo Casini Editore, 1954.

Andrews, Christopher. *Secret Service: The Making of the British Intelligence Community*. London: Sceptre, 1986.

Annan, Noel. "Book Review: No More an Enigma: Codebreakers: The Inside Story of Bletchley Park." *Independent*, August 22, 1993. www.independent.co.uk/arts-entertainment/book-review-no-more-an-enigma-codebreakers-the-inside-story-of-bletchley-park-ed-f-h-hinsley-alan-1462732.html.

"Architectural History Report of Bletchley Park." Bletchley Park Research. www.bletchleyparkresearch.co.uk/research-notes/architectural-history -report-bletchley-park.

Arielli, Nir. "Beyond 'Mare Nostrum.' Ambitions and Limitations in Fascist Italy's Middle Eastern Policy." *Geschichte und Gesellschaft* 37, no. 3 (2011): 385–407.

———. *Fascist Italy and the Middle East, 1933–40.* Houndmills, UK: Palgrave Macmillan, 2010.

———. "'Haifa Is Still Burning': Italian, German and French Air Raids on Palestine During the Second World War." *Middle Eastern Studies* 46, no. 3 (2010): 331–347.

———. "Italian Involvement in the Arab Revolt in Palestine, 1936–1939." *British Journal of Middle Eastern Studies* 35, no. 2 (2008): 187–204.

Armstrong, David. *At Close Quarters: SOE Close Combat Pistol Instructor Colonel Hector Grant-Taylor.* Stroud, UK: Fonthill, 2013. iBook.

Atkinson, Rick. *An Army at Dawn: The War in North Africa, 1942–1943.* New York: Henry Holt, 2002.

Avramski-Bligh, Irit, ed. *Pinkas Hakehillot; Luv; Tunisia.* Jerusalem: Yad Vashem, 5757 [1997].

"Aziz Ali al-Masri." al-hakawati. http://al-hakawati.net/en_personalities /PersonalityDetails/7406/Aziz-Ali-alMasri.

Bagnold, Ralph A. *Libyan Sands: Travels in a Dead World.* London: Howard and Stoughton, 1941.

———. *Sand, Wind and War: Memoirs of a Desert Explorer.* Tucson: University of Arizona, 1990.

Barr, Niall. *Pendulum of War: The Three Battles of El Alamein.* London: Jonathan Cape, 2004. Kindle.

Batey, Mavis. *Dilly: The Man Who Broke Enigmas.* London: Biteback, 2017. Kindle.

———. *From Bletchley with Love.* Milton Keynes, UK: Bletchley Park Trust, 2008.

Bauer, Yehuda. *From Diplomacy to Resistance: A History of Jewish Palestine, 1939– 1945.* New York: Atheneum, 1973.

Beaton, Cecil. *Near East.* London: B. T. Batsford, 1943.

Beckett, Ian F. W., ed. *Rommel: A Reappraisal.* London: Pen & Sword Military, 2013. iBook.

Behrendt, Hans-Otto. *Rommel's Intelligence in the Desert Campaign.* London: William Kimber, 1985.

Benbow, Tim. "The Dunkirk Evacuation and the German 'Halt' Order." Defense-in-Depth. https://defenceindepth.co/2016/07/11/the-dunkirk -evacuation-and-the-german-halt-order.

Bendersky, Joseph W. *The "Jewish Threat": Anti-Semitic Politics of the U.S. Army.* New York: Basic Books, 2006.

Ben-Dor, Yisrael. "Shloshah Degalim Ve'oyev Ehad." *Maarakhot* 463 (January 2015): 56–61.

Bennett, Ralph. *Intelligence Investigations: How Ultra Changed History*. London: Frank Cass, 1996.

———. *Ultra and Mediterranean Strategy*. New York: William Morrow, 1989.

Benson, Robert Louis. *A History of U.S. Communications Intelligence During World War II: Policy and Administration*. Fort Meade, MD: Center for Cryptological History, National Security Agency, 1997. www.nsa.gov/about/_files/cryptologic_heritage/publications/wwii/history_us_comms.pdf.

———. "SIGINT and the Holocaust." Undated NSA document. Internet Archive. https://archive.org/download/sigint_and_the_holocaust-nsa/sigint_and_the_holocaust.pdf.

Bernhard, Patrick. "Behind the Battle Lines: Italian Atrocities and the Persecution of Arabs, Berbers and Jews in North Africa During World War II." *Holocaust and Genocide Studies* 26, no. 3 (winter 2012): 425–446.

———. "Guerre et violences en Afrique du Nord." In *La guerre du desert, 1940–1943*, edited by David Reynolds, Olivier Wieviorka, and Nicola Labanca, 181–220. Paris: Perrin, 2019.

———. "Hitler's Africa in the East: Italian Colonialism as a Model for German Planning in Eastern Europe." *Journal of Contemporary History* 51, no. 1 (2015): 61–90.

"Besa: A Code of Honor: Muslim Albanians Who Rescued Jews During the Holocaust." Yad Vashem. www.yadvashem.org/yv/en/exhibitions/besa/index.asp.

Bierman, John. *The Secret Life of Laszlo Almasy: The Real English Patient*. London: Penguin, 2005.

Bletchley Park: Home of the Codebreakers. Briscombe Port, UK: Pitkin Publishing, 2015.

Bosworth, R. J. B. *Mussolini*. London: Bloomsbury, 2014.

Bouchnik-Chen, Raphael G. "Palestinian Arab Volunteers in the British Army in WWII: A Reality Check." BESA Center Perspectives Paper No. 1,367, December 9, 2019. https://besacenter.org/perspectives-papers/palestinian-arabs-british-army.

Boyle, David. *Alan Turing: Unlocking the Enigma*. Endeavour, 2014. Kindle.

Brenner, Uri. *Nokhah Ium Haplishah Hagermanit Le'eretz Yisrael Beshanim 1940–1942*. Ramat Efal: Yad Tabenkin, 1981.

Brigadier John Tiltman: A Giant Among Cryptanalysts. Fort Meade, MD: Center for Cryptologic History, National Security Agency, 2007.

Brighton, Terry. *Patton, Montgomery, Rommel: Masters of War*. New York: Crown Publishers, 2009.

Brin, Morik, and Raoul A. Biancardi. *Say It in Arabic and See Egypt: Manual and Guide-Book for the British and Imperial Forces*. Cairo: Horus, 1942.

Brown, Anthony Cave. *"C": The Secret Life of Sir Stewart Graham Menzies, Spymaster to Winston Churchill*. New York: Collier, 1987.

Browning, Christopher R. *The Origins of the Final Solution: The Evolution of Nazi Jewish Policy, September 1939–March 1942*. Lincoln: University of Nebraska, 2004.

Budiansky, Stephen. *Battle of Wits: The Complete Story of Codebreaking in World War II*. London: Viking, 2000.

———. "The Difficult Beginnings of US-British Codebreaking Cooperation." *Intelligence and National Security* 15, no. 2 (2000): 49–73.

Caanan, Haviv. *Matayim Yemei Haredah*. Tel Aviv: Mol Art, 5734 [1973–1974].

Calvocoressi, Peter. *Top Secret Ultra*. London: Cassell, 1980.

Cavallero, Ugo. *Diario, 1940–1943*. Rome: Ciarrapico, 1984.

Churchill, Winston S. *The Second World War*, vol. 3: *The Grand Alliance*. London: Cassell, 1950.

———. *The Second World War*, vol. 4: *The Hinge of Fate*. London: Cassell, 1951.

———. *The Second World War*, vol. 2: *Their Finest Hour*. London: Cassell, 1949.

Ciano, Galeazzo. *Ciano's Diplomatic Papers*. Edited by Malcolm Muggeridge. Translated by Stuart Hodd. London: Odhams Press, 1948.

———. *Diary, 1937–1943*. New York: Enigma, 2002.

Ciechenowski, Jan Stanislaw, et al., eds. *Marian Rejewski, 1905–1980: Living with the Enigma Secret*. Bydgoszcz: Bydgoszcz City Council, 2005.

Clark, Ronald. *The Man Who Broke Purple*. New York: Bloomsbury, 2011. iBook.

Clayton, Tim, and Phil Craig. *The End of the Beginning: From the Siege of Malta to the Allied Victory at El Alamein*. New York: Free Press, 2002.

Conti, Giuseppe. *Mussolini's Spies: A History of SIM Italian Military Intelligence, 1940–1943*. Translated by Brian Sullivan. Unpublished page proofs of the English translation.

Cooper, Artemis. *Cairo in the War, 1939–1945*. London: Hamish Hamilton, 1989.

Cooper, Diana. *Trumpets from the Steep*. Boston: Houghton, Mifflin, 1960.

"Count Galeazzo Ciano Executed." World War II Graves. https://ww2gravestone.com/count-galeazzo-ciano-executed.

Cowper, Marcus, and Christopher Pannell. *Tank Spotter's Guide*. Oxford, UK: Osprey, 2011.

Cox, Stephen Russell. "Britain and the Origin of Israeli Special Operations: SOE and PALMACH During the Second World War." *Dynamics of Asymmetric Conflict* 8, no. 1 (2015): 60–78.

Craven, Wesley Frank, and James Lea Cate, eds. *The Army Air Forces in World War II*. Vol. 7: *Services Around the World*. Washington, DC: Office of Air Force History, 1983.

Crompton, Paul. "King Farouk's Fabulous Wealth." *Al Arabiya News*, January 30, 2014, https://english.alarabiya.net/en/perspective/features/2014/01/30/King-Farouk-s-fabulous-wealth-1977.html.

Cüppers, Martin. *Walther Rauff—In deutschen Diensten: Vom Naziverbrecher zum BND-Spion*. Darmstadt: Wissenschaftliche Buchgesellschaft, 2013.

Currier, Prescott. "My 'Purple' Trip to England in 1941." *Cryptologia* 20, no. 3 (1996): 193–201.

Dalton, Hugh. *The Second World War Diary of Hugh Dalton, 1940–1945*. Edited by Ben Pimlott. London: Jonathan Cape, 1986.

Daly, M. W., ed. *The Cambridge History of Egypt*. Vol. 2: *Modern Egypt, from 1517 to the End of the Twentieth Century*. Cambridge: Cambridge University Press, 1998.

Davidson, Jason. "Italy, British Resolve and the 1935–1936 Italo-Ethiopian War." *Cahiers de la Méditerranée* 88 (2014): 1–17. https://journals.open edition.org/cdlm/7428.

Davis, Ronald W. "Jewish Military Recruitment in Palestine, 1940–1943." *Journal of Palestine Studies* 8, no. 2 (1979): 55–76.

De Felice, Renzo. *Jews in an Arab Land: Libya, 1835–1970*. Austin: University of Texas, 1985.

De Risio, Carlo. *Servizi segreti. Gli «uomini ombra» italiani nella seconda guerra mondiale e i (troppi) misteri insoluti della R. marina nel 1940–43*. Rome: Napoleone, 2014.

Documents on German Foreign Policy, Series D (1937–1945). Washington, DC: Government Printing Office. Multiple volumes.

Dovey, H. O. "Maunsell and Mure." *Intelligence and National Security* 8, no. 1 (1993): 60–77.

———. "Operation Condor." *Intelligence and National Security* 4, no. 2 (1989): 357–373.

Eban, Abba. *Personal Witness: Israel Through My Eyes*. New York: G. P. Putnam, 1992.

"Egypt-Libya: The U.S. Army Campaign of World War II." Last updated October 3, 2003. U.S. Army Center of Military History. https://history .army.mil/brochures/egypt/egypt.htm.

Elshahed, Mohamed. "Saving Cairo Station." *Egypt Independent*. May 2, 2011. www.egyptindependent.com/node/421491.

Eppler, John. *Operation Condor: Rommel's Spy*. Translated by S. Seago. London: MacDonald and Jane's, 1974.

Eran, Esther. "Redifat Yehudei Luv (Kefi Shehi Mishtakefet Bedivuhei Hakonsulia Hagermanit Betripoli)." *Yalkut Moreshet* 33 (June 1982): 153–156.

Fennell, Jonathan. "'Steel My Soldiers' Hearts': El Alamein Reappraised." *Journal of Military and Strategic Studies* 14, no. 1 (2011): 1–31.

Ferris, John. "The British Army, Signals and Security in the Desert Campaign, 1940–42." *Intelligence and National Security* 5, no. 2 (1990): 255–291.

———. *Issues in British and American Signals Intelligence, 1919–1932*. Fort Meade, MD: Center for Cryptologic History, National Security Agency, 2015.

———. Review of C. J. Jenner. "Turning the Hinges of Fate." H-Diplo Article Review No. 199. November 4, 2008. www.h-net.org/~diplo/reviews/PDF /Ferris-Jenner.pdf.

———. "The Road to Bletchley Park: The British Experience with Signals Intelligence, 1892–1945." *Intelligence and National Security* 17, no. 1 (2002): 53–84.

Fitzgerald, Penelope. *The Knox Brothers*. London: Flamingo, 2002.

Flicke, Wilhelm F. *War Secrets in the Ether, Part III*. Translated by Ray W. Pettengill. Washington, DC: National Security Agency, 1953. www.nsa .gov/public_info/_files/friedmanDocuments/Publications/FOLDER _265/41760949080010.pdf.

Foot, John. "Via Rasella, 1944: Memory, Truth, and History." *Historical Journal* 43 (2000): 1173–1181.

Foreign Relations of the United States. Washington, DC: Office of the Historian, Department of State. Multiple volumes and publication dates.

Fraser, David. *Knight's Cross: A Life of Field Marshal Erwin Rommel*. New York: Harper, 1995.

Friedman, William F. "A Brief History of the Signal Intelligence Agency." NSA. June 29, 1942, revised April 2, 1943. www.nsa.gov/public_info/_files /friedmanDocuments/ReportsandResearchNotes/FOLDER_224 /41760689079982.pdf.

Fuensanta, José Ramón Soler, Francisco Javier López-Brea Espiau, and Frode Weierud. "Spanish Enigma: A History of the Enigma in Spain." *Cryptologia* 34, no. 4 (2010): 301–328.

"Gas Vans." Yad Vashem. www.yadvashem.org/odot_pdf/Microsoft%20Word %20-%206236.pdf.

Gelber, Yoav. *Matzadah: Hahaganah Al Eretz Yisrael Bemilhemet Ha'olam Hash-niyah (Massada: The Defence of Palestine During World War II)*. Ramat Gan: Bar-Ilan University Press, 1990.

"Genevieve Grotjan Feinstein." NSA. www.nsa.gov/about/cryptologic-heritage /historical-figures-publications/women/Article/1621585/genevieve-grotjan -feinstein.

Gentzke, Ann Whitcher. "An American Hero." *At Buffalo* (spring 2018). www .buffalo.edu/atbuffalo/article-page-spring-2018.host.html/content/shared /www/atbuffalo/articles/Spring-2018/features/an-american-hero.detail .html.

Gershoni, Israel. *Milhemet Ha'umot Hahalashot (The War of the Weak Nations: Egypt in the Second World War, 1939–1945)*. Tel Aviv: Resling, 2017.

Gershoni, Israel, and James Jankowski. *Confronting Fascism in Egypt: Dictator-ship Versus Democracy in the 1930s*. Stanford, CA: Stanford University Press, 2010. iBook.

Gerwarth, Robert. *Hitler's Hangman: The Life of Heydrich*. New Haven, CT: Yale University Press, 2011. Kindle.

Gilad, Zerubavel, ed. *Magen Beseter*. Jerusalem: Jewish Agency: 5712 [1951–1952].

Gladwin, Lee A. "Alan Turing, Enigma, and the Breaking of German Machine Ciphers in World War II." *Prologue: The Journal of the National Archives* 29, no. 1 (1997): 203–217.

"The Glow-Lamp Ciphering and Deciphering Machine." *Cryptologia* 25, no. 3 (2001): 161–173.

Gordon, John W. *The Other Desert War: British Special Forces in North Africa, 1940–1943*. New York: Greenwood Press, 1987.

Greenberg, Joel. *Gordon Welchman: Bletchley Park's Architect of Ultra Intelligence*. London, Frontline, 2014.

Gross, Kuno, Michael Rolke, and András Zboray. *Operation Salam: Laszlo Almasy's Most Daring Mission in the Desert War*. Munich: Belleville, 2013.

Haag, Michael. "Ahmed Hassanein: Writer, Diplomat and Desert Explorer." *Michael Haag*. August 8, 2011, https://michaelhaag.blogspot.com/2011/08/ahmed-hassanein-diplomat-and-desert.html.

Haarr, Geirr H. *The German Invasion of Norway, April 1940*. Barnsley, UK: Seaforth, 2011.

Haggiag-Liluf, Yacov. *Yehudei Luv Bashoah*. Or Yehudah, Israel: Irgun Olami Shel Yehudim Yotzei Luv, 2012.

Haim, Rabbi Yosef. *Ben Ish Hai: Helek Hahalakhot*. Jerusalem: Merkaz Hasefer, 5746 [1985–1986].

Halder, Franz. *War Journal of Franz Halder*. Office of the Chief Counsel for War Crimes, 1948. Internet Archive. ia802805.us.archive.org/31/items/HalderWarJournal/Halder%20War%20Journal.pdf.

Halim, Nevine Abbas. *Diaries of an Egyptian Princess*. Cairo: Zaitouna, 2009.

Hanyok, Robert J. *Eavesdropping on Hell: Historical Guide to Western Communications Intelligence and the Holocaust, 1939–1945*. Fort Meade, MD: Center for Cryptologic History, National Security Agency, 2005.

Hart, Randle J. "There Comes a Time: Biography and the Founding of a Movement Organization." *Qualitative Sociology* 33, no. 1 (2010): 55–77.

Hassanein Bey, A. M. *The Lost Oases*. New York and London: Century, 1925.

Hastings, Max. *Finest Years: Churchill as Warlord 1940-45*. London: Harper Press, 2009. Kindle.

Herivel, John. *Herivelismus and German Military Enigma*. Cleobury Mortimer, UK: M&M Baldwin, 2008.

Hinsley, F. H., and Alan Stripp, eds. *Codebreakers: The Inside Story of Bletchley Park*. Oxford: Oxford University Press, 1993.

Hinsley, F. H., et al. *British Intelligence in the Second World War: Its Influence on Strategy and Operations*. Vol. 1. London: Her Majesty's Stationery Office, 1979.

Hirst, David, and Irene Beeson. *Sadat*. London: Faber and Faber, 1981.

Hodges, Andrew. *Alan Turing: The Enigma*. London: Vintage, 2014. Kindle.

Hoffman, Peter. *Hitler's Personal Security: Protecting the Führer, 1921–1945*. Boston: Da Capo, 2000.

Hofstadter, Richard. *The Paranoid Style in American Politics, and Other Essays*. Cambridge, MA: Harvard University Press, 1952.

Hugo, Victor. *Les Misérables*. Translated by Julie Rose. New York: New American Library, 2008.

Humphries, Ceri. "Our Rather Useless Hobby." Churchill College Cambridge. September 5, 2016. www.chu.cam.ac.uk/news/2016/sep/5/our-rather-useless-hobby.

Idriss, Nadania. "Architecture as an Expression of Identity: Abbas Hilmi II and the Neo-Mamluk Style." *International Conferences on Recent Advances in Geotechnical Earthquake Engineering and Soil Dynamics* 1 (2010): 1–6. https://scholarsmine.mst.edu/icrageesd/05icrageesd/session11/1.

Jackson, John, ed. *Solving Enigma's Secrets: The Official History of Hut 6*. Redditch, UK: BookTower, 2014. Kindle.

Jaggers, R. C. "The Assassination of Reinhard Heydrich." *Studies in Intelligence* 4, no. 1 (1960): 1–20. www.cia.gov/library/readingroom/docs/CIA-RDP78-03921A000300310001-0.pdf.

Jenner, C. J. "Turning the Hinge of Fate: Good Source and the UK-U.S. Intelligence Alliance, 1940–1942." *Diplomatic History* 32, no. 8 (2008): 165–205.

Jones, Daniel. "The Genius Still Embarrassed by His Success." *Milton Keynes on Sunday*, October 27, 2001.

Kahn, David. "The Black Code." *Quarterly Journal of Military History* 18, no. 1 (2005): 36–43.

———. *The Codebreakers: The Story of Secret Writing*. New York: Scribner, 1996.

———. *How I Discovered World War II's Greatest Spy, and Other Stories of Intelligence and Code*. Boca Raton, FL: CRC, 2014.

———. *Seizing the Enigma: The Race to Break the German U-boat Codes, 1939–1943*. London: Frontline Books, 2012. iBook.

Kasparek, Christopher, and Richard A. Woyak. "In Memoriam Marian Rejewski." *Cryptologia* 6, no. 1 (1982): 19–25.

Kéchichian, Joseph A. "The Military Officer Who Believed in a Muslim Empire." *Gulf News*. June 17, 2011. https://gulfnews.com/life-style/general/the-military-officer-who-believed-in-a-muslim-empire-1.821498.

Kelly, Saul. "A Succession of Crises: SOE in the Middle East, 1940–45." *Intelligence and National Security* 20, no. 1 (2005): 121–146.

———. *The Lost Oasis: The Desert War and the Hunt for Zerzura*. Oxford, UK: Westview, 2002.

Kimball, Warren F., ed. *Churchill and Roosevelt: The Complete Correspondence*. Vol. 1. Princeton, NJ: Princeton University Press, 1984.

Kingseed, Cole C. "Eisenhower and MacArthur: Toil, Trouble and Turbulence in the Philippines." Association of the United States Army. January 13, 2015. www.ausa.org/articles/eisenhower-and-macarthur-toil-trouble-and-turbulence-philippines.

Kitchen, Martin. *Rommel's Desert War*. Cambridge, UK: Cambridge University Press, 2009.

Knox, MacGregor. *Mussolini Unleashed, 1939–1941: Politics and Strategy in Fascist Italy's Last War*. Cambridge: Cambridge University Press, 1982.

Kozaczuk, Wladyslaw. *Enigma: How the German Machine Cipher Was Broken, and How It Was Read by the Allies in World War Two*. Edited and translated by Christopher Kasparek. Frederick, MD: University Publications of America, 1984.

Kozaczuk, Wladyslaw, and Jerzy Straszak. *Enigma: How the Poles Broke the Nazi Code*. New York: Hippocrene, 2004.

Krämer, Gudrun. *The Jews in Modern Egypt, 1914–1952*. London: I. B. Tauris, 1989.

Kruh, Louis. "British-American Cryptanalytic Cooperation and an Unprecedented Admission by Winston Churchill." *Cryptologia* 13, no. 2 (1989): 123–134.

———. "Stimson, the Black Chamber, and the 'Gentlemen's Mail' Quote." *Cryptologia* 12, no. 2 (1988): 65–89.

Kruh, Louis, and Cipher Deavours. "The Commercial Enigma: Beginnings of Machine Cryptography." *Cryptologia* 26, no. 1 (2002): 1–14.

Lababidi, Lesley. *Cairo's Street Stories: Exploring the City's Statues, Squares, Bridges, Gardens, and Sidewalk Cafés*. Cairo: American University in Cairo, 2007. iBook.

Landau, Jacob. *Parliaments and Parties in Egypt*. Tel Aviv: Israel Oriental Society, 1953.

Langhorne, Richard. "Francis Harry Hinsley, 1918–1998." *Proceedings of the British Academy* 120 (2003): 263–274.

Laqueur, Walter. "The Riegner Cable, and the Knowing Failure of the West to Act During the Shoah." *Tablet*. August 15, 2015. www.tabletmag.com /jewish-arts-and-culture/books/192421/riegner-cable-shoah.

"Lend Lease Act." Brian Loveman, San Diego State University. March 11, 1941. https://loveman.sdsu.edu/docs/1941LendLeaseAct.pdf.

Leutze, James. "The Secret of the Churchill-Roosevelt Correspondence: September 1939–May 1940." *Journal of Contemporary History* 10, no. 3 (1975): 465–491.

Lewin, Ronald. *Rommel as Military Commander*. Barnsley, UK: Pen & Sword, 1990.

Liddell, Guy. *The Guy Liddell Diaries: MI5's Director of Counter-Intelligence in World War II*. Vol. 1: *1939–1942*. Edited by Nigel West. London: Routledge, 2005.

Liddell Hart, B. H. *History of the Second World War*. London: Cassell, 1970.

———, ed. *The Rommel Papers*. New York: Harcourt, Brace, 1953.

Lindbergh, Charles A. *The Wartime Journals of Charles A. Lindbergh*. New York: Harcourt Brace Jovanovich, 1970.

Lintott, Brett Edward. "Confidence Men: The Mediterranean Double-Cross System, 1941–45." PhD diss., University of Toronto, 2015.

Lord Alanbrooke [Alan Brooke]. *War Diaries, 1939–1945*. London: Phoenix, 2001.

Lubienski, Mark. "The Zimmerman Telegram." *London Historians' Blog*. https://londonhistorians.wordpress.com/2018/03/23/the-zimmerman-telegram.

Lugol, Jean. *Egypt and World War II: The Anti-Axis Campaigns in the Middle East*. Translated by A. G. Mitchell. Cairo: Société Orientale de Publicité, 1945.

Mackenzie, W. J. M. *The Secret History of SOE: The Special Operations Executive, 1940–1945*. London: St. Ermin's, 2000.

Mallett, Robert. *Mussolini and the Origins of the Second World War, 1933–1940*. Houndsmills, UK: Palgrave, 2003.

Mallmann, Klaus-Michael, and Martin Cüppers. "'Elimination of the Jewish National Home in Palestine': The Einsatzkommando of the Panzer Army Africa, 1942." *Yad Vashem Studies* 35, no. 1 (2007): 1–31. www1.yadvashem .org/about_HOLocaust/studies/vol35/Mallmann-Cuppers2.pdf.

———. *Nazi Palestine: The Plans for the Extermination of the Jews in Palestine.* New York: Enigma and United States Holocaust Museum, 2010.

Manela, Erez. *The Wilsonian Moment: Self-Determination and the International Origins of Anticolonial Nationalism.* New York: Oxford University Press, 2007.

Markovitzki, Yaakov. *Hayehidot Hayevashtiot Hameyuhadot Shel Hapalmah.* Tel Aviv: Ministry of Defense, 1989.

Mason, Lt. Cdr. Geoffrey B., RN. "Service Histories of Royal Navy Warships in World War 2: HMS Resolution." Naval-History.net. www.naval-history .net/xGM-Chrono-01BB-Resolution.htm.

Matloff, Maurice, and Edwin M. Snell. *Strategic Planning for Coalition Warfare: 1941–1942.* Washington, DC: Center of Military History, 1999.

McBride, Barrie St. Clair. *Farouk of Egypt: A Biography.* London: Robert Hale, 1967.

McKay, Sinclair. *The Secret Life of Bletchley Park.* London: Aurum, 2011.

———. *The Lost World of Bletchley Park.* London: Aurum, 2013.

Miner, Samuel. "Planning the Holocaust in the Middle East: Nazi Designs to Bomb Jewish Cities in Palestine." *Jewish Political Studies Review* 27, no. 3/4 (2016): 7–33.

Mohi El Din, Khaled. *Memories of a Revolution: Egypt 1952.* Cairo: American University in Cairo, 1995.

Monelli, Paolo. *Mussolini: The Intimate Life of a Demagogue.* New York: Vanguard, 1954.

"Monty's Caravans: A Field Marshall's Home from Home." Imperial War Museums. www.iwm.org.uk/history/montys-caravans-a-field-marshals -home-from-home.

Moorehead, Alan. *African Trilogy.* Melbourne: Text, 1997.

Morris, Benny. *1948: A History of the First Arab-Israeli War.* New Haven, CT: Yale University Press, 2008.

———. *Righteous Victims.* New York: Vintage, 2001.

Morrison, Kathryn A. "'A Maudlin and Monstrous Pile': The Mansion at Bletchley Park, Buckinghamshire." *Transactions of the Ancient Monuments Society* 53 (2009): 81–106.

Morsy, Laila. "Farouk in British Policy." *Middle Eastern Studies* 20, no. 4 (1984): 193–211.

———. "The Military Clauses of the Anglo-Egyptian Treaty of Friendship and Alliance, 1936." *International Journal of Middle East Studies* 16, no. 1 (1984): 67–97.

Mosley, Leonard. *The Cat and the Mice.* London: Arthur Barkey, 1958.

Nafi, Basheer M. "The Arabs and the Axis." *Arab Studies Quarterly* 19, no. 2 (1997): 1–24.

Nasser, Gamal Abdul, and Walid Khalidi. "Nasser's Memoirs of the First Palestine War." *Journal of Palestine Studies* 2, no. 2 (winter 1973): 3–32.

Nell, Elizabeth. *Mr. Churchill's Secretary*. New York: Coward-McCann, 1958.

Neville, Peter. "The Foreign Office and Britain's Ambassadors to Berlin, 1933–39." *Contemporary British History* 18, no. 3 (2004): 110–129.

Nicosia, Francis R. *Nazi Germany and the Arab World*. New York: Cambridge University Press, 2014.

O'Connor, Derek. "Italy's Consummate Showman: Italo Balbo." *Aviation History Magazine*. March 8, 2017. www.historynet.com/italys-consummate-showman-italo-balbo.htm.

Parker, Frederick D. *Pearl Harbor Revisited: U.S. Navy Communications Intelligence, 1924–1941*. Fort Meade, MD: Center for Cryptological History, National Security Agency, 2013.

Pasqualini, Maria Gabriella. *Carte segrete dell' intelligence italiana il S.I.M. in archivi stranieri*. Rome: Ministero della Difesa, 2006.

———. "Manfredi Talamo e l'intelligence italiana tra le due guerre." *Notiziario Storico dell' Arma dei Carabinieri* 2, no. 6 (2017): 44–52.

Peace and War, United States Foreign Policy, 1931–1941. Washington, DC: US Government Printing Office, 1943. www.ibiblio.org/pha/paw/Peace%20and%20War.html.

Peck, Michael. "The M-3 Grant: America's Nazi Germany Tank-Killer." *National Interest*. January 22, 2017. https://nationalinterest.org/blog/the-buzz/the-m-3-grant-americas-nazi-germany-tank-killer-19126.

Piekalkiewicz, Janusz. *Rommel and the Secret War in North Africa, 1941–1943*. West Chester, PA: Schiffer Military History, 1992.

Pimlott, John, ed. *Rommel and His Art of War*. London: Greenhill, 2003.

Pitt, Barrie. *The Crucible of War 2: Auchinleck's Command*. London: Macmillan, 1986.

Playfair, I. S. O., et al. *The Mediterranean and Middle East*. Vol. 1: *The Early Successes Against Italy (to May 1941)*. London: HM Stationery Office, 1954. www.ibiblio.org/hyperwar/UN/UK/UK-Med-I/index.html.

———. *The Mediterranean and Middle East*. Vol. 3: *British Fortunes Reach Their Lowest Ebb (September 1941 to September 1942)*. Naval and Military Press: Uckfield, UK, 2004.

Porat, Dina, and Mordechai Naor, eds. *Ha'itonut Hayehudit Be'eretz Yisrael Nokhah Hashoah 1939–1945*. Tel Aviv: Ministry of Defense, 2002.

Portelli, Alessandro. *The Order Has Been Carried Out: History, Memory, and Meaning of a Nazi Massacre in Rome*. New York: Palgrave Macmillan, 2003.

Quinault, Roland. "Churchill and Democracy." *Transactions of the Royal Historical Society* 11 (2001): 201–220.

Ranfurly, Hermione. *To War with Whitaker*. Basingstoke, UK: Pan Macmillan, 2014. Kindle.

Ratcliff, R. A. *Delusions of Intelligence: Enigma, Ultra and the End of Secure Ciphers*. New York: Cambridge University Press, 2006.

Rejewski, Marian. "Mathematical Solution of the Enigma Cipher." *Cryptologia* 6, no. 1 (1982): 1–18.

———. "Remarks on Appendix I to British Intelligence in the Second World War by F. H. Hinsley." *Cryptologia* 6, no. 1 (1982): 75–83.

Reuth, Ralf Georg. *Rommel: The End of a Legend*. London: Haus, 2008.

Richelson, Jeffrey T. *A Century of Spies: Intelligence in the Twentieth Century*. New York: Oxford University Press, 1995.

"The Riegner Telegram." Holocaust Encyclopedia. United States Holocaust Memorial Museum. https://encyclopedia.ushmm.org/content/en/article /the-riegner-telegram.

Ritter, Nikolaus. *Code Name: Dr. Rantzau*. Translated by Katherine R. Wallace. Lexington: University of Kentucky, 2019.

Roberts, Andrew. *Masters and Commanders: The Military Geniuses Who Led the West to Victory in WWII*. London: Penguin, 2009.

Robinson, Jack. "The British Official Secrets Act: An Examination." Arlington, VA: Center for Naval Analyses, 1972. apps.dtic.mil/dtic/tr/fulltext /u2/745043.pdf.

Rodenbeck, Max. *Cairo: The City Victorious*. New York: Vintage, 2000.

Roumani, Maurice M. *The Jews of Libya: Coexistence, Persecution, Resettlement*. Eastbourne, UK: Sussex, 2008.

Rubin, Barry. "Anglo-American Relations in Saudi Arabia, 1941–45." *Journal of Contemporary History* 14 (1979): 253–267.

Russell-Jones, Mair, and Gethin Russell-Jones. *My Secret Life in Hut Six: One Woman's Experiences at Bletchley Park*. Oxford, UK: Lion, 2014.

al-Sadat, Anwar. *In Search of Identity: An Autobiography*. New York: Harper & Row, 1979.

———. *Revolt on the Nile*. New York: John Day, 1957. www.anwarsadat.org /project_img/book/4881.pdf.

Sadler, John. *Operation Agreement: Jewish Commandos and the Raid on Tobruk*. Oxford, UK: Osprey, 2016. iBook.

Sansom, A. W. *I Spied Spies*. London: George G. Harrap, 1965.

Satloff, Robert. *Among the Righteous: Lost Stories from the Holocaust's Long Reach into Arab Lands*. New York: Public Affairs, 2006. iBook.

Schewe, Eric Andrew. "State of Siege: The Development of the Security State in Egypt During the Second World War." PhD diss., University of Michigan, 2014. https://deepblue.lib.umich.edu/bitstream/handle/2027.42/107172 /eschewe_1.pdf.

Schneiderman, Harry, and Jullius B. Maller, eds. *American Jewish Yearbook 5707 (1946–47)*. Philadelphia: Jewish Publication Society of America, 5707/1946. www.ajcarchives.org/ajc_data/files/1946_1947_13_statistics.pdf.

Sebag-Montefiore, Hugh. *Enigma: The Battle for the Code*. London: Wiedenfeld & Nicholson, 2011. Kindle.

Segev, Tom. *1949: The First Israelis*. New York: Metropolitan, 1998.

Sells, Michael A. "Holocaust Abuse: The Case of Hajj Muhammad Amin al-Husayni." *Journal of Religious Ethics* 43, no. 4 (2015): 723–759.

Sharett, Moshe. *Ma'avak Medini 1942: Yanuar–Mai—Kovevetz Ne'umim Umis-makhim (Political Struggle 1942: January–May—an Anthology of Speeches and Documents)*. Edited by Shifra Kolat. Tel Aviv: Society to Commemorate Moshe Sharett, 2009.

Simon, Rachel. "Yehudei Luv Al Saf Shoah." *Peamim* 28 (5746 [1986]): 44–77.

Smith, Charles D. "4 February 1942: Its Causes and Its Influence on Egyptian Politics and the Future of Anglo-Egyptian Relations, 1937–1945." *International Journal of Middle East Studies* 10, no. 4 (1979): 453–479.

Smith, Jean. *FDR*. New York: Random House, 2007. Kindle.

Smith, Michael. *The Secrets of Station X*. London: Biteback, 2011. Kindle.

Smith, Michael, and Ralph Erskine, eds. *Action This Day*. London: Bantam, 2001.

Special Forces in the Desert War, 1940–1943. Kew, Richmond, Surrey, UK: National Archives, 2008.

Stillman, Norman. *The Jews of Arab Lands in Modern Times*. Philadelphia: Jewish Publication Society, 1991.

"The Story of the Palace Hotel." Royal Group. www.royalgroup.it /ambasciatoripalace/en/hotel.

Sullivan, Brian R. "Manfredi Talamo (January 1895–March 1944)." Author's ms.

———. "Roman Holiday for Spies: Episodes in Soviet, German and Italian Espionage Operations Against Britain and Each Other, 1924–1940." Author's ms.

"Sunday Times Reporter Interview with President Gamal Abdel Nasser." Nasser. https://nasser.bibalex.org/Common/pictures01-%20sira3_en.htm.

Sykes, Christopher. *Crossroads to Israel*. London: Collins, 1965.

Thornhill, Michael T. "Informal Empire, Independent Egypt and the Accession of King Farouk." *Journal of Imperial and Commonwealth History* 38, no. 2 (2010): 279–302.

———. Review of *Politics and Diplomacy in Egypt* by M. E. Yapp. *Contemporary British History* 12, no. 3 (1988): 143–145.

Turing, Dermot. *XY&Z: The Real Story of How Enigma Was Broken*. Stroud, Gloucestershire, UK: History Press, 2018.

"U.S. Entry into World War I, 1917." US Department of State, Office of the Historian. https://history.state.gov/milestones/1914-1920/wwi.

Van Creveld, Martin. "Rommel's Supply Problem, 1941–42." *RUSI* 119, no. 3 (1974): 67–73.

———. *Supplying War: Logistics from Wallenstein to Patton*. London: Cambridge University Press, 1977.

Von Clausewitz, Carl. *On War* [1874]. Translated by J. J. Graham. Project Gutenberg. February 25, 2006, last updated October 19, 2019. www .gutenberg.org/files/1946/1946-h/1946-h.htm.

Walton, Calder. *Empire of Secrets: British Intelligence, the Cold War, and the Twilight of Empire*. London: William Collins, 2012. Kindle.

Warburg, Gabriel. "The Sudan, Egypt and Britain, 1899–1916." *Middle Eastern Studies* 6, no. 2 (1970): 163–178.

Warner, Philip. *Auchinleck: The Lonely Soldier*. London: Sphere, 1986.

Weinberg, Gerhard L. *A World at Arms: A Global History of World War II*. 2nd ed. Cambridge: Cambridge University Press, 2005. Kindle.

Welchman, Gordon. "From Polish Bomba to British Bombe: The Birth of Ultra." *Intelligence and National Security* 1, no. 1 (1986): 71–110.

———. *The Hut Six Story: Breaking the Enigma Codes*. Harmondsworth, UK: Penguin, 1982.

West, Nigel. *GCHQ: The Secret Wireless War 1900–86*. London: Coronet, 1987.

———. *Historical Dictionary of World War II Intelligence*. Lanham, MD: Scarecrow, 2008.

———. *The Sigint Secrets: The Signal Intelligence War, 1900 to Today, Including the Persecution of Gordon Welchman*. New York: William Morrow, 1988.

Wichhart, Stefanie Katharine. "Intervention: Britain, Egypt and Iraq During World War II." PhD diss., University of Texas, Austin, 2007.

Wilkinson, Patrick. *Facets of a Life*. Privately published, 1986.

Williams, Caroline. "Twentieth-Century Egyptian Art: The Pioneers, 1920–52." In *Re-envisioning Egypt: 1919–1952*, edited by Arthur Goldschmidt Jr., Amy J. Johnson, and Barak A. Salmon, 426–447. Cairo: American University in Cairo, 2005.

Winterbotham, F. W. *The Ultra Secret*. New York: Harper & Row, 1974.

Woytak, Richard A. "A Conversation with Marian Rejewski." *Cryptologia* 6, no. 1 (1982): 50–60.

Yapp, M. E., ed. *Politics and Diplomacy in Egypt: The Diaries of Sir Miles Lampson, 1935–1937*. Oxford: Oxford University Press, 1997.

Young, Desmond. *Rommel*. London: Fontana, 1955.

Zerubavel, Yael. *Recovered Roots: Collective Memory and the Making of Israeli National Tradition*. Chicago: University of Chicago, 1995.

NEWSPAPERS AND WIRE SERVICES

Al Aharam
Argus, Melbourne
Guardian, London
Haaretz, Tel Aviv
JTA Daily News Bulletin
Life
London Gazette
New York Times
People
Telegraph, London
Times, London
Washington Post

WEBSITES

Alan Turing: The Enigma: www.turing.org.uk
American President: millercenter.org/the-presidency
Ancestry: ancestry.co.uk
BBC: www.bbc.co.uk
Bletchley Park: www.bletchleypark.org.uk
Bonner Fellers: www.bonnerfellers.com
Central Intelligence Agency Library: www.cia.gov/library
Charles Lindbergh: www.charleslindbergh.com
Christos Military and Intelligence Corner: chris-intel-corner.blogspot.com
Churchill Society, London: www.churchill-society-london.org.uk
Crusader Project: rommelsriposte.com
Encyclopaedia Britannica: www.britannica.com
Find My Past: findmypast.com
Google, All Newspapers: news.google.com/newspapers
Hansard: hansard.parliament.uk
Holocaust Encyclopedia: encyclopedia.ushmm.org
Ibiblio: www.ibiblio.org
IMDB: www.imdb.com
International Churchill Society, speeches: winstonchurchill.org/resources
    /speeches
Irgun Hahagana: www.irgon-haagana.co.il or hahagana.org.il
Shapell Manuscript Foundation: www.shapell.org
World War 2: www.mtholyoke.edu/acad/intrel/WorldWar2
World War II Today: ww2today.com
Yizkor: www.izkor.gov.il

INTERVIEWS AND CORRESPONDENCE

Alvarez, David
Avnery, Uri
Denzer, Tempe
Downes, Dorelle
Flemons, Pauline
Gouri, Haim
Hodsdon, James
Milvain, Lottie
Swinhoe, Nikki
Wiggin, Nicholas Fenn

Notes

ABBREVIATIONS

BPA: Bletchley Park Archive

CA: Churchill Archive

CD: Galeazzo Ciano, *Diary 1937–1943* (New York: Enigma, 2002); by date

CUOH: Columbia University Oral History Research Office

DFP: *Documents on German Foreign Policy, Series D (1937–1945)* (Washington, DC: US Government Printing Office, 1962); by volume and document number

FDR: Franklin D. Roosevelt Presidential Library

FFP: Fellers Family Papers

FRUS: *Foreign Relations of the United States*, Office of the Historian, Department of State; by volume and document number

HBF: Bonner Frank Fellers papers, Hoover Institution Archives

IWM: Imperial War Museums archive; by digital catalogue document number

KCLH: Liddell Hart Military Archives, King's College

KMC: Knox Mellon Collection, UCLA

MECA: Middle East Center Archive

MLD: Diary of Sir Miles Wedderburn Lampson, GB165-0176, Middle East Center Archive; by date

NCML: National Cryptological Museum Library

OH: oral history

PMA: Palmah Museum Archive

QDA: Qatar Digital Archive

RPP: Ranfurly Personal Papers

US NARA: United States National Archive and Records Administration

USSME: Archivio dell'Ufficio Storico dello Stato Maggiore dell'Esercito
YTA: Yad Tabenkin Archive
YVA: Yad Vashem Archives

United Kingdom National Archives Reference Groups

ADM: Admiralty
CAB: Cabinet Office
DEFE 3: Ministry of Defence: Intelligence from Intercepted German, Italian, and Japanese Radio Communications, WWII
FO: Foreign Office records
HS: Special Operations Executive
HW: Government Code and Cypher School (GC&CS) and its successor, Government Communications Headquarters (GCHQ)
KV: MI5 (Security Service)
PREM: Prime Minister's Office
WO: War Office

Ebooks are cited by page number or location number in editions in which those numbers are fixed and by chapter number in all other cases.

Diaries, published and unpublished, are cited by date.

For works in languages other than English, I have given translations of the titles only when they are provided by the publisher.

CURTAIN RISING: LAST TRAIN FROM CAIRO

1. Key sources on the "Flap" in Cairo include: Alan Moorehead, *African Trilogy* (Melbourne: Text, 1997), 383–389; Cecil Beaton, *Near East* (London: B. T. Batsford, 1943), 127–133; IWM, Document 1798, E. J. F. Watkins, *Underage and Overseas* (unpublished memoir, undated), chap. 1; IWM, Document 12979, diary of Lieutenant General Sir Charles Gairdner, July 3, 1942; W. J. M. Mackenzie, *The Secret History of SOE: The Special Operations Executive, 1940–1945* (London: St. Ermin's, 2000), 187; Artemis Cooper, *Cairo in the War, 1939–1945* (London: Hamish Hamilton, 1989), 192–197. Additional sources listed below.

2. IWM, Document 1798, E. J. F. Watkins, *Underage and Overseas*, chap. 1.

3. Beaton, *Near East*, 130; Cooper, *Cairo*, 195; IWM, Document 12979, diary of Lieutenant General Sir Charles Gairdner, July 3, 1942.

4. FO 371-31573, Lampson to Foreign Office, July 4, 1942. Cooper (*Cairo*, 197–198), citing *The National Bank of Egypt: A Short History, Produced on the 50th Anniversary of Its Foundation*, writes that the board of the Bank of Egypt decided on July 2, 1942, to meet the demand for cash by having the government Survey Office print banknotes. Watkins's account shows that before this date, banks were giving customers worn-out banknotes.

5. FO 954/5B, Appendix, Evacuation Policy, July 7, 1942, 2, notes the evacuation of the South African women soldiers and says that evacuation of female British soldiers was to take place only at the last minute. Watkins's account says that, in practice, many British women in uniform were evacuated. The official report to London appears to have understated the actions of the military in expectation of the possible fall of Cairo.

6. Beaton, *Near East*, 130.

7. Caroline Williams, "Twentieth-Century Egyptian Art: The Pioneers, 1920–52," in *Re-envisioning Egypt: 1919–1952*, ed. Arthur Goldschmidt Jr., Amy J. Johnson, and Barak A. Salmon (Cairo: American University in Cairo, 2005), 428–429; Lesley Lababidi, "Nahdat Misr—Egypt's Awakening," in *Cairo's Street Stories: Exploring the City's Statues, Squares, Bridges, Gardens, and Sidewalk Cafés* (Cairo: American University in Cairo, 2007), iBook; Mohamed Elshahed, "Saving Cairo Station," *Egypt Independent*, May 2, 2011, www.egyptindependent.com/node/421491 (accessed March 10, 2015).

8. Nadania Idriss, "Architecture as an Expression of Identity: Abbas Hilmi II and the Neo-Mamluk Style," *International Conferences on Recent Advances in Geotechnical Earthquake Engineering and Soil Dynamics* 1 (2010): 1–6, https://scholarsmine.mst.edu/icrageesd/05icrageesd/session11/1 (accessed August 6, 2018).

9. FO 954/5B, "Appendix, Evacuation Policy," July 7, 1942; "Evacuation of British and Allied Civilian Personnel," July 9, 1942. HW 12/278, Japanese Minister, Lisbon to Foreign Minister, July 14, 1942, carries a report from Mozambique of a single French steamer carrying four thousand refugees from Egypt to South Africa.

10. Ron Testro, "Cairo-Jerusalem Express in War Has Oppenheim Flavour," *Argus* (Melbourne), October 3, 1942, 3S, trove.nla.gov.au/ndp/del/article/11998336 (accessed March 10, 2015).

11. FO 371/31573, Weekly Appreciation, Lampson to Foreign Office, June 29, 1942; Moorehead, *African Trilogy*, 383.

12. Benny Morris, *Righteous Victims* (New York: Vintage, 2001), 158.

13. *JTA Daily News Bulletin*, June 30, 1942, pdfs.jta.org/1942/1942-06-30_148.pdf (accessed August 1, 2018).

14. HW 12/278, 106449, Turkish Minister Cairo to Minister for Foreign Affairs, Angora, July 3, 1942; 106678, Ministry of Foreign Affairs, Angora to Turkish Minister Cairo, July 6, 1942.

15. FO 954/5B, "Evacuation of British and Allied Civilian Personnel," July 9, 1942.

16. Christopher Sykes, *Crossroads to Israel* (London: Collins, 1965), 256. Sykes was a Special Operations Executive officer at the time of the events. He was stationed in Persia, but Beaton (*Near East*, 102) reports Sykes flying westward at least as far as Habbaniya in Iraq in early June 1942. It is not clear whether he was in Cairo on July 1 or later heard of the incident when he was reassigned to SOE in Cairo in November 1942. One detail of his account suggests he heard about it after the fact: he describes the officer as making "some

dozen . . . journeys between Cairo and Jerusalem in the course of two days" by car. Given the distance, this was physically impossible. However, SOE records show that the officer he identifies, Captain Albert Nacamuli, was in fact head of the SOE Italian section in Alexandria in 1942. In that capacity, he would almost certainly have worked with Italian Jews employed by the SOE and felt personally responsible for their safety. Moreover, Nacamuli himself was an Egyptian Jew, recruited locally by SOE. Following publication of the first edition of this book, Albert Nacamuli's nephew, Alec Nacamuli, contacted me and told me that his uncle had personally confirmed the essentials of Syke's account. See HS 9/1083/2, Nacamuli personnel file; HS 9/1433/9, Christopher Sykes personnel file; "Prominent Sephardic Jews Living in Egypt in 1942 & 1943," www.sephardicstudies.org/pdf/egyptjews.pdf (accessed December 3, 2018).

17. HW 12/278, 106185, The King, Riyadh, to Saudi Arabian Minister, June 29, 1942; 106272, Persian Legation, Cairo to Ministry of Foreign Affairs, Tehran, June 30, 1942; 106681, Turkish Minister, Cairo to Ministry of Foreign Affairs, Angora, July 6, 1942.

18. HS 3/123, SOE/Egypt 2: Policy and the 1942 Evacuation, passim.

19. Hermione Ranfurly, *To War with Whitaker* (Basingstoke, UK: Pan Macmillan, 2014), Kindle: June 26–July 6, 1942; Haviv Caanan, *Matayim Yemei Haredah* (Tel Aviv: Mol Art, 5734 [1973–1974]), 139.

20. *JTA Daily News Bulletin*, June 29, 1942, pdfs.jta.org/1942/1942-06 -29_147.pdf; July 1, 1942, http://pdfs.jta.org/1942/1942-07-01_149.pdf (both accessed August 1, 2018).

21. *JTA Daily News Bulletin*, June 26, 1942, pdfs.jta.org/1942/1942-06-26 _145.pdf (accessed August 1, 2018).

22. Dina Porat and Mordechai Naor, eds., *Ha'itonut Hayehudit Be'eretz Yisrael Nokhah Hashoah 1939–1945* (Tel Aviv: Ministry of Defense, 2002), 52–53.

23. Niall Barr, *Pendulum of War: The Three Battles of El Alamein* (London: Jonathan Cape, 2004), 70, Kindle; Philip Warner, *Auchinleck: The Lonely Soldier* (London: Sphere, 1986), 206–207.

24. FO 371/31573, Lampson to Foreign Office, June 25, 1942; Lampson to Foreign Office, June 29, 1942; Lampson to Foreign Office, July 1, 1942.

25. US NARA, RG 319 270/5/18/7, Box 380, File 370.2, June 28, 1942, Cable 1176.

26. WO 208/1561, Security Summary Middle East No. 58, June 30, 1942.

27. FO 371/31573, Lampson to Foreign Office, June 22, 1942; Foreign Office to Lampson, June 23, 1942; Weekly Appreciation, Lampson to Foreign Office, June 29, 1942; Lampson to Foreign Office, July 2, 1942.

28. Barr, *Pendulum*, 10.

29. Barr, *Pendulum*, 45; Moorehead, *African Trilogy*, 192.

30. Barr, *Pendulum*, 16; David Fraser, *Knight's Cross: A Life of Field Marshal Erwin Rommel* (New York: Harper, 1995), 337–338; Warner, *Auchinleck*, 188. Sources vary on the number of soldiers taken prisoner at Tobruk, especially in early reports. I have relied here on Barr's figures.

31. Moorehead, *African Trilogy*, 370–371; B. H. Liddell Hart, *History of the Second World War* (London: Cassell, 1970), 277; Barr, *Pendulum*, 34.

32. Winston S. Churchill, *The Hinge of Fate* (London: Cassell, 1951), 344.

33. PREM 3/290/6, Auchinleck to Prime Minister, June 21, 1942; Churchill to Auchinleck, June 22, 1942; Auchinleck to Prime Minister, June 24, 1942.

34. Barr, *Pendulum*, 23–26; Warner, *Auchinleck*, 191; FDR, Map Room, Box 93, File MR300, Sec. 1, Maxwell Cable No. 29, June 27, 1942.

35. Barr, *Pendulum*, 27–30; Warner, *Auchinleck*, 191–194.

36. MLD, June 29, 1942.

37. Ian F. W. Beckett, ed., *Rommel: A Reappraisal* (London: Pen & Sword Military, 2013), chap. 3, iBook.

38. WO 208/1561, Security Summary Middle East No. 57, June 25, 1942.

39. House of Commons Official Report, January 27, 1942, www.ibiblio.org /pha/policy/1942/420127a.html (accessed July 30, 2018).

40. Desmond Young, *Rommel* (London: Fontana, 1955), 23.

41. Beckett, *Rommel*, chap. 7. Praise of Rommel's extraordinary insight into the mind of his enemy continued and even increased after the war. A good example is B. H. Liddell Hart's introduction to *The Rommel Papers* (New York: Harcourt, Brace, 1953), xix.

42. FDR, Map Room, Box 93, File MR300, Sec. 1, June 21, 1942, Fellers Cable 1156. The cable was sent in six sections. Time stamps on sections two through six show they were sent after Fellers Cable 1157 on the fall of Tobruk. Wording quoted here is from the language of the cable as deciphered and distributed at the War Department. Cables were paraphrased when deciphered, so the language was slightly different from what Fellers sent from Cairo and sometimes less precise.

43. Liddell Hart, *Rommel Papers*, 239.

44. CD, June 29, 1942; Paolo Monelli, *Mussolini: The Intimate Life of a Demagogue* (New York: Vanguard, 1954), 9–10; Liddell Hart, *Second World War*, 277.

45. Fraser, *Knight's Cross*, 220, 342.

ACT I. CHAPTER 1. "REPORT FOR DUTY, IN ACCORDANCE WITH THE INSTRUCTIONS YOU HAVE RECEIVED"

1. Audio of Chamberlain announcement: "Britain Declares War on Germany," BBC Archive, www.bbc.co.uk/archive/ww2outbreak/7917.shtml (accessed August 22, 2018). Prepared text: www.bbc.co.uk/archive/ww2outbreak /7957.shtml (accessed August 22, 2018). The actual speech included a few words not in the prepared text.

2. Gerhard L. Weinberg, *A World at Arms: A Global History of World War II*, 2nd ed. (Cambridge: Cambridge University Press, 2005), chap. 1, Kindle.

3. "Evacuees Depart from Waterloo Station," BBC Archive, www.bbc.co.uk /archive/ww2outbreak/7921.shtml (accessed August 21, 2018).

4. The closing of places of entertainment and prohibition on public gatherings was announced on the BBC immediately after Chamberlain's announcement ("Britain Declares War on Germany").

5. Gordon Welchman, *The Hut Six Story: Breaking the Enigma Codes* (Harmondsworth, UK: Penguin, 1982), 7–13; Joel Greenberg, *Gordon Welchman: Bletchley Park's Architect of Ultra Intelligence* (London: Frontline, 2014), 5–14, and front jacket cover photo of Welchman.

6. BPA, Patrick Wilkinson, *Facets of a Life* (privately published memoir, 1986), 131.

7. Welchman, *Hut Six*, 12.

8. Peter Hoffman, *Hitler's Personal Security: Protecting the Führer, 1921–1945* (Boston: Da Capo, 2000), 135–138; Fraser, *Knight's Cross*, 141–142.

9. Beckett, *Rommel*, chap. 1; Ralf Georg Reuth, *Rommel: The End of a Legend* (London: Haus, 2008), 37–38.

10. Young, *Rommel*, 10. Erwin Rommel's son, Manfred Rommel, wrote in his introduction to Liddell Hart (*Rommel Papers*, xviii) that the United States returned to Rommel's wife the letters he had written to her. He notes that some remained missing. However, the letters to Lucie Rommel cited by Reuth (*Rommel*, 37–38) were found in the microfilm collection of captured German papers in the US National Archives, and the originals were likely among those returned to the family. Liddell Hart did not include material from before May 1940 in *The Rommel Papers*.

11. John Pimlott, ed., *Rommel and His Art of War* (London: Greenhill, 2003), 29; Reuth, *Rommel*, 33–36; Fraser, *Knight's Cross*, 98; Liddell Hart, *Second World War*, 3.

12. Welchman, *Hut Six*, 19–20.

13. "September 3, 1939: Fireside Chat 14: On the European War," Miller Center, https://millercenter.org/the-presidency/presidential-speeches /september-3-1939-fireside-chat-14-european-war (accessed December 24, 2018). On the ranking of the US Army, see *Peace and War, United States Foreign Policy, 1931–1941* (Washington, DC: US Government Printing Office, 1943), 55, www.ibiblio.org/pha/paw/Peace%20and%20War.html (accessed December 24, 2018).

14. Jean Smith, *FDR* (New York: Random House, 2007), chap 20, Kindle; Charles A. Lindbergh, "Let Us Look to Our Own Defense," ibiblio, www.ibiblio .org/pha/policy/1939/1939-09-15a.html (accessed December 25, 2018).

15. The main source on Rauff is Martin Cüppers, *Walther Rauff—In deutschen Diensten: Vom Naziverbrecher zum BND-Spion* (Darmstadt: Wissenschaftliche Buchgesellschaft, 2013). Additional information is found in Klaus-Michael Mallmann and Martin Cüppers, "'Elimination of the Jewish National Home in Palestine': The Einsatzkommando of the Panzer Army Africa, 1942," Yad Vashem, www1.yadvashem.org/about_HOLocaust/studies/vol35 /Mallmann-Cuppers2.pdf (accessed May 26, 2013), 4–5.

16. Robert Gerwarth, *Hitler's Hangman: The Life of Heydrich* (New Haven, CT: Yale University Press, 2011), 42–52, Kindle.

17. Plan LADYSHIP Progress Report, February 3, 1954, CIA name file for Walter [*sic*] Rauff, CIA, www.cia.gov/library/readingroom/docs/RAUFF %2C%20WALTER_0088.pdf (accessed July 23, 2018).

18. Gerwarth, *Hitler's Hangman*, 51.

19. Cüppers, *Rauff*, 81.

20. Cüppers, *Rauff*, 93–97; Gerwarth, *Hitler's Hangman*, 148; Christopher R. Browning, *The Origins of the Final Solution: The Evolution of Nazi Jewish Policy, September 1939–March 1942* (Lincoln: University of Nebraska, 2004), 25–26. Cüppers writes that Best conducted the meeting. Browning and Gerwarth state that Heydrich himself led this meeting, as he did the subsequent ones. However, Gerwarth also writes that Heydrich was on an inspection tour in Poland at the time, leaving Best in his place in Berlin (142).

21. Patrick Bernhard, "Hitler's Africa in the East: Italian Colonialism as a Model for German Planning in Eastern Europe," *Journal of Contemporary History* 51, no. 1 (2015): 61–90. I am grateful to Patrick Bernhard for sharing his insights with me in conversation and correspondence.

22. Gerwarth, *Hitler's Hangman*, 148–150; Cüppers, *Rauff*, 93–97.

23. Cüppers, *Rauff*, 97.

24. Jan Stanislaw Ciechanowski, "The Polish Contribution to Cracking the German Enigma Code," in *Marian Rejewski, 1905–1980: Living with the Enigma Secret*, ed. Jan Stanislaw Ciechanowski et al. (Bydgoszcz: Bydgoszcz City Council, 2005), 108–109.

25. Liddell Hart, *Second World War*, 30.

26. See, for instance, Ciechanowski et al., *Rejewski*, frontispiece.

27. Richard A. Woytak, "A Conversation with Marian Rejewski," *Cryptologia* 6, no. 1 (1982): 50–60; Christopher Kasparek and Richard A. Woyak, "In Memoriam Marian Rejewski," *Cryptologia* 6, no. 1 (1982): 20.

28. Woytak, "Conversation," 52.

29. Watkins, *Underage and Overseas*, chap. 1.

30. "The Glow-Lamp Ciphering and Deciphering Machine," *Cryptologia* 25, no. 3 (2001): 172.

31. "The Glow-Lamp," 161–169.

32. The description of Enigma's workings is based on numerous sources, including Marian Rejewski, "Mathematical Solution of the Enigma Cipher," *Cryptologia* 6, no. 1 (1982): 1–18; Welchman, *Hut Six*, 38–47; Greenberg, *Welchman*, 15–16, 201–203. The number of settings in the original Enigma was the multiple of 6 wheel orders, $26 \times 26 \times 26$ ring settings, and $26 \times 26 \times 26$ wheel settings, equaling 1,853,494,656.

33. Ciechanowski, "Polish Contribution," 99.

34. Marian Rejewski, "Remarks on Appendix I to British Intelligence in the Second World War by F. H. Hinsley," *Cryptologia* 6, no. 1 (1982): 76. The number of permutations for each wheel is the factorial of 26 (26!). For three wheels, the number of permutations is the cube of the number for a single wheel. In addition, the Enigma had a reflector wheel with contacts on one side only. Each contact was wired to another on that side. The number of permutations for this wheel equaled $25 \times 23 \times 21 \times 19 \times 17 \times 15 \times 13 \times 11 \times 9 \times 7 \times 5 \times 3$. Multiplying this by the total permutations for the three rotors produces the total for the device: 5.18568×10^{92}.

35. In Woytak ("Conversation," 52–55), Rejewski says he started at the Cypher Bureau in Warsaw at the start of September 1932 and began working on Enigma in late October or early November. Ciechanowski ("Polish Contribution," 103) states that by mid-January, the trio was reading intercepted Enigma messages. This includes the time to solve the daily settings. Rejewski's solution of the wiring may have taken as little as two months.

36. Kasparek and Woyak, "In Memoriam Marian Rejewski," 20.

37. Rejewski, "Remarks," 80.

38. Ciechanowski, "Polish Contribution," 109.

ACT I. CHAPTER 2. THE SEDUCTIVE CURVES OF THE DUNES

1. Ralph A. Bagnold, *Sand, Wind and War: Memoirs of a Desert Explorer* (Tucson: University of Arizona, 1990), 119.

2. Saul Kelly, *The Lost Oasis: The Desert War and the Hunt for Zerzura* (Oxford, UK: Westview, 2002), 15–16.

3. This is the date that Bagnold gives in his memoir *Sand, Wind* (49). In an earlier account, he gave the year as 1925: Ralph A. Bagnold, *Libyan Sands: Travels in a Dead World* (London: Howard and Stoughton, 1941), 19.

4. Bagnold, *Sand, Wind*, 51–60; Bagnold, *Libyan Sands*, 31–87.

5. Herodotus, *The Histories*, 3: 26.

6. Kelly, *Lost Oasis*, 11–12; Bagnold, *Libyan Sands*, 114–116, 141–146.

7. This was Bagnold's description (*Libyan Sands*, 165–166).

8. The detailed account of this journey is A. M. Hassanein Bey, *The Lost Oases* (New York and London: Century, 1925). See also Kelly, *Lost Oasis*, 9–10; Bagnold, *Libyan Sands*, 171–172.

9. Hassanein Bey, *Lost Oases*, 6.

10. Michael Haag, "Ahmed Hassanein: Writer, Diplomat and Desert Explorer," *Michael Haag*, August 8, 2011, https://michaelhaag.blogspot.com/2011/08/ahmed-hassanein-diplomat-and-desert.html (accessed October 9, 2017).

11. Bagnold, *Libyan Sands*, 112.

12. Bagnold, *Libyan Sands*, 67–71, 147. Instructions for use of the sand compass appear at Ceri Humphries, "Our Rather Useless Hobby," Churchill College Cambridge, September 5, 2016, https://www.chu.cam.ac.uk/news/2016/sep/5/our-rather-useless-hobby (accessed September 4, 2018).

13. Photo of Bagnold on 1929 expedition: *Sand, Wind*, plates after 118. For a typical photo of Bagnold, see Humphries, "Useless Hobby."

14. Bagnold, *Libyan Sands*, 135.

15. Bagnold, *Libyan Sands*, 128–129.

16. Bagnold, *Sand, Wind*, 102–104.

17. Bagnold, *Libyan Sands*, 166–168.

18. Bagnold, *Libyan Sands*, 177–178, 203; Kelly, *Lost Oasis*, 24–26.

19. Bagnold, *Libyan Sands*, 268–284.

20. Bagnold, *Libyan Sands*, 105–111, 179–180; László Almasy, *The Unknown Sahara*, trans. Andras Zboray (www.fjexpeditions.com, 2012) (originally published 1935), 22.

21. FO 371/15433 J1677/148/66, Enclosure of April 26, 1931; Kelly, *Lost Oasis*, 26–32; Bagnold, *Libyan Sands*, 197–205.

22. Bernhard, "Hitler's Africa," 68; Robert Mallett, *Mussolini and the Origins of the Second World War, 1933–1940* (Houndsmills, UK: Palgrave, 2003), 17; R. J. B. Bosworth, *Mussolini* (London: Bloomsbury, 2014), 205–207.

23. Kelly, *Lost Oasis*, 52; Almasy, *Unknown Sahara*, 8–37; L. E. de Almasy, "By Motor Car from Wadi Halfa to Cairo," *Sudan Notes and Records* 13, no. 2 (1930): 269–278; John Bierman, *The Secret Life of Laszlo Almasy: The Real English Patient* (London: Penguin, 2005), 47–57.

24. Kelly, *Lost Oasis*, 48.

25. See photo plates in Bierman, *Secret Life*, and Kelly, *Lost Oasis*.

26. Kelly, *Lost Oasis*, 39.

27. Bierman, *Secret Life*, 20–21.

28. Bierman, *Secret Life*, 22–25; Kelly, *Lost Oasis*, 42–43.

29. Kelly, *Lost Oasis*, 44–45.

30. "Gyula Gömbös," Encyclopaedia Britannica, www.britannica.com/biography/Gyula-Gombos (accessed September 8, 2018).

31. Almasy, *Unknown Sahara*, 2, 7. Almasy wrote that these words were a Beduin saying.

32. See Kelly, *Lost Oasis*, 51.

33. Kelly, *Lost Oasis*, 49. The byline "Count L. E. de Almasy" appears on his 1930 article "By Motor Car from Wadi Halfa to Cairo."

34. Almasy, *Unknown Sahara*, 1–4; Kelly, *Lost Oasis*, 46–52.

35. Almasy, *Unknown Sahara*, 63–69; Kelly, *Lost Oasis*, 53–62.

36. Kelly, *Lost Oasis*, 89–92.

37. Bagnold, *Sand, Wind*, 87 and photo plates after 118; Bagnold, *Libyan Sands*, 233. Bagnold does not give Lorenzini's first name, but it appears in other sources. See John Sadler, *Operation Agreement: Jewish Commandos and the Raid on Tobruk* (Oxford, UK: Osprey, 2016), chap. 12, iBook.

38. Kuno Gross, Michael Rolke, and András Zboray, *Operation Salam: Laszlo Almasy's Most Daring Mission in the Desert War* (Munich: Belleville, 2013), 165–168; Almasy, *Unknown Sahara*, 109; Kelly, *Lost Oasis*, 104.

39. Kelly, *Lost Oasis*, 63; Almasy, *Unknown Sahara*, 70.

40. Kelly, *Lost Oasis*, 87, 116.

41. Bagnold, *Libyan Sands*, 207; Kelly, *Lost Oasis*, 89.

42. Almasy, *Unknown Sahara*, 63–78.

43. Bierman, *Secret Life*, 133.

44. Bagnold, *Libyan Sands*, 268–284.

45. Bagnold, *Sand, Wind*, 100–117.

46. Ralph Bagnold, *Libyan Sands* (London: Eland Publishing, 2012), Epilogue 1987, Kindle.

47. Bagnold, *Sand, Wind*, 106, 119.

48. Bierman (*Secret Life*, 131) writes that the last documentary evidence of Almasy's presence in Egypt is a flight he logged from the Almaza airfield outside Cairo on July 22, 1939. His actual departure from the country more likely took place after the war began.

49. CUOH, Laszlo Pathy, 1976, 23–25.

ACT I. CHAPTER 3. NEXT KING OF THE NILE

1. Sources for this brief history of Egypt leading up to World War II are too numerous to list. Of particular value were M. W. Daly, ed., *The Cambridge History of Egypt*, vol. 2: *Modern Egypt, from 1517 to the End of the Twentieth Century* (Cambridge: Cambridge University Press, 1998); Max Rodenbeck, *Cairo: The City Victorious* (New York: Vintage, 2000); Lababidi, *Cairo's Street Stories*; James Aldridge, *Cairo* (London, Macmillan, 1970); M. E. Yapp, ed., *Politics and Diplomacy in Egypt: The Diaries of Sir Miles Lampson, 1935–1937* (Oxford: Oxford University Press, 1997); Michael T. Thornhill, "Informal Empire, Independent Egypt and the Accession of King Farouk," *Journal of Imperial and Commonwealth History* 38, no. 2 (2010): 279–302; Laila Morsy, "Farouk in British Policy," *Middle Eastern Studies* 20, no. 4 (1984): 193–211; Gabriel Warburg, "The Sudan, Egypt and Britain, 1899–1916," *Middle Eastern Studies* 6, no. 2 (1970): 163–178; Eric Andrew Schewe, "State of Siege: The Development of the Security State in Egypt During the Second World War" (PhD diss, University of Michigan, 2014), https://deepblue.lib.umich.edu/bitstream/handle /2027.42/107172/eschewe_1.pdf (accessed October 8, 2018); Stefanie Katharine Wichhart, "Intervention: Britain, Egypt and Iraq During World War II" (PhD diss, University of Texas, Austin, 2007), www.lib.utexas.edu/etd/d/2007 /wichharts70798/wichharts70798.pdf (accessed June 18, 2014).

2. Paul Crompton, "King Farouk's Fabulous Wealth," *Al Arabiya News*, January 30, 2014, https://english.alarabiya.net/en/perspective/features/2014/01 /30/King-Farouk-s-fabulous-wealth-1977.html (accessed October 8, 2018). The weapons collected by Fouad and Farouk are on display at the Abdeen Palace Museum in Cairo.

3. Erez Manela, *The Wilsonian Moment: Self-Determination and the International Origins of Anticolonial Nationalism* (New York: Oxford University Press, 2007), 141ff.; Aldridge, *Cairo*, 224–226; Rodenbeck, *Cairo: The City*, 143–144.

4. IWM, Document 4829, R. J. Maunsell, unpublished memoir, 2–3.

5. Bagnold, *Libyan Sands*, chap. 2–4.

6. On the lives of the royals, see Nevine Abbas Halim, *Diaries of an Egyptian Princess* (Cairo: Zaitouna, 2009); CUOH, Laszlo Pathy, 1976, 22.

7. Halim, *Diaries*, 54, 86.

8. Yapp, *Politics*, 4–6; Michael Thornhill, Review of *Politics and Diplomacy in Egypt* by M. E. Yapp, *Contemporary British History* 12, no. 3 (1988): 143–145.

9. "The Dowager Lady Killearn—Obituary," *Telegraph*, October 12, 2015, www.telegraph.co.uk/news/obituaries/11926858/The-Dowager-Lady -Killearn-obituary.html (accessed April 25, 2018); Yapp, *Politics*, 35, 44.

10. MLD. See, for instance, entries for January 27, 1942, February 21, 1942, June 4, 1942, July 3, 1942.

11. On Farouk's accession, see Morsy, "Farouk in British Policy"; Thornhill, "Informal Empire."

12. Barrie St. Clair McBride, *Farouk of Egypt: A Biography* (London: Robert Hale, 1967), 76, 83. On Queen Nazli, cf. CUOH, Laszlo Pathy, 1976, 22; Halim, *Diaries*, 110.

13. Yapp, *Politics*, especially 25ff.; Morsy, "Farouk in British Policy"; Laila Morsy, "The Military Clauses of the Anglo-Egyptian Treaty of Friendship and Alliance, 1936," *International Journal of Middle East Studies* 16, no. 1 (1984): 67–97.

14. Treaty text: Yapp, *Politics*, 984–993.

15. Mallett, *Mussolini*, 83.

16. Bosworth, *Mussolini*, 250.

17. Mallett, *Mussolini*, 83–101; Kelly, *Lost Oasis*, 92.

18. Israel Gershoni and James Jankowski, *Confronting Fascism in Egypt: Dictatorship Versus Democracy in the 1930s* (Stanford, CA: Stanford University Press, 2010), chap. 1, iBook.

19. Thornhill, "Informal Empire," 295.

20. IWM, Document 4829, Maunsell memoir, 4–5.

21. Morsy, "Military Clauses," 76–77.

22. Khaled Mohi El Din, *Memories of a Revolution: Egypt 1952* (Cairo: American University in Cairo, 1995), 12.

23. Anwar al-Sadat, *In Search of Identity: An Autobiography* (New York: Harper & Row, 1979), 2–16.

24. Mohi El Din, *Memories*, 12–13; "Sunday Times Reporter Interview with President Gamal Abdel Nasser," Nasser, https://nasser.bibalex.org/Common/pictures01-%20sira3_en.htm (accessed October 4, 2018). The original interview took place in 1962.

25. IWM, Document 4829, Maunsell memoir, 22.

26. "Farouk First King of Modern Egypt," *New York Times*, July 30, 1937, 21.

27. Gershoni and Jankowski, *Confronting Fascism*, chap. 1.

28. Gershoni and Jankowski, *Confronting Fascism*, chap 1.

29. On Verucci, see Morsy, "Farouk in British Policy," 197.

30. Jean Lugol, *Egypt and World War II: The Anti-Axis Campaigns in the Middle East*, trans. A. G. Mitchell (Cairo: Société Orientale de Publicité, 1945), 15–17; Wichhart, "Intervention," 82–83.

31. "Aziz Ali al-Masri," al-hakawati, http://al-hakawati.net/en_personalities/PersonalityDetails/7406/Aziz-Ali-alMasri (accessed October 8, 2018); Joseph A. Kéchichian, "The Military Officer Who Believed in a Muslim Empire," *Gulf News*, June 17, 2011, https://gulfnews.com/life-style/general/the-military-officer-who-believed-in-a-muslim-empire-1.821498 (accessed October 2, 2018).

32. Wichhart, "Intervention," 81ff.

33. Lampson's cables from the early days of September 1939 on his meetings with Ali Maher are in FO 371/23368 and FO 407/223. See also Wichhart, "Intervention," 81–87. Lugol (*Egypt*, 19) gives a highly sanitized version of events.

34. CD, August 30–31, 1939.

35. Mallett, *Mussolini*, 83ff.; CD, November 6, 1937, November 20, 1937.

36. CD, September 9, 1937.

37. Bosworth, *Mussolini*, 253–254.

38. CD, March 16–17, 1939, August 11, 1939, August 13, 1939, August 27, 1939. On Hitler's disappointment with Munich and hurry to go to war before he got any older, see Weinberg, *World at Arms*, chap. 1.

39. CD, August 20, 1939.

40. CD, September 1, 1939.

41. US NARA, RG 226, Entry 171A, Box 59, "Report on the Penetration Activities of the 'P' Squad of the Italian Military Intelligence Service, Counter Espionage Section," 4. On the Maffey Report, cf. Jason Davidson, "Italy, British Resolve and the 1935–1936 Italo-Ethiopian War," *Cahiers de la Méditerranée* 88 (2014), https://journals.openedition.org/cdlm/7428 (accessed October 10, 2018).

42. "Report on the Penetration Activities," 4; US NARA, RG 226, Entry 108B, Box 306, "Penetration of Diplomatic Premises by SIM CS Prior to the Armistice," August 14, 1944; Maria Gabriella Pasqualini, "Manfredi Talamo e l'intelligence italiana tra le due guerre," *Notiziario Storico dell' Arma dei Carabinieri* 2, no. 6 (2017): 44–52; Maria Gabriella Pasqualini, *Carte segrete dell' intelligence italiana il S.I.M. in archivi stranieri* (Rome: Ministero della Difesa, 2006), 212–237. I am grateful to Maria Gabriella Pasqualini for her generosity in sharing the archival materials cited above.

43. The name is consistently misspelled in British records as Constantini.

44. Brian R. Sullivan, "Roman Holiday for Spies: Episodes in Soviet, German and Italian Espionage Operations Against Britain and Each Other, 1924–1940," author's ms., 3–6. I am grateful to Brian Sullivan for sharing his manuscript and his insights with me.

45. "Penetration of Diplomatic Premises," 2.

46. "Report on the Penetration Activities," 6ff.

47. "Report on the Penetration Activities," 5–6; "Penetration of Diplomatic Premises," 3.

48. Giuseppe Conti, *Mussolini's Spies: A History of SIM Italian Military Intelligence, 1940–1943*, trans. Brian Sullivan, 365. Unpublished page proofs of the English translation courtesy of Brian Sullivan.

49. HW 40/75, "Penetration of Diplomatic Premises by SIM/CS," August 14, 1944; "Report on the Penetration Activities," 8; "Penetration of Diplomatic Premises," 1, 4.

50. "Report on the Penetration Activities," 8.

51. FO 850/2 Y775, "Security of Documents in H. M. Embassy, Rome," February 20, 1937. While various writers have identified the necklace as belonging to Drummond's wife, FO 850/2, Smith to Osborne, draft of March 15, 1937, says it belonged to Drummond's daughter.

52. HW 40/75, C/7541, September 6, 1944.

53. FO 850/2 Y832, "Security Measures at H. M. Embassy, Berlin," July 22, 1937.

54. Peter Neville, "The Foreign Office and Britain's Ambassadors to Berlin, 1933–39," *Contemporary British History* 18, no. 3 (2004): 119–120.

55. "Report on the Penetration Activities," 4–8; "Penetration of Diplomatic Premises," 2–5.

56. Sullivan, "Roman Holiday," 39.

57. "Report on the Penetration Activities," 6.

58. Lugol, *Egypt*, 22–23.

59. Wichhart, "Intervention," 87–88.

60. Gershoni and Jankowski, *Confronting Fascism*, chap. 1.

61. Bagnold, *Sand, Wind*, 119–120; I. S. O. Playfair et al., *The Mediterranean and Middle East*, vol. 1: *The Early Successes Against Italy (to May 1941)* (London: HM Stationery Office, 1954), 31–33, 41, 457–459, www.ibiblio.org/hyperwar /UN/UK/UK-Med-I/index.html (accessed October 16, 2018); *London Gazette*, no. 34650, August 1, 1939, 5311, www.thegazette.co.uk/London/issue/34650 /page/5311 (accessed October 16, 2018).

ACT I. CHAPTER 4. THE MACHINE IS THE FUTURE

1. Wilkinson, *Facets*, 132.

2. Welchman, *Hut Six*, 31; "Architectural History Report of Bletchley Park," chap. 5.1, Bletchley Park, www.bletchleypark.org.uk/resources/filer .rhtm/683101/eh+-+chapter+5.1.pdf (accessed Mar 15, 2016); Mavis Batey, *Dilly: The Man Who Broke Enigmas* (London: Biteback, 2017), loc.1682, Kindle; Kathryn A. Morrison, "'A Maudlin and Monstrous Pile': The Mansion at Bletchley Park, Buckinghamshire," *Transactions of the Ancient Monuments Society* 53 (2009): 81–106.

3. Batey, *Dilly*, loc. 1670 ff.; Welchman, *Hut Six*, 31; Michael Smith, *The Secrets of Station X* (London: Biteback, 2011), loc. 500ff., Kindle; Wilkinson, *Facets*, 132; Sinclair McKay, *The Secret Life of Bletchley Park* (London: Aurum, 2010), 12; Morrison, "Maudlin and Monstrous," 103–104.

4. Smith, *Station X*, loc. 480ff.; Batey, *Dilly*, loc.1682; Richard Aldrich, *GCHQ: The Uncensored Story of Britain's Most Secret Intelligence Agency* (London: Harpers, 2010), 22–24; Morrison, "Maudlin and Monstrous," 103–104.

5. Aldrich, *GCHQ*, 22–23; Smith, *Station X*, 291ff.

6. Wilkinson, *Facets*, 132.

7. Stephen Budiansky, *Battle of Wits: The Complete Story of Codebreaking in World War II* (London: Viking, 2000), 26–27; John Ferris, *Issues in British and American Signals Intelligence, 1919–1932* (Fort Meade, MD: Center for Cryptologic History, National Security Agency, 2015), 51.

8. William F. Friedman, "A Brief History of the Signal Intelligence Agency," NSA, June 29, 1942, revised April 2, 1943, www.nsa.gov/Portals/70 /documents/news-features/declassified-documents/friedman-documents/reports -research/FOLDER_528/41771299081038.pdf (accessed February 3, 2019).

9. John Ferris, "The Road to Bletchley Park: The British Experience with Signals Intelligence, 1892–1945," *Intelligence and National Security* 17, no. 1 (2002): 75.

10. "U.S. Entry into World War I, 1917," US Department of State, Office of the Historian, https://history.state.gov/milestones/1914-1920/wwi (accessed October 22, 2018); Mark Lubienski, "The Zimmerman Telegram," *London Historians' Blog*, https://londonhistorians.wordpress.com/2018/03/23/the-zimmerman-telegram/ (accessed October 22, 2018); "Text of Germany's Proposal to Form an Alliance with Mexico and Japan Against the United States," *New York Times*, March 1, 1917, 1; Batey, *Dilly*, loc. 618ff.; Aldrich, *GCHQ*, 15.

11. Jack Robinson, "The British Official Secrets Act: An Examination" (Arlington, VA: Center for Naval Analyses, 1972), apps.dtic.mil/dtic/tr/fulltext/u2/745043.pdf (accessed November 11, 2018); Aldrich, *GCHQ*, 17; Smith, *Station X*, 130ff.; Ferris, "Road to Bletchley Park," 67, 73; Jeffrey T. Richelson, *A Century of Spies: Intelligence in the Twentieth Century* (New York: Oxford University Press, 1995), 65. Cf. FO 1093/313, C/4278, April 3, 1940.

12. Welchman, *Hut Six*, 8; Greenberg, *Welchman*, 10.

13. *Brigadier John Tiltman: A Giant Among Cryptanalysts* (Fort Meade, MD: Center for Cryptologic History, National Security Agency, 2007).

14. BPA, unnumbered file. Handwriting tentatively dates photo as spring 1939. *Brigadier John Tiltman* shows the same image of Tiltman but dates it as 1942. The London location makes an earlier date more likely.

15. Welchman, *Hut Six*, 33–34; Penolope Fitzgerald, *The Knox Brothers* (London: Flamingo, 2002), 126ff., 188–189, 230; Smith, *Station X*, loc. 240ff., 366ff.; McKay, *Secret Life*, 13–14; Batey, *Dilly*, loc. 618ff.

16. Smith, *Station X*, loc. 371, 531.

17. Smith, *Station X*, loc. 240ff., 374; Ferris, "Road to Bletchley Park," 73; Greenberg, *Welchman*, 28; José Ramón Soler Fuensanta, Francisco Javier López-Brea Espiau, and Frode Weierud, "Spanish Enigma: A History of the Enigma in Spain," *Cryptologia* 34, no. 4 (2010): 301–328.

18. Welchman, *Hut Six*, 12–13, 31 ff.; Fitzgerald, *Knox Brothers*, 230.

19. Wilkinson, *Facets*, 137–140; Welchman, *Hut Six*, 35; Smith, *Station X*, 561ff.; Morrison, "Maudlin and Monstrous," 103–104.

20. I have based my account of Welchman's early work mainly on his own: Welchman, *Hut Six*, 34ff. As he was working from memory, he made some minor errors. For instance, he says that German operators connected eleven pairs of letters daily on the plugboard. Logically this would have provided the maximum number of permutations, but the actual practice was ten connections. See Greenberg, *Welchman*, 212. Terminology for various aspects of Enigma varies from source to source. I have sought to use the simplest terms that are faithful to the time, while avoiding the foreign words that were sometimes used at Bletchley Park.

21. HW 14/1, "Enigma: A Position," Appendix 1, refers to the "main discriminant" as being German air force traffic. This was the Red key.

22. Jacek Tebinka, "Account of the Former Chief of Polish Intelligence on Cracking the Enigma Code of 31 V 1974," in Ciechanowski et al., *Rejewski*, 210; HW 25/12, Denniston report on Pyry conference, May 11, 1948, via Stanislaw Ciechanowski and Eugenia Maresch, "Disclosure of the Enigma Secret to the

Allies (Pyry, July 1939): Documents in the British Archives," in Ciechanowski et al., *Rejewski*, 221, 226ff.

23. Hugh Sebag-Montefiore, *Enigma: The Battle for the Code* (London: Wiedenfeld & Nicholson, 2011), loc. 655 ff., Kindle.

24. Woytak, "Conversation," 54–55.

25. Woytak, "Conversation," 57; Gordon Welchman, "From Polish Bomba to British Bombe: The Birth of Ultra," *Intelligence and National Security* 1, no. 1 (1986): 89–92. Sebag-Montefiore, *Enigma*, loc. 1139ff.

26. Sebag-Montefiore, *Enigma*, loc. 962ff.

27. Ciechanowski, "Polish Contribution," 105–106.

28. HW 25/12, Denniston report, 220–230. There was a third member of the British delegation, a naval officer in charge of radio interception named Humphrey Sandwith. Afterward, some participants recalled a man named "Sandwich," whom they suspected was really Stewart Menzies, the deputy of dying MI6 chief Hugh Sinclair. So myths are born. Menzies wasn't there. See Woytak, "Conversation," 57, where Rejewski recounts the suspicion that the man was Menzies.

29. HW 25/12, Denniston report, 226.

30. Welchman wrote of his view in 1939: "To discover the internal wiring of the rotors by purely cryptanalytical means appeared to be an insoluble problem." Even after learning decades later of Rejewski's work, Welchman doubted that Rejewski could have worked out the wiring for the newly added wheels of Enigma, writing, "It seems to me that the Poles must have obtained the new five-wheel Enigma by capture or some other nefarious means." Welchman, *Hut Six*, 12, 16.

31. HW 25/12, Denniston to Bertrand, August 3, 1939, in Ciechanowski and Maresch, "Disclosure," 236.

32. HW 25/12, Denniston report, 226; HW 25/12, Knox on Pyry Conference, August 4, 1939, in Ciechanowski and Maresch, "Disclosure," 239; Woytak, "Conversation," 56–57.

33. Sebag-Montefiore, *Enigma*, loc. 9070ff.; Tebinka, "Account of the Former Chief," 211; HW 25/12, Bertrand to Denniston, August 4, 1939, in Ciechanowski and Maresch, "Disclosure," 238.

34. Rejewski, "Remarks," 81; Ciechanowski, "Polish Contribution," 108.

35. "Hitler, in Warsaw, Cites It as a Warning," *New York Times*, October 6, 1939, 5.

36. Gerwarth, *Hitler's Hangman*, 141ff.; Browning, *Origins*, 25–35.

37. Fraser, *Knight's Cross*, 142–143; Reuth, *Rommel*, 37–40.

38. On the handicaps that Hitler created by commanding from the front, see Hoffman, *Hitler's Personal Security*, xi. On the shared love of danger, see Reuth, *Rommel*, 15–16; Fraser, *Knight's Cross*, 142–143.

39. "Hitler, in Warsaw"; Reuth, *Rommel*, 39.

40. Welchman, *Hut Six*, 71–72; Mavies [*sic*] Batey, "Marian and Dilly," in Ciechanowski et al., *Rejewski*, 72.

41. Andrew Hodges, *Alan Turing: The Enigma* (London: Vintage, 2014), 30–32, 73–74, 99–100, 263–265, Kindle; David Boyle, *Alan Turing: Unlocking the Enigma* (Endeavour, 2014), 17, 21–27, 55–59, Kindle.

42. HW 14/2, "Enigma—Position," November 1, 1939.

43. HW 14/2, "Investigation of German Military Cyphers: Progress Report," November 7, 1939.

44. HW 14/1, Denniston to "The Director" [Sinclair], September 16, 1939.

45. Welchman, *Hut Six*, 75–77. Unsigned version of Welchman's plan: HW 14/2, November 18, 1939. It refers to Welchman in the third person, is addressed to Denniston, and was likely written by Travis following his discussion with Welchman. See Greenberg, *Welchman*, 33–35.

46. Beckett, *Rommel*, chap. 1; Reuth, *Rommel*, 22, 35ff.; Fraser, *Knight's Cross*, 142–143.

47. Reuth, *Rommel*, 43; Beckett, *Rommel*, chap. 1; Pimlott, *Rommel and His Art of War*, 36; Fraser, *Knight's Cross*, 151.

ACT I. CHAPTER 5. THE FLAW IN THE MACHINE IS THE MAN

1. Lugol, *Egypt and World War II*, 38–39.

2. FO 407/224, J131/92/16, Lampson to Halifax, January 5, 1940; J580/92/16, Lampson to Halifax, February 7, 1940.

3. FO 407/224, J457/92/16, Lampson to Halifax, February 3, 1940; J580/92/16, Lampson to Halifax, February 7, 1940; J582/582/16, Lampson to Halifax, February 8, 1940, Enclosure, "Political Review of the Year 1939."

4. IWM, Document 4829, Maunsell memoir, 6–7, 13.

5. Nir Arielli, *Fascist Italy and the Middle East, 1933–40* (Houndmills, UK: Palgrave Macmillan, 2010), 160.

6. Bagnold, *Sand, Wind*, 121–123; CAB 44/151, "The History of the Long Range Desert Group (June 1940–March 1943)," reprinted in *Special Forces in the Desert War, 1940–1943* (Kew, Richmond, Surrey, UK: National Archives, 2008), 14.

7. "Architectural History Report of Bletchley Park," chap. 7, Bletchley Park, www.bletchleyparkresearch.co.uk/research-notes/architectural-history -report-bletchley-park (accessed March 12, 2016); Smith, *Station X*, loc. 600ff.; *Bletchley Park: Home of the Codebreakers* (Briscombe Port, UK: Pitkin Publishing, 2015).

8. Stuart Milner-Barry, "Hut 6: Early Days," in *Codebreakers: The Inside Story of Bletchley Park*, ed. F. H. Hinsley and Alan Stripp (Oxford: Oxford University Press, 1993), 89–90; Welchman, *Hut Six*, 84–85.

9. Joan Murray, "Hut 8 and Naval Enigma, Part I," in Hinsley and Stripp, *Codebreakers*, 113–114. HW 14/6 X4228/G, August 8, 1940, lists F. H. Hinsley's pay as £260 per year, a low rate because of his young age. The memo states that the standard pay for this rank was £300 for men and £260 for women. HW 14/6, Denniston to Moore, August 31, 1940, lists Clarke's raise from her starting pay of £3 to £3 15s. The film *The Imitation Game* shows Clarke reaching Bletchley Park after answering an advertisement

for crossword puzzle buffs. Like much else in the film, this is a cinematic fiction.

10. John Herivel, *Herivelismus and German Military Enigma* (Cleobury Mortimer, UK: M&M Baldwin, 2008), 76–77; BPA, Daniel Jones, "The Genius Still Embarrassed by His Success," *Milton Keynes on Sunday*, October 27, 2001; Peter Calvocoressi, *Top Secret Ultra* (London: Cassell, 1980), 13; Welchman, *Hut Six*, 86.

11. HW, 14/6 X4228/G, August 8, 1940, lists Margaret and Penelope Storey as being promoted from Grade III to Grade II clerks, with a pay of five shillings per week. Neither Cambridge nor Oxford has records of Margaret Storey studying there. "Storey Household," entry from 1939 UK population register, Find My Past, https://search.findmypast.com/record?id=TNA%2FR39%2F2464%2F2464B%2F007%2F30 (accessed September 26, 2016); "Margaret Elizabeth Storey," Ancestry, https://person.ancestry.co.uk/tree/12985624/person/26451775027/facts (accessed December 5, 2016); "Harry Storey," Ancestry, https://person.ancestry.co.uk/tree/12985624/person/13691236196/story (accessed December 5, 2016); Nikki Swinhoe, interview, December 7, 2016; Pauline Flemons, interview, December 21, 2016; James Hodsdon, email correspondence, December 2016; Dorelle Downes, interview, February 26, 2017; Nicholas Fenn Wiggin, interview, October 1, 2017. Late in the war, Storey wrote a rhymed spoof of her own reports, in which various forms of intelligence were each known by a single letter. A red stamp at the top labels it "Top Secret 'U.'" One section reads,

> *The 'O' reports of 16/3*
> *And 10th of April; and the 'K'*
> *Report of 7/2; the 'P'*
> *Report sent out on Saturday*
> *Had nothing that seemed to be*
> *Worth mentioning in any way.*

HW 8/19, "Enemy Intelligence Report Nr. 1000," April 11, 1944.

12. CD, January 3, 1940, January 10, 1940, January 15, 1940, January 17, 1940, February 3, 1940, February 14, 1940, February 18, 1940, February 26, 1940, February 28, 1940.

13. Herivel, *Herivelismus*, 78–79.

14. Rejewski ("Remarks," 81) says the sheets were sent from Bletchley Park to the Polish team at Gretz-Armainvilliers in December 1939. Batey ("Marian and Dilly") says Turing brought them in January 1940.

15. HW 14/1, To Denniston, October 18, 1939; HW 14/3, Denniston to Menzies, January 9, 1940; Menzies to Rivet, January 10, 1940; Greenberg, *Welchman*, 40; Ciechanowski, "Polish Contribution," 109; John Jackson, ed. *Solving Enigma's Secrets: The Official History of Hut 6* (Redditch, UK: Book-Tower, 2014), chap. 2, Kindle. (This is a published edition of HW 43/70,

the official and secret history of Hut 6 written immediately after the war. Despite being an internal history, it is based in part on memory rather than documentation.)

16. HW 14/3, January 25, 1940.

17. Eugenia Maresch, "The Radio-Intelligence Company in Britain," in Ciechanowski et al., *Rejewski*, 188, 189n3.

18. Jackson, *Solving Enigma's Secrets*, chap 2.

19. Herivel, *Herivelismus*, 77; Greenberg, *Welchman*, 40. HW 14/3, To C. S. S., January 25, 1940, refers obliquely to the first breaks. There are conflicting accounts of when the break was achieved in France and for the keys of what date. January 17 is the date most commonly given for the key and possibly for when it was broken.

20. Batey, *Dilly*, loc. 1859ff.; Welchman, *Hut Six*, 98–103, 120; Greenberg, *Welchman*, 44, 253–255. Dilly's method made use of instances where both errors appeared in order to find which wheel orders, combined with the indicator of the first message (the cillie), could produce the indicator of the second message. With the number of possible wheel orders reduced to a few, using the Zygalski sheets was much faster.

21. HW 3/119, "The History of Hut Three (January 1940–May 1945)," 1:27; HW 43/64, "The History of Hut 3 (1940–1945)," 2:356; Milner-Barry, "Hut 6: Early Days," 91–93; Welchman, *Hut Six*, 88.

22. HW 3/119, "History," 21.

23. Welchman, *Hut Six*, 81; Greenberg, *Welchman*, 47, 206–207; Sebag-Montefiore, *Enigma*, loc. 1428. Welchman, working from memory, wrote that he had the idea for his improvement, known as the diagonal board, in autumn 1939. If that were correct, however, it would almost certainly have been incorporated in the first bombe, delivered in March 1940. It is more likely that he came up with the idea around the latter date, as other sources state.

24. Herivel, *Herivelismus*, 78–79.

ACT I. CHAPTER 6. THE ORACLES

1. F. H. Hinsley, "Bletchley Park, the Admiralty, and Naval Enigma," in Hinsley and Stripp, *Codebreakers*, 78; David Kahn, *Seizing the Enigma: The Race to Break the German U-boat Codes, 1939–1943* (London: Frontline Books, 2012), chap. 9, iBook; Richard Langhorne, "Francis Harry Hinsley, 1918–1998," *Proceedings of the British Academy* 120 (2003): 263–274.

2. Christopher Morris, "Navy Ultra's Poor Relations," in Hinsley and Stripp, *Code Breakers*, 238; Weinberg, *World at Arms*, chap. 2. Cf. Noel Annan, "Book Review: No More an Enigma: Codebreakers: The Inside Story of Bletchley Park," *Independent*, August 22, 1993, www.independent.co.uk/arts-entertainment /book-review-no-more-an-enigma-codebreakers-the-inside-story-of-bletchley -park-ed-f-h-hinsley-alan-1462732.html (accessed December 15, 2018). In his account, Morris says the ships were to report to the "German War Office." No such office existed in 1940; context indicates that he is referring to the German

equivalent of the British War Office, which was responsible for the army but not the navy.

3. Geirr H. Haarr, *The German Invasion of Norway, April 1940* (Barnsley, UK: Seaforth, 2011), chap. 3, https://books.google.co.il/books/about/The _German_Invasion_of_Norway.html?id=BqaeuAAACAAJ&redir_esc=y (accessed December 13, 2018); F. H. Hinsley et al., *British Intelligence in the Second World War: Its Influence on Strategy and Operations* (London: Her Majesty's Stationery Office, 1979), 1: 113–125.

4. HW3/119, "History," 1: 25–34; Jackson, *Solving*, chap. 3; Calvocoressi, *Top Secret*, 69; Smith, *Station X*, loc. 936–937.

5. CD, April 20, 1940, April 26, 1940, May 1, 1940, May 3, 1940, May 4, 1940.

6. Jackson, *Solving*, chap. 3.

7. "Conduct of the War (Hansard, 7 May 1940)," UK Parliament, https:// api.parliament.uk/historic-hansard/commons/1940/may/07/conduct-of-the -war#S5CV0360P0_19400507_HOC_329 (accessed December 18, 2018).

8. "Churchill Becomes Prime Minister," *BBC*, www.bbc.co.uk/history/ events/churchill_becomes_prime_minister (accessed December 18, 2018); Max Hastings, *Finest Years: Churchill as Warlord 1940-45* (London: Harper Press, 2009), chap. 1, Kindle.

9. James Leutze, "The Secret of the Churchill-Roosevelt Correspondence: September 1939–May 1940," *Journal of Contemporary History* 10, no. 3 (1975): 478–480.

10. Liddell Hart, *Rommel Papers*, 6.

11. This brief account of Rommel's part in the May–June 1940 campaign draws on Beckett, *Rommel*, chap. 2; Reuth, *Rommel*, 43–44, 122–126; Fraser, *Knight's Cross*, 186–187; Liddell Hart, *Rommel Papers*, 3–6. On the portrait, see Terry Brighton, *Patton, Montgomery, Rommel: Masters of War* (New York: Crown Publishers, 2009), 3–6.

12. Beckett, *Rommel*, chap. 2; Tim Benbow, "The Dunkirk Evacuation and the German 'Halt' Order," Defense-in-Depth, https://defenceindepth .co/2016/07/11/the-dunkirk-evacuation-and-the-german-halt-order (accessed December 24, 2018); Fraser, *Knight's Cross*, 187–189.

13. Herivel, *Herivelismus*, 100–106; Hinsley et al., *British Intelligence*, 1: 144– 145. Herivel estimates that the first break with his method was on May 11 or 12. Hinsley gives the date of the first break as May 22. Hinsley's description of one thousand messages being decrypted daily appears exaggerated.

14. HW 14/5, Denniston to "all," May 23, 1940.

15. Hinsley et al., *British Intelligence*, 1: 144–145.

16. Christopher Andrews, *Secret Service: The Making of the British Intelligence Community* (London: Sceptre, 1986), 627–628.

17. Herivel, *Herivelismus*, 105.

18. FRUS, "Secretary of State to the Ambassador in Italy," May 26, 1940, *General and Europe*, II: 710–711; CD, May 27, 1940.

19. Monelli, *Mussolini*, 187; Bosworth, *Mussolini*, 298.

20. Monelli, *Mussolini*, 186–187. Text of Mussolini's speech: Bosworth, *Mussolini*, 299. My thanks to historian Ciro Paoletti for explaining the carefully created Fascist symbolism of the piazza.

21. CD, June 10, 1940.

22. WO 201/2119, "Personal to General Wavell from CIGS," June 10, 1940; "To CIGS from General Wavell," June 11, 1940.

ACT II. CHAPTER 1. THE KEYSTONE IN THE ARCH

1. Winston Churchill, "Their Finest Hour," International Churchill Society, June 18, 1940, winstonchurchill.org/resources/speeches/1940-the-finest-hour/their-finest-hour (accessed December 27, 2018).

2. The main source for this and following paragraphs on the Lampson-Farouk clash is MLD, June 12–30, 1940. Other sources are noted separately.

3. Arielli, *Fascist Italy*, 160.

4. Cf. CAB 65/7/56, June 11, 1940, War Cabinet conclusions, para. 7; CAB 65/7/57, June 12, 1940, para. 6; CAB 65/5/70, June 22, 1940, para. 9.

5. See Nir Arielli, "Beyond 'Mare Nostrum.' Ambitions and Limitations in Fascist Italy's Middle Eastern Policy," *Geschichte und Gesellschaft* 37, no. 3 (2011): 397.

6. McBride, *Farouk*, 57.

7. FO 407/224, J1604/208/16, Lampson to Halifax, June 22, 1940.

8. McBride, *Farouk*, 100.

9. For general accounts of the origins of the Long Range Desert Group, see Bagnold, *Sand, Wind*, 123–128; *Special Forces*, 14–17.

10. On sandstorms, see Moorehead, *African Trilogy*, 7–8. In the first months, the name of the unit was the Long Range Desert Patrol; with expansion, it became the Long Range Desert Group, the name by which it was known thereafter.

11. WO 201/2119, Wavell to Gort, August 24, 1939; Wavell, "Notes on Strategical Situation in Middle East," August 24, 1939; Wavell to Ironside, September 27, 1939; Wavell to Ironside, December 28, 1939; Wavell, "Note for CIGS," June 6, 1940; WO 201/2218, Wavell to Pownall, September 3, 1939.

12. Ranfurly, *To War*, September 3, 1939, January 10, 1940, January 18, 1940, July 9, 1940.

13. Winston S. Churchill, *The Second World War*, vol. 2: *Their Finest Hour* (London: Cassell, 1949), 125.

14. Moorehead, *African Trilogy*, 4–12; Bagnold, *Sand, Wind*, 126; Playfair et al., *The Mediterranean*, 1: 81–105, 185–191.

15. CAB 65/14/17, July 31, 1940, War Cabinet Conclusions: Confidential Annex.

16. Lord Alanbrooke, *War Diaries, 1939–1945* (London: Phoenix, 2001), 93–98.

17. CAB 65/14/21, August 13, 1940, War Cabinet Conclusions: Confidential Annex.

18. The literature on Churchill's extreme imperialism, even relative to his time, his class, and his political context, and on the contradiction between these

views and his ardent defense of democracy is too vast to list here. For a brief overview, see Johann Hari, "Not His Finest Hour: The Dark Side of Winston Churchill," *Independent*, October 27, 2010, www.independent.co.uk/news/uk /politics/not-his-finest-hour-the-dark-side-of-winston-churchill-2118317 .html (accessed June 16, 2020), and for comparison, Roland Quinault, "Churchill and Democracy," *Transactions of the Royal Historical Society* 11 (2001): 201–220.

19. Churchill, *Finest Hour*, 379.

20. The main source for this and the following paragraphs on Roosevelt's actions in May–September 1940 is Smith, *FDR*, chaps. 20–21. Other sources are noted separately.

21. "Address Delivered by President Roosevelt to the Congress, May 16, 1940," Mount Holyoke College, www.mtholyoke.edu/acad/intrel/WorldWar2 /fdr16.htm (accessed January 11, 2019); "Defense Measures of the United States 1940," Mount Holyoke College, www.mtholyoke.edu/acad/intrel/WorldWar2 /defense.htm.

22. On Roosevelt's relations with Woodring, see "President Franklin D. Roosevelt Fires His Isolationist Secretary of War During WWII: June 19, 1940," Shapell Manuscript Foundation, www.shapell.org/manuscript/fdr-fires -isolationist-secretary-of-war-woodring (accessed January 12, 2019).

23. "June 10, 1940: 'Stab in the Back' Speech," Miller Center, https:// millercenter.org/the-presidency/presidential-speeches/june-10-1940-stab -back-speech (accessed December 24, 2018).

24. *Life*, June 24, 1940, 16–19. (The date of the magazine indicates the last day it was on newsstands. It appeared a week earlier.)

25. *Life*, May 27, 1940, 30.

26. Charles A. Lindbergh, *The Wartime Journals of Charles A. Lindbergh* (New York: Harcourt Brace Jovanovich, 1970), 374–375, 380–382; Charles A. Lindbergh, "Our Relationship with Europe," Charles Lindbergh: An American Aviator, August 4, 1940, www.charleslindbergh.com/americanfirst/speech3.asp (accessed December 25, 2018).

27. The biography of Bonner Fellers is based on numerous documents in the Bonner Frank Fellers Papers at the Hoover Institution Archives including, HBF B17 F1, Military Record and Report of Separation, November 30, 1946; B17 F5, Oral History Interview, 1967; B17 F6, Oral History Interview, 1973; B17 F13, Travel Documents, 1923–1938; B19 F19, Fellers to Clarke, May 7, 1940; B21 F6–8, Frazier Hunt Correspondence; 29/36, "We Are Headed for War" (notes for a lecture); B20 F31, Herbert Hoover Correspondence; B21 F4, Frederick Howe Correspondence; B30 F3, Travel Notes, 1922–1939; B38 F12, Military Career Correspondence, 1940–1941. Additional sources include the Bonner Fellers website, www.bonnerfellers.com (accessed March 25, 2015); Megan Rosenfeld, "Brig. Gen. Bonner Fellers, Ret., Dies," *Washington Post*, October 10, 1973, B8.

28. Budiansky, *Battle of Wits*, 38.

29. On "scientific" racism, anti-Semitism, and fear of the "yellow peril" in the US Army in the first half of the twentieth century, especially in military intelligence and at the War College and West Point, see Joseph W. Bendersky, *The*

"Jewish Threat": Anti-Semitic Politics of the U.S. Army (New York: Basic Books, 2006).

30. Derek O'Connor, "Italy's Consummate Showman: Italo Balbo," *Aviation History Magazine*, March 8, 2017, www.historynet.com/italys-consummate -showman-italo-balbo.htm (accessed January 16, 2019); Maurice M. Roumani, *The Jews of Libya: Coexistence, Persecution, Resettlement* (Eastbourne, UK: Sussex, 2008), 21–26; Renzo De Felice, *Jews in an Arab Land: Libya, 1835–1970* (Austin: University of Texas, 1985), 168–174; Irit Abramski-Bligh, ed., *Pinkas Hakehillot; Luv; Tunisia* (Jerusalem: Yad Vashem, 5757 [1997]), 94ff.; Saviona Mane, "Opening Italy's 'Closet of Shame,'" *Haaretz*, November 16, 2018, www.haaretz.com/world-news/europe/.premium.MAGAZINE-opening-italy -s-closet-of-shame-1.6657425 (accessed November 16, 2018).

31. Moorehead, *African Trilogy*, 17.

32. CD, July 5, 1940, July 22, 1940, August 8, 1940.

33. CD, August 18–September 7, 1940; MacGregor Knox, *Mussolini Unleashed, 1939–1941: Politics and Strategy in Fascist Italy's Last War* (Cambridge: Cambridge University Press, 1982), loc. 2712–2742.

ACT II. CHAPTER 2. WAR OF SHADOWS

1. Main sources for this account: Budiansky, *Battle of Wits*, 29–32, 81–88, 159–170; Ronald Clark, *The Man Who Broke Purple* (New York: Bloomsbury, 2011), passim, iBook; Theodore M. Hannah, "Frank B. Rowlett, A Personal Profile." *Cryptologic Spectrum*, Spring 1981, 5–20; Friedman, "Brief History"; William Friedman, "Preliminary Historical Report," October 14, 1940, www .nsa.gov/Portals/70/documents/news-features/declassified-documents/friedman -documents/reports-research/FOLDER_211/41760789079992.pdf (accessed January 30, 2019).

2. Budiansky, *Battle of Wits*, 32.

3. NSA OH-17-82, Solomon Kullback, August 26, 1982, NSA, www.nsa .gov/Portals/70/documents/news-features/declassified-documents/oral -history-interviews/nsa-oh-17-82-kullback.pdf (accessed September 5, 2019), recounts the episode of tossing the cards without specifying which code was developed. Kullback does note that the Military Intelligence Code, used by attachés, was the only one of the codes they developed that went into use. The number of code groups, fifty thousand, matches the description of this code in HW 40/91, May 11, 1945, "Japanese MA Berlin Reports on Different Types of American Cipher," translation of Cable 318, January 22, 1942, Japanese Military Attaché Berlin to Tokyo.

4. NSA NSA-OH-1976-(1-10), Frank Rowlettt, NSA, www.nsa.gov /public_info/_files/oral_history_interviews/nsa_OH_1976_1-10_rowlett.pdf (accessed December 20, 2015).

5. On Grotjan, see Ann Whitcher Gentzke, "An American Hero," *At Buffalo*, spring 2018, www.buffalo.edu/atbuffalo/article-page-spring-2018.host .html/content/shared/www/atbuffalo/articles/Spring-2018/features/an

-american-hero.detail.html (accessed February 7, 2019); "Genevieve Grotjan Feinstein," NSA, www.nsa.gov/about/cryptologic-heritage/historical-figures -publications/women/Article/1621585/genevieve-grotjan-feinstein (accessed January 2, 2019).

6. On Hitler's goals in the pact with Japan, see Weinberg, *World at Arms*, chap. 3.

7. The main sources on the Polish codebreakers after the fall of France are Wladyslaw Kozaczuk, *Enigma: How the German Machine Cipher Was Broken, and How It Was Read by the Allies in World War Two*, ed. and trans. Christopher Kasparek (Frederick, MD: University Publications of America, 1984), 108–121; Wladyslaw Kozaczuk and Jerzy Straszak, *Enigma: How the Poles Broke the Nazi Code* (New York: Hippocrene, 2004), 36–41; Tebinka, "Account of the Former Chief," 214.

8. Greenberg, *Welchman*, 47–49; Welchman, *Hut Six*, 101, 119–121; McKay, *Secret Life*, 96–98, 107–109.

9. Decrypted Enigma messages from August 4 to October 10, 1940, are overwhelmingly German air force material. HW 5/4, HW 5/5. Later sources, especially those based on memory, give a wide range of views on the significance of Enigma intelligence in the British victory in the Battle of Britain. Welchman (*Hut Six*, 120) and others (e.g., Calvocoressi, *Top Secret*, 72) state that Bletchley Park deciphered almost immediately Hitler's September 17, 1940, decision to postpone Operation Sea Lion, the planned invasion of Britain, a postponement that became permanent. However, no message to that effect appears in HW 5/5 in the second half of September. In fact, messages after September 17, 1940, continue to report invasion preparations. On September 26 (CX/JC/355), a daily report includes a note that it is now certain that Sea Lion "is a code-name for a sea-borne operation" but does not definitely state that it is the invasion of Britain. On the other hand, the decrypted Enigma messages do provide a steady stream of information on German air force operations and on the directional radio beams used to guide German bombers to their targets—information that was certainly of high value for the RAF.

10. For an account of the difficulty in breaking naval Enigma and of the German security measures, see Kahn, *Seizing*, chap. 9 and appendix.

11. ADM 223/463, Fleming to DNI, September 12, 1940, via "Operation Ruthless, October 1940," Alan Turing: The Enigma, www.turing.org.uk /sources/ruthless.html (accessed August 21, 2018); Mavis Batey, *From Bletchley with Love* (Milton Keynes, UK: Bletchley Park Trust, 2008), 4–7.

12. ADM 223/463, Frank Birch to Admiralty, October 20, 1940, via "Operation Ruthless."

13. HW 8/24, Nigel de Grey to Vivian, April 13, 1942.

14. CD, August 3, 1940.

15. Carlo De Risio, *Servizi segreti. Gli «uomini ombra» italiani nella seconda guerra mondiale e i (troppi) misteri insoluti della R. marina nel 1940–43* (Rome: Napoleone, 2014), 22n1; "The Story of the Palace Hotel," Royal Group, www .royalgroup.it/ambasciatoripalace/en/hotel (accessed November 1, 2017).

16. HW 40/75, From Quirinal Rome, July 29, 1944; SCI/370/3, "Penetration of Diplomatic Premises by SIM/CS," August 14, 1944; DS/5(B)/1391, August 12, 1945; USNARA, RG 226, Entry 108B, Box 306, "Penetration of Diplomatic Premises by SIM CS Prior to the Armistice," August 14, 1944, 3; David Alvarez, *Spies in the Vatican: Espionage and Intrigue from Napoleon to the Holocaust* (Lawrence: University of Nebraska, 2002), 215–219; David Alvarez, interview, July 7, 2017, and personal correspondence, July 6, 2017.

17. KV 2/88, "Final Report on Obstlt. Fritz Adolf Ritter," January 16, 1946; Nikolaus Ritter, *Code Name: Dr. Rantzau*, trans. Katherine R. Wallace (Lexington: University of Kentucky, 2019), 105–113; Gross, Rolke, and Zboray, *Salam*, 32–35; Kelly, *Lost Oasis*, 160ff.

ACT II. CHAPTER 3. SANDSTORM

1. Knox, *Mussolini Unleashed*, loc. 2674–2741.

2. Moorehead, *African Trilogy*, 12–20. On "Hellfire Pass," cf. MLD, September 17, 1940.

3. Knox, *Mussolini Unleashed*, 2742–2755; Moorehead, *African Trilogy*, 50–53.

4. CAB 65/9/23, War Cabinet conclusions, September 30, 1940.

5. CD, September 27, 1940, September 30, 1940, October 2, 1940, October 12, 1940.

6. US NARA, RG165, Entry 65, M1194, Reel 77, Frames 2083ff. War Department Correspondence Index, Col. Bonner Fellers, entries for October 5 and October 12, 1940; HBF B39 F5, Secretary of State Cordell Hull to Fellers, September 27, 1940; War Department special orders for Fellers, October 10, 1940.

7. HBF B39 F8, Fellers via Cairo Legation to Department of State, December 30, 1940, requesting "code books and all regulations including those for finance for Military Attaché." Until early April 1941, Fellers was still sending his telegrams via the legation to the State Department for forwarding to the War Department, meaning that they would have been encoded in diplomatic rather than military codes.

8. US NARA, RG165, Entry 65, M1194, Reel 77, Frames 2083ff. War Department Correspondence Index, Col. Bonner Fellers, entry for November 5, 1940; HBF B18 F11, U.S military attaché Budapest to Mrs. Bonner Fellers, October 29, 1940; FFP, Military Attaché Cairo Report 1810, April 14, 1941, 7.

9. CAB 65/15/15, War Cabinet conclusions, confidential annex, October 9, 1940.

10. HBF B39 F8, Fellers to War Department via State Department, Cable 1799, November 4, 1940.

11. HBF B40 F13, Military Attaché Report 1, November 20, 1940.

12. Mohi El Din, *Memories*, 13–15.

13. Anwar al-Sadat published two memoirs, twenty years apart. They are not consistent, and both contain obvious confusion in chronology. According to both, though, he originally made his connection to Masri through Hassan al-Banna, leader of the Muslim Brotherhood. Anwar al-Sadat, *Revolt on the Nile*

(New York: John Day, 1957), 25, 33, 38ff., www.anwarsadat.org/project_img /book/4881.pdf (accessed June 19, 2014); Sadat, *Identity*, 24–31.

14. Ranfurly, *To War*, entries for the length of 1940. On Pollock's ambiguous relation to military command, see the internal history of the SOE, published as W. J. M. Mackenzie, *The Secret History of SOE: The Special Operations Executive, 1940–1945* (London: St. Ermin's, 2000), 172.

15. On Italian financial support for the Arab Revolt, see Nir Arielli, "Italian Involvement in the Arab Revolt in Palestine, 1936–1939," *British Journal of Middle Eastern Studies* 35, no. 2 (2008): 187–204. On the air raids and local reactions, see Nir Arielli, "'Haifa Is Still Burning': Italian, German and French Air Raids on Palestine During the Second World War," *Middle Eastern Studies* 46, no. 3 (2010): 331–347. Ranfurly's description of the raids on Haifa fits those that Arielli dates as July 15 and 24, 1940, though her published diary gives later dates. The reason for the discrepancy is unclear.

16. Morris, *Righteous Victims*, 150–160.

17. Yoav Gelber, *Matzadah: Hahaganah Al Eretz Yisrael Bemilhemet Ha'olam Hashniyah (Massada: The Defence of Palestine During World War II)* (Ramat Gan: Bar-Ilan University Press, 1990), 14ff.; Uri Brenner, *Nokhah Ium Haplishah Hagermanit Le'eretz Yisrael Beshanim 1940–1942* (Ramat Efal: Yad Tabenkin, 1981), 22ff.; Yehuda Bauer, *From Diplomacy to Resistance: A History of Jewish Palestine, 1939–1945* (New York: Atheneum, 1973), 79–92.

18. KV 2/2085, "Palestine. The Mufti's Propaganda at Nabi Musa," May 10, 1940; "Palestine. Miscellaneous Arab Information," March 15, 1940.

19. Mustafa Abbasi, "Palestinim Nilhamim Benatzim: Sippuram Shel Hamitnadvim Hapalestinim Bemilhemet Ha'olam Hashniyah," *Katedra* 171 (Nissan 5779 [April–May 2019]): 125–147. Predictably, the history of Palestinian Arab and Jewish enlistment in the British army is subject to intense historical disputes. Ronald W. Davis, "Jewish Military Recruitment in Palestine, 1940–1943," *Journal of Palestine Studies* 8, no. 2 (1979): 55–76; Raphael G. Bouchnik-Chen, "Palestinian Arab Volunteers in the British Army in WWII: A Reality Check," BESA Center Perspectives Paper No. 1,367, December 9, 2019, https://besacenter.org/perspectives-papers/palestinian-arabs-british -army (accessed January 7, 2020).

20. WO 201/2014, Personal for CIGS from General Auchinleck, Situation Review, June 19, 1942.

21. Uri Avnery, interview, May 15, 2015; Abbasi, "Palestinim Nilhamim Benatzim," 134.

22. As John Ferris writes, "Only a traitor used radio, only a fool did not; this dilemma haunted all commanders of the Second World War." John Ferris, "The British Army, Signals and Security in the Desert Campaign, 1940–42," *Intelligence and National Security* 5, no. 2 (1990): 256.

23. Churchill, *Finest Hour*, 480.

24. Moorehead, *African Trilogy*, 59–61.

25. HBF B39 F8, Fellers to War Department via State Department, Cable 346, December 12, 1940, 12 p.m.; Cable 349, 8 p.m.

26. CD, December 10–13, 1940.

27. Moorehead, *African Trilogy*, 62–66, 73–74.

28. *Special Forces*, 36–43; Bagnold, *Sand, Wind*, 131–134; Kelly, *Lost Oasis*, 149–154; MECA GB155–0185, Longrigg papers, Report on Occupied Enemy Territory Administration, Cyrenaica, for the Period October 14, 1941, to January 31, 1942, Appendix B.

29. Moorehead, *African Trilogy*, 79–88. MECA GB155–0185, Longrigg papers, Occupied Enemy Territory Administration, April 3, 1941, 2, notes that Tobruk was "completely depopulated."

30. HBF B39 F8, Fellers to War Department via State Department, Cable 1807, December 30, 1940; Cable 1809, January 25, 1941.

31. HBF B39 F8, Fellers to War Department via State Department, Cable 1815, February 8, 1941.

32. MECA GB155–0185, Longrigg papers, Occupied Enemy Territory Administration, April 3, 1941; Abramski-Bligh, *Pinkas Hakehillot*, 118; Moorehead, *African Trilogy*, 108.

33. Yacov Haggiag-Liluf, *Yehudei Luv Bashoah* (Or Yehudah, Israel: Irgun Olami Shel Yehudim Yotzei Luv, 2012), 140–141.

34. Ranfurly. *To War*, February 10, 1941.

35. HBF B39 F8, Fellers to War Department via State Department, Cable 1815, February 8, 1941.

ACT II. CHAPTER 4. HALF-SHARED SECRETS

1. Ranfurly, *To War*, March 11, 1941; "Lend Lease Act," March 11, 1941, https://loveman.sdsu.edu/docs/1941LendLeaseAct.pdf (accessed June 12, 2019).

2. Weinberg, *World at Arms*, chap. 4; Smith, *FDR*, chap. 22.

3. "Our Aid and Britain's Need," *New York Times*, January 26, 1941, Section 4, 1.

4. FO 1093/308, Cable 3154, Butler to Hopkinson, December 18, 1940, identifies the two expected US Army representatives in garbled form as "Lt. Col. Freeman and Lt. Col. Rosen." Cf. HW 14/9, DNI to Flag Officer, Commanding, 3rd Battle Squadron, Halifax, December 20, 1940. FO 1093/308, Cable 508, Halifax to Hopkinson, February 2, 1941, says that the delegation's baggage included twelve boxes, the heaviest of which was "about 200 lbs." This was almost certainly the replica of the Purple machine. The description of Sinkov is based on photos in US NARA, RG 457 HCC, Box 1359.

5. David Alvarez, *Secret Messages: Codebreaking and American Diplomacy, 1930–1945* (Lawrence: University of Kansas, 2000), 83–85.

6. Prescott Currier, "My 'Purple' Trip to England in 1941," *Cryptologia* 20, no. 3 (1996): 193–201: posthumously published text of an undated talk by Currier; Alvarez, *Secret Messages*, 85.

7. Alvarez, *Secret Messages*, 82.

8. FO 1093/308, Cable 2416, Butler to Hopkinson, October 25, 1940.

9. FO 1093/308, C/5249, Menzies to Hopkinson, October 30, 1940; Cable 2914, Butler to Hopkinson, November 5, 1940.

10. FO 1093/308, C/5392, Menzies to Beaumont-Nesbitt, November 22, 1940; C/5415, Menzies to Churchill, November 29, 1940, and proposed Draft A, initialed by Churchill. Menzies's response about reading US codes is not in the file.

11. Currier, "My 'Purple' Trip," 196; Smith, *Station X*, loc. 2241.

12. Alvarez, *Secret Messages*, 85.

13. HW 1/2, C/5906, Menzies to Churchill, February 26, 1941; NCML, NSA OH 04-78, Oral History Interview with John Tiltman, November 1, 1978; 07-78, Oral History Interview with John Tiltman, December 17, 1978.

14. HW 14/9, GC and CS Personnel, December 2, 1940.

15. Mair Russell-Jones and Gethin Russell-Jones, *My Secret Life in Hut Six: One Woman's Experience at Bletchley Park* (Oxford, UK: Lion, 2014), describes the life of the women who worked these and other machines in the decoding assembly line.

16. NCML, NSA OH 07-78, Tiltman Oral History; Robert Louis Benson, *A History of U.S. Communications Intelligence During World War II: Policy and Administration* (Center for Cryptological History, National Security Agency, 1997), 19–20, www.nsa.gov/about/_files/cryptologic_heritage/publications/wwii /history_us_comms.pdf (accessed January 10, 2015); Russell-Jones, *My Secret Life*.

17. Tempe Denzer, daughter of John Tiltman, interview.

18. Biography of Russell Dudley-Smith on his personal papers, generously shared by his daughter, Lottie Milvain, and on interviews with her (November 21, 2016) and with Tempe Denzer (October 20, 2016), daughter of John Tiltman, with additional material from Lt. Cdr. Geoffrey B. Mason, RN, "Service Histories of Royal Navy Warships in World War 2: HMS Resolution," Naval-History.net, www.naval-history.net/xGM-Chrono-01BB-Resolution. htm (accessed June 7, 2018); HW 50/22, Chronology of Inter-Service Cypher Security Committee; "Security Allied Cyphers," Section D, "The Enemy Naval 'Y' Service."

19. HW 50/22, "W/T Security and Deception"; "Interservice Cypher Security Committee and Cypher Policy Board" entry for 19.2.41; "The Enemy Naval Wire Service"; CAB 116/29, "Staff Dealing with Security of Codes and Cyphers"; ADM 223/882. The full file shows the wider history of this affair, including interception of German messages showing that the German navy's B-Dienst cryptographic service was reading American messages in this cipher.

20. FO 1093/314, Vickers to Cavendish-Bentinck et al., May 20, 1941; EWT to CSS, May 24, 1941.

21. FO 1093/314, Cable 518, Cadogan to Hoare, March 29, 1941; Hoare to Foreign Office, April 2, 1941; Cadogan to Johnson, April 7, 1941, with handwritten approval from C, April 5, 1941. Cf. US NARA, RG 457, Entry 9032, Box 1384, File NR 4400, "Report of Special Committee to Investigate Security of State Department Communications," June 26, 1941.

22. Jackson, *Solving*, chap. 20; Ralph Erskine, "Breaking Air Force and Army Enigma," in *Action This Day*, ed. Michael Smith and Ralph Erskine (London: Bantam, 2001), 69–72; Budiansky, *Battle of Wits*, 186–188; Weinberg, *World at Arms*, chap. 4; HW 14/30, "Appreciation of Present Position of 'E,'" March 10, 1942.

23. Greenberg, *Welchman*, 125, 138–139.

24. Liddell Hart, *Rommel Papers*, 98–111.

25. Winston S. Churchill, *The Second World War*, vol. 3: *The Grand Alliance* (London: Cassell, 1950), 13–27, 83–97; Weinberg, *World at Arms*, chap. 4.

26. HBF, B39 F8, Fellers to War Department via State Department, Cable 1822, February 24, 1941.

27. HBF, B39 F8, Fellers to War Department via State Department, Cable 1824, March 1, 1941.

28. Ranfurly, *To War*, February 17, 1941.

29. Wavell to Churchill, March 2, 1941; Wavell to Churchill, March 27, 1941, both in Churchill, *Grand Alliance*, 174–179; Liddell Hart, *Rommel Papers*, 104.

30. Liddell Hart, *Rommel Papers*, 105–111; DEFE 3/686 OL27 15:30, April 2, 1941.

31. Liddell Hart, *Rommel Papers*, 109–111.

32. Martin van Creveld, *Supplying War: Logistics from Wallenstein to Patton* (London: Cambridge University Press, 1977), 185, citing German general staff evaluations of February 11, 1941.

33. Liddell Hart, *Rommel Papers*, 111.

34. Moorehead, *African Trilogy*, 139–144; Fraser, *Knight's Cross*, 232–233.

35. Ranfurly, *To War*, April 4, 1941, April 8, 1941.

36. Liddell Hart, *Rommel Papers*, 114–119.

37. HBF B39 F8, Fellers to War Department, Cable 1857, April 19, 1941.

38. Fellers was still sending via the State Department on April 7. By April 14 his cables show he was sending directly to the War Department. HBF B39 F8.

39. Van Creveld, *Supplying War*, 187; Liddell Hart, *Rommel Papers*, 133–134.

40. *War Journal of Franz Halder* (Office of the Chief Counsel for War Crimes, 1948), April 23, 1941, http://ia802805.us.archive.org/31/items/Halder WarJournal/Halder%20War%20Journal.pdf (accessed June 24, 2019); Reuth, *Rommel*, 134–136. German air force messages paraphrased in DEFE 3/686 detail the supply crisis of Rommel's forces, including the lack of aircraft fuel.

41. DEFE 3/686 OL34, 04:34, April 5, 1941, OL35, 08:20, April 5, 1941.

42. HBF, Declassified files HIA-R 5C-11-714-9.

43. HBF, B39 F8, Cable 1861, April 19, 1941.

44. Ranfurly, *To War*, April 17, 23, 28, 30 and May 2, 3, 1941; RPP, unpublished fragment marked Cairo 1940, actually describing 1941; HBF, Declassified files HIA-R 5C-7-554-2; HBF B39, F8, Cable 1868, April 23, 1941; "U.S. Flier Killed on Study of R.A.F," *New York Times*, April 23, 1941, p. 9.

45. RPP, unpublished typescript fragment from Ranfurly's diary, marked in pencil "Cairo, May 1941." Kirk had become ambassador in March.

46. HW 1/3 C/6112, Menzies to Churchill, March 28, 1941, with Churchill annotation, March 29, 1941; CX/JQ/799/T7, March 28, 1941. The orders to move the divisions followed Yugoslavia's joining the Tripartite Alliance; when Yugoslavia reversed direction, the troop movement was apparently delayed for the brief Yugoslavia campaign.

47. Churchill, *Grand Alliance*, 319–323.

48. HW 1/3, CX/JQ/923/T19, May 7, 1941.

49. HBF B39 F8, Cable 1857, part 7, April 19, 1941.

50. Wichhart, "Intervention," 105, 122–132; Basheer M. Nafi, "The Arabs and the Axis," *Arab Studies Quarterly* 19, no. 2 (1997); Norman Stillman, *The Jews of Arab Lands in Modern Times* (Philadelphia: Jewish Publication Society, 1991), 116–117; "The Iraqi Government Committee for the Investigation of the Events of June 1 and 2, 1941," in Stillman, *Jews of Arab Lands*, 405–417.

51. DEFE 3/686 OL 261, May 9, 1941; OL 272, May 11, 1941; OL 367, May 15, 1941; OL 400, May 22, 1941.

52. DEFE 3/687 OL 302, May 13, 1941; DEFE 3/686 OL 339, May 16, 1941; OL 341, May 16, 1941; OL 370, May 19, 1941; OL 394, May 21, 1941; HBF, Declassified files HIA-R 5C-1-519-7, Fellers, Report 9900, "Airborne Invasion of Crete," September 8, 1941; Moorehead, *African Trilogy*, 155–167; Welchman, *Hut Six*, 129. There is a long debate on Freyberg's handling of Crete's defense, especially the defense of the Melame airfield. Ralph Bennett, *Intelligence Investigations: How Ultra Changed History* (London: Frank Cass, 1996), 195–203, argues persuasively that the charges against Freyberg are based on hindsight.

53. On the perception that "special intelligence" had failed, see Ralph Bennett, *Ultra and Mediterranean Strategy* (New York: William Morrow, 1989), 51.

54. *War Journal of Franz Halder*, May 28, 1941.

55. Brenner, *Ium Haplishah*, 39–41; Gelber, *Matzadah*, 25–34.

56. Ritter, *Code Name*, 172–175; KV 2/88, "Final Report on Obstlt. Fritz Adolf Ritter," Appendix D, January 16, 1946.

57. Kelly, *Lost Oasis*, 169–172; cf. FO 141/852 983/17/429, "A Report on Two Interviews with Aziz El Masri Pasha," August 24, 1942.

58. QDA Coll 17/10(4) [IOR/L/PS/12/2863], Cornwallis to Eden, July 29, 1941; "The Iraqi Government Committee for the Investigation of the Events of June 1 and 2, 1941" and Boyd to Driver, April 29, 1942, in Stillman, *Jews of Arab Lands*, 405–418. For Rabbi Yosef Haim's rulings, see his *Ben Ish Hai: Helek Hahalakhot* (Jerusalem: Merkaz Hasefer, 5746 [1985–1986]).

59. Warren F. Kimball, ed., *Churchill and Roosevelt: The Complete Correspondence* (Princeton, NJ: Princeton University Press, 1984), 1: 178–197: Roosevelt to Churchill, May 1, 1941; Churchill to Roosevelt, May 3, 1941; Roosevelt to Churchill, May 10, 1941, May 28, 1941.

60. HBF, B39 F8, Cable 1857, part 11, April 20, 1941.

61. Ritter, *Code Name*, 177–191; KV 2/88, "Final Report on Obstlt. Fritz Adolf Ritter," January 16, 1946; HW 19/8, ISOS 6861A, June 26, 1941, via Gross, Rolke, and Zboray, *Salam*, 356. The account of Almasy's argument with Ritter on

the tarmac is in KV 2/1467, "Third Detailed Interrogation Report of: Eppler, Johann," August 2, 1942. Eppler's testimony is secondhand, based on conversations with Almasy and perhaps others, and includes a number of questionable details.

62. Liddell Hart, *Rommel Papers*, 148.

63. Churchill, *Grand Alliance*, 319–323. Both Churchill's motives and Stalin's response have been discussed in scholarly accounts too numerous to list. Weinberg's reading in *World at Arms*, chap. 4, is persuasive.

64. See Weinberg, *World at Arms*, chap. 4.

ACT II. CHAPTER 5. THE LADY WHO SPIED ON SPIES

1. CD, June 21–23, 1941.

2. RPP, unpublished typescript fragment from Ranfurly's diary. In pencil it is marked "1943," but references in the text suggest that earlier dating is possible.

3. DFP 12:350, Ettel to Ribbentrop, April 15, 1941.

4. DFP XII:427, Ribbentrop to Ettel, April 30, 1941.

5. DFP XIII:66, Ettel to Ribbentrop, July 3, 1941.

6. RPP, unpublished fragment marked Cairo 1940, actually describing 1941; Ranfurly, *To War*, diary entries from December 1, 1940, to June 28, 1941.

7. HS 3/192. Entitled "Anti-SO2 Dossier," the file is devoted to scathing reports on SO2 operations in the Balkans and Middle East directed from Cairo, along with rebuttals and countercharges. As of May 2019, some sections remained redacted. Cf. Mackenzie, *Secret History of SOE*, 175–176. On the ship, known as the *Darien*, see Bauer, *From Diplomacy*, 193.

8. Barry Rubin, "Anglo-American Relations in Saudi Arabia, 1941–45," *Journal of Contemporary History* 14 (1979): 253–267.

9. HS 8/266, CD to Jebb, February 14, 1941.

10. Saul Kelly, "A Succession of Crises: SOE in the Middle East, 1940–45," *Intelligence and National Security* 20, no. 1 (2005): 126.

11. Report by Moshe Dayan on the operation in Lebanon; undated, attached to an undated letter to which he received a reply on October 29, 1941; sold at auction in 2015: "Lot #1: Moshe Dayan Archive of Signed Letters & Documents Related to the Famous Loss of His Eye," Nate D. Sanders Auctions, natedsanders.com/moshe_dayan_archive_of_signed_letters___documents _-lot37277.aspx (accessed July 8, 2019); PMA 1/1/4, Reports on Actions of Groups 1–10, June 7, 1941; Gelber, *Matzadah*, 36–37.

12. Weinberg, *World at Arms*, chap. 4.

13. HS 2/192, Pollock to Wavell, "Report on SO2 Activities in Syria, Other Than Propaganda, in Connection with the Occupation by Allied Forces," June 12, 1941.

14. Robert Louis Benson, "SIGINT and the Holocaust," undated NSA document, Internet Archive, https://archive.org/download/sigint_and_the _holocaust-nsa/sigint_and_the_holocaust.pdf (accessed July 10, 2019); Robert J. Hanyok, *Eavesdropping on Hell: Historical Guide to Western Communications*

Intelligence and the Holocaust, 1939–1945 (Fort Meade, MD: Center for Cryptologic History, NSA, 2005), 82; Budiansky, *Battle of Wits*, 197–200; Jackson, *Solving*, chap. 26.

15. HW 1/30, "German Police," original message August 23, 1941, decrypt August 27, 1941.

16. "Prime Minister Winston Churchill's Broadcast to the World About the Meeting with President Roosevelt," ibiblio, August 24, 1941, www.ibiblio.org /pha/timeline/410824awp.html (accessed July 10, 2019).

17. Smith, *FDR*, chap. 22.

18. "Prime Minister Winston Churchill's Broadcast to the World About the Meeting with President Roosevelt."

19. HW 50/22, "Official Breaches and Use of Material," undated; Budiansky, *Battle of Wits*, 199–201.

20. Cüppers, *Walther Rauff*, 110–142. Cüppers concludes that 400,000 to 500,000 people were murdered in gas vans. Other sources give even higher estimates. See "Gas Vans," Yad Vashem, www.yadvashem.org/odot_pdf /Microsoft%20Word%20-%206236.pdf (accessed July 10, 2019).

21. US NARA, RG 165/390/31/30/7, Box 749, file 2200, March 25, 1941, James T. Scott, "Fellaheen Living on Four Cents a Day"; Schewe, *Siege*, 178–183.

22. Moorehead, *African Trilogy*, 182–200.

23. Warner, *Auchinleck*, 35–38; Moorehead, *African Trilogy*, 222–223. Photo of Wavell and Fellers: FFP.

24. Churchill, *Grand Alliance*, 153–160.

25. Liddell Hart, *Rommel Papers*, 134–139, 149–151.

26. Sebag-Montefiore, *Enigma*, chap. 10; McKay, *Secret Life*, 13–14.

27. DEFE 3/688 OL 861, August 1, 1941; OL 888, August 6, 1941; OL 897, August 8, 1941; Bennett, *Ultra and Mediterranean Strategy*, 70–79.

28. Sebag-Montefiore, *Enigma*, chap.11–15.

29. R. A. Ratcliff, *Delusions of Intelligence: Enigma, Ultra and the End of Secure Ciphers* (New York: Cambridge University Press, 2006), 131–135.

30. WO 208/5520, 1st Consolidated Report on Activities of a) Eppler Johann (alias Hussein Gaafar) b) Sandstede Heinrich Gerd (alias Peter Muncaster), July 29, 1941; 5th Consolidated Report, August 23, 1941; Gross, Rolke, and Zboray, *Salam*, 284–287, 336–337. The latter pages are from Sandstede's previously unpublished memoir, written in diary form but years later. The account here depends as much as possible on Sandstede's testimony rather than Eppler's, which is less reliable. In British documents, the spelling of Eppler's Egyptian last name and that of his half brother sometimes appears as Gafaar. In various accounts, Sandstede's name has also appeared as Sandstete, Sandstette, or Sandstetter.

ACT II. CHAPTER 6. THE ORACLES SPEAK GIBBERISH

1. HW 8/129, entries for December 3, 1941; HW 1/288, 1/290, 1/294, 1/296, 1/297, 1/298, 1/303.

2. HW 1/298; HW 8/129, entries for December 5, 1941.

3. Smith, *FDR*, chap. 23; David Kahn, *The Codebreakers: The Story of Secret Writing* (New York: Scribner, 1996), 1–3, 44–59; Frederick D. Parker, *Pearl Harbor Revisited: U.S. Navy Communications Intelligence, 1924–1941* (Fort Meade, MD: Center for Cryptological History, National Security Agency, 2013), 43–45, www.nsa.gov/Portals/70/documents/about/cryptologic-heritage /historical-figures-publications/publications/wwii/pearl_harbor_revisited.pdf (accessed July 18, 2019).

4. HBF B15, F7, Fellers to Kimmel, March 6, 1967.

5. On the racial bias that led American commanders, especially those at Pearl Harbor, to underestimate the Japanese and therefore fed conspiracy theories after the fact, see Weinberg, *World at Arms*, chap. 4.

6. HBF B39, F8, Cable 297, December 3, 1941; Cable 309, December 5, 1941; Cable 316, December 6, 1941; Cable 318, December 6–10, 1941; Ranfurly, *To War*, January 2, 1941.

7. *Special Forces*, 276–283, 416–419. Cf. Liddell Hart, *Rommel Papers*, 156. British and German accounts of the raid predictably differ; both are based on very few surviving witnesses.

8. Laszlo Almasy, *With Rommel's Army in Libya*, trans. Gabriel Francis Horchler (Bloomington, IN: 1st Books Library, 2001), 35–39. Many of the details in Almasy's memoir, written in Hungarian during the war, are certainly mistaken.

9. In parallel with this raid, the nascent Special Air Service attempted to land fifty-five commandos by parachute in order to attack Axis airbases in Libya. The LRDG was to pick up the commandos after the raids. Parachuting proved a failure. The men were scattered and never carried out the raids. Twenty-one of the fifty-five made it to rendezvous points with the LRDG. This, together with the Beda Littoria raid, led to the conclusion that it was more effective to exploit the LRDG to deliver commandos. See *Special Forces*, 308–310.

10. Bagnold, *Sand, Wind*, 136–137. Bagnold attributes the appellation "mosquito army" to Wavell.

11. "Panzergruppe Afrika Intelligence Assessment—18 November 1941," located and translated by Andreas Biermann, The Crusader Project, rommel sriposte.com/2013/11/19/panzergruppe-afrika-intelligence-assessment-18 -november-1941 (accessed September 15, 2015); Hans-Otto Behrendt, *Rommel's Intelligence in the Desert Campaign* (London: William Kimber, 1985), 99. On Seebohm, see HW 73/6.

12. Moorehead, *African Trilogy*, 234; Beckett, *Rommel*, chap. 3; Fraser, *Knight's Cross*, 279–280.

13. HBF B39 F8, Cable 318, December 6–8, 1941.

14. Moorehead, *African Trilogy*, 242–244.

15. FFP, Cable 587, Fellers to Military Intelligence Division, January 14, 1942; Beckett, *Rommel*, chap. 3.

16. See FDR, PSF Box 147, William J. Donovan, "Memorandum for the President," February 2, 1942, in which Donovan's "man in Cairo" reports on

an early-January conversation with Admiral Andrew Cunningham. Despite the intense rivalry between the Military Intelligence Division and William Donovan's Office of the Coordination of Information, Fellers appears to have reported to both.

17. DEFE 3/745, messages from November 23–25, 1941; M. van Creveld, "Rommel's Supply Problem, 1941–42," *RUSI* 119, no. 3 (1974): 69. Accounts of these battles written after the Ultra secret became known may have exaggerated the intelligence available to Auchinleck from German army Enigma. HW 14/30, "Appreciation of Present Position of 'E,'" March 10, 1942, Appendix II, says the army group of keys labeled Chaffinch was broken fifteen days in November but none in the following months. Jackson, *Solving*, chap. 21, states that Hut 6 ceased breaking the army Enigma keys for North Africa on November 23, 1941. Many of the breaks for earlier dates were based on captured materials, so the messages were decoded at too great a delay to have operational value.

18. Liddell Hart, *Rommel Papers*, 168.

19. Liddell Hart, *Rommel Papers*, 175.

20. HBF B39 F8, Cable 406, December 18, 1941; Cable 419, December 22, 1941.

21. Moorehead, *African Trilogy*, 258.

22. Liddell Hart, *Rommel Papers*, 178.

23. HBF B39 F8, Cable 260, November 27, 1941.

24. DFP XIII:385, Papen to Foreign Ministry, October 6, 1941; FO 371/63073, "Telegram from Angora No. 1415 of 10th November 1941," from a dossier of German documents, captured at the end of the war, on Egyptian contacts with the Axis.

25. Smith, *FDR*, chap. 23.

26. Kimball, *Churchill and Roosevelt*, 283–284; Alanbrooke, *Diaries*, December 8, 1941; CD, December 8–11, 1941.

27. Andrew Roberts, *Masters and Commanders: The Military Geniuses Who Led the West to Victory in WWII* (London: Penguin, 2009), 70–76; Alanbrooke, *Diaries*, January 27, 1942; Elizabeth Nell, *Mr. Churchill's Secretary* (New York: Coward-McCann, 1958), 72–73.

28. Maurice Matloff and Edwin M. Snell, *Strategic Planning for Coalition Warfare: 1941–1942* (Washington, DC: Center of Military History, 1999), 102–105; Alanbrooke, *Diaries*, January 14, 1942, February 4, 1942, February 9, 1942, April 9, 1942; Rick Atkinson, *An Army at Dawn: The War in North Africa, 1942–1943* (New York: Henry Holt, 2002), 11–14; Roberts, *Masters*, 68–84, 123, 139; Smith, *FDR*, chap. 23. Contrasting portrayals of the abilities of US and British leaders and generals in histories written decades later are so striking, it seems the historians are still fighting the War of 1812.

29. Menzies's text: HW 1/362, January 22, 1942. Churchill's typed text: CA CHAR 20/52/17-18. Text received by Roosevelt: Louis Kruh, "British-American Cryptanalytic Cooperation and an Unprecedented Admission by Winston Churchill," *Cryptologia* 13, no. 2 (1989): 126–127. Kruh does not give an archival reference.

30. Holburn had been stationed before the war in Berlin and afterward in Moscow and had been embedded with the Nationalist army during the Spanish Civil War. If there was anything unimpressive in his record, it was falling for Nationalist propaganda that Guernica was torched by the Republicans, not bombed.

31. Lampson diary, January 24, 1942, January 21, 1942.

32. Moorehead, *African Trilogy*, 259–269; Warner, *Auchinleck*, 131–133; Fraser, *Knight's Cross*, 298–299; HBF B39 F8, Cable 468, December 31, 1941; FFP, Cable 503, January 3, 1942; Cable 616, Fellers to Military Intelligence Division, January 17, 1942.

33. Liddell Hart, *Rommel Papers*, 179–181.

34. Fraser, *Knight's Cross*, 292–293, 299–302; Janusz Piekalkiewicz, *Rommel and the Secret War in North Africa, 1941–1943* (West Chester, PA: Schiffer Military History, 1992), 102, 110.

35. Almasy, *With Rommel's Army*, 57–65.

36. WO 208/1561, Security Summary Middle East No. 11, January 5, 1942.

37. MLD, January 22, 1941, January 29, 1941; Cooper, *Cairo*, 162.

38. The main sources for the account that follows are MLD entries from January 5 to February 5, 1942, Lampson's cables in FO 371/31567 from February 4 to February 10, 1942, and his report on political events in Egypt, March 12, 1942, in FO 403/466. Other sources are noted below.

39. *Al Abaram*, January 25, 1942.

40. CUOH, Laszlo Pathy, 1976, 21.

41. Walter Monckton had been legal adviser to Edward VIII. Andrew Walker, "Profile: Walter Monckton," *BBC*, January 29, 2003, http://news.bbc.co.uk/2/hi/uk_news/2702371.stm (accessed June 12, 2017).

42. Wichhart, "Intervention," 173; FFP, Cable 778, Part 3, February 8, 1942; Diana Cooper, *Trumpets from the Steep* (Boston: Houghton, Mifflin, 1960), 149.

43. FFP, Cable 778, Part 3, February 8, 1942.

44. Cooper, *Trumpets*, 150.

45. Mohi El Din, *Memories*, 16; FO 371/31567, Lampson to Foreign Office, February 10, 1942; FO 141/841, Jenkins to Tomlyn, February 9, 1942, and attached agents' reports. Jenkins was the district security officer, the MI5 representative in Egypt. One of his informants put the number of officers present at "about 1,000."

46. Sadat, *Identity*, 32.

47. FFP, Cable 778, Part 3, February 8, 1942.

48. CD, February 7, 1942.

49. Barrie Pitt, *The Crucible of War 2: Auchinleck's Command* (London: Macmillan, 1986), 167–168; cf. van Creveld, *Supplying War*, 193.

50. Weinberg, *World at Arms*, chap. 6.

51. The main sources for Almasy's journey are Gross, Rolke, and Zboray, *Salam*, including primary sources first published there: Almasy's diary for the operation, Sandstede's memoir-diary, and decrypted Abwehr messages from HW 19. Also KV/2/1467, 1st Consolidated Report on Activities of a) Eppler,

Johann (alias Hussein Gaafar) b) Sandstede, Heinrich Gerd (alias Peter Muncaster), July 29, 1941; Kelly, *Lost Oasis*, 192–219; Almasy, *With Rommel's Army*, 96–109. Other sources are noted below.

52. Batey, *Dilly*, chap. 10.

53. "Jean Howard: Wartime Intelligence Officer," *Times* (London), July 9, 2007, www.thetimes.co.uk/article/jean-howard-wartime-intelligence-officer -mgmjh7vj5mp (accessed August 8, 2019).

54. Gross, Rolke, and Zboray, *Salam*, 294; HW 19/30, ISOS 28341, via Gross, Rolke, and Zboray, *Salam*, 373; Kelly, *Lost Oasis*, 202.

ACT III. CHAPTER 1. THE WOMAN OF DAUNTING INTELLIGENCE

1. Copies of CX/MSS/919/T4 exist in HW 5/84 and HW 1/521. The version in the latter file is the one that MI6 director Stewart Menzies gave to Winston Churchill and shows Churchill's markings in red ink. However, some of the time markings and the notation of the Enigma key in which the message was sent appear only in the HW 5/84 version. These differences are typical of HW 1 and HW 5 files. Sources for the workings of Hut 6 and 3 in spring 1942 include HW 77/12, Hut 6 Weekly Reports; Calvocoressi, *Top Secret*, 54–57; Welchman, *Hut Six*, 128–131, 145–148; Ralph Bennett, "The Duty Officer, Hut 3," in Hinsley and Stripp, *Codebreakers*, 30–40; Erskine, "Breaking Air Force and Army Enigma," 57.

2. HW 14/46, "Following from CSS," February 19, 1942. Originally, it appears, the diplomatic section was to remain in the countryside at Wavendon.

3. Photos of Travis: Greenberg, *Welchman*, plate after 142; "Sir Edward Wilfrid Harry Travis," National Portrait Gallery, November 21, 1946, www .npg.org.uk/collections/search/portraitZoom/mw110783/Sir-Edward-Wilfrid -Harry-Travis (accessed August 20, 2019).

4. Welchman, *Hut Six*, 121, 127.

5. HW 14/36, "Secrecy," filed with material from early May 1942.

6. Russell-Jones, *My Secret Life*, 80–81, 137–144.

7. HW 50/22, "Security: Personnel, Vetting, Breaches, Official Secrets Act," 2, notation for May 1, 1943.

8. Martin Kitchen, *Rommel's Desert War* (Cambridge, UK: Cambridge University Press, 2009), 204–205.

9. Aleric W. Rowntree, *The Hungry Ones* (unpublished memoir, undated), IWM, Document 11910, 56–96; Churchill, *Hinge of Fate*, 260–270; Moorehead, *African Trilogy*, 331–336.

10. Churchill, *Hinge of Fate*, 261–262. The quoted words are Churchill's paraphrase of Auchinleck.

11. HW 1/537, CX/MSS/886/T18, April 14, 1942, plus response, unsigned but certainly from Menzies, and subsequent response from RAF HQ in Cairo. C. J. Jenner implies that the information in this cable came from the same source as the other leaked information from Cairo. While the timing makes

this possible, I have not found proof that is the case in the form of a cable from the source or the language of the German message. C. J. Jenner, "Turning the Hinge of Fate: Good Source and the UK-U.S. Intelligence Alliance, 1940–1942," *Diplomatic History* 32, no. 8 (2008): 195–196.

12. US NARA, RG 319, Entry 47, 270/5/18/7, Box 379, File 350.07–350.09, Report 6000, May 8, 1942, "Diary of Colonel Fry's Visit to British Armored Units in the Western Desert."

13. US NARA, RG 319, Entry 47, 270/5/13/5, Box 125, File 315–452.1, Fellers to Assistant Chief of Staff, G-2, "Organizational Chart," January 21, 1942; A. Khairi, "Places Occupied by the United States Mission in Cairo (Historical)," July 14, 1988. My thanks to the US embassy in Cairo for this document.

14. "Egypt-Libya: The U.S. Army Campaign of World War II." Last updated October 3, 2003. U.S. Army Center of Military History. https://history .army.mil/brochures/egypt/egypt.htm (accessed May 8, 2015). Associated Press reported Maxwell's arrival in Cairo on November 22, 1941. See "American Military Mission in Cairo," *Ellensburg Daily Record*, November 22, 1941, 1, https:// news.google.com/newspapers?nid=860&dat=19411122&id=pbo0AAAAIBAJ &sjid=Q4MFAAAAIBAJ&pg=4735,3636331&hl=en (accessed April 28, 2016). Maxwell's radiograms carried Fellers's numbering and were often signed by Fellers. See, e.g., FDR, Henry L. Hopkins Papers, Box 139, Egypt file.

15. FDR, Map Room, Box 45, Army Dispatches, April 7–15, 1942, Cable 963, April 11, 1942. On Fellers's official status as US liaison officer to the Middle East Command, see WO 201/2158.

16. FFP, Cable 987, April 22–25, 1942; Cable 1018, May 5, 1942; Cable 1080, May 30, 1942; HBF, Declassified files HIA-R 5C-11-714-9, Fellers Report 2437, May 13, 1942.

17. Roberts, *Masters*, 120–196, passim.

18. Cole C. Kingseed, "Eisenhower and MacArthur: Toil, Trouble and Turbulence in the Philippines," Association of the United States Army, January 13, 2015, www.ausa.org/articles/eisenhower-and-macarthur-toil-trouble-and -turbulence-philippines (accessed November 12, 2019); Ranfurly, *To War*, November 26, 1943. Fellers's daughter, Nancy Finch, in a letter describing an unpublished biography of her father that she had written, wrote that Fellers was the "only witness" to the falling out between Eisenhower and MacArthur. HBF B45 F12. The archive does not contain Finch's manuscript.

19. HBF, Declassified files HIA-R 5C-7-553-3, Marshall to Fellers, Cable 875, June 6, 1942.

20. Interviews and correspondence, Swinhoe, Flemons, Hodsdon, Downes, Wiggin.

21. HW 50/22, "W/T Security and Deception"; "Security Allied Cyphers," Section D, "The Enemy Naval Y Service"; HW 43/11, Frank Birch, *GC&CS Naval Sigint*, vol. 2: *The Organization and Evolution of British Naval Sigint*, 141; US NARA, RG 457 HCC, Box 92, V. Cole et al., *GC&CS Air and Military History*, vol. 11: *Special Studies*, 232–233. An appendix to the last of these works, on page 286, lists the Kesselring message of April 24, CX/MSS/919/T4, as the

first of a series of German signal intelligence successes. The list includes serial numbers for two messages that would appear to be earlier: CX/MSS/853/T11 and CX/MSS/853/T20. In fact, the numbers were miscopied when this history was written after the war. The correct numbers are CX/MSS/993/T11 and CX/MSS/953/T20.

22. Copies of CX/MSS/919/T4 exist in HW 5/86 and HW 1/537. The former version includes handwritten notations of when the intercept came in and what Enigma key was used. The latter version went to Churchill; he made no notations.

23. HW 50/22, "Security: Sigint Dissemination and Breaches of Security (Ultra Regulations)," notation for April 23, 1942.

24. Welchman, *Hut Six*, 123–124.

25. HW 14/30, "Appreciation of the Present Position of 'E,'" March 10, 1942; HW 14/32, "Classification of Headings Under Which MSS Information Is Obtained," filed for last third of March 1942.

26. Jackson, *Solving*, chap. 21; HW 14/36, "Proportion of Bombe Time Spent on Various Colours for April, 1942," May 3, 1942; HW 77/12, Hut 6 weekly report for week ending May 2, 1942.

27. Liddell Hart, *Rommel Papers*, 138–139.

28. Patrick Bernhard, "Behind the Battle Lines: Italian Atrocities and the Persecution of Arabs, Berbers and Jews in North Africa During World War II," *Holocaust and Genocide Studies* 26, no. 3 (winter 2012): 425–446; Patrick Bernhard, "Guerre et violences en Afrique du Nord," in *La guerre du desert, 1940–1943*, ed. David Reynolds, Olivier Wieviorka, and Nicola Labanca (Paris: Perrin, 2019), 181–220.

29. Sources on deportation of the Jews of Cyrenaica include Esther Eran, "Redifat Yehudei Luv (Kefi Shehi Mishtakefet Bedivuhei Hakonsulia Hagermanit Betripoli)," *Yalkut Moreshet* 33 (June 1982): 153–156; Rachel Simon, "Yehudei Luv Al Saf Shoah," *Peamim* 28 (5746 [1986]): 44–77; Abramski-Bligh, *Pinkas Hakehillot*, 87–92, 114–121, 131–136, 198–201; Roumani, *Jews of Libya*, 28–35; and oral histories from the YVA testimony collection, including that of Rahamim Bukra, 1984, file 8464.

30. HW 14/46, "Report by Lt. Colonel J. H. Tiltman on His Visit to North America, March and April 1942"; Friedman to Tiltman, May 13, 1942; NSA OH 07-78 Tiltman Oral History; *Brigadier John Tiltman*, 35–40. On breaking JN-25, see Budiansky, *Battle of Wits*, passim.

31. HW 14/36, CBME to Denniston, May 6, 1942; Denniston to Jacob, May 8, 1942.

32. Zerubavel Gilad, ed. *Magen Beseter* (Jerusalem: Jewish Agency, 5712 [1951–1952]), 177–178; "Eliahu Ernst Gottlieb," Irgun Hahagana, www.irgon-haagana.co.il/info/n_show.aspx?id=24290 (accessed August 25, 2019).

33. Sources on Buck and the SIG include WO 201/727, Haselden to Graham, April 1942; WO 201/732, "Transport for Special Interrogation Group," April 1, 1942; WO 416/45/1, "Buck, Herbert Cecil"; "Maurice Tiefenbrunner," *Telegraph*, August 2, 2013, www.telegraph.co.uk/news/obituaries/10219109

/Maurice-Tiefenbrunner.html (accessed June 25, 2017); John Sadler, *Operation Agreement: Jewish Commandos and the Raid on Tobruk* (Oxford, UK: Osprey, 2016), chap. 1, iBook.

34. FDR, Map Room, Box 44, Army Dispatches, From M/A Cairo, March 6, 1942.

35. Warner, *Auchinleck*, 163–174; Churchill, *Hinge of Fate*, 277–278.

36. WO 201/202, 201/227; Gelber, *Matzadah*, 48–51. Trenches, emplacements, and tank barriers on the Carmel remained intact as of August 2017.

37. Moshe Sharett, *Ma'avak Medini 1942: Yanuar–Mai—Kovevetz Ne'umim Umismakhim (Political Struggle 1942: January–May—an Anthology of Speeches and Documents)*, ed. Shifra Kolat (Tel Aviv: Society to Commemorate Moshe Sharett, 2009), 441–463.

38. YTA 15-46/169/4/14, Yisrael Galili to Tziporah Galili, March 23, 1942.

39. Haim Gouri, interview, May 6, 2015.

40. YTA 15-46/169/4/14, Yisrael Galili to Tziporah Galili, March 20, 1942; HS 7/266, SOE War Diary, July 1942, 36–38.

41. Brenner, *Ium Haplishah*, 10, gives the date as April 26. Sources on the Mishmar Ha'emek camp include YTA 12/3/132/2, Abba Eban OH, February 15, 1960; Gouri interview; Stephen Russell Cox, "Britain and the Origin of Israeli Special Operations: SOE and PALMACH During the Second World War," *Dynamics of Asymmetric Conflict* 8, no. 1 (2015): 70–73; Richard Clogg, "Nicholas Hammond," *Guardian*, April 5, 2001, www.theguardian.com/news/2001/apr/05/guardianobituaries1 (accessed August 28, 2019); David Armstrong, *At Close Quarters: SOE Close Combat Pistol Instructor Colonel Hector Grant-Taylor* (Stroud, UK: Fonthill, 2013), chap. 5, iBook; Yaakov Markovitzki, *Hayehidot Hayevashtiot Hameyuhadot Shel Hapalmah* (Tel Aviv: Ministry of Defense, 1989), 60–64. The formative role of the Palmah in the lives of many of Israel's founders created an almost instant mythology around the Mishmar Ha'emek camp and an extensive nostalgic literature. The loss of the Palmah's early records and of a large portion of the SOE's records has impeded efforts for an account based on contemporary documents.

42. HS 7/266, SOE War Diary, July 1942, 36; August 1942, 116. Possibly explaining the discrepancy, Galili wrote in advance that 150 Palmah fighters would be mobilized full-time by the SOE, and another 250 would be reservists training for a week a month. YTA 15-46/169/4/14, Yisrael Galili, March 20, 1942. The numbers 150 and 400 likewise appear in a memorandum by Palmah commander Yitzhak Sadeh from June 15, 1942: Brenner, *Ium Haplishah*, 90.

43. YTA 12/3/132/2, Abba Eban OH, February 15, 1960; Gouri interview; Abba Eban, *Personal Witness: Israel Through My Eyes* (New York: G. P. Putnam, 1992), 30–43; HS 9/466/6, Eban, Major Aubrey S. (Mr. Abba Eban) personnel file; HS 7/234, SOE War Diary, June 1942, 4239; KV 2/3860/3 Eban, Aubrey Solomon—MI5 file.

44. YTA 15-46/169/4/14, Yisrael Galili, March 23, 1942; Gelber, *Matzadah*, 50–54. On pilgrimages to Masada and the site's role in memory of 1942, see

Yael Zerubavel, *Recovered Roots: Collective Memory and the Making of Israeli National Tradition* (Chicago: University of Chicago, 1995), 62–75, 119–127.

45. For later testimony that the "Northern Plan" or "Tobruk on the Carmel" was an operational plan, see Brenner, *Ium Haplishah*, 145–160. Gelber (*Matzadah*, 50–56) convincingly shows that this testimony is misleading and the proposal was never more than theoretical.

46. HW 5/87, CX/MSS/945/T8, CX/MSS/945/T3.

47. On inaccurate German intelligence on the British order of battle, see US NARA, RG 457 HCC, Box 92, V. Cole et al., *GC&CS Air and Military History*, 11: 231–242. On Thirteenth Corps, see, e.g., FFP, Cable 999, Part 4, April 28, 1942.

48. HW 5/89, CX/MSS/968/T15. The German message was sent on May 9, 1942; the decrypt is dated May 11.

49. Cf. HW 1/642, where Menzies explicitly avoids informing Churchill of a related problem until he has answers.

50. NCML, SHR-025, Colonel McCormack's Trip to London, May–June 1943, Bluebird Incident, 271.

ACT III. CHAPTER 2. *MARE INCOGNITUM*

1. HW 8/24 AI/MSS/13, "German Intentions in the Mediterranean," May 6, 1942. Cf. the follow-up report, HW 14/37, AI/MSS/14, May 18, 1942, which confirms these conclusions.

2. HW 14/37, Commanders in Chief to DMI for Chiefs of Staff, May 13, 1942.

3. HW 14/37, Tedder to Chief of Air Staff, May 17, 1942.

4. HW 13/52, CX/MSS/S/12, "Axis Preparations for Operations in the Mediterranean," May 26, 1942. On the Hut 3 research section, see HW 43/64, *The History of Hut 3 (1940–1945)*, 2: 356.

5. Fraser, *Knight's Cross*, 304–306; *War Journal of Franz Halder*, entries for March 1942. On March 25, Halder listed German dead, wounded, and missing at 1,073,066 out of an army originally numbering 3.2 million.

6. Liddell Hart, *Rommel Papers*, 191–192.

7. CD, May 12–13, 1942.

8. CD, April 29–May 2; Kitchen, *Rommel's Desert War*, 205–214.

9. Carl von Clausewitz, "Friction in War," chap. 7 of *On War*, trans. J. J. Graham, Project Gutenberg, www.gutenberg.org/files/1946/1946-h/1946-h.htm (accessed September 25, 2019).

10. Main sources used here on Husseini's relations with the Nazis include KV 2/2085, passim; Francis R. Nicosia, *Nazi Germany and the Arab World* (New York: Cambridge University Press, 2014), 180–205; Klaus-Michael Mallmann and Martin Cüppers, *Nazi Palestine: The Plans for the Extermination of the Jews in Palestine* (New York: Enigma and United States Holocaust Museum, 2010), 88–94; Michael A. Sells, "Holocaust Abuse: The Case of Hajj Muhammad Amin al-Husayni," *Journal of Religious Ethics* 43, no. 4 (2015): 724–725; Samuel

Miner, "Planning the Holocaust in the Middle East: Nazi Designs to Bomb Jewish Cities in Palestine," *Jewish Political Studies Review* 27, no. 3/4 (2016): 20–22; Mallmann and Cüppers, "Elimination of the Jewish National Home," 6–7; Weinberg, *World at Arms*, chap. 10.

11. DFP 13:515, "Record of the Conversation Between the Führer and the Grand Mufti of Jerusalem on November 28, 1941, in the Presence of the Reich Foreign Minister and Minister Grobba in Berlin"; 13:516, "Memorandum by the Director of the Political Department," November 28, 1941.

12. CD, April 14, 1942.

13. Weinberg, *World at Arms*, chaps. 6, 10.

14. HW 1/573, "Arab Independence: Japanese Ambassador, Rome, Forwards Letter from Mufti and Gailani to Ciano," May 16, 1942; HW 1/575, "Arab Independence: Japanese Ambassador, Rome, Forwards Letter from Ciano to Mufti," May 17, 1942.

15. Mallmann and Cüppers, "Elimination of the Jewish National Home," 6–7.

16. HW 77/12, Hut 6 weekly report for week ending May 23, 1942.

17. HW 5/91, CX/MSS/988/T15.

18. HW 5/92, CX/MSS/993/T11.

19. This is the second Bluebird message described in NCML, SHR-025, Colonel McCormack's Trip to London, May–June 1943, Bluebird Incident, 271. The information is based on a meeting between McCormack and Dudley-Smith. It is unclear whether McCormack took notes or reported based on his memory of the conversation. It is possible that his list is incomplete.

20. KCLH GB0099, papers of Maj. Gen. Henry Maughan ("Bill") Liardet, letter to his wife, February 18, 1943, published as Guy Liardet, "The Gazala Battles," *Tank Journal*, August 1996. Liardet writes that his unit was to move up on July 1 but also that he had a fortnight from May 15 to train them. "July" is almost certainly a substitution for "June," an extremely common error.

21. IWM, Document 25879, R. G. Hurlock, letter to his father, May 25, 1942.

22. IWM, Document 7876, E. H. Wilmott, *Nothing Spectacular: 41–45* (transcribed journal), 12.

23. HW 5/93, CX/MSS/1003/T9.

24. DEFE 3/756, MK 5749, May 24, 1942, based on decrypt CX/MSS/1008/T5.

25. HW 5/94, CX/MSS/1014/T16, intercepted May 22, 1942.

26. Morik Brin and Raoul A. Biancardi, *Say It in Arabic and See Egypt: Manual and Guide-Book for the British and Imperial Forces* (Cairo: Horus, 1942).

27. The account here is based on interrogations of Eppler, Sandstede, and others in the summer of 1942, which corroborate each other and differ greatly from wildly embellished postwar accounts by Eppler and others. In the interrogations, they recalled the date when they were left at Assiut and took the train to Cairo as May 24. However, Almasy recorded the date as May 23 in the diary he was keeping at the time. See Almasy's diary in Gross, Rolke, and Zbo-

ray, *Salam*, 326–327. Interrogations: HW 14/40, "Special Report on German Intelligence in Egypt and Libya," based on the statements of Waldemar Weber and Walter Aberle, June 18, 1942; KV 2/1467, "Report on the Interrogation of Victor Hauer," July 22–23, 1942; "First Consolidated Report on Activities of Eppler, Johann and Sandstede, Heinrich Gerd," July 29, 1942; "Second Consolidated Report on the Activities of Eppler, Johann and Sandstede, Heinrich Gerd," July 31, 1942; "Further Report on Sandy and Eppler Case," August 5, 1942; KV 3/5, J. C. Curry, "The German Secret Services: Supplement to the Report on the German Secret Service Issued in August 1942," July 1944, 67–71.

28. Almasy's diary in Gross, Rolke, and Zboray, *Salam*, 326–331.

29. KV 2/1467, "Second Consolidated Report," says that Albert Wahda had "apparently been working for Mme. Therese as a pimp." In the unsigned "Further Report," the writer refers to him as "a Jew boy called Albert Wahba." The overt anti-Semitism of the investigators toward Wahda/Wahba may have led to their assumption that he was Therese's pimp.

30. Almasy's message: His diary for May 18, 1942; Gross, Rolke, and Zboray, *Salam*, 322. Message from Tripoli to Berlin: HW 19/30, ISOS 27806, May 20, 1942, via Gross, Rolke, and Zboray, *Salam*, 369. Mideast Headquarters to Kaid Khartoum: WO 201/2139, May 25, 1942. On the bottleneck in transmitting Abwehr decrypts, see Brett Edward Lintott, "Confidence Men: The Mediterranean Double-Cross System, 1941–45" (PhD diss, University of Toronto, 2015), 59–63.

31. Bagnold, *Libyan Sands*, 10.

32. Fraser, *Knight's Cross*, 313ff.; Warner, *Auchinleck*, 182ff.; Liddell Hart, *Rommel Papers*, 191ff.; WO 201/2014, Personal for CIGS from General Auchinleck, Situation Review, May 27, 1942.

33. FFP, Cable 1090, June 1, 1942.

34. Liddell Hart, *Rommel Papers*, 203–208; Fraser, *Knight's Cross*, 323–328; Marcus Cowper and Christopher Pannell, *Tank Spotter's Guide* (Oxford, UK: Osprey, 2011), 27–29; Michael Peck, "The M-3 Grant: America's Nazi Germany Tank-Killer," *National Interest*, January 22, 2017, https://nationalinterest .org/blog/the-buzz/the-m-3-grant-americas-nazi-germany-tank-killer-19126 (accessed September 23, 2019); cf. FDR, Map Room, Box 93, File MR300, Section 1, Fellers Cable 1076, May 30, 1942.

35. WO 201/632, To Mideast from HQ Main Eighth Army, Cositrep 322, May 30, 1942; Cositrep 323, May 30, 1942; Cositrep 325, May 31, 1942.

36. IWM, Document 15623, 4/5 W. B. Kennedy-Shaw papers, Wbk 8, "The Almasy Commando," June 5, 1942; WO 201/2139, To Mideast from Kaid Khartoum, June 8, 1942; To Main Eighth Army from Mideast, June 9, 1942; "Enemy Intelligence Unit," June 9, 1942; HW 51/26, message of June 9, 1942; HW 14/40, "Special Report on German Intelligence in Egypt and Libya," based on the statements of Waldemar Weber and Walter Aberle, June 18, 1942. The documentation clearly indicates that Weber and Aberle were captured on May 27 and that some of Weber's papers were found separately on May 29.

There is no mention in the British records of the novel *Rebecca* or of any other English-language novel. The report on the interrogation of Weber and Aberle does note that Weber was carrying "a number of incriminating documents."

37. KV 2/1467, 1st Consolidated Report on Activities of a) Eppler, Johann (alias Hussein Gaafar) b) Sandstede, Heinrich Gerd (alias Peter Muncaster), July 29, 1941.

38. The key sources for the legend are Leonard Mosley, *The Cat and the Mice* (London: Arthur Barkey, 1958); A. W. Sansom, *I Spied Spies* (London: George G. Harrap, 1965); John Eppler, *Operation Condor: Rommel's Spy*, trans. S. Seago (London: MacDonald and Jane's, 1974).

39. IWM, Document 15623, 4/5 W. B. Kennedy-Shaw papers, Wbk 8, "The Almasy Commando," June 5, 1942; HW 14/40, "Special Report on German Intelligence in Egypt and Libya," based on the statements of Waldemar Weber and Walter Aberle, June 18, 1942.

40. Cüppers, *Walther Rauff*, 142; Mallmann and Cüppers, *Nazi Palestine*, 119–120; Gerwarth, *Hitler's Hangman*, 218–276; R. C. Jaggers, "The Assassination of Reinhard Heydrich," *Studies in Intelligence* 4, no. 1 (1960): 1–20, www.cia.gov/library/readingroom/docs/CIA-RDP78-03921A0003003100010.pdf (accessed September 24, 2019).

41. HW 1/641, CX/MSS/1027/T17, decrypted and translated on May 30, 1942. The version in HW 5/95 gives the key as Red. Note that CX/MSS/1030/T24, also in HW 5/95, provides more of the original German message, including information from the same source on May 5, but was not given to Churchill.

42. This is the third Bluebird message described in NCML, SHR-025, Colonel McCormack's Trip to London, May–June 1943, Bluebird Incident, 271.

ACT III. CHAPTER 3. SPIES, EVERYWHERE

1. HW 1/612, CX/MSS/1032/T7.

2. HW 1/615, CX/MSS/1037/T6. The Enigma key appears in handwriting on the version in HW 5/96.

3. Bennett, "The Duty Officer," 34.

4. WO 201/632, To Mideast from HQ Main Eighth Army, Cositrep 322, May 30, 1942.

5. Greenberg, *Welchman*, 71.

6. Jackson, *Solving*, chap. 21.

7. Erskine, "Breaking Air Force and Army Enigma," 69–70; Calvocoressi, *Top Secret*, 78–79; HW 14/38, Colman to Travis, "Middle East 'E' Interception," May 25, 1942; HW 14/39, "Scorpion II," June 7, 1942; "Operational Intercepts, Middle East. Scorpion II," June 7, 1942; From Travis to DDMI (O), June 9, 1942; HW 77/12, Hut 6 reports for weeks ending May 30, June 6, June 13, 1942.

8. Welchman, *Hut Six*, 166–169.

9. HW 8/17, "B-Dienst 26/5–2/6." The report does not include CX/MSS /1027/T17 on the failure of RAF technicians, which was under investigation outside Bletchley Park. See NCML, SHR-025, Colonel McCormack's Trip to London, May–June 1943, Bluebird Incident. On Welchman's feelings: *Greenberg*, Welchman, 138–139.

10. The main sources for Eppler and Sandstede's early days in Cairo are KV 2/1467, "Report on the Interrogation of Victor Hauer," July 22–23, 1942; "First Consolidated Report on Activities of Eppler, Johann and Sandstede, Heinrich Gerd," July 29, 1942; "Second Consolidated Report on the Activities of Eppler, Johann and Sandstede, Heinrich Gerd," July 31, 1942; "A Report on the Eppler and Sandy Case," undated, likely from August 1 or 2, 1942; "Third Report," August 3, 1942; "Further Report on Sandy and Eppler Case," August 5, 1942; "Aziz El Masri and His Connection with the 2 German Spies Now in Custody in British Hands," August 11, 1942. Other sources noted below.

11. KV 1/1467, "Further Report"; Halim, *Diaries*, 48–54, 71; WO 208/1561, Security Summary Middle East No. 43, May 7, 1942.

12. WO 2019/2139, DMI to DDO, June 7, 1942; "Operation Claptrap," June 7, 2019; cf. IWM, Document 15623, 4/5 W. B. Kennedy-Shaw papers, Wbk 8, "The Almasy Commando," June 5, 1942.

13. US NARA, RG 165, 390/31/30/7, Box 753, File 3850, Fellers Report 2376, "Anglo-Egyptian Relations," May 27, 1942.

14. WO 208/1561, Security Summary Middle East No. 36, April 13, 1942; No. 38, April 21, 1942. On opposition to the Axis in Egypt, see Israel Gershoni, *Milhemet Ha'umot Hahalashot* [The War of the Weak Nations: Egypt in the Second World War, 1939–1945] (Tel Aviv: Resling, 2017).

15. HBF B40 F13, Military Attaché Report 1, November 20, 1940; B19 F4, correspondence with Azzam, Abdul Rahman.

16. Moorehead, *African Trilogy*, 350–355; WO 201/632, To Mideast from HQ Main Eighth Army, Cositrep 327, June 1, 1942; Cositrep 329, June 2, 1942.

17. Liardet, "The Gazala Battles."

18. FDR, Map Room, Box 93, File MR300, Sec. 1, Fellers Cable 1105, 3:46 p.m., June 6, 1942; Fellers Cable 1107, 5:40 p.m., June 6, 1942. On the responsibilities of assistant attaché Lt. Col. Gooler, see US NARA, RG 319, Entry 47, 270/5/13/5, Box 125, File 315–452.1, Fellers to Assistant Chief of Staff, G-2, "Organizational Chart," January 21, 1942.

19. Kitchen, *Rommel's Desert War*, 231–235, 495n44; Moorehead, *African Trilogy*, 359–363; Liddell Hart, *Rommel Papers*, 213–220; WO 201/632, Cositreps 330–342, June 3–9, 1942. Moorehead (*African Trilogy*, 360) reported that there was a second woman in the French forces at Bir Hakeim.

20. HW 5/97, CX/MSS/1048/T17, CX/MSS/1048/T27. The latter message is also in HW 1/626.

21. HW 8/17, "'B-Dienst 3/6–9/6."

22. Weinberg, *World at Arms*, chap. 6; Budiansky, *Battle of Wits*, 1–21, 255–257.

23. HW 14/47, Hastings to Godfrey, June 30, 1942, and attached retyped copy of June 7, 1942, article from the *Washington Times Herald*; HW 69/9, Godfrey to Hastings, July 7, 1942; Stephen Budiansky, "The Difficult Beginnings of US–British Codebreaking Cooperation," *Intelligence and National Security* 15, no. 2 (2000): 51–53.

24. Ranfurly, *To War*, July 16, 1941, May 28, 1942.

25. HS 7/234, SOE War Diary, June 1942, 4239–4240; Cox, "Britain and the Origin," 73; Brenner, *Ium Haplishah*, 11.

26. HS 7/266, SOE War Diary, Mideast and Balkans, July–August 1942, 36–38.

27. HW 1/641, For ACASI, from Duty Officer, Hut 3, June 8, 1942. Tedder is identified as the author of this message in a subsequent note in the same file from Chief of Air Staff Charles Portal.

28. WO 201/214, Personal for CIGS from General Auchinleck, Situation Review, June 5, 1942.

29. WO 201/2139, "Operations, Cyrenaica," May 30, 1942; *Special Forces*, 144–153, 302–310, 319–322.

30. HW 5/98, CX/MSS/1060/T24.

31. HW 5/99, CX/MSS/1062/T7.

32. US NARA, RG 226, Entry 171A, Box 59, "Report on the Penetration Activities of the 'P' Squad of the Italian Military Intelligence Service, Counter Espionage Section," 3, 7; CD, June 9, 1942; Brian R. Sullivan, "Manfredi Talamo (January 1895–March 1944)," unpublished manuscript courtesy of the author; David Alvarez and Robert A. Graham, *Nothing Sacred: Nazi Espionage Against the Vatican, 1939–1945* (Portland, OR: F. Cass, 1997), 125–126.

ACT IV. CHAPTER 1. COMPROMISED

1. FFP, Cable 1118, Parts 1 and 2. Over the next three days, Fellers wrote seven more parts to this cable. Parts 1 and 3 are also in FDR, Map Room, Box 93, File MR300, Sec. 1, Warfare-North Africa, Mid East, Mediterranean (1), May–June 1942.

2. IWM, Document 25879, R. G. Hurlock. A newspaper clipping, with no date preserved, states that he was killed on June 10, 1942.

3. HW 5/99, CX/MSS/1066/T10, CX/MSS/1065/T18, CX/MSS/1066/T11; Liddell Hart, *Rommel Papers*, 218.

4. HW 5/99, CX/MSS/1067/T21; Moorehead, *African Trilogy*, 361.

5. HW 5/100, CX/MSS/1078/T12; WO 201/2014, Personal for CIGS from General Auchinleck, Situation Reviews, June 11 and 19, 1942; WO 201/632, To Mideast from HQ Main Eighth Army, Cositreps 346–347, June 11, 1942; FFP, Cable 1147, June 18, 1942; "Susan Travers," *Telegraph* (London), December 23, 2003, www.telegraph.co.uk/news/obituaries/1450081/Susan-Travers.html (accessed October 17, 2019); Alan Riding, "A Legionnaire, She Was Never Timid in Amour or War," *New York Times*, April 21, 2001, B7; Kitchen, *Rommel's Desert War*, 495n44.

6. HW 1/640, CX/MSS/1069/T8.

7. HW 1/636, CX/MSS/1062/T17, and attached note from Menzies, June 10, 1942. The message also appears in HW 5/99, where it is marked as having been sent in Chaffinch II.

8. HW 50/22, "W/T Security and Deception," states that in the spring of 1942 the Naval Section at Bletchley Park "set aside a research specialists" [*sic*] to track German successes in codebreaking. From context, the singular rather than plural is correct, and the research specialist is Storey. In the same file, the "Interservice Cypher Security Committee and Cypher Policy Board" entry for February 19, 1941, refers to Dudley-Smith's appointment.

9. HW 8/132. The log of cables is incomplete, and Tiltman's cable is missing. However, the content and approximate timing can be derived from Friedman's urgent response, addressed to Tiltman and received at 4:35 a.m. in England.

10. HW 8/132, A80, Friedman to Tiltman, received 0435 June 11, 1942.

11. HW 8/132, R135, Tiltman and Kullback to Friedman, received 1103 June 11, 1942.

12. HW 8/132, A82, For Tiltman [unsigned, presumably from Friedman], received 0157, June 12, 1942.

13. HW 8/132, A83, For Tiltman [unsigned, presumably from Friedman], received 0820, June 12, 1942.

14. NSA OH-17-82, Kullback. Kullback's recounting in 1982 implies that Friedman accepted that the code was compromised but believed it had been stolen rather than solved. Travis's reply in 1942, however, implies that Friedman was asserting that the Germans' source was an agent, an assertion Travis disputes.

15. HW 1/641, C/9743, June 12, 1943, with Churchill annotation of June 13, and attachments.

16. HW 1/642, C/9744, Menzies to Portal, June 12, 1942.

17. HW 8/132, T767, Travis to Friedman, received 1705 June 12, 1942; R137 (unmarked, presumably Travis to Friedman), received 2210 June 12, 1942; HW 5/99, CX/MSS/1069/T21.

18. HW 8/132, R139, Kullback to Friedman, marked "personal," received 1345 [text of time unclear], June 13, 1942.

19. WO 201/2139, Dennys to DMI et al., June 10, 1942; DMI to G(O), June 10, 1942.

20. Churchill, *Hinge of Fate*, 326–327.

21. HW 5/100, CX/MSS/1071/T17, CX/MSS/1073/T8.

22. HW 5/100, CX/MSS/1078/T11.

23. HW 5/99, CX/MSS/1069/T16; WO 201/632, To Mideast from HQ Main Eighth Army, Cositrep 352, June 14, 1942; Liddell Hart, *Rommel Papers*, 220–224; Barr, *Pendulum*, chap. 1.

24. HW 1/646, C/9761, Menzies to Churchill, June 14, 1942.

25. HW 8/132, R140, Travis to Friedman, received 1930 June 14, 1942. The decrypted message cited is HW 5/100, CX/MSS/1078/T5.

26. The message cited is CX/MSS/1078/T7, found in HW 1/648 and HW 5/100, sent in Chaffinch II.

27. FFP, Cable 1118, Part 2.

28. NCML, David Kahn Collection, DK 66/33, Cable 1119. This is the text as deciphered and paraphrased at the receiving end, where it was mistakenly numbered 11119 by a clerk who struck the numeral "1" too many times. The grammatical error is most likely also a product of the Washington code room.

29. HW 5/100, CX/MSS/ZTPI/10922(1072/4), repeated in HW 1/644, Naval Headlines 644, June 13, 1942, section 1a; HW 5/100, CX/MSS/1073/T12; HW 5/102, CX/MSS/1094/T15.

30. HW 5/100, CX/MSS/1073/T12.

31. Primary sources for the account of the raids from the perspective of the participants: *Special Forces*, 147–149 (from the official "History of the Long Range Desert Group," CAB 44/151), 319–322 (from the official "History of Commandos and Special Service Troops in the Middle East and North Africa," CAB 44/152); WO 201/727, "Capt. Buck's Party," July 7, 1942; Zerubavel, *Magen Beseter*, 174–178; "Rav Turai Petr Haas," Izkor, www.izkor.gov.il/פטר האז/en_5e01a22f0ef7df5c9ee5ce5063100b7c (accessed October 31, 2019). The two British official histories differ on some details. Additional sources are noted below.

32. An additional account, however, states that Gottlieb was captured, then executed. "Turai Eliahu-Ernst Gottlieb," Izkor, www.izkor.gov.il/ארנסט-אליהו גוטליב/en_5b237d6472ed0424a7cd96e98a69f52a (accessed October 31, 2019).

33. WO 201/727, Bill [Kennedy Shaw] to John [Haselden], June 19, 1942.

34. The Martuba pilot also conveyed a hearsay account of the raid at Derna, though he had not been there. He claimed that the SIG's German driver had driven right up to the commander's office at the Derna base, gone in, and revealed who was in the truck. This hints strongly at a story embellished in retelling.

35. WO 201/727, Supplementary Report on Leutnant Friedrich Körner, Supplementary Report on Oberleutnant Ernst Klager, July 7, 1942.

36. US NARA, RG 242, Microfilm Publication T-321, Oberkommando der Luftwaffe, Roll 236, Frame 6298760, Morgenmeldung vom 15.6.42. A slightly more detailed Luftwaffe report in TNA HW 1-645, CX/MSS/1073/T29, states explicitly that there were "no raids" at Martuba. At Derna, "on the basis of a report by a German soldier, an enemy sabotage lorry was captured." It is impossible to know if this refers to betrayal by the SIG's German instructor.

37. See, for example, *Special Forces*; John W. Gordon, *The Other Desert War: British Special Forces in North Africa, 1940–1943* (New York: Greenwood Press, 1987), 105–108.

38. Cesare Amè, *Guerra segreta in Italia, 1940–1943* (Rome: Gherardo Casini Editore, 1954), 103–105.

39. *Special Forces*, 409–412.

40. US NARA, RG 242, Microfilm Publication T321, Oberkommando der Luftwaffe, Roll 236, Bericht über die Untersuchung des Sabotagfälle auf dem Flugplatz in Iraklion am 13. und 14. Juni 1942, July 19, 1942; cf. Microfilm

Publication T321, Oberkommando der Luftwaffe, Roll 236, Frame 6298760, Morgenmeldung vom 15.6.42.

41. IWM, Document 25664, journal of J. H. Jackman, 1; Document 15363, W. Morris, letter dated to approximately September–October 1942.

42. IWM, Document 3583, Commander A. E. Sutcliff, Newcastle logbook IV, entries for June 14, 1942.

43. IWM, Document 7696, Capt. W. F. N. Gregory-Smith, undated account, 32.

44. IWM, Document 25664, Jackman, 2–3.

45. I. S. O. Playfair et al., *The Mediterranean and Middle East*, vol. 3: *British Fortunes Reach Their Lowest Ebb (September 1941 to September 1942)* (Uckfield, UK: Naval & Military Press, 2004), 307–313.

46. Amè, *Guerra segreta*, 102–105.

47. Playfair et al., *The Mediterranean*, 1: 314.

48. FFP, Cable 1134, June 14, 1942.

49. WO 201/2014, Personal for CIGS from General Auchinleck, Situation Review, June 19, 1942; Moorehead, *African Trilogy*, 365–367.

50. Churchill, *Hinge of Fate*, 331–332; FFP, Cable 1134, June 14, 1942; Barr, *Pendulum*, chap. 1; Warner, *Auchinleck*, 187–188.

51. RG 242, Microfilm Publication T321, Oberkommando der Luftwaffe, Roll 83, Item 270, Frame 385, June 15, 1942, translation of Cable 1385 from Maxwell to Arnold, June 10, 1942. On the air ferry route, see Wesley Frank Craven and James Lea Cate, eds., *The Army Air Forces in World War II*, vol. 7: *Services Around the World* (Washington, DC: Office of Air Force History, 1983), x, 46–48, 73.

52. HW 1/648, CX/MSS/1078/T5, CX/MSS/1078/T7.

53. HW 1/653, C/9782, Menzies to Portal, June 16, 1942. Menzies reports on a conversation with Churchill the previous day.

54. NCML, SHR-025, Colonel McCormack's Trip to London, May–June 1943, Bluebird Incident, 271.

55. HW 1/652, C/9779, Menzies to Churchill, June 16, 1942.

ACT IV. CHAPTER 2. INSIDE INFORMATION

1. FFP, Cable 1145, June 17, 1942. Cf. FFP, Cable 1149, June 19, 1942.

2. WO 201/632, To Mideast from HQ Main Eighth Army, Cositrep 358, June 17, 1942; Cositrep 359, June 17, 1942; Cositrep 362, June 19, 1942. Cf. FFP, Cable 1148, June 18, 1942.

3. FFP, Cable 1148, June 18, 1942.

4. WO 201/2014, Personal for CIGS from General Auchinleck, Situation Review, June 19, 1942.

5. Alanbrooke, *Diaries*, June 13–18, 1942; Roberts, *Masters*, 185–186.

6. Kimball, *Churchill and Roosevelt*, 509–514; Smith, *FDR*, chap. 24; Alanbrooke, *Diaries*, June 26, 1942.

7. Smith, *FDR*, chap. 24; Roberts, *Masters*, 185–199.

8. Alanbrooke, *Diaries*, June 21, 1942.

9. FDR, Map Room, Box 93, File MR300, Sec. 1, Fellers Cable 1157. This is the text as paraphrased in the War Department code section and brought to the president. Fellers's original text (in FFP) is slightly different. Brooke and Churchill reaction: Alanbrooke, *Diaries*, June 21, 1942.

10. Roberts, *Masters*, 200–201; Alanbrooke, *Diaries*, June 21, 1942.

11. Moorehead, *African Trilogy*, 373–381; Liddell Hart, *Rommel Papers*, 225–231.

12. HW 5/104, CX/MSS/1111/T18.

13. HW 8/17, Appendix to Enemy Intelligence Report No. 3 (22/6–28/6/42).

14. FDR, Map Room, Box 93, File MR300, Sec. 1, Fellers Cable 1156, in six parts. Part 1, missing in this file, is partially preserved, with likely errors due to translation to Italian and back to English, in US NARA, RG 457, 190/37/7/1, Box 1035, File NR 3324, "The Contribution of the Information Service to the May–June Offensive in North Africa," Appendix 8. While Part 1 was sent on June 20, the remainder is dated June 21. Dating is further confirmed by British decrypts of German messages based on this cable: HW 5/104, CX/MSS/1111/T18, CX/MSS/1114/T10; HW 5/105, CX/MSS/1127/T4.

15. CD, June 23, 1942; *War Journal of Franz Halder*, June 22, 1942.

16. CD, June 22, 1942; Barr, *Pendulum*, 18; Kitchen, *Rommel's Desert War*, 246–247.

17. Liddell Hart, *Rommel Papers*, 235–236; Fraser, *Knight's Cross*, 343; Kitchen, *Rommel's Desert War*, 249.

18. The SIM (Italian) decrypt and translation of Fellers Cable 1156 is dated June 23, 1942: US NARA, RG 457, 190/37/7/1, Box 1035, File NR 3324, "Contribution of the Information Service to the May–June Offensive," Introduction and Appendix 8. Kesselring forwarded key points from the cable, attributed to "a Good Source," in the Red key of Enigma, also on June 23: HW 5/104, CX/MSS/1114/T10. The German army version of the message in Chaffinch was apparently either not intercepted or not decoded. By this time many Good Source reports were decoded and sent within one day. If that was the case, Rommel would have received the information on June 22.

19. RG 165, NM84–42, 390/37/31/5, Box 357, documents from June 20–25, 1942; Alanbrooke, *Diaries*, June 21–26, 1942; Roberts, *Masters*, 200ff.; Matloff and Snell, *Strategic Planning*, 243–254.

20. KV 2/1467, "First Consolidated Report," July 29, 1942; "Second Consolidated Report on the Activities of Eppler, Johann and Sandstede, Heinrich Gerd," July 31, 1942; "Third Report," August 3, 1942; "Interrogation of Persons Connected with the 'Eppler and Sandy' Case," Parts I and II, undated; KV 2/1468, summary, January 5, 1943.

21. US NARA, RG 457, 190/37/7/1, Box 1035, File NR 3324, "Contribution of the Information Service to the May–June Offensive," Appendices 4–11; HW 5/104, CX/MSS/1111/T18, CX/MSS/1114/T10; HW 5/105, CX/MSS/1127/T4. On discrepancies between Fellers's assessment and actual Brit-

ish strength, see Barr, *Pendulum*, 20–21. Part but not all of the discrepancy is due to Italian mistranslation of Fellers Cable 1156.

22. Barr, *Pendulum*, 34–35.

23. WO 201/727, "Notes on Conversation with Col. Bagnold on Subject of Qattara Depression," June 25, 1942.

24. Barr, *Pendulum*, 25–27.

25. WO 208/1561, Security Summary Middle East No. 57, June 25, 1942; No. 58, June 30, 1942.

26. FO 371/63073, Weizäcker to Neurath, June 23, 1942.

27. CD, June 26, 1942.

28. Sadat, *Identity*, 32–33. David Hirst and Irene Beeson, in *Sadat* (London: Faber and Faber, 1981), 62–63, raise questions about Sadat's involvement. However, as the investigation of the Eppler-Sandstede affair shows, Sadat was indeed aware of and apparently involved in the effort to contact Rommel.

29. Mallmann and Cüppers ("Elimination of the Jewish National Home") state that planning accelerated after the fall of Tobruk. The plan was presented to Himmler on July 1 and probably to Hitler on the same day. The phrase "executive measures" is from the orders issued for Rauff's unit on July 13 (Cüppers, *Walther Rauff*, 150). Jewish population of Egypt, Palestine, Syria, Lebanon, and Iraq: Harry Schneiderman and Jullius B. Maller, eds. *American Jewish Yearbook 5707 (1946–47)* (Philadelphia: Jewish Publication Society of America, 5707/1946), 609, www.ajcarchives.org/ajc_data/files/1946_1947_13 _statistics.pdf (accessed November 24, 2019). The figures for Palestine, based on government calculations, do not include significant illegal immigration.

30. The message itself, CX/MSS/1122/T9, is in HW 5/105 with the key indicated and in HW 1/676 with Churchill's question. The latter file contains Menzies's answer, C/9871, June 29, 1942. Menzies wrote that leakage would end "as from 25th July"; in context, July is clearly a typographic error, and the intent is June.

31. Beaton, *Near East*, 122.

32. Barr, *Pendulum*, 31.

33. Liddell Hart, *Rommel Papers*, 237–239.

ACT V. CHAPTER 1. EL ALAMEIN

1. Moorehead, *African Trilogy*, 383; Barr, *Pendulum*, 69–70.

2. Beaton, *Near East*, 126–132; Watkins, *Underage and Overseas*, chap. 1.

3. MLD, July 1, 1942.

4. HW 5/106, CX/MSS/1134/T17, CX/MSS/1135/T28, CX/MSS/1136/ T16, CX/MSS/1136/T34, CX/MSS/1137/T18, 1139/T3. On Rommel's failed feint, see Pitt, *Crucible of War 2*, 286–288.

5. US NARA, RG 242, Records of Headquarters, German Army Command, Microfilm Publication T-78, Roll 451, Generalstab des Heeres, Abteilung Fremde Heere West, Nr. 786/42 Geheime Reichssache Kommandos Chefs,

June 29, 1942. It is not clear whether Rommel himself received a copy of this message. However, this is also the date later given by Rommel's deputy chief intelligence officer for the end of the Good Source messages, indicating that, in one form or another, he was informed on June 29 not to expect more. There had actually been no messages for several days at this point. Behrendt, *Rommel's Intelligence*, 166–167.

6. Ugo Cavallero, *Diario, 1940–1943* (Rome: Ciarrapico, 1984), 297; USSME, "FRONTE CIRENAICO: Rilievi sulle operazione britanniche ed elementi informative tratti da un rapporto di un osservatore Americano," December 23, 1941, N-3/520/B. I am grateful to John Gooch for sharing this document with me. The information is drawn from HBF B39 F8, Fellers Cable 406, December 18, 1941.

7. US NARA, RG 457, 190/37/7/1, Box 1035, File NR 3324, "The Contribution of SIM to the Second Counteroffensive of Cyrenaica (January 21–February 5, 1942)," App. 1–15; HW 40/91, "Japanese MA Rome Forwards Report Derived from Intercepted American Cipher Telegram," May 11, 1945, decrypt of January 24, 1942, Cable 558, Japanese Military Attaché Rome to Summer Tokyo; "Der Deutsche General beim Hauptquartier Ital. Wehrmacht," Ic Nr. 206/42, to OBS, Duetsches Marine-Kommando Italien, translation of Fellers's cable misdated as January 19, 1942. I am grateful to Andreas Bierman for sharing this document. His translation is at "The Good Source," The Crusader Project, May 10, 2009, https://rommelsriposte.com/2009/05/10/the-good-source (accessed August 30, 2015). Sources for the Axis documents include Fellers Cable 616, January 17, 1942; Cable 699, January 27, 1941; Cable 723, January 31, 1942; Cable 741, February 2, 1941, all via FFP; Fellers Cable 640, January 20, 1942, reproduced in David Kahn, *How I Discovered World War II's Greatest Spy, and Other Stories of Intelligence and Code* (Boca Raton, FL: CRC, 2014), 251.

8. Kitchen, *Rommel's Desert War*, 194–196.

9. On June 29, Menzies informed Churchill that with "U.S. authorities having now changed their cypher, no further leakage should occur as from 25th July, 1942" (HW 1/676, C/9871). As noted above, July is a typographic error for June. While Menzies's US sources had been mistaken in previous claims of changes in the code, additional evidence shows that the Military Intelligence Code (MIC) ceased being used between Cairo and London on or very close to June 25.

- The last messages sent to Rommel as recorded in "Contribution of the Information Service to the May–June Offensive" and in British decrypts are from Fellers Cable 1156, the final part of which was radioed on June 21 or early on June 22. Thus, the code was still in use up to this time. Neither of these sources, however, is a complete record of Axis interceptions.
- Cavallero was aware of the plan to send a US armored division to Egypt, which was under active consideration in Washington on June 23–25. He never learned of the cancellation of the plan late on June 25. We can con-

clude that a message to Cairo about the plan was intercepted; a message cancelling it was not.

• By June 27 at the latest, Fellers was no longer signing cables from Cairo. His messages were signed by Maxwell, indicating that the shared code room was now under Maxwell's command. The change appears to have taken place at the same time that the new cipher machine went into use.

• An enigmatic cable from Fellers for the chief signal officer on June 24 (FDR, Map Room, Box 93, File MR300, Sec. 1, Cable 1168) asks if the latter has "received notification of destruction" of certain materials. A message for the chief signal officer on June 27 from Fellers but signed by Maxwell confirms arrival of new cryptographic materials (US NARA, RG 319, 270/5/13/5, Box 125, File 311.5, Cable 1174). How messages were sent between these dates is unclear, but it was evidently not in MIC.

• As noted, German military intelligence was certain on June 29 that its Cairo source was no longer available. Such a conclusion would only have been reached after several days of silence.

10. Cavallero's testimony on this point is from his diary entry for July 25, 1942. Summing up SIM's "indistinct" information on reinforcement of Egypt, Cavallero wrote that it included the arrival of the US "15th" Armored Division, according to the published version of his diary. "15th" is most likely a transcription error for *l'2o*, "the 2nd" in Italian. Cavallero, *Diario*, 436.

11. Fellers himself only became aware of this decision on June 27 when Ritchie returned to Cairo. FDR, Map Room, Box 93, File MR300, Sec. 1, Maxwell Cable No. 29, June 27, 1942. The text of the cable states that it was "prepared by Fellers and concurred in by Maxwell."

12. NCML, David Kahn Collection, DK 64/1, David Kahn interview of Hans-Otto Behrendt, November 18, 1978, Stuttgart.

13. HW 5/107, CX/MSS/1141/T7, indicates that on June 29, after the fall of Mersa Matruh, German intelligence was still in the dark about the El Alamein line. CX/MSS/1141/T11 shows that on June 30 German intelligence underestimated the forces at El Alamein.

14. NCML, SHR-025, Colonel McCormack's Trip to London, May–June 1943, Bluebird Incident, 273–275. According to Jenner, "Turning the Hinge of Fate," 198–199, Marshall gave orders on June 21, 1942, for a change in the encryption system used with Fellers. If so, the order either was not sent immediately or was not carried out for several more days.

15. The number of soldiers captured at Tobruk varies in different accounts, based in part on estimates of how many British troops were actually in the town on the eve of the battle. The number here is from Barr, *Pendulum*, 16.

16. Monelli, *Mussolini*, 9–11.

17. Bernhard, "Behind the Battle Lines," 435–436.

18. Roumani, *Jews of Libya*, 34–35; Simon, "Yehudei Luv," 66–68; Bernhard, "Behind the Battle Lines," 434–435. There are conflicting accounts of when the

imprisonment of Cyrenaica's Jews reached completion. The date here is from Roumani.

19. "1,000,000 Jews Slain by Nazis, Report Says," *New York Times*, June 30, 1942, 7; cf. details of the smuggled report in *JTA Daily News Bulletin*, June 26, 1942, pdfs.jta.org/1942/1942-06-26_145.pdf (accessed August 1, 2018).

20. Cüppers, *Walther Rauff*, 148–149.

21. HW 5/107, CX/MSS/1141, para. 11; CX/MSS/1142/T43; CX/MSS/1142/T27.

22. Barr, *Pendulum*, 71–81.

23. HW 5/107, CX/MSS/1144/T19, CX/MSS/1144/T21, CX/MSS/1144/T24, CX/MSS/1146/T33, CX/MSS/1147/T4, CX/MSS/1147/T31, CX/MSS/1141/T5, CX/MSS/1142/T16, CX/MSS/1148, para. 8; Barr, *Pendulum*, 87.

24. Barr, *Pendulum*, 93.

25. CD, July 3, 1942.

26. US NARA, RG 165, 390/31/30/7, Box 751, File 2900–2950, "Axis Formally Declares Egypt Free," July 3, 1942, 3:50 p.m. EWT.

27. Mallmann and Cüppers, "Elimination of the Jewish National Home," 14. The conversation took place on July 9.

28. US NARA, RG 165, 390/31/30/7, Box 759, File 5970, "Letter in English (extracts)," July 15, 1942.

29. HW 12/278, 106449, Turkish Minister Cairo to Minister for Foreign Affairs, Angora, July 3, 1942.

30. Haim Gouri, interview, June 21, 2013. Recalling the events after seven decades, Gouri could not give a precise date. However, his description fits the movement of the Ninth Australian Division, as described by Barr (*Pendulum*, 100). Gouri's memory of conversations, in my experience, was uniquely accurate.

31. HW 8/17, Enemy Intelligence Report No. 4, 28/6–5/7/42.

32. WO 201/2158, documents from January 9 to May 19, 1942; FFP, Cable 882, March 5, 1942, Cable 929, March 26, 1942; FDR, Map Room, Box 45, Army Dispatches, April 7–15, 1942, Cable 963, April 11, 1942.

33. US NARA, RG 165, NM84/42, 390/37/31/5, Box 357, File 381, Memorandum for General Wedemeyer, September 26, 1942, quoting Maxwell cable of July 7, 1942.

34. HBF B39 F5, Kunzler to Fellers, Travel Orders, July 20, 1942, citing orders in War Department Cable 72, July 14, 1942; US NARA, RG 165, 488 390/37/13/7, Box 4717, Strong to Marshall re Colonel Bonner F. Fellers, July 8, 1942. Fellers actually left Cairo on July 17. FDR Official Files, File 283, Kirk to Undersecretary of State, July 21, 1942.

35. US NARA, RG 165, NM84/42, 390/37/31/5, Box 357, File 381, Memorandum for General Wedemeyer, September 26, 1942. Cf. HS 7/234, 4195, in which the SOE reports instructions from the British Security Coordination office in New York that "care should be taken in any discussion" with Compton and that "a general watch should be kept on the activities of this mission."

36. HBF B38 F12, Fellers to Marie Broach, August 13, 1942.

37. FO 371/31573, Clayton and Maunsell to DMI and Snuffbox [MI5], July 6, 1942; WO 208/1561, Security Summary Middle East No. 30, March 23, 1942; No. 34, April 7, 1942; No. 64, July 23, 1942.

38. WO 208/1561, Security Summary Middle East No. 61, July 13, 1942; FO 371/31573, Cable 1784, Lampson to Foreign Office, July 10, 1942; MLD, July 9, 1942; FO 371/63073, Foreign Office to UK representative to UN, August 13, 1947, quoting captured report from Ettel to Ribbentrop, July 24, 1942; Sadat, *Identity*, 32–33; Hirst and Beeson, *Sadat*, 62–63.

39. FO 371/31573, Cable 1749, Lampson to Foreign Office, July 6, 1942; Cable 1793, Lampson to Foreign Office, July 11, 1942; Cable 1818, Lampson to Foreign Office, July 15, 1942; MLD, July 8, 1942, July 13, 1942.

40. Brenner, *Ium Haplishah*, 105–106.

41. Ranfurly, *To War*, July 4, 1942; Bauer, *From Diplomacy*, 183–184.

42. Gelber, *Matzadah*, 68–69; Bauer, *From Diplomacy*, 190–191.

43. Barr, *Pendulum*, 95, 116–117.

44. HW 1/711, CX/MSS/1168/T8, CX/MSS/1168/T10, CX/MSS/1168/T11, CX/MSS/1168/T34, CX/MSS/1168/T52.

45. HW 73/6 contains the immediate, extensive reports on the capture of Seebohm's unit and later reports on its impact. See also HW 40/8, "Security of British and Allied Communications," November 1, 1944–February 28, 1945. On the battle: Barr, *Pendulum*, 103–111.

46. The account of Eppler and Sandstede's final activities is based on extensive documents in KV 2/1467, KV 2/1468, and FO 141/852. The two KV (MI5) files were declassified only in 2004 and contain information that was missing in earlier accounts of the affair. By the nature of an investigation, the testimony of various figures is contradictory, and later interrogations contain information lacking in earlier ones. Spellings of names also vary. See especially FO 141/852, "Further Report on Sandy and Eppler," with cover note, Jenkins to Tomlyn, August 5, 1942; KV 2/1467, "Report on Interrogation of Victor Hauer on 22 & 23 July, 1942"; "First Interrogation of Hassan Gafaar," undated; "1st Consolidated Report on Activities of Eppler, Johann and Sandstede, Heinrich Gerd," July 29, 1942; "Second Consolidated Report on the Activities of Eppler, Johann and Sandstede, Heinrich Gerd," July 31, 1942; "Interrogation of Persons Connected with the 'Eppler and Sandy' Case," July 26–31, 1942; KV 2/1468, "Weber, Waldemar; Aberle, Walter; Sandstede, Heinrich; Eppler, Johann," January 5, 1943.

47. FO 141/852, 983/8/429, August 12, 1942.

48. The story is told, with variations, in war correspondent Leonard Mosley's 1958 book *The Cat and the Mice*; Sansom's 1965 memoir *I Spied Spies*; and Eppler's memoir *Operation Condor*, published in English under the name "John Eppler" in 1977. For an overview of additional earlier versions, see H. O. Dovey, "Operation Condor," *Intelligence and National Security* 4, no. 2 (1989): 357–373. Dovey had access to the Foreign Office file on the case, but the MI5 files were still classified. Examples of anachronisms include Sansom's claim to

have arrested Ezzet before Eppler, and his claim to have met and known Sadat before Eppler's arrest, when investigation records show that Sadat's surname emerged only later. British banknotes counterfeited by the Germans showed up in Egypt only later in the war. See KV 4/465, "Supplementary Report of Payment of German Agents by Bank of England Notes," August 1, 1945. Attempts to identify the supposed Jewish Mata Hari have included identifying her with Ruth Aliav-Klüger of Hamossad Le'Aliya Bet, the Jewish Agency's illegal immigration arm, but Aliav-Klüger was only stationed in Cairo from the very end of 1942. Contrary to the many accounts of the spies using *Rebecca* for their cipher key, Sandstede "admitted that the book they were to use to encode their messages was 'The Unwarranted Death.'" Unless this was the title of an obscure edition of *Rebecca*, the use of that novel is a later invention that became a fixed part of memory of the case. See KV 2/1467, "First Consolidated Report," July 29, 1942. A full list of discrepancies would be much longer.

49. FO 141/852, 983/3/429, July 25–27, 1942; 983/5/429, Jenkins to Tomlyn, August 2, 1942; 983/6/429, Jenkins to Tomlyn, August 5, 1942.

50. KV 2/1467, Jenkins to Sir David [Petrie], August 1, 1942, and attached reports on interrogation of Hauer, July 22–23 and 24, 1942.

51. WO 208/1561, Security Summary Middle East No. 87, October 14, 1942; KV 2/1467, Jenkins to Sir David [Petrie], October 19, 1942.

52. KV 2/1467, "3rd Report," August 3, 1942; IWM, Document 4829, Maunsell memoir, 30–31.

53. Mallmann and Cüppers, "Elimination of the Jewish National Home," 3–27.

54. WO 208/1561, Security Summary Middle East No. 63, July 20, 1942; No. 64, July 23, 1942; No. 65, July 27, 1942; No. 67, August 3, 1942, and attached "Appendix A: The 'Fifth Column' and the Middle East."

55. Albania went from Italian occupation to German occupation in 1943. All but one family of the country's small Jewish community were hidden and saved, along with the several hundred Jewish refugees from elsewhere in Europe. See "Besa: A Code of Honor: Muslim Albanians Who Rescued Jews During the Holocaust," Yad Vashem, www.yadvashem.org/yv/en/exhibitions /besa/index.asp (accessed December 20, 2019); Joseph Berger, "Casting Light on Little-Known Story of Albania Rescuing Jews from Nazis," *New York Times*, November 18, 2013 (accessed December 20, 2019).

56. Cüppers, *Walther Rauff*, 155.

57. Liddell Hart, *Rommel Papers*, 257.

58. CD, July 20–23, 1942.

59. Barr, *Pendulum*, 154–168; Moorehead, *African Trilogy*, 402–403.

60. CAB 121/284, Butler to Bracken, June 25, 1942; "Draft Telegram to Washington," June 26, 1942; Radcliffe to Butler, June 27, 1942.

61. Moorehead, *African Trilogy*, 410–411.

62. FDR Official Files, File 283, Kirk to Undersecretary of State, July 21, 1942; Welles to Roosevelt, July 21, 1942.

63. US NARA, RG 165, NM84/15, 390/30/15/3, Box 6, File 381, Roosevelt to Hopkins, Marshall, and King, "Instructions for London Conference," July 16,

1942; Roosevelt to Hopkins, Marshall, and King, undated [July 22, 1942, or after]; Roosevelt to Hopkins, Marshall, and King, July 25, 1942; Alanbrooke, *Diaries,* July 17–20, 1942; Matloff and Snell, *Strategic Planning,* 266–297; Roberts, *Masters,* 230–259. The phrase "to drive in against the backdoor of Rommel's armies" is from Roosevelt's memo of July 16.

64. Matloff and Snell, *Strategic Planning,* 297.

65. Matloff and Snell, *Strategic Planning,* 283; Atkinson, *Army at Dawn,* 26.

66. Van Creveld, *Supplying War,* 196–199; van Creveld, "Rommel's Supply Problem," 71–72.

67. Winston Churchill, "The End of the Beginning," The Churchill Society, November 10, 1942, www.churchill-society-london.org.uk/EndoBegn.html (accessed December 25, 2019).

68. Auchinleck "expressed the opinion that, had we not had the 'U' [Ultra] service, Rommel would certainly have got through to Cairo." Lee A. Gladwin, "Alan Turing, Enigma, and the Breaking of German Machine Ciphers in World War II," *Prologue: The Journal of the National Archives* 29, no. 1 (1997): 214, citing US NARA, RG 457, Box 1424, File NR 4686, Brig. Williams and Grp. Capt. Humphreys, "Reports Concerning Ultra," 7.

69. US NARA, RG 59, 119.25/1398–99, Cable 3405, Harrison to Shaw, July 24, 1942; Cable 802, Hull to Kirk, July 25, 1942; Wilson to Adams, "Alleged Deciphering by Axis Agents of Telegram Sent to Washington from Cairo," July 25, 1942; Cable 1322, Kirk to Hull, July 27, 1942. I am grateful to Brian Sullivan for sharing these papers.

70. The extant logbooks of cables between Bletchley Park and the War and Navy Departments end on July 9, 1942 (HW 8/132) and resume on November 17, 1942 (HW 8/133).

ACT V. CHAPTER 2. UNKNOWN SOLDIERS

1. Alanbrooke, *Diaries,* August 3–9, 1942; Jonathan Fennell, "'Steel My Soldiers' Hearts': El Alamein Reappraised," *Journal of Military and Strategic Studies* 14, no. 1 (2011): 1–31, https://jmss.org/article/view/58014 (accessed December 26, 2019); Barr, *Pendulum,* 192–213; Warner, *Auchinleck,* 202–220; Ronald Lewin, *Rommel as Military Commander* (Barnsley, UK: Pen & Sword, 1990), 169–170; "Monty's Caravans: A Field Marshall's Home from Home," Imperial War Museums, www.iwm.org.uk/history/montys-caravans-a-field-marshals-home-from-home (accessed December 30, 2019); Brighton, *Patton, Montgomery, Rommel,* 6.

2. Fennell, "Steel My Soldiers' Hearts," 22. On Auchinleck's reserved character, see Warner, *Auchinleck.*

3. Jackson, *Solving,* chaps. 6, 21; F. H. Hinsley, "Introduction: The Influence of Ultra in the Second World War," in Hinsley and Stripp, *Codebreakers,* 4–6; Bennett, "The Duty Officer," 37; Calvocoressi, *Top Secret,* 78–79; Erskine, "Breaking Air Force and Army Enigma," 70–71.

4. Hinsley, "Influence of Ultra," 3–5; Barr, *Pendulum,* 211, 219.

5. Rommel's health: HW 5/126, CX/MSS/1339/T12. Pilots' intestinal problems: HW 5/127, CX/MSS/1248/T4. Both HW 5/126 and 5/127 contain messages too numerous to list regarding the fuel crisis.

6. Gladwin, "Alan Turing, Enigma," 214; Barr, *Pendulum*, 223–252.

7. Liddell Hart, *Rommel Papers*, 283.

8. Barr, *Pendulum*, 255–267, 296–298, 307ff.; Fraser, *Knight's Cross*, 382–383; Liddell Hart, *Rommel Papers*, 319.

9. Atkinson, *Army at Dawn*, 59–159.

10. Fraser, *Knight's Cross*, 387–396; Barr, *Pendulum*, 408; Roumani, *Jews of Libya*, 34–35; Simon, "Yehudei Luv," 68; "The British Enter Benghazi," World War II Today, ww2today.com/20th-november-1942-the-british-enter-benghazi (accessed January 2, 2020).

11. Weinberg, *World at Arms*, chap. 8; Atkinson, *Army at Dawn*, 163–167.

12. Robert Satloff, *Among the Righteous: Lost Stories from the Holocaust's Long Reach into Arab Lands* (New York: Public Affairs, 2006), passim, iBook; Mallmann and Cüppers, *Nazi Palestine*, 167–184; Cüppers, *Walther Rauff*, 157–178; Michel Abitbol, *The Jews of North Africa During the Second World War*, trans. Catherine Tihanyi Zentelis (Detroit, MI: Wayne State University Press, 1989), 116–140.

13. Fraser, *Knight's Cross*, 410–413; Weinberg, *World at Arms*, chap. 8; Mallmann and Cüppers, *Nazi Palestine*, 183–184.

14. Kozaczuk, *Enigma: How the German Machine Cipher Was Broken*, 136–208; Kozaczuk and Straszak, *Enigma: How the Poles Broke the Nazi Code*, 46.

15. Porat and Naor, *Ha'itonut*, 45–47, 56–57; "The Riegner Telegram," Holocaust Encyclopedia, United States Holocaust Memorial Museum, https://encyclopedia.ushmm.org/content/en/article/the-riegner-telegram (accessed January 7, 2020); "Wise Gets Confirmation," *New York Times*, November 25, 1942, 10. Even with official confirmation, news of the genocide continued to appear on the inside pages of almost all US newspapers. Walter Laqueur, "The Riegner Cable, and the Knowing Failure of the West to Act During the Shoah," *Tablet*, August 15, 2015, www.tabletmag.com/jewish-arts-and-culture/books/192421/riegner-cable-shoah (accessed January 7, 2020).

16. Yisrael Ben-Dor, "Shloshah Degalim Ve'oyev Ehad," *Maarakhot* 463 (January 2015), 56–61.

17. Billy Wilder, *Five Graves to Cairo*, 1943; "Five Graves to Cairo: Filming and Production," IMDB, www.imdb.com/title/tt0035884/locations (accessed January 7, 2020).

18. Bosworth, *Mussolini*, 321–331; Monelli, *Mussolini*, 208–237; Fraser, *Knight's Cross*, 437–451; Weinberg, *World at Arms*, chap. 11; "Count Galeazzo Ciano Executed," World War II Graves, ww2gravestone.com/count-galeazzo-ciano-executed (accessed January 8, 2020); "Italy," Holocaust Encyclopedia, United States Holocaust Memorial Museum, https://encyclopedia.ushmm.org/content/en/article/italy (accessed January 8, 2020).

19. Bierman, *Secret Life*, 193–232.

20. Ranfurly, *To War*, entries from November 16, 1942, to May 13, 1944. Ranfurly does not mention the rumors about the nature of Eisenhower's relationship with Kay Summersby, which remained a subject of controversy long after their deaths.

21. *Brigadier John Tiltman*, 43–45; Michael Smith, "Bletchley Park, Double Cross and D-Day," in Smith and Erskine, *Action This Day*, 280–281; Maurice Miles, "Japanese Military Codes," in Hinsley and Stripp, *Codebreakers*, 283–284. On Rommel's plans, cf. Fraser, *Knight's Cross*, 460–468.

22. Fraser, *Knight's Cross*, 457–554. On the debate on Rommel's role in the failed plot, see Reuth, *Rommel*, 165–222; Beckett, *Rommel*, chap. 6.

23. *New York Times*, June 6, 1944. The front page has a three-deck lead headline on the landings in France, beneath which is a one-column headline in much smaller type devoted to the fighting in Italy and a similar headline for Roosevelt's radio address.

24. HW 40/75, CXG 4, from Quirinal Rome, July 29, 1944, referencing cable from 92,700, July 22, 1944.

25. HW 40/75, "Penetration of Diplomatic Presences by SIM/CS," September 7, 1944, based on cable CX 32619, August 14, 1944; C/7599, September 18, 1944. One of these refers to the second agent as 32,000; the other refers to the same agent as 32,700.

26. US NARA, RG 226, Entry 108B, Box 306, "Penetration of Diplomatic Premises by SIM CS Prior to the Armistice," August 14, 1944; Entry 171A, Box 59, "Report on the Penetration Activities of the 'P' Squad of the Italian Military Intelligence Service, Counter Espionage Section." An American cover note is dated January 31, 1945, but the report itself is undated and may have been written before the August 14, 1944, report. The reports indicate that the P Squad had little success penetrating the German and Spanish embassies but succeeded against the Japanese embassy.

27. I am grateful to the staff of the US embassy in Rome in 2017 for historical material on the buildings and for a tour of the grounds.

28. De Risio, *Servizi segreti*, 22n1. In "Report on the Penetration Activities," former NCOs of the P Squad were able to recall the names of two contacts within the US embassy: Mario Bosi, a footman, and Paesano, a messenger for Fiske. Paesano may be a nickname or codename. In the full Italian transcript of a 1970 BBC interview, the wartime head of SIM, Cesare Amè, stated that four Italian employees of the embassy collaborated with the P Squad. He named one of them by the surname Gherardi. NCML, David Kahn Collection, DK 69/19. Kahn (*Codebreakers*, 472) gives the full name as Loris Gherardi.

29. These were the official names of the codes. See "The Compromise of the Communications of General Barnwell R. Legge, US Military Attache to Switzerland," Christos Military and Intelligence Corner, https://chris -intel-corner.blogspot.com/2015/05/the-compromise-of-communications-of .html (accessed September 17, 2015). NSA OH-17-82, Kullback, 65, refers to the higher-level code stolen in Rome as "MI-10," meaning version 10 of

the Military Intelligence Code. Frank Rowlett likewise later referred to the theft of "military intelligence code No. 10." See NCML, NSA OH-01-74, Oral History Interview with Mr. Frank B. Rowlett, 21. HW 40/91, ULTRA/POP/ JMA/508, translated May 11, 1945, text of message from January 22, 1942, refers to the theft of the US "intelligence" and "secret" codes; "secret" here is a translation of "confidential."

David Kahn, in *Codebreakers*, 472, and in "The Black Code," *Quarterly Journal of Military History* 18, no. 1 (2005), 37, says that the Military Intelligence Code was commonly known as the "Black Code" after the color of the binding. Other writers have used the same name. While a source for this may exist, I have not seen it. The State Department did have a Brown Code and a Grey Code, named for their bindings, but the Military Intelligence Code was a War Department system. The US military attaché in Rome until 1941, Norman Fiske, wrote to Kahn, "I have never heard of a 'black'" code. (David Kahn Collection, Kahn-Fiske correspondence, Fiske to Kahn, May 24, 1964.) I have therefore refrained from using the term "Black Code."

30. "Report on the Penetration Activities," 7. The report gives the timing of the operation only as "prior to the entry of the United States into the war." Amè (*Guerra segreta*, 96), in his 1954 memoir, gives the timing as "in the days immediately preceding" the US entry into the war. Various accounts have given more specific dates, some based on questionable reasoning. I have not seen a basis for a date in a contemporary document. As discussed below, therefore, the exact date remains unknown.

31. Martin S. Alexander, "Safes and Houses: William C. Bullitt, Embassy Security and the Shortcomings of the US Foreign Service Before the Second World War," *Diplomacy and Statecraft* 2, no. 2 (1991): 194–203.

32. US NARA, RG 457, Entry 9032, Box 1384, File NR 4400, "Report of Special Committee to Investigate Security of State Department Communications," June 26, 1941. I am grateful to Christos Triantafyllopoulos for sharing this file.

33. US NARA, RG 457, Entry 9032, Box 1384, File NR 4400, "Summary Report of Committee Appointed to Resurvey Cryptographic Systems Employed by the Department of State," January 14, 1944. The committee began its work before the end of 1943.

34. CD, October 31, 1941.

35. HW 40/219, "Draft: The Italian 'Y' Service Organisation." I am grateful to Brian Sullivan for sharing this document and to Ciro Paoletti for a personal guided tour of SIM sites in Rome.

36. NCML, David Kahn Collection, Kahn-Fiske correspondence, Fiske to Kahn, May 24, 1964.

37. Cavallero, *Diario*, 297, entry for December 22, 1941; USSME, "FRONTE CIRENAICO: Rilievi sulle operazione britanniche ed elementi informative tratti da un rapporto di un osservatore Americano," December 23, 1941, N-3/520/B; HBF B39 F8, Cable 406, December 18, 1941.

38. US NARA, RG 457, 190/37/7/1, Box 1035, File NR 3324, "The Contribution of SIM to the Second Counteroffensive of Cyrenaica (January 21–February 5, 1942)"; Der Deutsche General beim Hauptquartier der Ital. Wehrmacht, IC Nr.206/42, "Deutsche Luftangriffe auf Malta," January 29, 1942, translation of FFP, Fellers Cable 616, January 17, 1942. A redacted version appears as Appendix 1 in "Contribution of SIM to the Second Counteroffensive." Full translation at "The Good Source," The Crusader Project, May 10, 2009, https://rommelsriposte.com/2009/05/10/the-good-source (accessed August 30, 2015). I am grateful to Andreas Biermann for sharing the original German document.

39. Postwar interrogations of German and Italian cryptographers, and writings by them, produced a series of conflicting accounts on how their agencies obtained the codebooks and the cipher tables. The accounts have some historical value, but show the signs of compartmentalization within agencies, of blurred memory, and on occasion of boasting. I have worked on the principle that documents from the time of events, even when incomplete, provide a more accurate picture.

40. TICOM DF-187D, Army Security Agency, "Relations of OKW/Chi with Foreign Cryptologic Bureaux," https://docs.google.com/file/d/0B_oIJ bGCCNYeeDcyZ2pIUVFRM1dURENqd2ZxRkU2Zw/edit (accessed February 11, 2018).

41. HW 40/91, ULTRA/POP/JMA/645, translated January 12, 1946, text of message from Tokyo to Hayashi, January 14, 1942. Hayashi's message, to which this is a response, is not in the file.

42. HW 40/91, ULTRA/POP/JMA/508, translated May 11, 1945, text of message from January 22, 1942. A message to Hayashi on July 14, 1944, after his appointment as Japanese military attaché in Hungary, indicates that the tables photographed in Rome were issued in July 1941. It is not clear from the Hayashi-Tokyo exchange if these tables were still valid in January 1942, or if SIM had reconstructed the tables that replaced them. See HW 40/8, ULTRA/ZIP/SAC/R.12B., "Security of British and Allied Communications," July 15–November 1, 1944, 7.

43. HW 40/195, "Correspondence Between OKW/Chi and Intercept Stations on the Interception of Diplomatic Traffic," February 24, 1946, message No. 4, Kempf to FSR Station, Lauf, "Traffic Cairo-Washington," January 19, 1942.

44. US NARA, RG 242, Records of the German Air Force (OKL), T-321, Roll 83, Item No. 270, Frame 398.

45. US NARA, RG242, Records of the German Foreign Office, T120, "Telegramm, gerichtet an das Kriegsdepartment in Washington durch die Gesandschaft in Kairo," February 7, 1942, Roll 2484, Frame E261632–E261634, translated in FO 371/63073. Source is FFP, Fellers Cable 778, parts 1 and 2, February 7, 1942. Cf. Cavallero, *Diario*, 340, entry for February 10, 1942, in which he complains that he has only received three political cables from Cairo, no military material.

46. CD, February 12, 1942.

47. The clearest evidence that the Axis agencies ceased reading the code in February comes from British decrypts. In late April, German messages showed a delay of a week in decrypting current messages from Cairo, and subsequent German messages carried information from Cairo messages as far back as February 19 and possibly earlier, meaning that OKW/Chi was going through back traffic as it reconstructed the new tables. The Italian decrypt of Fellers Cable 778 covers parts 1 and 2 of the message, which Fellers dated February 7, but not parts 3 and 4, dated February 8, possibly giving a precise date for the change of tables.

48. Jenner, "Turning the Hinge of Fate," 171.

49. HW 40/174, "Report on the Interrogation of Wilhelm Fenner," September 17, 1946.

50. Reading did not mean understanding. The German translator took Fellers's recommendations to be British plans.

51. US NARA, RG 457, 190/37/7/1, Box 1035, File NR 3324, "The Contribution of the Information Service to the May–June Offensive in North Africa."

52. An exception was the Italian message, HW 5/100, CX/MSS/ZTPI/10922(1072/4), warning of the commando raids against Axis airfields. This was a rare case of information from a Fellers cable being sent in the Italian naval code, which the Naval Section at Bletchley Park tracked closely.

53. Sullivan, "Manfredi Talamo"; John Foot, "Via Rasella, 1944: Memory, Truth, and History," *Historical Journal* 43 (2000): 1173–1181; Alessandro Portelli, *The Order Has Been Carried Out: History, Memory, and Meaning of a Nazi Massacre in Rome* (New York: Palgrave Macmillan, 2003), 175–176; "Ardeatine Caves Massacre," Holocaust Encyclopedia, United States Holocaust Memorial Museum, https://encyclopedia.ushmm.org/content/en/article/ardeatine-caves -massacre (accessed January 11, 2020).

54. HW 49/7, 26256B/April, April 26, 1945.

EPILOGUE

1. Sources from the HBF include Box 17, File 1, Military Record and Report of Separation: Certificate of Service; Box 43, File 4, For America documents; Box 36, File 9, Bonner Fellers, "Only Americans Can Defend America"; Box 6, File 10, Citizens Foreign Aid Committee; Box 37, File 8, "Foreign Aid: A Communist Plot to Bankrupt America"; Box 37, File 14, "Foreign Aid Is Financing Global Socialism." Additional sources include NMC, Box 17, Citizens Foreign Aid Committee; "Gen. Fellers Gets 'For America' Post," *New York Times*, November 17, 1954, 17; "M'Carthy Praises Role of M'Arthur," *New York Times*, February 23, 1953, 11; Megan Rosenfeld, "Brig. Gen. Bonner Fellers, Ret., Dies" *Washington Post*, October 10, 1973; Richard Hofstadter, *The Paranoid Style in American Politics, and Other Essays* (Cambridge, MA: Harvard University Press, 1952), 27–29; Randle J. Hart,

"There Comes a Time: Biography and the Founding of a Movement Organization," *Qualitative Sociology* 33, no. 1 (2010): 55–77.

2. Victor Hugo, *Les Misérables*, trans. Julie Rose (New York: New American Library, 2008; original French publication, 1862), 261–277.

3. Winston Churchill, "Speech at the Lord Mayor's Day Luncheon at the Mansion House, London," International Churchill Society, November 10, 1942, www.winstonchurchill.org/resources/speeches/1941-1945-war-leader/the -end-of-the-beginning (accessed April 17, 2015).

4. Benny Morris, *1948: A History of the First Arab-Israeli War* (New Haven, CT: Yale University Press, 2008), chap. 1–2.

5. Gamal Abdul Nasser and Walid Khalidi, "Nasser's Memoirs of the First Palestine War," *Journal of Palestine Studies* 2, no. 2 (winter 1973): 3–32; Mohi El Din, *Memories*, 41–44.

6. On the unreadiness of Arab armies in 1948, see Morris, *1948*, 183–187.

7. Tom Segev, *1949: The First Israelis* (New York: Metropolitan, 1998), 84–85. On the Jewish side's greater preparedness for war, see Morris, *1948*, 28, 81–88, 197–198. Morris gives a figure of "more than twenty-six thousand" Palestinian Jews having served in the British army during World War II. He notes that "more than 4,000" foreign volunteers, Jewish and non-Jewish, almost all of whom had served during World War II, joined the Jewish forces in Palestine.

8. Sadat, *Revolt*, 227–228.

9. Mohi El Din, *Memories*, 108–112; McBride, *Farouk*, 190–223.

10. Mosley, *The Cat and the Mice*.

11. Sansom, *I Spied Spies*, 108–132.

12. Eppler, *Operation Condor*.

13. Pamela Andriotakis, "The Real Spy's Story Reads Like Fiction and 40 Years Later Inspires a Best-Seller," *People*, December 15, 1980, https://people .com/archive/the-real-spys-story-reads-like-fiction-and-40-years-later-inspires -a-best-seller-vol-14-no-24 (accessed December 25, 2017).

14. Sansom, *I Spied Spies*, 88.

15. Mallmann and Cüppers, *Nazi Palestine*, 204–205; Cüppers, *Walther Rauff*, 394; Robert D. McFadden, "Walter Rauff, 77, Ex-Nazi, Dead; Was an Accused War Criminal," *New York Times*, May 15, 1984, B8; Plan LADYSHIP Progress Report, February 3, 1954, CIA name file for Walter [*sic*] Rauff, CIA, www.cia.gov/library/readingroom/docs/RAUFF%2C%20WALTER_0088 .pdf. The CIA file includes an early postwar report alleging that Rauff briefly had ties with Israeli intelligence in 1949; a 1984 document refers to the allegation as "spotty, unconfirmed," and Cüppers debunks it.

16. GC&CS Naval Sigint, Volumes I–XV, HW 43/10-25. Margaret Storey wrote Volume VI, *German and Italian Naval Sigint*.

17. Interviews with Nikki Swinhoe, Pauline Flemons, and Nicholas Fenn Wiggin; last will and testament of Margaret Elizabeth Storey, via the Cheltenham Local History Society.

18. Interviews with Lottie Milvain (née Dudley-Smith) and Tempe Denzer; "Death of Cdr. R. Dudley-Smith," *Gloucestershire Echo*, October 3, 1967, courtesy of Lottie Milvain, page number not preserved.

19. Dermot Turing, *XY&Z: The Real Story of How Enigma Was Broken* (Stroud, Gloucestershire, UK: History Press, 2018), 277–281.

20. Hodges, *Alan Turing*, chap. 6–8; Boyle, *Alan Turing*, chap. 6–7.

21. "Cdr Edward Wilfred Harry 'Jumbo' Travis," Bletchley Park, https://rollofhonour.bletchleypark.org.uk/search/record-detail/9170 (accessed August 31, 2015); "The End of Denniston's Career, and His Legacy," GCHQ, www.gchq.gov.uk/features/end-dennistons-career-and-his-legacy (accessed January 11. 2018).

22. F. W. Winterbotham, *The Ultra Secret* (New York: Harper & Row, 1974). On the Japanese systems, see 86–87.

23. Greenberg, *Welchman*, 136. Winterbotham made the claim in private correspondence with Welchman.

24. Turing, *XY&Z*, 279–283.

25. Greenberg, *Welchman*, 164–198.

26. Nigel West, *The Sigint Secrets: The Signal Intelligence War, 1900 to Today, Including the Persecution of Gordon Welchman* (New York: William Morrow, 1988), 25–28, 255–256.

27. Turing, *XY&Z*, 281.

28. "Royal Pardon for Codebreaker Alan Turing," *BBC*, December 24, 2013, www.bbc.com/news/technology-25495315 (accessed January 14, 2020).

29. Haim Gouri, interview, May 6, 2015. Gouri died in January 2018 at age ninety-four.

Index

YASMIN GORENBERG

GERSHOM GORENBERG is a historian and journalist who has been covering Middle Eastern affairs for over thirty-five years. He is the author of three critically acclaimed books, *The Unmaking of Israel*, *The Accidental Empire*, and *The End of Days*, and coauthor of *Shalom, Friend: The Life and Legacy of Yitzhak Rabin*, winner of the National Jewish Book Award. A columnist for the *Washington Post*, Gorenberg has also written for the *New York Times Magazine*, *Atlantic Monthly*, *New York Review of Books*, *New Republic*, and *Foreign Policy*, and in Hebrew for *Haaretz*. He has been a visiting professor at Columbia University's Graduate School of Journalism, where he led a workshop on writing history. He lives in Jerusalem.